THE HIDDEN HISTORY OF THE JFK ASSASSINATION

The Hidden History of the JFK Assassination

The Definitive Account of the Most Controversial Crime
of the Twentieth Century

Lamar Waldron

COUNTERPOINT
BERKELEY

Library of Congress Cataloging-in-Publication Data

Waldron, Lamar, 1954-
The hidden history of the JFK Assassination : the definitive account of the most controversial crime of the twentieth century / Lamar Waldron.

Includes bibliographical references and index.
ISBN 978-1-61902-226-3 (alk. paper)
1. Kennedy, John F. (John Fitzgerald), 1917-1963--Assassination. 2. Mafia--United States. 3. Conspiracies--United States--History--20th century. I. Title.

E842.9.W274 2013
973.922092--dc23

2013035745

ISBN 978-1-61902-226-3

Cover design by Charles Brock, Faceout Studios
Interior design by meganjonesdesign.com

COUNTERPOINT
1919 Fifth Street
Berkeley, CA 94710
www.counterpointpress.com

Printed in the United States of America
Distributed by Publishers Group West

10 9 8 7 6 5 4 3 2 1

To Abraham Bolden, selected by JFK as the first black presidential Secret Service agent. Bolden is still fighting to clear his name after being framed by the Mafia almost fifty years ago.

Table of Contents

PREFACE

F IFTY YEARS HAVE passed since the murder of President John F. Kennedy, yet even with millions of words written about the case, *The Hidden History of the JFK Assassination* provides the final pieces to that puzzle for the first time. While several hundred books about President Kennedy's assassination have been published over the past five decades, fewer than two dozen have seriously dealt with the tidal wave of new information and evidence that has emerged in recent years. Many of those new revelations resulted from the 4.5 million pages of JFK assassination files released throughout the 1990s as a result of the 1992 JFK Act.

Even fewer books have presented that information in a clear, concise way accessible to readers not already steeped in the sometimes arcane and always complex terminology of JFK assassination research. Previous books that provided ample, credible documentation to prove their claims had the additional problem of extreme length. I have personal experience with that, since my first two books on JFK's murder—*Ultimate Sacrifice* and *Legacy of Secrecy*—were each more than nine hundred pages. They had a combined total of almost four thousand endnotes documenting sources, hardly the type of book that most readers can easily digest.

New revelations about the case continue to emerge, both from previously released government files and from participants in operations for which the files are still mostly withheld. For example, in 2008 *Legacy of Secrecy* first revealed and named the FBI's daring undercover CAMTEX operation, which lasted from 1985 to 1986. On December 15, 1985, that operation obtained godfather Carlos Marcello's confession that he had ordered JFK's murder. More information about the CAMTEX operation, including the name of the FBI's undercover informant, Jack Van Laningham, appeared for the first time in the updated trade paperback of *Legacy of Secrecy* in 2009.

Most of that book's information came from uncensored FBI files I uncovered from officials involved in the operation. However, since that time, I have had dozens of interviews and conversations with Van Laningham. His observations illuminated many aspects of Marcello's involvement with JFK's murder—as well as with Lee Oswald and Jack Ruby—that weren't completely clear from the files alone. In addition, I uncovered independent corroboration for many of Van Laningham's observations, originally made when he was Marcello's cellmate and confidante for many months in 1985 and 1986.

For the first time, that documented information allows the full story of JFK's assassination to be told in a clear, concise manner, one backed up by the most important earlier discoveries about JFK's murder.

The story of Carlos Marcello, Jack Van Laningham, and JFK's assassination will be told in the upcoming film *Legacy of Secrecy*, currently being produced by—and starring—Leonard DiCaprio, with Robert De Niro slated to play Marcello. However, that film can tell only a small portion of the whole story of JFK's murder. This book provides a much fuller account and provides the supporting documentation backing it up.

Credibility is always important in evaluating information about JFK's murder and in deciding which books or revelations to believe.

Because I have presented documented information from credible sources, buttressed by independent corroboration, my work has received more mainstream press coverage than most books documenting a conspiracy in JFK's murder. This includes appearing numerous times on CNN and in television documentaries about my work produced by a division of NBC News for the Discovery Channel and by German Public Television. Those organizations have been able both to verify the authenticity of the declassified files I showed on those programs and to interview some of my key sources. Other coverage has come from hundreds of newspapers, magazines, radio stations, and television stations, in this country and others. Moreover, I aided the staff of the Presidentially appointed JFK Assassination Records Review Board in the 1990s, identifying important government files that were not being turned over to the Board by US agencies as the law required.

Many of the key disclosures in this book came from more than two dozen key associates of John and Robert Kennedy, interviewed by me and by my original research collaborator, radio and television commentator Thom Hartmann. I then found or helped get declassified files that verified their accounts. In addition, my research was aided by many of the best writers, historians, and former government investigators in the field, many of whom are cited throughout the book and all of whom are named in this book's extensive Acknowledgments.

For twenty-five years, I have been building on their work and advancing the findings of the five government investigating committees that came after the Warren Commission. I spent most of that time working full-time on the case, and this book is the first compact culmination of all that research.

In response to requests from readers, this book features an Annotated Bibliography, making it easy for readers to refer to the books, articles, and documents used as source material. The Bibliography identifies books with additional well-documented information about certain aspects of JFK's assassination and specifies which websites have major document collections, where readers can view online many of the important files cited in the text. In my previous books, bibliographic information lay instead in thousands of endnotes. Though *The Hidden History of the JFK Assassination* has the same high level of documentation as my earlier works, we have dispensed with endnotes for this book. Now, it's easy to simply Google most quotations to find more information about their source. Also, because of its shorter length, this book focuses on only the most important people involved in these events—in contrast to my earlier works, which contained hundreds of names of officials, witnesses, participants, journalists, and sources, often dozens in a single chapter. Those wanting more in-depth information about any of the topics dealt with in this book can find it in the updated trade paperbacks of *Ultimate Sacrifice* (2006) and *Legacy of Secrecy* (2009) and in my 2013 edition of *Watergate: The Hidden History*, which devotes almost two hundred pages to JFK's assassination.

When I began researching the case in 1988, I started with no preconceived conclusions and looked at the evidence against all the individuals and organizations that some considered suspects. Focusing on credible sources, information, and documentation for which there is independent corroboration—and that have stood the test of time—led me to new discoveries and to a cohesive story of what really happened to President Kennedy. The final result of that research is in this book.

Since 1966, dozens of carefully researched and well-documented books have thoroughly debunked every aspect of the Warren Commission's conclusion and process, often using the Commission's own evidence as well as information that was withheld from the Commission. (The best books are listed in the Annotated Bibliography.) The most recent books to do so are 2005's *Breach of Trust* by noted historian Gerald D. McKnight and *A Cruel and Shocking Act,* veteran *New York Times* reporter Philip Shenon's 2013 book about the Warren Commission. Chapter Two of *The Hidden History of the JFK Assassination* debunks some of the Warren Commission's most glaring errors, but the rest of the book focuses primarily on telling the documented story of what led to the murder of John F. Kennedy as simply and as concisely as possible.

The Hidden History of the JFK Assassination first gives a brief overview of the overwhelming amount of evidence for a conspiracy in JFK's murder. It then describes the Warren Commission's 1964 conclusion about JFK's murder (largely adopted by authors such as Bill O'Reilly, Vincent Bugliosi, Gerald Posner, and Stephen King) and shows how that conclusion is demonstrably wrong. It also presents well-documented information that will show accused assassin Lee Oswald in a whole new light for most readers.

After revealing new information about the FBI's CAMTEX operation and Carlos Marcello, this account begins the chronological story of Marcello's rise to power. It explains why he came to be targeted by John and Robert Kennedy and how he—and his criminal associates— became involved in CIA operations against Fidel Castro without the knowledge of the Kennedys.

Step by step, the book discloses how JFK was assassinated in a way that forced several top US officials, including Attorney General Robert Kennedy, to withhold key information from the press, the public, and the Warren Commission. They did so to prevent another dangerous US confrontation with the Soviet Union just a year after the tense nuclear standoff during the Cuban Missile Crisis. Three CIA agents, officers, and assets who were involved in JFK's murder—two of whom confessed before they died—are also named. The book also reveals new information from Carlos Marcello about Lee Oswald, Jack Ruby, and the Mafia hit men in Dealey Plaza when JFK was killed.

We will also explore the hidden history of the aftermath of JFK's murder, including just how close the truth came to being exposed on several occasions. This history includes secret investigations conducted by the CIA, Naval Intelligence, and Robert Kennedy. The account shows why Robert Kennedy's associates pushed for the creation of the Warren Commission and why it was limited to essentially endorsing a conclusion that had been publicly proclaimed within hours of JFK's murder. That section includes the tragic story of Abraham Bolden, chosen by JFK to be the first black Presidential Secret Service agent, who was framed by the Mafia and then arrested when he tried to tell the Warren Commission about two earlier attempts to kill JFK, in Tampa and Chicago. The book also identifies the five later government investigating committees that had access to far more information than the Warren Commission. Those investigations eventually led Congress to conclude in 1979 that JFK had likely been killed as the result of a conspiracy, in which Carlos Marcello "had the motive, means, and opportunity."

The book reveals what happened after Marcello made his JFK confession, unveiling details about JFK's assassination in words recorded on undercover FBI audiotape. It shows why the 1992 JFK Act unanimously passed by Congress requires the Bureau to release those tapes and transcripts and why the CIA and Naval Intelligence should release their remaining files related to JFK's assassination. According to NBC News, those agencies have still not released "millions" of pages of records involving JFK's assassination. (Some of the most important files that have been released are shown in the book's photo-document section, some published for the first time.) However, *The Hidden History of the JFK Assassination* explains what is in the unreleased files, since much of the story came directly from Kennedy associates and others who experienced crucial events firsthand.

Along the way, the book also debunks some of the more pervasive myths about JFK's murder that continue to surface on the internet, years after they were proven false. The book identifies those who were involved in JFK's assassination, as well as those whose involvement—or lack of it—is less clear and may be determined only when the CIA, FBI, and Naval Intelligence release the rest of their JFK assassination files.

Releasing all the JFK assassination files is important because US–Cuba relations have been essentially frozen since the time of JFK's assassination. In part, that's because high US officials such as President Lyndon Johnson and CIA Director John McCone—and those involved in Cuban operations in 1963 who later became high officials, such as Ronald Reagan's Secretary of State Alexander Haig—believed fragmentary CIA reports that Fidel Castro was somehow behind JFK's assassination. However, historians and researchers have shown that all the "Castro killed JFK" CIA reports were either debunked and/or can be traced back to the mob bosses and their CIA associates who later confessed their roles in JFK's murder. Helping to expose that—and other parts of the hidden history of JFK's murder—readers of this book can help to remove one of the last remaining obstacles to finally ending America's fifty-two-year-long Cold War with Cuba.

CHAPTER 1

Evidence of Conspiracy

D RAMATIC NEW EVIDENCE in *The Hidden History of the JFK Assassination*, much of it from government sources and associates of John and Robert Kennedy, proves clearly and simply for the first time that President John F. Kennedy was killed by a small, tightly held conspiracy directed by two Mafia godfathers. Using critical facts never reported before, this book documents exactly who was involved, why, and how they got away with it.

It builds on the findings of Robert Kennedy and his own secret investigations, as well as those of the House Select Committee on Assassinations. The House Committee concluded in 1979 that JFK "was probably assassinated as a result of a conspiracy" and that two Mafia godfathers who were close associates—Carlos Marcello and Santo Trafficante*—"had the motive, means, and opportunity to assassinate President Kennedy."

Using exclusive interviews and newly declassified files not available to that Committee, this book provides detailed proof of that conspiracy. In addition to Marcello and Trafficante, others involved included their associates Mafia don Johnny Rosselli and mobster John

---

*Officially Santo Trafficante Jr.

Martino. Few realize that all four men made credible confessions to JFK's murder, with Marcello providing by far the most detailed account, according to FBI files and sources that for the first time are fully detailed in this book.

All four mobsters had also been assets of the Central Intelligence Agency in the early 1960s, working on the Agency's plots to kill Fidel Castro—plots that began in September 1960 at the direction of then Vice President Richard Nixon, before JFK was elected President. Those CIA–Mafia plots against Castro continued into 1963 without the knowledge of President Kennedy, Attorney General Robert Kennedy, or even JFK's CIA director, John McCone.

Marcello and Trafficante used two active-duty CIA men in their assassination plan: CIA agent Bernard Barker and CIA officer David Morales. A Congressional investigator for the House Committee discovered that Morales—in 1963 a close friend of Johnny Rosselli—had confessed involvement in JFK's murder to two close associates. Barker admitted under oath that he had watched JFK's shooting as it happened, even though JFK's motorcade through Dealey Plaza was not broadcast live, even in Dallas. Barker was also identified as being behind the picket fence on the grassy knoll at the time of JFK's shooting by two credible eyewitnesses who encountered him, one of them a Dallas Deputy Sheriff.

Important new material from FBI files and personnel allows this book to detail for the first time Carlos Marcello's own account of how he planned JFK's murder and used trusted associates to carry it out. This new information finally connects all the dots, tying Marcello to the shooters, to Lee Oswald, and to Jack Ruby. What had formerly been a mass of compelling evidence—with a few key parts missing and some connections murky—now becomes a clear, coherent, and concise story of JFK's murder.

For almost fifty years, polls have consistently shown that a majority of the American public believes JFK was killed as the result of a conspiracy. Distinguished tenured historians—among them CBS News consultant Dr. Douglas Brinkley, Dr. David Kaiser of the Naval War College, Dr. Gerald McKnight, Dr. David Wrone, and Dr. Michael Kurtz—have publicly expressed their belief that the historical evidence for a conspiracy in JFK's murder is conclusive. Yet much of the US news media still reports on this topic as if only one official government committee, the Warren Commission, ever looked into JFK's murder, and there has been only one "official" verdict: that a single assassin—depicted at the time and ever since as a "lone nut"—killed JFK. For the "lone nut" thesis to work, a bullet found in almost pristine condition had to have caused two wounds to JFK while also shattering Texas governor John Connally's rib and wrist bones. The following chapter debunks this "single bullet theory," long derided by its critics as the "magic bullet theory," and shows how anyone can easily demonstrate the physical impossibility of the single bullet theory for him- or herself.

In reality, over the course of three decades, a half dozen government committees—including the House Select Committee and most recently, in the 1990s, the JFK Assassination Records Review Board, appointed by President Clinton—investigated JFK's murder. Among the 4.5 million pages of government records the Review Board released during the 1990s was the uncensored FBI file with Carlos Marcello's clear, direct confession to JFK's murder, which I first uncovered at the National Archives in 2006. Several years earlier, I had helped high-level Review Board staff identify crucial JFK records that had not been released.

The news media rarely report that Robert F. Kennedy himself, along with numerous government officials who were associates of

RFK and JFK, voiced the belief that President Kennedy was killed as a result of a conspiracy. Robert Kennedy told aide Richard Goodwin that he thought "that mob guy in New Orleans"—Marcello—was behind his brother's death, as Goodwin confirmed to me. RFK learned about Marcello's role because he directed several trusted aides to conduct small, secret investigations into his brother's murder for him. RFK's investigators included the head of the Justice Department's "Get Hoffa Squad," Walter Sheridan, and his press secretary, Frank Mankiewicz. Both concluded that a conspiracy had killed JFK.

Other well-documented believers in an assassination conspiracy included President Lyndon Johnson, CIA Director John McCone, JFK's personal physician Admiral George Burkley (the only doctor with JFK's body at both Parkland Hospital and his autopsy at Bethesda Naval Hospital), JFK's press secretary Pierre Salinger, and JFK aides Ted Sorensen, Arthur Schlesinger Jr., and Harris Wofford. Also expressing belief in a conspiracy were LBJ aides Joseph A. Califano Jr. and Alexander Haig, plus numerous Justice Department Mafia prosecutors for RFK, including Ronald Goldfarb and Robert Blakey—the last also authored the RICO Act, used in prosecuting organized crime, and directed the House Select Committee's investigation. According to *Vanity Fair*, even Dallas Police Chief Jesse Curry "believed two gunmen were involved," while Kennedy aide Arthur Schlesinger Jr. wrote that CIA Director John McCone told Robert Kennedy he "thought there were two people involved in the shooting."

JFK's two closest aides, Dave Powers and Kenneth O'Donnell, actually witnessed two shots from the grassy knoll, from their perfect vantage point in the limousine directly behind JFK's. (One of the Secret Service agents in their limo testified that he also thought that JFK's fatal head shot came from the grassy knoll.) Powers and

O'Donnell both confirmed the grassy knoll shots to House Speaker Tip O'Neill, as O'Neill described in his 1987 autobiography, *Man of the House*. Later, in an exclusive interview with my research collaborator Thom Hartmann, Powers detailed how he was pressured to change his Warren Commission testimony "for the good of the country." As I first discovered (with the help of the National Archives), Powers's perjured affidavit was taken by Commission counsel Arlen Specter, the leading proponent of the single bullet theory, an important detail the Warren Commission omitted when it published Powers's affidavit.

It's important to stress that much of my information came not only from exclusive interviews with more than two dozen associates of John and Robert Kennedy but also from former FBI, Secret Service, military intelligence, and Congressional personnel, including those critical of how their agencies handled the investigation. All of those sources provided crucial firsthand information. While some of their disclosures have been detailed in my previous books dealing with the Kennedys—*Ultimate Sacrifice* (2005; updated 2006), *Legacy of Secrecy* (2008; expanded 2009), and several chapters in *Watergate: The Hidden History* (2011)—many important new revelations are detailed in this book for the first time.

It has taken almost fifty years for the full story of JFK's assassination to emerge, for reasons of national security that are detailed later, compounded by the reluctance of agencies such as the FBI and CIA to reveal their own intelligence failures and unauthorized operations.

Government agencies and officials withheld many hundreds of thousands of pages of relevant files and information on covert operations from the Warren Commission, but neither the public nor most journalists knew that when the *Warren Report* was issued in September 1964. The sheer volume of information publicly available today that was hidden from the Warren Commission is staggering: the CIA's plots with dangerous mob bosses to kill Fidel Castro, the attempt to kill JFK in Tampa four days before Dallas and in Chicago before that, Jack Ruby's work for the Mafia, Oswald's many links to Carlos Marcello, and much more. Instead, the American news media embraced and helped to disseminate the *Report* since it had been approved by a distinguished panel headed by Supreme Court Chief Justice Earl Warren.

Many people don't realize that in addition to the best-selling one-volume *Warren Report*, the Commission also issued twenty-six volumes of supporting material. By 1966 authors and journalists were pointing out that the evidence contained in those twenty-six volumes didn't support the *Warren Report*'s own conclusions. A flurry of critical books began to appear, starting with former Congressional investigator Harold Weisberg's *Whitewash: The Report on the Warren Report*, followed by *The Unanswered Questions about President Kennedy's Assassination* by veteran reporter Sylvan Fox, who soon joined the *New York Times*. Next came Edward Jay Epstein's *Inquest*, which even former JFK aides found compelling. Best-selling books followed: Mark Lane's *Rush to Judgment* and Harvard professor Josiah Thompson's *Six Seconds in Dallas*, as well as Sylvia Meagher's *Accessories after the Fact*. All of those authors used the Warren Commission's own information, along with fresh interviews and overlooked news accounts, to undermine the Warren Report's "lone nut/ single bullet" conclusion.

Those efforts helped to spark major investigations by the *New York Times* and major weekly magazines such as *Life*, *Look*, and the *Saturday Evening Post*. However, declassified files now show that FBI Director J. Edgar Hoover and CIA Director Richard Helms immediately began a significant public relations counteroffensive, issuing detailed instructions on how to smear critics of the *Warren Report*. For example, in a January 4, 1967, CIA memo in which the Agency gives fifty-three pages of specific instructions on how to counter the growing tide of books and articles questioning the "lone nut" conclusion, a domestic operation far outside the bounds of the Agency's charter. In many ways, those PR counteroffensives by the FBI and CIA would last for decades, and some writers make the case that they continue even today.

Also hindering the 1966 and early 1967 investigations by mainstream news organizations was the JFK murder probe begun in late 1966 by New Orleans District Attorney Jim Garrison (portrayed by Kevin Costner in the film *JFK*). Though Garrison first focused on Carlos Marcello's pilot and investigator in 1963—David Ferrie—Marcello's name never publicly surfaced in Garrison's probe. FBI files show that Garrison came close to publicly naming Marcello twice but never did.

After Ferrie's sudden death early in Garrison's investigation, the District Attorney took his inquiry far from the Mafia, and it soon became a media circus. None of the hundreds of articles in the mainstream press about it mentioned Ferrie's work for Marcello in 1963 or raised the possibility of Mafia involvement in the assassination.

By mid-1967 the mainstream media had ended serious investigations of JFK's assassination and had become highly critical of Garrison. Mainstream journalists didn't resume writing about the assassination until late 1974 and early 1975, in the aftermath of Watergate investigations, when the first widespread reports emerged about CIA–Mafia plots to kill Fidel Castro in the early 1960s emerged. Those revelations spawned new investigations such as the Rockefeller Commission and the Senate Church Committee, which eventually added a JFK assassination subcommittee that included Senator Gary Hart. In the summer of 1975, the mob stymied those investigations by murdering two key figures in the CIA–Mafia plots—Rosselli's former boss Sam Giancana and Jimmy Hoffa—before they could testify. The investigations were also hindered by the massive amount of relevant information withheld by the FBI and CIA. When Johnny Rosselli, who was central to the CIA–Mafia plots, was gruesomely murdered the following year, the resulting media firestorm led to the creation of the House Select Committee on Assassinations. The House Committee also found itself thwarted by a spate of sudden deaths of mob-connected potential witnesses—some murders, some suicides, some (such as Martino and Morales) by natural causes—and the CIA, FBI, and military intelligence withheld even more relevant information. In the case of both the House Select Committee and the Church Committee, the CIA assigned as its Committee liaison an Agency veteran of the 1963 anti-Castro plotting who actually should have been called as a witness.

Still, due to books such as Dan Moldea's *The Hoffa Wars* and the House Select Committee's investigation, the press finally linked Marcello and Trafficante to JFK's assassination. Surprisingly, only in the late 1970s did Jack Ruby first become widely identified in the press as a mobster, even though some journalists had known of his mob ties for years. After the House Committee ended with its 1979 conclusion of conspiracy, more books and lengthy mainstream articles with evidence of conspiracy followed, including works by former Senate and House investigator Gaeton Fonzi and former FBI agent William Turner, who had been the first agent to publicly confront J. Edgar Hoover. Both men gave me important, early assistance when I began researching JFK's murder in the late 1980s.

In 1985 the FBI finally obtained Carlos Marcello's confession to JFK's assassination, including details of how it was carried out and the godfather's meetings with Oswald and Ruby. Yet none of that information was released to the public at the time or during the intense media coverage of the twenty-fifth anniversary of JFK's murder in November 1988—and in fact it wouldn't reach the public for years. Nonetheless, mainstream documentaries and articles casting suspicion on Marcello and the Mafia appeared at the time.

Oliver Stone left the Mafia—including the extensive work that David Ferrie (memorably played in the film by Joe Pesci) performed for Carlos Marcello in 1963—almost completely out of his 1991 film *JFK*. Still, it was superior filmmaking, using many documented facts, except for some of the remarks by District Attorney Jim Garrison (an associate of Marcello's brother Joe) and all of the remarks by the fictional character "Mr. X."*

However, the popularity and cultural impact of Stone's film did lead directly to passage of the 1992 JFK Records Act, designed to release all of the JFK assassination records. It took three years for the first releases to begin, and in the meantime, Gerald Posner's 1993 *Case Closed* was part of a well-orchestrated media campaign to push back against the views of *JFK* and the conspiracy books by Mark Lane and others that had become best sellers in its wake. Posner was criticized for presenting essentially a one-sided case against Oswald in championing the *Warren Report*'s "lone nut/single bullet" theory. (It would take seventeen years for Posner to issue a 2010 news release admitting

---

*Mr. X, played by Donald Sutherland, was based on retired Colonel L. Fletcher Prouty, an advisor to the film. He was caught providing false information before filming was complete, as verified by the book of the *JFK* screenplay. His claims were later debunked in his interview with the JFK Assassination Records Review Board.

". . . I've always believed that had Mark Lane represented Oswald, he would have won an acquittal.") Similar criticisms were leveled fourteen years later against Vincent Bugliosi's massive *Reclaiming History,* which—far from being an objective account—grew out of Bugliosi's work as Oswald's prosecutor in a televised mock trial.

Even today, some authors continue to ignore the Mafia's confessed role in JFK's murder, the findings of the House Select Committee, and the new file releases. That's true for Bill O'Reilly's *Killing Kennedy,* which basically accepts the *Warren Report*'s conclusion, and for Brian Latell's 2012 *Castro's Secrets.* Latell, who admits his work for the CIA's Cold War against Cuba goes back to the 1960s, also implies that Fidel Castro's government was somehow linked to JFK's assassination, something CIA personnel have been unsuccessfully claiming for decades.

The evidence of Carlos Marcello's guilt in JFK's murder was extensive even before his confession, but the new information makes his motivation and methods even clearer. Marcello was far more powerful than any other godfather, and he remained so for an unusually long period of time. For almost forty years, he was the unchallenged ruler of a territory that included all of Louisiana, most of Texas, and much of Mississippi. Unlike the leaders of warring Mafia factions in cities like New York, Marcello didn't need to fight with the surrounding mob bosses; he became partners with them, expanding his reach even farther. For example, government investigators showed that Marcello played a key role in the ruthless, highly lucrative French Connection heroin network run by Santo Trafficante—which is one reason several members of that network played roles in JFK's murder.

Investigators determined that by the 1960s, the revenue of Marcello's vast criminal empire was equal to that of the largest

American corporation of the time, General Motors. This vast wealth allowed Marcello to own mayors, judges, governors, members of Congress, and senators. Marcello even employed his own high-powered Washington lobbyist (the same one used by countries such as Nicaragua) and a powerful Washington law firm. Yet he maintained a very low public profile and managed to remain out of the spotlight— until John and Robert Kennedy dragged him in front of the TV cameras covering their Senate crime hearings in 1959. That started the Kennedys' war against the Mafia, and against Marcello in particular. As described in later chapters, that war resulted in the Kennedys' April 1961 deportation of Marcello to Central America.

This unprecedented—and apparently extralegal—act involved a law-enforcement convoy rushing Marcello to the New Orleans airport, where a waiting plane took him to Guatemala, where Marcello had obtained a fake birth certificate. Marcello, who had seemed untouchable under the Eisenhower–Nixon Administration, was furious over the Kennedys' action. After Guatemala ordered Marcello out, his hatred of the Kennedy brothers soon became even more intense. The godfather had to trudge through the jungle in his Gucci shoes, accompanied only by his lawyer, all the while swearing eternal vengeance against President Kennedy and his brother. After sneaking back into the United States with the aid of his pilot, David Ferrie, Marcello faced increasing pressure from the President and Attorney General Robert Kennedy, culminating in his federal trial in New Orleans in November 1963.

Thanks to bribing a key juror, Marcello made sure he was acquitted on November 22, 1963, just after JFK's murder. Knowing he would be acquitted, Marcello had even planned a celebration with his family and associates for the evening of JFK's assassination. (The night of JFK's murder, Marcello's partner in the crime, Santo Trafficante, publicly toasted JFK's assassination with his attorney, Frank Ragano, at a posh restaurant in the same Tampa hotel where JFK had spoken just four days earlier.)

Because Marcello ruled the oldest mob family in the United States, he didn't have to get approval from the national Mafia commission before undertaking major hits. Unlike most mob families (except for Chicago), Marcello and his close associates also had a history of targeting government officials who posed a threat, including the 1954 assassination of Alabama's anti-mob Attorney General–elect.

AFTER BECOMING PRESIDENT and Attorney General, John and Robert Kennedy had tried in vain to convict Marcello as part of their massive war against organized crime. Their war against the mob became Marcello's reason for killing JFK, in order to end Attorney General Robert Kennedy's power and prosecution of him. For years, historians believed the FBI had not followed up on the House Committee's 1979 recommendation to investigate Marcello further for JFK's murder. I was the first to discover the FBI's uncensored CAMTEX files about Marcello in the National Archives in 2006 and revealed them in about a dozen pages of *Legacy of Secrecy* in 2008. However, the files contained so much information—and there was so much more from my exclusive interviews with the FBI supervisor for CAMTEX, with an additional key CAMTEX FBI official, and with another individual involved—that there wasn't room to include all the CAMTEX revelations. NBC News tracked down CAMTEX informant Jack Van Laningham for a Discovery Channel special featuring me and *Legacy*. But there was room—and time—to insert only a few additional sentences naming Van Laningham in the updated trade paperback of *Legacy* because three new chapters of other important new information had already been added.

However, since that time, I have had more than a dozen exclusive, probing talks with Van Laningham about Marcello, fleshing out even more material in the FBI's CAMTEX files. Van Laningham—an ordinary businessman who went to prison after one drunken escapade (robbing a bank with a TV remote control and a bag of laundry, which he claimed were a detonator and a bomb)—was eventually made Marcello's cellmate by the FBI. He drew Marcello out in numerous conversations over many months as the two became friends, all while Van Laningham was reporting to the FBI and recording Marcello's remarks via a court-authorized, bugged transistor radio, supplied by the FBI.

Later chapters quote Marcello describing for the first time exactly how he had JFK killed, using Marcello's own descriptions given to FBI informant Van Laningham, backed up with independent corroboration for many of the godfather's statements. Marcello ordered the murder because of his often-voiced hatred of John and Robert Kennedy over his deportation, his ongoing prosecution, and their unrelenting and ever-escalating war against the Mafia, especially against his allies such as Santo Trafficante and Jimmy Hoffa. Yet Marcello had not reached and maintained his powerful position by taking rash action, especially where hits were concerned. The House Committee found evidence that Marcello and Trafficante had carefully planned the JFK hit for more than a year.

Mafia don Johnny Rosselli, the Chicago Mafia's man in Hollywood and Las Vegas, soon joined the godfathers' plot, since his boss, Sam Giancana, was also under intense pressure from the Kennedy Justice Department. Ever cautious, Marcello, Trafficante, and Rosselli developed one plan for shooting JFK in a motorcade that could be used in any of three cities: Chicago, home of Rosselli's mob family, Trafficante's base of Tampa, or Dallas, in Marcello's territory. That way, even their backup plan (Tampa) had a backup (Dallas). Since the medical evidence in JFK's murder shows at least two gunmen were involved—and the evidence against Oswald as a shooter falls apart under close examination, as the next chapter starts to show—who pulled the triggers?

Carlos Marcello said that he imported two of the hit men from Europe for the JFK assignment; an independent account shows this was a favored technique for Marcello in other hits as well—a way to use difficult-to-trace shooters for especially sensitive hits. Later chapters explain why the two men were chosen, how they obtained travel documents and aliases, and what the FBI was able to learn about their actual identities. They also detail why Marcello said the two shooters came into the United States from Canada, through Michigan, instead of making a border crossing much closer to Dallas.

Michigan was logical because the mob bosses planned their first attempt to kill JFK for Chicago, on November 2, 1963. JFK's Chicago motorcade route passed by a warehouse that employed an ex-Marine with recent parallels to Oswald. After Chicago-based Secret Service agents learned that four hit men were at large in the city, the ex-Marine was arrested and the attempt called off. As detailed later, JFK canceled not just his motorcade but his entire visit at the last minute, and news of the threat was kept out of the press by the White House and Secret Service, even though it was known to some reporters.

Marcello's next attempt was planned for Trafficante's home base of Tampa, where the longest domestic motorcade of JFK's Presidency was scheduled for November 18, 1963. However, Tampa's police chief, J. P. Mullins, told me that federal authorities learned about a plot to shoot JFK in the motorcade. Security precautions were intense as JFK (without Jackie) bravely went ahead with the motorcade for national security reasons. Once again, the President's men insisted that no word of the threat appear in the press. Only one small article slipped out the day after JFK died, but it was quickly suppressed and never seen by the Warren Commission or the House Select Committee.

That meant JFK had to be assassinated in Dallas, Marcello's territory. As revealed later in this book for the first time, Carlos Marcello explained how his second-in-command lieutenant in Dallas—mobster and restaurateur Joe Campisi Sr.—played a key role in managing the shooters for JFK's murder. The House Committee had been suspicious of Campisi, a close associate of Jack Ruby. (Ruby went to Campisi's restaurant the night before JFK's assassination, and Campisi visited Ruby in jail soon after Oswald was shot.) Ruby has long been reported to have been the Mafia's "payoff man" for the Dallas Police, but the Dallas Chief of Detectives regularly conducted mob business with Campisi every Sunday night for years.

The book documents other associates of Marcello and Trafficante who were reportedly in Dallas to help with JFK's assassination. They include Michel Victor Mertz, Trafficante's French Connection heroin kingpin and a former assassin who had intelligence connections, as well as CIA agent and Cuban exile Bernard Barker, then working on the CIA's most sensitive authorized anti-Castro operation.

Carlos Marcello's own words, confided to his trusted friend, FBI informant Van Laningham, provide the final pieces to the JFK assassination puzzle. As part of setting up Oswald, Marcello had his pilot, David Ferrie, bring Oswald to meet the godfather personally—and secretly. The House Committee uncovered evidence that Oswald had met Ferrie years earlier when Ferrie helped supervise Oswald's Civil Air Patrol unit and that in the summer of 1963 Oswald was actually working with Ferrie.

Marcello also told Van Laningham about his meetings with Jack Ruby and said that Ruby's club in Dallas was one of several in that city secretly owned by Marcello's organization. Ruby just fronted the club for Marcello, and when Ruby was caught stealing from the till to pay his back taxes, Marcello summoned him to Churchill Farms and made the trembling Ruby an offer he couldn't refuse. Essentially, Ruby had to arrange for a Dallas policeman to kill Oswald soon after JFK's murder or else Ruby would have to do the job himself. Marcello's meetings with Ruby and Oswald are contained in the declassified CAMTEX FBI files.

In addition, Marcello's accounts of the two shooters and his meetings with Oswald and Ruby are backed up by much additional independent evidence, as described in later chapters. It all forms a consistent and credible story that finally makes sense of what until now has been a sprawling mass of evidence with several key gaps.

Much of the CAMTEX information appears for the first time in this book, since I am the only author to have extensively interviewed Van Laningham, CAMTEX FBI Supervisor Thomas Kimmel, and the CAMTEX FBI official who heard all the secretly recorded tapes of Marcello.

Further confirmation for Marcello's story comes from my exclusive interviews with two noncriminal businessmen in Louisiana, men who had befriended Carlos Marcello in one case and his family in another. The interviews include the account of a friend of Carlos Marcello's who heard an outburst very similar to the first time Marcello confessed to murdering JFK during CAMTEX. In addition, a Louisiana man who dated Marcello's daughter and shared a large fishing boat with the godfather, heard from a Marcello employee about the godfather's plan to assassinate JFK.

Another new source is a businessman who became friends with Marcello's brother Joe. The businessman was actually with Joe Marcello when Carlos first learned that Van Laningham was really an informant for the FBI. Carlos Marcello's discovery of Van Laningham's role eventually resulted in a documented hit attempt on the FBI's CAMTEX informant when Van Laningham was on parole in Tampa.

In addition to Marcello's explicit JFK confession, made in front of two witnesses, Santo Trafficante also confessed his involvement in JFK's murder, and later chapters have new revelations about Trafficante's admission. Also detailed are the confessions of two mob associates of Marcello's, Johnny Rosselli and John Martino, who were both CIA assets, as were Marcello and Trafficante. According to former Justice Department prosecutor William Hundley, shortly before Rosselli was brutally murdered (following his last meeting with Trafficante), Rosselli confessed his involvement to his attorney. Not long before CIA asset John Martino died from natural causes, he also confessed to a reporter for *Newsday*. As the book shows, most of the mobsters Marcello and Trafficante used in the plot had worked for the CIA on anti-Castro operations, as did the two godfathers themselves. This enabled them to feed disinformation into US intelligence networks before and after JFK's murder to force a government cover-up.

Marcello and Trafficante used their inside knowledge of covert US operations to topple Fidel Castro in order to kill JFK in a way that forced high US officials—including President Johnson, Robert Kennedy, J. Edgar Hoover, and the CIA—to withhold key information from the press, public, and investigators. The officials did so to prevent another nuclear confrontation with the Soviets, just a year after the Cuban Missile Crisis, because Marcello, Trafficante, and their allies had planted phony evidence implicating Fidel Castro in JFK's murder. In the fall of 1963, the godfathers knew from their CIA associates that John and Robert Kennedy had formed a secret subcommittee of the National Security Council to make contingency plans in case Fidel attempted the "assassination of American officials" in response to US efforts to overthrow him. US officials were primed and ready when the phony evidence implicating Fidel in JFK's murder quickly surfaced, triggering a cover-up to protect national security—a cover-up that in some ways continues today.

Also triggering cover-ups for national security reasons was the fact that JFK had a top-secret plan with the head of the Cuban Army, Commander Juan Almeida, to overthrow Fidel Castro on December 1, 1963—ten days after Dallas. JFK's Secretary of State Dean Rusk first revealed that plan to me; it has since been confirmed in great detail by other JFK associates and hundreds of pages of files declassified in the 1990s. JFK had barred the Mafia from the coup and from reopening their casinos, but Marcello and Trafficante managed to penetrate the highly secret operation via their CIA associates who worked on it, such as Bernard Barker and David Morales. Later chapters quote FBI files showing that a surprising number of Marcello associates— including Jack Ruby, John Martino, and David Ferrie—knew about the top-secret coup plan, even though it was so secret that government committees, from the Warren Commission to the House Select Committee, never learned of it.

JFK's goal for the coup was a democratic Cuba with no Mafia influence, but Marcello saw a way to use parts of the secret coup plan to force a massive government cover-up after JFK's murder. If made public, JFK's role in the plan to overthrow Castro could have triggered World War III in those tense Cold War times. Even years later, the plan's exposure could have cost the lives of JFK's ally, Commander Almeida. That's one reason the government kept so much about JFK's murder so secret for so long, since Almeida remained in place and unexposed for decades, passing away in 2009 when he was still a revered figure and a high official in Cuba.

The secret coup plan, and the Contingency Plans to protect it, helps explain why reporters in Dallas were warned off, for national security reasons, when they were pursuing leads that could have led to the exposure of US covert actions against Cuba. According to an NBC cameraman, when Oswald's link to David Ferrie began to surface two days after JFK's assassination, "[a]n FBI agent said that I should never discuss what we discovered for the good of the country." "For the good of the country" is the same phrase officials used to pressure Powers and O'Donnell to change their Warren Commission testimony about having seen shots from the grassy knoll. The same principle was at work in Dallas, and "members of NBC News" there told veteran TV journalist Peter Noyes that "they were convinced their superiors wanted certain evidence suppressed at the request of someone in Washington."

In the same way, preventing World War III was the real goal of the Warren Commission, and in that it succeeded. It's also one reason that even though a dozen of Marcello's lieutenants and family were interviewed about JFK's assassination or even arrested by law enforcement, Marcello's name is nowhere to be found in the *Warren Report*.

As the fiftieth anniversary of the tragic events in Dallas approaches, it's ironic to look back and realize how much important information the FBI had back in 1985, much of it from Marcello himself in the

CAMTEX undercover operation. Had it been released by the twenty-fifth anniversary of JFK's murder in 1988, the public's view of JFK's murder would have been vastly different then and certainly would be today. Instead, the Bureau initially withheld the information from the JFK Assassination Records Review Board for several years, giving Board members only a few dozen pages about CAMTEX and Marcello's confession at the last minute, as their terms expired and their operation closed. I discovered those uncensored files seven years later, and this book represents the first full account of that operation and of Marcello's startling admissions.

CHAPTER 2

"Single Bullet Theory" Demolished and a New Look at Oswald

T HE TWO CORNERSTONES of the 1964 *Warren Report* are the "single bullet theory" and its depiction of Oswald as a "lone nut"* Communist who fired the only shots at JFK's motorcade, all from the sixth floor of his workplace, the Texas School Book Depository. However, considerable evidence that calls into question both theories has been available to the general public since 1966. Additional information and files that demolish those key assertions have emerged in the succeeding decades. This chapter shows why the single bullet theory is impossible and then uses well-documented facts to present a completely different view of Oswald—the only one that accounts for all the known facts about him.

First, the single bullet theory of the 1964 *Warren Report*—and authors supporting it since that time—maintains that only three shots were fired at the limousine on Elm Street holding President Kennedy and his wife, Jackie; Governor Connally and his wife, Nellie, in the seat in front of them; and two Secret Service agents in the front seat. The Warren Commission's theory says that one shot not only completely missed the

---

*A term first applied to Oswald by FBI Director J. Edgar Hoover.

limo but missed the entire street, hitting a curb and knocking a piece of concrete (or a bullet fragment) up to hit a bystander, James Teague. The Commission said that another bullet, the first to strike Kennedy, entered his back, exited his throat just below his Adam's apple, and then dived down to hit Governor Connally, who was sitting in front of JFK. That bullet caused multiple wounds in Connally—including shattering four inches of his rib, smashing into his wrist bones, and plowing into his thigh—before emerging in almost pristine condition. That remarkable bullet was supposedly found on Governor Connally's stretcher at Parkland Hospital just over an hour after the shooting and was later matched to Oswald's cheap, mail-order Mannlicher-Carcano rifle, cinching the case against the ex-Marine marksman, as the Commission indicated it had unanimously concluded. The third and final shot—according to the Commission—was the horrible, fatal head shot, which the Commission said Oswald fired from behind the President.

In the *Warren Report* itself, the Commissioners—and the staff of lawyers that actually wrote the Report, primarily based on the FBI's original investigation and additional testimony—claimed that the single bullet theory wasn't essential to this conclusion, but that's simply not correct. The only thing almost all authors and historians who have written about JFK's murder agree on is that the single bullet theory is required for the Warren Commission's conclusion that Oswald did all the shooting. Given the timing of the shots, it was simply impossible for Oswald and his old rifle to have fired more than three shots quickly enough—and that's not even giving him time to aim again for his second and third shots. So if there were four shots, or if any of the shots came from a location other than the "sniper's nest" on sixth floor of the Texas School Book Depository far behind President Kennedy's limo, then there was at least one other shooter, and thus a conspiracy.

Even among the seven members of the Warren Commission, the belief in the single bullet theory was not unanimous. It's now well documented that arch-conservative Senator Richard B. Russell of Georgia strenuously objected to its inclusion and wanted to issue a dissenting opinion about it, until he was talked into compromise wording of the Report at the last minute. Commission members Senator Sherman Cooper of Kentucky and Senator Hale Boggs of Louisiana also doubted the theory.

Others who actually witnessed the shooting or its aftermath opposed the single bullet theory even more adamantly, and they understood that without it there must have been at least two shooters. Governor John Connally always stated that he was struck by the first shot and that a separate shot struck JFK, and Nellie Connally agreed in her testimony. JFK's personal physician, Admiral George Burkley, the only doctor present at both Parkland Hospital in Dallas and in the autopsy room at Bethesda Naval Hospital, just outside Washington, DC, filled out Kennedy's death certificate. He described JFK's back wound as being too low for the bullet to have exited just below his Adam's apple, as the autopsy photos clearly show. Even the three official autopsy doctors—James Humes, Pierre Finck, and J. Thornton Boswell—testified to the Commission under oath that they did not believe the bullet that shattered Connally's rib and wrist was the same one that struck JFK in the back. Noted forensic pathologist Cyril Wecht shared that conclusion when he served on the Forensic Pathology Panel of the House Select Committee on Assassinations in 1978.[*]

---

[*] Wecht was reportedly the only member of the Panel without personal or professional ties to the original autopsy doctors and was the only one to disagree with the magic bullet theory.

JFK's two closest aides, Dave Powers and Kenny O'Donnell, both riding in the limousine behind JFK's, said that two shots came from the right front of the motorcade—the area of the "grassy knoll" with its picket fence—and many other witnesses in Dealey Plaza also saw or heard shots from that area. These witnesses included Abraham Zapruder, who made the famous film of the assassination, standing to the left and in front of the grassy knoll, and who testified that he thought the shots "came from back of me." According to investigative journalist Anthony Summers, "a dozen people were actually on the grassy knoll when the President was shot, and almost all of them believed some of the gunfire came from behind them, high up on the knoll itself," though "many were never called by the Warren Commission." He notes that even "sixteen people, in or outside the Book Depository, indicated some shooting came from the knoll." While the number of shots claimed by all the known Dealey Plaza witnesses ranged from two to five, in 1966 author Josiah Thompson found that "with no exceptions, all those witnesses who were deep inside the Depository (either at work or in hallways) report hearing fewer than three shots"—either just one shot or two. When single bullet theory supporters claim that most people in Dealey Plaza heard three shots and that they came from the Book Depository, they're including witnesses such as Powers and O'Donnell, who later admitted that they were pressured to change their testimony. It's important to remember while reading this book that even before the release of 4.5 million pages of files, author Henry Hurt discovered in 1986 that "at least 60 witnesses claimed that the FBI in some way altered what the witnesses had reported." Many more such claims have emerged since then, and the witness intimidation/alteration always favored the theory—stated as fact by the FBI within hours of the crime—that Oswald was the lone assassin.

JFK's autopsy records and clothes show that his back wound was almost six inches below his collar. Even the 1964 attempt to restage the shooting by the FBI—which always slanted its investigation toward Oswald as a single assassin—depicted the wound on its test subject accurately, about six inches below the collar. The Warren volumes even included a photo of that FBI reenactment with the back wound accurately placed, yet the Commission ignored it when adopting the single bullet theory.

Any bullet fired from the sixth floor of the Book Depository that entered JFK's back would have been traveling downward at a steep angle. Yet for the "lone nut/magic bullet theory" to work, that same bullet had to cause the wound just below JFK's Adam's apple—a wound that is significantly higher than the wound in JFK's back. Even if the bullet somehow ricocheted off one of JFK's bones, theoretically turning upward to exit JFK's throat, it would have been impossible for the bullet to change course in midair to dive down to hit Connally. In 1997 Warren Commissioner Gerald Ford admitted to the Associated Press that he had changed the description of the "back wound" in the *Warren Report* into a "back of the neck" wound. Raising the back wound almost six inches made the single bullet theory appear more viable.

Anyone can disprove the single bullet theory by simply sitting a person (preferably a six-foot-tall male) in a chair. With your test subject in a chair, measure six inches below the top of his collar and put a mark there. Then put another small mark just below his Adam's apple. You don't even need to figure the exact downward angle of the bullet, which is a matter of some debate. The autopsy physician who probed JFK's back wound said the downward angle was 45 to 60 degrees, but all experts agree that the angle was downward at least 15 to 20 degrees, possibly much more. On a normal-sized adult male, the wound just under the Adam's apple would be significantly higher than a back wound almost six inches below the collar. Thus the single bullet theory is physically impossible and should rightly be called the "magic bullet" theory. Historian Gerald D. McKnight points out:

> A theory is a well-supported and well-tested hypothesis or set of hypotheses. [But] the [Warren] Commission's one-bullet construction never met these demanding standards. It was an ad-hoc invention or fabrication to meet the Commission's requirements for a lone-assassin, no conspiracy explanation of the Kennedy assassination.

Since that's the case, this book will henceforth refer to the almost pristine bullet as the "magic bullet."

Dr. McKnight devoted many pages of his acclaimed Warren Commission critique *Breach of Trust* to the many other reasons the "magic bullet" theory is impossible. Some of this information comes from files unavailable until recent years, but most of it has been known for decades yet ignored or glossed over by "magic bullet" theorists.

One obvious disproof of the "magic bullet" theory is visible to anyone watching the Zapruder film. Notice JFK, when he emerges from behind a sign, clearly shot in the throat as he raises his arms to his neck. At that exact instant—and for several moments more—John Connally is seen just as clearly holding his white Stetson hat with his right hand, even though the "magic bullet" has supposedly already smashed his rib and shattered his right wrist. In addition, doctors testified that more small bullet fragments were removed from Connally's wounds than were missing from the almost pristine bullet. The amount of material missing from the "magic bullet" was about the weight of a postage stamp, far less than the weight of those bullet fragments.

As for JFK's throat wound, the Dallas doctors called it a small wound of "entrance," meaning JFK was shot from the front. Chapter Sixteen explains how that tiny (3–5mm) neat entrance wound seen by the Dallas doctors became the much larger, jagged wound seen in JFK's Bethesda autopsy photos. Since the Bethesda doctors couldn't find a bullet while probing JFK's back wound during the autopsy, they were relieved to hear that the almost pristine "magic bullet" had been found in Dallas. However, Dr. David Osborne—later an Admiral and Deputy Surgeon General of the Navy—told Congressional investigators that he saw "an intact bullet roll . . . onto the autopsy table" when JFK was first removed from his casket, before the start of the official autopsy. "I had that bullet in my hand and looked at it," he said, and it was "reasonably clean [and] unmarred," but "the Secret Service took it." An X-ray technician at the autopsy also saw "a pretty good-sized bullet . . . when we lifted [JFK] up . . . that's when it came out." The Commanding Officer of the Naval Medical School at the time, Captain John Stover, told two authors "there was a bullet in the Bethesda morgue." However, the "magic bullet" wasn't at Bethesda but many miles away at the FBI laboratory. Like so much other crucial evidence, including JFK's brain, the Bethesda bullet vanished from the official record, for reasons explained in later chapters.

FBI and other scientific claims that the "magic bullet" could be matched to the same batch of ammunition as the bullet fragments found in JFK's limo were finally debunked to the scientific community in 2007 by Texas A&M researchers Cliff Spiegelman and Dennis James. When the Army provided the Warren Commission with its top wound ballistic expert, Dr. Joseph R. Dolce, he and his associate Dr. Fredrick Light Jr. said that the "magic bullet" couldn't "have shattered Connally's wrist and still retained its virtually pristine condition."

When they fired Oswald's actual Mannlicher-Carcano "into ten cadaver wrists . . . in each and every instance the bullet was 'markedly deformed'" and not pristine. Dolce and his tests were not mentioned in the *Warren Report*. Instead, Warren Commission assistant counsel Arlen Specter—the creator of the "magic bullet" theory—relied on a veterinarian's tests, which involved shooting into horse meat, gelatin blocks, and goat carcasses, to "prove" his theory. Decades later, a wound ballistics expert said he was finally able to produce a relatively unmarred bullet after firing into a cadaver's wrist, but only by reducing the bullet's speed by half and not firing it through a rib first.

In a desperate attempt to make the "magic bullet" theory work, some authors claim that JFK was leaning very far forward in his seat or had his suit coat and shirt greatly bunched up along the back of his head, but photos and the Zapruder film show that that was clearly not the case. The bunching was minor, which is why the wound in the autopsy drawing and photograph lined up perfectly with the bullet holes in JFK's shirt and suit coat, all almost six inches below the top of the collar. When computer animation was used in a major television special to try to make the "magic bullet" theory work, JFK's neck and shoulders were so distorted that he almost didn't look human. In one Discovery Channel special (not one of mine), when JFK's shooting was restaged accurately, it showed that the bullet striking JFK in the back would have exited through his heart, not just below his Adam's apple.

In addition, that Discovery crew had trouble getting its Mannlicher-Carcano rifle to fire, even though it had been worked on by a top gunsmith, unlike Oswald's cheap mail-order rifle. The problem wasn't just the rifle's age, since a 1967 special by CBS had the same problems, even though CBS used a rifle that fired faster and was in better condition than Oswald's weapon. More than a third of the attempts had to be disqualified "because of trouble with the rifle," as documented by author Michael T. Griffith. Not only that, but in the case of CBS, "not one of the eleven participating expert marksmen scored at least two hits (as the 'magic bullet' theory requires) on his first attempt. A majority, seven of them, failed to do so on ANY of their attempts. Oswald would have had only one attempt."

Accounts supporting the "magic bullet" theory and Oswald as the lone assassin usually mention that Oswald earned a rating of "marksman" when he was in the Marines, leaving the impression that he was a crack shot. That's an important part of the "magic bullet/lone nut" theory since in all the years since the assassination, no sharpshooter has ever duplicated the shooting attributed to Oswald on his first try and with an accurate moving target. However, the reality is that "marksman" is the lowest of the three Marine shooting titles. The lowest possible score on the test is 190, with the highest being 250. In other words, almost anyone could get a score of at least 190 and be considered a "marksman" on that test. Before Oswald left the Marines, he scored only one point above the minimum and sometimes missed not just the bull's-eye but the entire target.

Finally, the evidence is clear that the "magic bullet" was not even found on Governor Connally's stretcher. At Dallas's Parkland Hospital, an hour and fifteen minutes after JFK was shot, Senior Engineer Darrell Tomlinson found the nearly pristine bullet. It was on one of two stretchers close together in a hallway, one of which had probably been used to transport Connally. The other hadn't been used for either Kennedy or Connally but instead for either a female adult patient who had been "bleeding from the mouth" or a "two-and-a-half-year-old [patient] with a deep cut on his chin."

Tomlinson initially told Arlen Specter that he had found the bullet on the stretcher that had NOT held Connally. But after being pressured and intimidated by Specter to reverse his testimony, Tomlinson claimed uncertainty, still refusing to say the bullet came from Connally's stretcher. However, Dr. McKnight's recent analysis of the testimony of Parkland nurse Jane C. Wester and orderly R. J. Jamison corroborates Tomlinson's initial statement "and strongly supported the conclusion that" the bullet had NOT been found on Connally's stretcher.

Both stretchers had probably been unattended for thirty minutes, in a hall where various people were milling about. The non-Connally stretcher might have had enough bloodstains to cause a person to think it had been Connally's or even Kennedy's stretcher. Someone could have easily planted the "magic bullet" to incriminate Oswald.

Around 1:30 p.m., about fifteen minutes before the "magic bullet" was discovered, two reliable witnesses at Parkland Hospital saw Jack Ruby, a lower-level member of Carlos Marcello's organization. One of the two witnesses, journalist Seth Kantor, even spoke to Ruby, as he later told authorities and confirmed to me. However, Ruby later lied to authorities about the encounter, saying that he hadn't gone to Parkland that day. That raises the question of why Ruby would deny his presence there—unless he was engaged in some illegal activity, such as planting evidence. Ruby might have planted the "magic bullet" or might have given it to someone else to plant. Regardless of who placed the pristine bullet on the non-Connally stretcher, it was used to link Oswald's rifle to the shooting of JFK and Connally.

Since the Warren Commission's version of the "magic bullet" theory is impossible to physically support and since someone planted the bullet to incriminate Oswald—and much evidence and testimony shows that there were at least two shooters—where does that leave the *Warren Report*'s "lone nut" scenario?

THE WARREN REPORT went out of its way to stress that Oswald's "commitment to Marxism and communism appears to have been another important factor in his motivation" to kill President Kennedy. The Commission related information saying that Oswald had become a Marxist/Communist when he was a teenager and had continued a fascination with Russia when he joined the United States Marines. According to the official story, after getting an early discharge by claiming he needed to financially provide for his mother, he defected to Russia in 1959. After marrying a Russian woman, Marina Prusakova, he returned to the United States in 1962. He worked at a photographic map firm in Dallas in the fall and moved to New Orleans in the spring to live with his uncle, after ordering the rifle and pistol he would allegedly use on November 22, 1963. Marina eventually joined him in New Orleans, where he worked for a relatively short time at a coffee company before being unemployed during August 1963. In that month he got a surprising amount of publicity for his local chapter of the pro-Castro Fair Play for Cuba Committee.

After sending Marina and their child to live with a friend in Dallas, Oswald made a mysterious trip to Mexico City, visiting the Russian and Cuban Embassies there before heading to Dallas himself. He lived for a time in a Dallas YMCA before moving to a rooming house in the Oak Cliff section of the city, visiting Marina on the weekends. He also got a job at the Texas School Book Depository, one of dozens of tall buildings that overlooked JFK's planned motorcade route. From there, according to the *Warren Report,* he alone would shoot JFK and soon after kill Dallas patrolman J. D. Tippit. From teenage Communist to Presidential assassin and murderer, Oswald's story was readily accepted by an American audience in the middle of the Cold War, just one year after the tense nuclear showdown with Russia during the Cuban Missile Crisis. For decades, authors ranging from Gerald Posner to Bill O'Reilly have repeated and expanded on this version of the story.

However, questions about that scenario—and Oswald's motivation, or lack of it—surfaced soon after his murder by Jack Ruby, and they've been growing ever since.

The *Warren Report*'s depiction of Oswald as a teenage Marxist who grew into a troubled, murderous loner doesn't stand up to modern scrutiny. In addition to the Warren Commission's Report and twenty-six volumes of evidence, thousands of additional pages of Warren Commission documents were eventually released. These make it clear that the FBI—and especially Naval Intelligence and the CIA—withheld much crucial information about Oswald. Today we have thousands of pages of additional material from the House Select Committee's investigation, and those have been supplemented by millions of pages of additional files. These documents help to cast Oswald in a very different light.

It's shockingly easy to debunk the *Warren Report* depiction of Oswald as a teenage Marxist. How many teenage Marxists joined the Civil Air Patrol as Oswald did, especially in the McCarthy era? How many teenage Marxists in the 1950s joined the US Marines? Oswald had even been so desperate to join that he tried to enlist before he was legally old enough. How many US Marines in the conservative Nixon/McCarthy fifties were like Oswald, allegedly going around his base publicly spouting a supposed love of all things Russian and allegedly teaching himself to speak fluent Russian? Even the *Warren Report* admits that his fellow Marines called him Oswaldskovitch. Yet not once was Oswald ever written up or disciplined for his outrageously pro-Russian behavior, not even when he was based at the sensitive U-2 spy plane base in Atsugi, Japan. G. Robert Blakey, the former Mafia prosecutor for Robert Kennedy who directed the House Select Committee on Assassinations, repeatedly asked during a PBS interview:

> Why was no action taken against him? Why, when this came to the attention of his Marine superiors, was action not initiated? This man was a man with a security clearance; this man was a man who had access to highly sophisticated materials; and he is now showing an interest in Marxism.

Blakey was right to be concerned since Oswald had been a radar operator for the Marines at Atsugi, where the CIA's supersecret U-2 spy planes were based for their flights over Russia.

Even more bizarre, soon after "defector" Oswald made a well-publicized 1962 return to the United States, with a Russian wife in tow, US authorities allowed him to get a job at a Dallas firm that made maps from U-2 spy plane photos for the US government—at the height of the Cuban Missile Crisis! The firm made the lettering used on the large display maps shown in televised presentations by US officials, including President Kennedy. The Warren–Posner–Bugliosi–O'Reilly version asks us to believe that the FBI and CIA saw no problem with former defector Oswald working at the U-2 map firm at that dangerous time. Yet, later Congressional investigations showed that that was a time when thousands of American Communists, leftists, Socialists, progressives, and liberals in nonsensitive jobs were routinely subjected to domestic surveillance.

Oswald's actions make perfect sense only when viewed in light of all the facts, not just a select few. To be fair, it's also easier to evaluate Oswald accurately now that we're decades removed from the Cold War and the "better dead than Red" mind-set of many, if not most, Americans of the early 1960s.

Before Oswald was born, his father died. He looked up to his older brothers, both of whom joined the military, with one serving in an intelligence service that ferreted out Communists. Oswald's favorite TV show when he was young was *I Led Three Lives,* based on a true story about a seemingly ordinary American who went under deep cover for years as an apparent Communist only to emerge to fame and fortune when it was revealed that he was really a US government agent. Oswald had an above-average IQ, but learning disabilities apparently hindered his schooling, so his prospects were limited. He grew up in less-savory parts of New Orleans, where his mother knew members of the Marcello crime organization and where his only father figure was a favorite uncle—"Dutz" Murret—who worked as a bookie for Marcello. Oswald's limited options apparently led him to follow in the footsteps of the protagonist of *I Led Three Lives,* and there is a great deal of evidence, including statements from fellow Marines, that he was recruited by military intelligence while in the Marines.

Oswald told a fellow Marine that he had a "civilian . . . intelligence contact at the Atsugo (U-2) base" who was "believed . . . to be [in] with the CIA." Also, author Dick Russell points out that when Oswald went to Russia in 1959, he was one of seven young American men who "defected" around the same time, and six of those later returned to the United States with Russian wives. For years the CIA denied debriefing Oswald when he returned to the

United States, even though the Agency routinely debriefed other far less potentially damaging travelers to Russia. After all, Oswald did have high security clearances in the Marines. Wouldn't the CIA want to at least ask Oswald if he shared any information with the Soviets?

Years later, after decades of denial, former CIA Director Richard Helms admitted to historian (and retired military intelligence Major) John Newman that Oswald had been debriefed by the CIA. Helms and other officials had lied about that to government committees from the Warren Commission to the House Select Committee on Assassinations. But why?

Bill O'Reilly's book *Killing Kennedy* acknowledges that an unusual Dallas man—an erudite and sophisticated anti-Communist White Russian named George DeMohrenschildt—helped Oswald get his job at the U-2 map firm in Dallas. But O'Reilly leaves out the well-documented fact that DeMohrenschildt was an admitted and well-documented CIA asset who was in contact with the head of the CIA office in Dallas about Oswald's activities.*

As I first disclosed in 2005, using information mostly withheld from the House Select Committee on Assassinations, Oswald was under "tight" surveillance by Naval Intelligence from the time he returned from Russia until he was arrested for JFK's murder. According to my source, who helped file reports of that surveillance, the CIA assisted in tracking Oswald's movements and associates,

---

*George DeMohrenschildt knew both Jackie Kennedy and George H. W. Bush. On the day an investigator for the House Select Committee on Assassinations was trying to interview him, DeMohrenschildt committed suicide. That same day, Chicago hit man Charles Nicoletti—who worked with Johnny Rosselli on the CIA–Mafia plots in 1963 and was alleged to be in Dallas when JFK was assassinated—was murdered, gangland style. He had also been scheduled to talk to investigators for the House Select Committee.

as at times did the FBI. In addition, one of Oswald's files prominently included a CIA phone number to call in case he was ever in
trouble, indicating that the CIA was utilizing or planning to utilize
Oswald in some fashion. The monitoring of Oswald couldn't be obvious, because Naval Intelligence wanted to see how the KGB might
try to recruit Oswald or his wife. That was probably also true for
most of the other recently returned defectors.* CIA asset George
DeMohrenschildt apparently helped Oswald get the job at the U-2
map firm to make him more attractive for the Russians to recruit.
Because Oswald was working for Naval Intelligence and had some
CIA role, Helms and the Agency used that justification to essentially
lie to the Warren Commission and Congressional investigators about
debriefing Oswald—and, as Newman learned, about other matters
as well.

However, just as it had in Russia, the KGB saw through the ruse
of having Oswald work at the U-2 map firm and made no contact
with Oswald. Perhaps the KGB noticed what stands out today when
we look back at Oswald's activities once he returned to the United
States: that Oswald avoided real American Communists, Marxists,
and Socialists like the plague, even though he could have easily found
them around the colleges and hipper parts of New Orleans and Dallas.
That Oswald was willing to contact such people and organizations
only by mail smacks of building a cover for himself by leaving a paper
trail at the direction of his handlers. That's especially true when we
consider that his best friend in Dallas was the staunchly anti-Communist George DeMohrenschildt and that Oswald would soon find

*While the House Select Committee looked for US intelligence ties to other defectors in the late 1970s,
that was before Blakey wrote for PBS in 2003, "I am no longer confident that the Central Intelligence
Agency cooperated with the Committee."

himself working for two men who were stridently anti-Communist and anti-Castro.

By early 1963, Oswald was no doubt looking for another assignment. Ironically, buried in the twenty-six Warren volumes are Oswald's own notes for his "big reveal," in which he admits hating Communism, something he could publicly proclaim only after the success of his anti-Castro work, when he emerged from his deep undercover work to (hoped-for) fame and fortune.

After being fired from his job at the map firm on April 6, Oswald made a well-documented move to New Orleans on April 24, 1963. He left Marina in Dallas and went to live with his uncle Dutz Murret, a bookie for Carlos Marcello. However, even before his move to the Crescent City, an INS agent interviewed Oswald in the New Orleans jail. The interview had to have been in February or March—and before Oswald's move and even before he lost his job—because the INS agent was transferred away from New Orleans on April 1, 1963. The INS agent didn't recall why Oswald was in jail, but the charge—if any—must have been minor, since no record of it was kept. During the interview, Oswald, probably using a Hispanic-sounding alias, pretended to be a Cuban national even though he couldn't speak Spanish. It sounds absurd, except that Oswald would soon join (by mail) the tiny national pro-Castro organization known as the Fair Play for Cuba Committee, a group that the CIA had targeted for harassment and penetration since at least 1961.

Also in early 1963, Oswald ordered through the mail the cheap rifle and pistol he would later be accused of using to kill JFK and Officer Tippit. Conveniently, Oswald had photos taken of himself holding each weapon, along with copies of two Communist newspapers of opposing views: *The Worker* of the Communist Party USA and the Trotskyite paper *The Militant*. The late Dr. Philip Melanson, Chairman of Political Science at the University of Massachusetts–Dartmouth, wrote that holding two such opposing papers would be like trying to present a coherent American political view by holding up copies of the conservative *National Review* and the liberal icon *The Nation*. For any type of true believer—especially someone like Oswald who had lived in Russia—it made no sense.

However, here and throughout his life, all of Oswald's activities (and claimed activities) related to Communism and Marxism are consistent with someone building and maintaining a cover, like his childhood idol who inspired *I Led Three Lives*. Who could have been directing Oswald's activities in 1963? It's well documented that a few months after his April move to New Orleans, Oswald worked at least part-time for and with two associates of Carlos Marcello: Marcello's private detective, Guy Banister, and Marcello's pilot and investigator, David Ferrie.

Both loom large in assassination literature, yet much of it ignores their connection to Carlos Marcello, who admitted to Congressional investigators that he knew both men. Ferrie had been an Eastern Airlines pilot who had known Oswald as a teenager, when Ferrie helped supervise Oswald's Civil Air Patrol unit. There is also some evidence that Ferrie originally encouraged Oswald to join the Marines. By 1963 Ferrie had lost his job at Eastern Airlines because he had been accused of molesting a fifteen-year-old boy. Ferrie officially worked for Marcello's New Orleans attorney, but Marcello admitted working with Ferrie directly on the two weekends prior to JFK's assassination. In addition, Victor Marchetti, former Executive Assistant to the Deputy Director of the CIA, confirmed that "Ferrie had been a contract agent to the Agency in the early sixties . . . in some of the Cuban activities." Marchetti said that his boss "[Richard] Helms stated that David Ferrie was a CIA agent" in the fall of 1963. According to historian Dr. Michael Kurtz, Deputy Chief of the New Orleans CIA Station Hunter Leake confirmed Ferrie's 1963 CIA work to him. Leake also confirmed that Guy Banister performed work for the CIA related to Cuba.

Banister had many more, and more highly placed, intelligence connections than his associate David Ferrie, and they were developed before both men began working for Carlos Marcello. A former FBI Chief of Chicago in the early 1950s, the hard-drinking Banister had been Assistant Superintendent of the New Orleans Police Department for two and a half years before being fired for erratic behavior caused by his drinking.

Banister then opened a detective agency, though he focused far more on intelligence work, strident anti-Communism, and white supremacist causes than any traditional private detective. He maintained good relations with the New Orleans office of the FBI and with Naval Intelligence, as well as taking on work for the CIA—tasks that revolved around Cuba. The New Orleans *States-Item* newspaper reported that Banister "participated in every anti-Communist South and Central American revolution that came along, acting as a key liaison man for the U.S. government-sponsored anti-Communist activities in Latin America." Banister led his own group, the Anti-Communist League of the Caribbean, which was involved in a plot against Fidel Castro in December 1960. Four months earlier, when the CIA–Mafia plots with Trafficante and Marcello were in the planning stage, the CIA had considered Banister for a covert assignment providing cover for a sensitive CIA operation. That job went instead to Howard Hughes aide Robert Maheu, who only a few years earlier had been

Banister's partner, before Banister went to New Orleans. (Their other partner had been Carmine Bellino, by 1963 a close Kennedy aide in their fight against the Mafia.) While in the FBI in the 1930s, Banister had even served on two cases with General Joseph Carroll, who in 1963 was heading the recently created Defense Intelligence Agency, which was supposed to oversee Naval Intelligence and the other military intelligence agencies.

Banister and Ferrie are both said to have helped with the CIA's Bay of Pigs operation in early 1961, when New Orleans was a little-known site for one of the operation's Cuban-exile training camps, run by the CIA. On January 20, 1961 (three months before the Bay of Pigs), one of Banister's organizations even bought trucks in New Orleans for an anti-Castro operation using the name "Oswald," a safe alias since the real Oswald was still in the Soviet Union.

Banister and Ferrie's work on Cuban operations for the CIA continued into 1963, and by that summer Oswald was working for them. When he was a student that year, Dr. Michael Kurtz actually saw Guy Banister with Oswald at the University of New Orleans, debating students about integration. In 1999 scholar and former Arizona Secretary of State Richard Mahoney published a book about John and Robert Kennedy—*Sons and Brothers*—after gaining special access to files at the John F. Kennedy Presidential Library. Mahoney wrote that six witnesses saw Oswald with Ferrie or Banister in the summer of 1963, when Oswald garnered an unusual amount of TV, radio, and newspaper publicity for his phony one-man New Orleans chapter of the Fair Play for Cuba Committee. Two witnesses said Oswald was working for Banister at that time.

Since that time, Kurtz has added another three people to the list of witnesses who saw Ferrie and Banister together, including Deputy

New Orleans CIA Chief Hunter Leake. Leake said that not only did Ferry and Banister work together but that Lee Oswald did small jobs for the CIA as well. In fact, "Leake [said that he] personally paid Oswald various sums of cash for his services." Kurtz later interviewed Richard Helms about this and other assertions. Helms was essentially the CIA's highest operational officer in 1963 and later became CIA Director. "Helms neither confirmed nor denied Leake's story" when Kurtz asked Helms about it.

Years later, a CIA-generated file card that linked Oswald to Banister and Ferrie was declassified. It said Othat in the CIA, "there had been no secret as far as anyone was concerned in regard to the fact that Banister [and] David William Ferrie and subj [Oswald] may have known or been acquainted with one another." That was an understatement, but what happened to the CIA's extensive files in New Orleans about Oswald, Ferrie, and Banister is explained in a later chapter.

Banister and Ferrie could have manipulated Oswald in a variety of ways. He always needed money, he had no car or driver's license, and he was stuck with a "less than honorable" discharge because of his "defection." And he needed another intelligence assignment if he ever wanted to profit from a successful "big reveal," after his long years of undercover work. However, Congress was holding hearings about mail-order gun sales around the time Oswald ordered his guns through the mail—and hearings about the Fair Play for Cuba Committee around the time he started his one-man New Orleans chapter of that organization. So the well-connected Banister may have initially told Oswald that ordering guns and joining Fair Play for Cuba could help those hearings.

It's also possible—even likely given that at least nine people saw them together in New Orleans just months before JFK's murder—that

Ferrie and Banister were helping to monitor Oswald for the CIA and Naval Intelligence. Someone was monitoring Oswald for Naval Intelligence, and doing so would put Banister and Ferrie in the perfect position to manipulate Oswald, who would think he was simply getting ready for his next intelligence assignment. In reality, though, Ferrie and Banister could have been controlling Oswald to set him up as the fall guy for the murder of President Kennedy. As we will see, just a few months before Oswald ordered—or was told to order—the rifle and pistol, Carlos Marcello had made a threat to kill JFK to end RFK's prosecution of him. An FBI informant heard Marcello's threat and reported it to his contact at the Bureau. Though that report has yet to surface in any released FBI files, the House Select Committee looked into the informant's account and concluded that the incident did occur.

If Banister and Ferrie were manipulating Oswald for Marcello, under the nose of the CIA and Naval Intelligence, this would resolve many of the lingering mysteries about Oswald's unusual activities in 1963. In August of that year, while being seen with Banister and Ferrie, Oswald received a surprising amount of TV, radio, and newspaper publicity from a fight Oswald provoked with a Cuban exile leader on the streets of New Orleans. The publicity Oswald secured seems highly unusual given how hard it was for left-wing groups to get any type of press coverage in the early 1960s in politically conservative states like Louisiana and Texas. When Oswald was arrested after the fight, an associate of Carlos Marcello bailed him out of jail. Oswald, Banister, and Ferrie did make one small mistake by using the address of a side entrance to Banister's office building (544 Camp Street) on some of the pro-Castro flyers that Oswald made a big show of distributing on the streets of New Orleans.

The CIA had a media-propaganda expert who easily could have arranged such publicity for Oswald. He was David Atlee Phillips, an expert in overthrowing Latin American governments for the CIA and a good friend to CIA officer E. Howard Hunt. In fact, Guy Banister had met with Phillips a couple of years earlier about anti-Castro publicity. Remarkably, Phillips would also reportedly meet with Oswald and Cuban exile leader Antonio Veciana in Dallas in late August or early September to discuss killing Fidel Castro. Congressional investigator Gaeton Fonzi confirmed that meeting, as did my research associate in an interview with Veciana. It's important to note that Richard Helms was continuing the CIA–Mafia plots in 1963 without telling his own CIA Director (John McCone), Robert Kennedy, or President Kennedy. Those plots included Marcello and Trafficante, as well as their confessed partner in JFK's murder, Johnny Rosselli, who also visited Guy Banister that summer.

Oswald's unusual adventures in Mexico City—David Atlee Phillips's primary base, though he did missions for Washington that didn't involve the Mexico City CIA Station Chief—can be explained the same way. Oswald spoke fluent Russian and poor Spanish, but after he visited the Russian and Cuban embassies in an attempt to get to Cuba, someone made calls in excellent Spanish and poor Russian that seemed designed to ensure that Oswald would not get permission to travel to Cuba. It was as if someone wanted him to stay in the United States so he could be of use to them later in the fall. Marcello had the means to make something like that happen. The Mexican Federal Police (DFS) helped the CIA monitor phone surveillance of the Russian and Cuban embassies. However, the DFS was corrupt and involved in the same heroin network used by Trafficante and Marcello. In addition, a CIA asset involved in the CIA–Mafia plots with Trafficante and

Marcello had actually bugged a Communist embassy in Mexico City for the CIA not long before, so he would have known much about the monitoring and bugging of Communist embassies there.

Oswald's exact actions on the day of the assassination are detailed in Chapters 14 and 15. Here we'll note that something important happened as soon as his name surfaced as a suspect: Naval Intelligence staff in charge of monitoring secret surveillance reports on Oswald began destroying their files on him. My Naval Intelligence source was called back to his office in Washington and ordered to sanitize and destroy much of their Oswald surveillance file. That destruction continued until midday Sunday, November 24, and confirmation for that can be found in an FBI memo from several months later. In it, FBI agent T. N. Goble stated that three of Oswald's fellow Marines "said they had been interviewed about Oswald." However, "Goble noted that no such statements or interview reports had been located" in Oswald's Marine or Office of Naval Intelligence files provided to the FBI. "In a postscript for the" FBI headquarters file, "Goble did not suggest any doubt that such interviews had taken place. Their absence from USMC and ONI files 'indicates that perhaps they have been destroyed.'"

However, the destruction of files ended after Washington received word that Oswald had been killed. Since no trial lay ahead, the rest of the records wouldn't have to be destroyed, just hidden from the prying eyes of other agencies. Longtime researcher Paul Hoch, who has assisted several of the government's JFK investigations, later found indications in declassified government memos that there were more Naval Intelligence files on Oswald than were provided to the Warren Commission. He found references to three files as well as a "supplemental file" on Oswald—one that was never explained or provided to any government committee.

After Jack Ruby murdered Oswald and it was clear there would be no trial, Naval Intelligence and Marine Intelligence decided to conduct their own secret investigation of Oswald. To maintain strict secrecy, even within Naval Intelligence, they used the same men who had been compiling the "tight" surveillance of Oswald, including my confidential source.

The investigation began on November 24, 1963, immediately after Oswald's death, and lasted for six weeks. Given that Oswald had been under top-secret surveillance by Naval Intelligence, it's not surprising that the organization wanted to know how he could have been involved in JFK's murder. Even without a trial, if word ever leaked to the press or public about Oswald's intelligence work or the tight surveillance, it would have been a public relations nightmare for military intelligence and for agencies such as the CIA that had assisted with Oswald's surveillance. Military intelligence leaders would have to be ready with as many facts as possible in case President Johnson or Congressional leaders called them to account. The military investigation was highly secret, even within Naval and Marine Intelligence circles, and all of the investigators had to sign strict confidentiality agreements that threatened them with court-martial for any disclosure. No word leaked about the military investigation at the time, and the Warren Commission was never told about it.

In 1978 the wife of a military navigator who had helped fly the investigators to their destinations finally tipped off the House Select Committee on Assassinations about the secret military investigation of Oswald. When the former Marine navigator testified to House Committee staff, he confirmed his participation in the military investigation and provided Committee staff with a great deal of specific information about his former commanders, the size of the investigation force, and their travel while they probed Oswald's history. However, as recounted in the House Committee's report, when Congressional staff tried to run down those leads, Defense Department officials stonewalled them until the Committee's term was almost over. The first piece of official confirmation for the existence of the military investigation was provided only when the Committee's efforts were ending. The Committee never received the military's findings or report. However, the former Marine navigator had read the military's report and testified that it concluded that one person "was incapable of committing the assassination alone."

My Naval Intelligence source, who worked on the investigation, provided more detail, saying that the military intelligence report concluded that "Oswald was not the shooter, due to his skills, the gun, etc." and that the report stressed that "Oswald was incapable of masterminding the assassination or of doing the actual shooting."

I later located an additional independent ex-Navy source, who confirmed the report's existence and its conclusion that "Oswald was not the shooter" and "was incapable of masterminding the assassination." This confidential ex-Navy source was the son of an Admiral who, thanks to his father's high position, had been assigned to a comfortable office job at a major US naval base in the Pacific. While handling files, he noticed the report and, intrigued, read the entire file. He told me that the report was probably being kept so far from Washington to ensure that word of it didn't leak and so it wasn't seen by civilian political officials who might talk to journalists.

Those conclusions meshed with off-the-record comments of US officials who expressed doubts about the evidence against Oswald in private conversations, even as they publicly proclaimed his ironclad guilt. These comments came from the highest levels of government, as shown by a private, taped conversation between President Lyndon Johnson and J. Edgar Hoover soon after the assassination. In the call, Hoover admitted to Johnson that "the evidence" against Oswald "is not very strong." At the same time, Hoover was pushing Oswald's guilt to journalists, the public, and other officials.

Years later, Dallas Police Chief Jeff Curry, who had been in JFK's motorcade, was blunt in his assessment of the lack of real evidence against Oswald: "We don't have any proof that Oswald fired the rifle, and never did. Nobody's yet been able to put him in that building with a gun in his hand." Right after JFK's murder, Curry's public statements—like Hoover's—had shown no such doubt. But to himself at the time, and in public years later, Curry admitted that he thought "Oswald had been trained in interrogation techniques and resisting interrogation" and that Oswald was some type of agent.

In hindsight, it's easy to see why the public initially accepted the reassuring public pronouncements of Hoover, Curry, and other officials that a Communist "lone nut" had killed JFK. After all, it was the height of the Cold War. Then, too, on the surface Oswald *looked* guilty: He had a job along the motorcade route, he'd left the building after the assassination, he was a member of the Fair Play for Cuba Committee, and he appeared guilty of the murder of Officer J. D. Tippit.

However, as has been well documented since the publication in 1966 and 1967 of the first critical analyses of the Warren Commission's own twenty-six volumes of supporting materials, the evidence fails to support the Commission's most important claims about Oswald's guilt. For example, other employees also left the building after the shooting, Oswald had no getaway car (or even a driver's license) and initially left by public transit bus, and he had only $13.87 in his pocket when he was arrested at the Texas Theatre.

More important, as Police Chief Curry said, there was no credible evidence to place Oswald in the Book Depository's sixth-floor "sniper's nest." In contrast, much compelling evidence—including testimony from the Warren Commission volumes—places him in the Depository's lunchroom at the time of the shooting, near a pay phone, as if waiting to receive or make a call. As detailed later, all the evidence and eyewitness testimony against Oswald in Dealey Plaza and the Tippit case are very problematic and far from conclusive, while Oswald's actions at the Texas Theatre, where he was arrested, smack of someone trying to locate a prearranged contact. In fact, John Martino—a mobster associate of Marcello and Trafficante—confided to a friend that "Oswald was to meet his contact at the Texas Theatre. They were to meet Oswald in the theatre, and get him out of the country."

When we look at Oswald in isolation as a suspect in JFK's murder, he can appear unusual. However, as noted earlier and as will be detailed in later chapters, Dallas wasn't the only city where the godfathers planned to kill JFK—and Oswald wasn't the only ex-Marine arrested and investigated for trying to kill JFK. In Chicago, Thomas Vallee, a seemingly troubled former Marine, was arrested on November 2, 1963, on the morning of JFK's planned motorcade through that city. As people started to line the streets in anticipation of seeing JFK, the motorcade was suddenly called off—with two different phony excuses hurriedly given—because the Secret Service had learned that four possible assassins were at large. When arrested, Vallee had "an M-1 rifle, a handgun, and 3,000 rounds of ammunition in his car," according to the House Select Committee. In interesting parallels with Oswald in Dallas, Vallee had recently taken a job in a warehouse overlooking JFK's Chicago motorcade route, had moved into a YMCA in the fall of 1963 around the same time as Oswald, and had contact with a CIA-supported anti-Castro Cuban exile group, as had Oswald earlier in 1963.

For the attempt to kill JFK in Tampa on November 18, 1963, there were even more parallels between Oswald and Gilberto Lopez, a young man living there at the time. On the day of JFK's Tampa motorcade, Lopez was working not far from the motorcade route. Oswald and Lopez were about the same age and had the same general physical description. (The description of a suspect issued in Tampa prior to the attempt to kill JFK in that city fits Oswald—and Lopez— much better than the initial description issued by the police in Dallas after JFK was shot.) In all, government files and sources show there were nineteen parallels between the two men, including having highly unusual ties to the Fair Play for Cuba Committee, getting into fist-fights over seeming pro-Castro sympathies, making an unusual trip to Mexico City to try to get into Cuba, not owning a car or even being able to drive, and moving to a new city and leaving a wife at the same time, just a few months before JFK's assassination. After the attempt to kill JFK in Tampa was called off and JFK successfully completed his motorcade, Lopez left Trafficante's home base and reportedly went to Dallas, which was in Marcello's territory. Lopez would be secretly investigated for JFK's murder by both the FBI and the CIA, and their reports on Lopez were provided to Naval Intelligence.

Had JFK been killed on November 2, 1963, in Chicago (home of Rosselli's mob family) or in Trafficante's base of Tampa on November 18, 1963, someone remarkably like Oswald was apparently positioned to "take the fall" in either of those cities, just like Oswald in Dallas. The conspirators had only one basic plan: to shoot JFK in an open motorcade, a plan that could be applied in all three cities. Aside from someone to take the blame, the other personnel were mostly the same, regardless of which city would be the scene of the assassination. (For example, Jack Ruby—part of Marcello's organization in Dallas—had well-documented ties to his hometown of Chicago, where he received a large payoff shortly before the attempt to kill JFK there, and also to Tampa).

Oswald has been a mystery to many on all sides of the JFK assassination controversy, but when looked at through the lens of Carlos Marcello and his associates—and that of US intelligence—his documented actions as they unfold in this book finally make sense. The only viable explanation for why Oswald worked for strident anti-Castro anti-Communists like Banister and Ferrie and was friends with anti-Communist George DeMohrenschildt is that he was an anti-Communist US intelligence asset. (Many liberals in the early 1960s, including JFK, were anti-Communist, so such a role didn't require Oswald to be as ultraconservative as Banister and Ferrie.) In that role, he was one of several US intelligence assets sent to the Soviet Union to come back to America with a Russian wife. When the KGB failed to take the bait in the US, Oswald soon began focusing on an upcoming anti-Castro Cuban operation for Naval Intelligence and/or the CIA. Meanwhile, intelligence assets Banister and Ferrie began to manipulate Oswald for nonintelligence reasons. Both were also working for Carlos Marcello, who was planning to kill President Kennedy to end Robert Kennedy's war against the godfather and his mob allies.

Oswald would have been focused on what he thought was his impending mission to Cuba—and his "big reveal," when he would finally emerge from years of undercover work to fame and fortune. Yet the very actions that helped him build a pro-Castro, pro-Communist image in public for his intelligence work would also make him look instantly guilty if he were ever accused of murdering the President. Confessed conspirator John Martino, an associate of Marcello and Trafficante, described the tragic scenario perfectly, telling a trusted associate that Oswald "didn't know what he was involved in" or "who he was [really] working for—he was just ignorant of who was really putting him together."

CHAPTER 3

A Mafia Godfather Confesses

O N DECEMBER 15, 1987, godfather Carlos Marcello sat in a gazebo in a prison yard with two close associates, as he railed against John and Robert Kennedy. Aside from those two, no one was in earshot as he hurled curses at the long-dead Kennedy brothers. He had done that before, but this time—since Marcello trusted the two men—he went further than usual in his anti-Kennedy tirade. Normally in careful control of his emotions, Marcello became more and more agitated as he talked about the Kennedys' crusade against him: First they'd hauled him before Congress, then briefly deported him to Central America, and finally they had him prosecuted in New Orleans, the center of his multistate criminal empire.

Marcello's anti-Kennedy rant reached a crescendo as he blurted out to his two friends a startling admission about John F. Kennedy: "Yeah, I had the son of a bitch killed. I'm glad I did." Marcello's only regret seemed to be that he didn't get to pull the trigger, since he told his two stunned associates, "I'm sorry I couldn't have done it myself."

Carlos Marcello had become America's most powerful godfather by being not just ruthless but also cautious and discreet, and he paused his diatribe after his remarkable confession. Realizing that even though he trusted his two associates he had crossed a line, Marcello turned away from them and simply walked off.

After Marcello left, his deadly admission hung in the air between the two stunned men who'd heard it. They knew Marcello well enough to know what could happen to them if they ever revealed what they'd just heard. One man told the other, "I don't know about you, but I did not hear anything." With that, he walked away as well, leaving fifty-six-year-old Jack Van Laningham alone in the prison yard's gazebo to ponder the gravity of his situation.

Van Laningham was Marcello's cellmate at the Texarkana Federal Correction Institute, where both men were incarcerated. The two men had grown close, and Marcello had come to regard Van Laningham almost like a son, as someone he protected and to whom he dispensed fatherly advice.

But Van Laningham was far more than just Marcello's good friend—he was also an active undercover informant for the FBI.

After the House Select Committee on Assassinations officially concluded in 1979 that Carlos Marcello—along with his closest mob ally, godfather Santo Trafficante—had the "motive, means, and opportunity to assassinate President Kennedy," it referred the matter to the Justice Department for further investigation. It appeared to the press and public that nothing was done with the Committee's referral and that Justice officially closed the matter in 1988.

However, we now know that a major, extremely secret undercover investigation of Marcello—code-named CAMTEX (for CArlos Marcello, TEXas)—did go forward from 1985 to 1986. CAMTEX used FBI informant Jack Van Laningham not only to obtain Marcello's 1985 JFK confession but to glean additional details as well, including some in conversations secretly taped by the FBI. The tapes include

Marcello describing how he committed the crime, including his pre-assassination meetings with Lee Oswald and Jack Ruby. However, apparently, for political reasons, high officials in the Reagan–Bush Administration and Justice Department decided not to reveal CAMTEX and Marcello's JFK confession to Congress, the press, or the public—either in 1986 when CAMTEX ended or in 1992 when Congress passed the JFK Assassination Records Act to release all government files about the crime.

The Review Board created by the JFK Act was set to expire in September 1998, and the FBI waited until near the end to dump almost a hundred pages of CAMTEX files on the Board staff. It's doubtful that any Review Board members saw Marcello's confession files or that any of the Board's staff—overwhelmed by even larger last-minute document dumping by the CIA—got more than a cursory glance at a few pages of CAMTEX files before their office closed for good.

Over the next seven years, researchers found less than a handful of scattered pages at the National Archives, some with more than 90 percent of the page blacked out, making them impossible to understand. Finally, in 2006, after months of intense effort and with the help of National Archives staff, I located the main trove of CAMTEX files given to the Review Board, and they were almost completely uncensored. The public first heard about Marcello's JFK confession files in TV news and newspaper coverage accompanying the 2008 publication of the hardcover of my book *Legacy of Secrecy*, which also contained interviews with key CAMTEX FBI personnel. In 2009 I partnered with a division of NBC News for a Discovery Channel special (*Did the Mob Kill JFK?*), which also involved locating Jack Van Laningham, who had maintained a very low profile since his release from prison.

This book contains startling new revelations about Marcello's confession and CAMTEX from declassified FBI files, from former Bureau
informant Jack Van Laningham, and from key FBI personnel involved
in the undercover operation. Since 2009 I have conducted numerous
exclusive in-person and phone interviews with Van Laningham, adding
to and clarifying important parts of the story told by the FBI files and
by the FBI agents involved. It's remarkable how much of that information confirms many of the most crucial discoveries of the House Select
Committee and of historians such as Marcello's biographer, John H.
Davis (whose 1989 book *Mafia Kingfish* remains the only definitive
biography of the godfather). In turn, the Committee's findings, other
government investigators, and noted historians and journalists but-
tress almost all the key points of the new CAMTEX revelations.

Credibility is always important in evaluating information about
JFK's assassination, and the CAMTEX revelations about Marcello
are extremely reliable. As noted, all the CAMTEX files referenced in
this book came from FBI files at the National Archives, and all had
been officially declassified. CAMTEX involved several FBI agents and
supervisors, as well as court-authorized wiretaps on Marcello. The
dangerous undercover operation was fully authorized by the FBI and
Justice Department. CAMTEX lasted from 1985 to early 1987 and
targeted not only Carlos Marcello but also members of his family,
including his brother Joe. The operation succeeded in persuading a
Marcello family member to pay two bribes to an undercover FBI agent
who posed as a crooked friend of Van Laningham.

As for Jack Van Laningham, more than twenty-five years later, he
retains an excellent memory of those events, which can be verified by
comparing his comments now with his extensive remarks contained
in FBI files from the 1980s. When first interviewed by NBC and me,

Van Laningham hadn't seen his own notes—now in the FBI files—in over two decades. In fact, I extensively interviewed Van Laningham on many occasions before giving him copies of those notes, yet his unaided recollection was very much in sync with what he had typed up all those years before.

In addition, after his release from prison in early 1989, Van Laningham took and passed an FBI polygraph test regarding Marcello's JFK confession. Moreover, Van Laningham was not a career criminal. In fact, until shortly before meeting Marcello in prison, Van Laningham was a successful family man with no criminal record at all.

In 1985 Jack Van Laningham was fifty-six years old and had spent much of his adult life as a civilian air traffic controller for the US Air Force. In the 1970s, he'd switched to selling cars in California and was successful at that as well, supporting his English-born wife and three children. However, Jack's wife was a troubled alcoholic who left him in the early 1980s. That sent Jack on a downward spiral. By the time he hit bottom, he was regularly drinking heavily and living in a small motel in Tampa, Florida. When his money ran out, he committed his first—and only—crime during a drinking spree, robbing a small bank branch using a bag of dirty laundry and a TV remote control, which he told the tellers were a bomb and a detonator.

Van Laningham got away scot-free but was soon so overcome with guilt that he called the authorities to turn himself in. When he was taken into custody, a Tampa FBI agent admitted that they would have never found Jack on their own. Nonetheless, Van Laningham was sentenced to eight years in federal prison for armed robbery and wound up at the federal prison in Texarkana to serve his sentence.

Soon after entering Texarkana, Van Laningham first saw the "little man," a short, stout inmate named Carlos Marcello, who another inmate said "runs this place." Jack was surprised to see that even in prison, "Marcello went where he pleased and did what he wanted [and] was big time." Van Laningham wrote that while he shared "a crowded dorm with a hundred other guys," Marcello was one of the few lucky inmates who shared a two-man cell. In addition, Marcello's "clothes were new and pressed and his shoes were shined. This guy was really sharp."

Van Laningham had no idea who Marcello really was and knew nothing about his criminal empire. Jack hadn't followed the news about Marcello's recent trial, and he hadn't paid attention to news reports about the House Select Committee six years earlier since he had no special interest in JFK's assassination, though he'd liked JFK. He didn't know that in the late 1970s the FBI and Justice Department had targeted Marcello as part of a larger undercover operation code-named BRILAB, which grew out of investigations related to several Watergate figures.

The BRILAB charges were obtained with the help of an earlier Bureau informant, a business associate of Marcello named Joe Hauser. Hauser wore a wire for the FBI when he met with Marcello in the late 1970s, a major accomplishment since the Bureau—for reasons that will shortly become clear—hadn't wiretapped or bugged Marcello at all in the 1950s, 1960s, or most of the 1970s.* Hauser's information eventually resulted in multiple convictions for Marcello, who was finally sent to prison on April 15, 1983. The godfather was initially incarcerated at the US Medical Center for Federal Prisoners in Springfield, Missouri. Twelve years earlier, Marcello had spent

---

*According to former Justice Department prosecutor John Diuguid, the only exception was a single visit to Marcello in the 1960s by a very frightened, wired informant for the Bureau of Narcotics.

a comfortable and unusually short sentence there, serving only five months when he was supposed to serve two years. The prison grounds at Springfield have been described as "park-like." The prison was minimum security (level one), and after his original stay in the early 1970s, Marcello emerged in improved physical condition and ready for his most prosperous decade of crime.

However, in the 1980s things were different for Carlos Marcello. After a year at Springfield, he was moved to the far more secure and harsher level-three federal prison at Texarkana. The move may have been occasioned because officials suspected that Marcello was continuing to run his vast criminal empire from prison. He had left his younger brother Joe Marcello nominally in charge, but Carlos still made the major decisions for a domain that included all of Louisiana, much of Texas, and the lower half of Mississippi. In addition, Marcello had built his power by forging alliances with surrounding Mafia godfathers, such as the boss of the Kansas City mob and Trafficante in Florida, stretching his clout and influence even farther. Marcello's recent trials and imprisonment—and the changing nature of organized crime in the 1980s—had no doubt taken a financial toll on his huge enterprise, which had grossed $2 billion a year at its peak but was still massive.

Jack Van Laningham didn't know any of that when he first saw Marcello in prison, since the godfather was not then as well known as he is today. In 1985 there had as yet been no books devoted to—or TV documentaries about—Marcello. Instead, the media focused on high-profile mob figures such as John Gotti. But Van Laningham's own observations, coupled with the comments and actions of other inmates, quickly made it clear to him that Marcello was a figure to be reckoned with, even in prison. Marcello received special gourmet food, wore the aforementioned pressed clothes, and even held sway over work assignments and who got the coveted two-man cells instead of being placed in the massive dorms.

Van Laningham noticed that some "of the inmates hung around [Marcello], trying to get his attention." They constantly gave Marcello their coveted phone time and tried to curry favor with the godfather since—as one inmate told Van Laningham—Marcello was "a good friend to have."

However, Van Laningham stood in stark contrast to the other inmates. He didn't seek favors from Marcello or even try to meet him. In addition, Van Laningham, like Marcello, was much older than the typical inmates at Texarkana, many of whom were in their twenties. In fact, Van Laningham was the second-oldest inmate at Texarkana, and Marcello—nineteen years older—was the oldest.

One day in March 1985, Van Laningham just happened to sit next to Marcello. The godfather surprised him by introducing himself: "Hello, I'm Carlos Marcello." Marcello was holding a newspaper and asked if Van Laningham had heard anything about the trial of a political figure then in the news. They chatted briefly and then Marcello "got up to leave and said 'If you need anything look me up.'"

The two men soon struck up an acquaintance, and not long after, Marcello had Van Laningham read him the newspaper each day. Because of Marcello's age and relative lack of formal education, reading was difficult for the godfather. Marcello was interested not only in news about the political figure's trial but also in reports of criminal activity from other parts of his empire. Since he was closer in age to Van Laningham than any other inmate, they had similar tastes in things like music. Like Marcello, Van Laningham was part of the "big band" generation, and neither was a fan of the rock music preferred by the other inmates. Instead they remembered—and could reminisce with each other about—radio shows, movie palaces, World War II, and a dozen car companies no longer in business by the 1980s. In addition, the first crime both men had been arrested for was bank robbery, and while Marcello laughed at Jack's hopelessly amateur effort, he admired the courage of anyone willing to rob a bank with nothing but a bag of laundry and a TV remote.

Also in Van Laningham's favor were that he had lived in Tampa, the city run by Marcello's closest mob ally, Trafficante, and that unlike the other inmates, he wasn't constantly trying to curry favor with Marcello. Finally, Marcello felt he could trust Van Laningham because—much to Jack's surprise—his power was such that he could show Jack his own prison file, which had the details of Jack's arrest and personal history.

Not all the prison staff had been corrupted by Marcello's influence, and one reported the growing closeness of Van Laningham and Marcello to an official at the prison. That word eventually reached Thomas Kimmel, a Unit Director at FBI headquarters in Washington whose territory included Texas.

I was the first to interview Thomas Kimmel about CAMTEX, and he confirmed and illuminated much of the material in the FBI file. In 1985 Thomas Kimmel was a twelve-year veteran of the Bureau. He had a special interest in organized crime and would eventually head the FBI's Labor Racketeering Section. Kimmel's territory included three prisons, and he was well aware of Marcello's presence at Texarkana and the fact that the House Select Committee had focused attention on Marcello's possible role in JFK's murder. Kimmel knew he couldn't sell FBI headquarters on an investigation focused on the assassination since the FBI had publicly maintained since soon after JFK's shooting that there was no conspiracy.

Instead, Kimmel proposed to his superiors an operation designed to see how "Marcello was still running" his organization from prison, something the godfather had done during his brief 1971 incarceration. FBI headquarters approved, and Kimmel became "the driving force behind" the new CAMTEX operation targeting Marcello at Texarkana. Kimmel learned of Van Laningham's friendship with Marcello when he was already looking for a way to get to the godfather. Kimmel could use Van Laningham to pierce the normally impenetrable wall of secrecy that surrounded the hypercautious godfather.

For decades, most former FBI officials were reluctant to talk in public about anything contrary to the FBI's long-held official position that a lone, unaided Oswald assassinated JFK. However, there were several reasons Kimmel was willing to go on record as the first FBI veteran ever interviewed about CAMTEX and Marcello's confession. First, since so many pages of uncensored files had already been released, Kimmel agreed to discuss what was in those files. After all, the daring CAMTEX operation had been successful in some ways, yet the public, Congress, and even most in the Bureau knew nothing about it. In addition, Kimmel had seen how excessive secrecy could actually hinder national security. In 1999—two years prior to the arrest of Robert Hanssen, an FBI agent and Soviet spy—Kimmel tried to alert FBI Director Louis Freeh about a possible "mole" in the Bureau. His warning was ignored, and FBI officials stonewalled his efforts and refused him access to important files, as detailed by the *New York Times* and *60 Minutes*.* For all those reasons, Kimmel agreed to talk

---

*Thomas Kimmel's grandfather was Admiral H. E. Kimmel, Commander of the US Naval Base at Pearl Harbor when it was attacked on December 7, 1941. Admiral Kimmel was scapegoated for the disaster, which was the subject of excessive government secrecy at the time and for many decades afterward.

with me, and he even appeared in my 2009 Discovery Channel special that also featured Van Laningham.

Kimmel used a "terrific" FBI agent based in Texas as one of those to handle the operation for him locally. (I have interviewed that agent, but he asked not to be identified.) Completing the team was an older FBI agent, Tom Kirk, who was assigned to work undercover with Jack Van Laningham. Before meeting him, Jack was called to his cell block manager's office and "asked if I would help the Feds." Jack was reluctant, but he was told that on visiting day at the prison, someone would talk with him. When visiting day came around, FBI agent Tom Kirk posed as an old friend of Van Laningham's. He pretended to be a shady businessman looking for opportunities, even if they weren't legal. Using that cover, Kirk tried to talk Van Laningham into becoming an informant for the FBI.

When Kirk first approached him, Van Laningham was initially very apprehensive about the operation. But the agent pressed him, saying, "It would be a great help to the FBI if [he] would become an informant against Carlos Marcello." Jack said that Kirk then "started telling me things about Marcello that were not nice at all, [saying] he would have a book sent in to me that would tell me all about 'the little man.'"

The book, about organized crime, had fewer than a dozen pages about Carlos Marcello, since only a few books at that time had even that much information about the godfather. After receiving it, Jack "read up on Carlos Marcello [and] all the things that this man had done. He had raped the people of Louisiana, he had bribed and cheated and if that did not work, he resorted to murder. New Orleans was his home, and he ruled it with an iron hand . . . he was into everything crooked [at] one time or the other, and had made millions running the Mafia in Louisiana." Van Laningham said that "the book . . . had some things in it that led me to believe that [Marcello] was responsible for the murder [of JFK]." Surprisingly, Van Laningham revealed that "I read pages of the book to Marcello and he would listen, completely engrossed. The only thing he said to me" at that time "was that he had been kidnapped" on the Kennedys' orders "and that he hated the Kennedys." These and many other quotes from Jack Van Laningham come directly from his declassified FBI file, from letters and summaries soon after the events described that he either wrote by hand or later had a trusted inmate type up for him.

The information in the book Kirk sent had the effect that Kimmel had hoped for. Van Laningham said, "The next time Kirk came to see me, I told him that I would help if I could." Van Laningham said there were three conditions:

1. That "the FBI would have to protect me, if I got in trouble."

2. That a small amount of "money would be [put] up on my [prison] account."

3. The most important: that he would receive an early release for helping the FBI with its dangerous undercover operation.

Van Laningham "was convinced that no matter what the FBI said, I must be careful or I would be dead. If Marcello found out that I was working with the FBI I would not have time to call for help." Van Laningham would eventually be proven right, but that was still several years in the future.

Once Van Laningham became an FBI informant, he continued growing closer to Marcello, who talked more and more to Jack about his array of criminal activities. After a few weeks of seeing Kirk on visiting days, Van Laningham casually introduced Kirk to Marcello, noting that "Kirk thought that it was great that he could meet Marcello." FBI files show that Van Laningham and Kirk gradually tried to draw Marcello into a series of illegal business schemes based upon ongoing criminal operations that Marcello had revealed to Jack. Marcello didn't go for any of the schemes for various reasons, including the innate caution he had developed during his more than fifty years of successful criminal activity.

To get Van Laningham even closer to Marcello, Jack wrote, "[T]he FBI asked the [prison's] Unit Manager to move me into Marcello's room with him. Some days later, this was accomplished." Jack now shared Marcello's two-man cell. Van Laningham was soon told by Kirk that reports about his work were going all the way up to the US Attorney General, Edwin Meese.

To fill the long hours in their cell, Marcello began opening up even more to Jack, giving him fatherly advice while revealing more of his crimes and even telling Jack his hopes for the future. In contrast to the shady deals Kirk had proposed to Marcello, Van Laningham learned that "the only thing Marcello was really interested in was getting out of prison. He had a standing offer with any attorney of a million dollars if they could get him released from prison."

That knowledge gave Kimmel a new goal for his operation, and Van Laningham soon told Marcello a new cover story: that Kirk had a friend in the Bureau of Prisons who could transfer Marcello to a much more comfortable prison—and eventually do even more—for the right price. The new CAMTEX plan was to get Marcello to pay a bribe to Kirk to get to a nicer and less-secure level-two prison and then another bribe to get to a level-one "country club" prison. Finally—once

Marcello saw that Kirk's "friend" could get results—Marcello would get his family or close associates to pay a $1 million bribe to get him "released." After payment of the third and final bribe, the trap would be sprung: Marcello and his associates would be charged. The hope was that either Marcello—facing essentially a life sentence—a family member, or an associate would "flip" at that point and start providing information to the FBI in return for reduced or dropped charges. But even before the FBI's plan got to the final stage, the agents would also learn how Marcello communicated with his subordinates.

To help document Marcello's words and actions, Kirk told Van Laningham "he was going to report to his boss and try for a wiretap of the prison" cell that Marcello shared with Jack. "Two weeks later, Kirk came to see me. He said, 'Well, a judge is going to give us a wire-tap [based] on the evidence [Jack had provided].'" Van Laningham was told that "the Unit phone in the hall would be bugged" and more importantly "that I would have a bug in the room that I shared with Marcello. I was told to buy a Panasonic radio in the [prison] store. I bought the radio and [the Unit Manager] said that he would have to take the radio away to see if it was legal for me to have. I called Kirk and he told me that the bug was being installed in the radio and it would be returned when they were finished. On the 17th of September [1985, the Unit Manager] brought the radio back and told me that I could have it. . . . [I] thought to myself, here I am in this little room with the head of the Mafia from New Orleans, with a radio with a bug inside. I was really scared. If I was found out, I was dead."

The bugging operation described by Van Laningham was confirmed by Kimmel and the FBI files, which include a "Priority" memo sent to the Director of the FBI, William Sessions, confirming that Van Laningham "was roommate of New Orleans organized crime boss Carlos Marcello at Federal Correctional Institution, Texarkana, Texas," and "was instrumental in furnishing probable cause to initiate Title III coverage of Marcello and prison telephone." The same memo also confirms that Van Laningham "successfully introduced FBI undercover agent to Marcello." Van Laningham wrote at the time—and told NBC News for the Discovery Channel—that the Marcello bugging operation yielded "hundreds of hours" of tapes, which Kimmel confirmed. Kimmel told me that while the FBI listened to every tape, they would transcribe a tape only if Marcello mentioned something of interest. Another CAMTEX FBI agent I interviewed said he was the one who actually listened to every secretly recorded tape.

Even as their private conversations were being recorded, Marcello continued to grow closer to Van Laningham. Marcello "would talk for hours about his early life in New Orleans [and] how he had got started running the Mafia in Louisiana." Marcello shared with Jack intimate aspects of his personal life, from his many girlfriends and mistresses to details about his family. The godfather also saw that Van Laningham got well-fitting clothes, avoided bad work assignments, and gained protection from the other inmates, including those jealous of Jack's close friendship with the godfather. Marcello even dispensed fatherly advice to Van Laningham about his future outside of prison.

For all those reasons, Van Laningham grew to like some aspects of Marcello's personality. Yet all that changed once Jack heard Carlos Marcello's chilling confession to JFK's assassination. It brought home to Jack just how much Marcello had come to trust him—and how deadly the godfather could be. If Marcello could find a way to kill a president and get away with it, what chance did Jack have if Marcello learned that he had betrayed him to the FBI?

CHAPTER 4

Carlos Marcello's Rise to Power

I N MANY WAYS, Carlos Marcello was unique among Mafia god-fathers. He ruled his empire without challenge from the late 1940s to the early 1980s, a remarkable tenure for such a deadly profession. A close look at Marcello's early life shows how he developed the incredible confidence needed to order JFK's assassination and how he gained the experience to get away with it.

Marcello wasn't like Mafia chiefs in other cities, because the history of his mob "family" was very different. The New Orleans Mafia is the oldest Mafia family in the United States, having begun in the 1860s. As a result, the New Orleans mob could conduct some critical business, such as carrying out major hits, without approval of the national Mafia "commission." The New Orleans Mafia was also monolithic and under Marcello's sole control once he became a godfather, in stark contrast to the Mafia in New York City, whose several mob families often competed—and sometimes fought—among themselves.

In addition, the New Orleans Mafia was one of the few mob families to conduct hits on government officials; the only others who dared to take such measures even occasionally were Trafficante's Tampa mob and the Chicago Mafia, both allies of Marcello in drug trafficking and the JFK hit.

In the 1800s, soon after the Civil War, New Orleans became a favored American destination for immigrants from Sicily, the birthplace of the Mafia, because the climates of the two regions were so similar. Marcello biographer John H. Davis found that "between 1869 and 1889, the New Orleans police attributed over a hundred murders to the [local] Sicilian Mafia."

One hundred was also the number of members in the New Orleans Mafia by October 15, 1890, when mob hit men shot the city's Police Chief, David Hennessey, using a shotgun and a revolver. He died the following day, and though nineteen mobsters were indicted for the hit, all were acquitted thanks to witness intimidation and bribed jurors. In response to Hennessey's assassination and the resulting acquittals, the public rioted and killed eleven of the Mafia men. But within two years, the New Orleans Mafia had fully recovered and was stronger than ever.

By 1922 the new head of the New Orleans Mafia was Sam Carolla, a narcotics trafficker born in Sicily who, as Davis noted, had shot and killed "a federal narcotics agent by the name of Cecil Moore." Carolla served only two years in federal prison for the crime and emerged to continue heading the organization into the 1930s and mid-1940s.

Carlos Marcello was born Calogero Minacore on February 6, 1910, in Tunisia, the son of a Sicilian mother who soon joined her husband in New Orleans. After dropping out of school at age fourteen, Carlos helped his large family of six brothers and two sisters by delivering vegetables from the family's farm to the New Orleans market, which was controlled by the Mafia. Carlos soon saw crime as a greater opportunity than farming, and at age nineteen he and three friends robbed a bank of $7,000. However, after they were caught and forced to return the money, all the charges were dropped.

Marcello quickly learned that it was better to have others commit his crimes, so he had two teenagers rob a grocery store. While Marcello was planning a follow-up crime with the two—another bank robbery—the teens were arrested. One of them told the authorities everything, and the police also arrested Marcello. In the future, Marcello would come to rely on only close family members and associates who could be trusted not to talk. He had a lot of time to think about such things after "he was sentenced to nine to twelve years in prison," a term he began serving in May 1930 when he was just twenty. Thanks to a corrupt governor, Marcello was pardoned after only four years.

After leaving prison, Marcello bought his first bar, beginning a pattern that would eventually see him owning or controlling dozens of bars, clubs, and restaurants in cities ranging from New Orleans to Dallas, where he would secretly control even gay bars and Jack Ruby's Carousel Club. The following year, in 1936, the twenty-six-year-old Marcello officially joined the New Orleans Mafia and married the daughter of one of Sam Carolla's underbosses. Less than two years later, Marcello was arrested again, this time for selling twenty-three pounds of marijuana from his bar. He was sentenced to a year and a day and ordered to pay a fine of $76,830, but thanks to the mob's influence, he paid only $400 and was released after just nine months. In the future, Marcello would leave the actual trafficking of drugs to others to insulate himself from risk of arrest.

After his release, Marcello focused on a music company he owned with one of his brothers. It was just a front for putting their jukeboxes and pinball machines in bars, restaurants, and clubs in the cities of Gretna and Algiers, just outside New Orleans. Any owners who didn't want Marcello's machines were dealt with brutally.

Those machines—and Marcello's ruthless powers of persuasion—proved to be his ticket to the big time because Sam Carolla had just closed a deal with New York mob boss Frank Costello to put a thousand of Costello's slot machines in and around New Orleans. Carolla ordered Marcello to get a fourth of the machines into New Orleans's west side. In return, Marcello would keep two-thirds of the money while Costello got one-third. The deal was incredibly profitable for both thanks to Marcello's fearsome reputation among bar and club owners. At this time Marcello made his first steps at large-scale bribery of public officials. He later boasted that he gave the Gretna Police Chief "$50,000 in cash every few months," as well as distributing much smaller bribes to lower-level police.

Marcello was so ruthlessly efficient and the slots so profitable that when Costello and Meyer Lansky decided to build a plush gambling casino called the Beverly Country Club near New Orleans, they made Marcello a 12.5 percent partner. The club opened in 1945 and soon featured top nightclub acts of the day, including such Hollywood stars as Jimmy Durante. Marcello was soon managing not only the club but all of Costello's gambling operations in the New Orleans area. All of that was in addition to his other highly profitable activities, which ranged from having "the largest racing wire service in New Orleans" to "reaping huge profits from the narcotics trade for Sam Carolla."

When it came to keeping his men in line, as well as the many other business owners he dealt with, Carlos Marcello could rely on his violent reputation. John H. Davis pointed out that "Carlos had been the prime suspect in several murders for which he had never been charged." One victim was a hoodlum who used the names Constantine Masotto and (according to FBI files) Thomas Siracusa. In 1943 Marcello sent a clear message to mobsters, business owners, and law enforcement when he personally helped torture and murder Siracusa in semi-public fashion at the Willswood Tavern, a rustic restaurant just outside New Orleans owned by Marcello's family.

Davis briefly mentioned the torture/murder in his landmark 1989 biography of Marcello, a key source for information about Marcello's history in this chapter. But here, quoted from FBI files for the first time, is an eyewitness account from a woman who had been dining at the restaurant that evening. Twenty-four years later, when she finally told the FBI what she had seen, she was still so afraid that she refused to testify in court and requested that the FBI not identify her.

The woman said that Marcello was part of a large dinner party at the restaurant and that when Siracusa "arrived [he] appeared surprised and then afraid." When "Siracusa walked . . . back into the kitchen," Marcello and three other men "immediately" followed him. After hearing shouting and fighting, a customer "opened the kitchen door," and the witness "observed Siracusa sitting in a metal chair." One of Marcello's men "was holding a snub-nose revolver which was pressed against Siracusa's temple. Carlos Marcello was slapping Siracusa [who] appeared afraid for his life and was shouting in Italian."

The "terrified" witness and her companions fled. A day or two later, the witness noticed "all the newspapers were carrying front-page stories about the disappearance of Siracusa," so she notified "the New Orleans Police Department." She was sent "to see Sheriff Clancy . . . and told him what she had seen and that she was scared. Sheriff Clancy told her that if she kept her mouth shut, she would not get hurt. She later went to see [a police] Captain at his home [who] told her to keep her mouth shut about what she had told him, as they would kill her. Several weeks later [a] Deputy [for Clancy] also told her to keep her mouth shut," adding that he already knew "Carlos Marcello worked [Siracusa] over [and] that Siracusa was killed."

The willingness of public officials to intimidate the witness and aid Marcello is remarkable, especially considering that the witness told the FBI that the man she had seen holding the gun on Siracusa for Marcello was the "Chief Investigator" for the local "District Attorney." John H. Davis cited a different FBI report stating that "a year after [Siracusa went] missing . . . his lime-encrusted skeleton was discovered in the swamp behind [Willswood] Tavern." That report said that Siracusa "had been beaten to death with rubber hoses by Carlos Marcello and an accomplice. The body was then thrown into a tub of lye and after decomposition, the partially liquefied remains were poured into the swamp." That type of murder (usually by "one of his guards") and body dumping became standard retaliation for anyone in Marcello's organization who displeased, disobeyed, or withheld money from the crime boss.

Word of Marcello's murder of Siracusa spread throughout the criminal underworld and beyond, to those who did business with Marcello and to all levels of law enforcement, helping to keep all of them in line. That use of fear and corruption was a template for many of Marcello's future crimes, though the mob boss later kept his hands technically clean by relying on his men and professionals to take care of the actual murders.

At the same time, Carlos Marcello could also be extremely personable with family, friends, and business associates. Given the many murders for which he was responsible, it's tempting to say that Marcello combined the traits of both a sociopath and a psychopath. However, a better analogy might be that Marcello was simply like a great white shark, which must keep swimming forward or die. Jack

Van Laningham later characterized Marcello by saying, "[A] more cruel and vicious egomaniac I have never met. If he liked you, he would take care of you. But if he did not—well, I'm sure that you know what happens to you." He added that Marcello "seemed to want to win all the time, even if he had to cheat," and this impulse applied even to the friendly games of gin rummy they played in prison. So for Marcello, killing may simply have been part of winning, of always moving ahead. After all, he hadn't achieved his position in the Mafia by inheriting it from his father, as had his friend Santo Trafficante. Instead, Marcello had to earn his own power and then keep earning it to fend off potential local rivals and mob bosses from other areas.

As Marcello gained experience, he also became better at avoiding prosecution. John H. Davis points out that in the late 1930s and early 1940s, "Carlos had been charged with two more assaults and robberies, violation of the federal Internal Revenue laws, assault with intent to kill a New Orleans police officer, sale of narcotics, and armed assault of a New Orleans investigative reporter. None of these charges were ever prosecuted, and the records of several of the arrests mysteriously disappeared." Not bad for a man described as "almost illiterate."

Marcello's rise was also aided by his mentor and partner from New York, Frank Costello. The top Mafia figure of the 1930s had been Charles "Lucky" Luciano, who eventually left Costello temporarily in charge while Luciano was in prison. In return for the aid Luciano offered Naval Intelligence during World War II (ostensibly to help protect New York docks from sabotage and to help restore order in Italy and Sicily after the Allied invasion), Luciano was released from prison. He went into permanent exile in Italy. This solidified Costello's

New York and national mob power even more, a development that also helped Marcello.

Costello and the other high-ranking mob bosses clearly liked what they saw in Carlos Marcello because when local boss Sam Carolla was slated for deportation back to Sicily in May 1947, Marcello was chosen to take over the Mafia in Louisiana. Ostensibly, Marcello was to be Carolla's "*de facto* successor," since Carolla would still technically be the local godfather. But with the same merciless determination that had taken him that far, Marcello continued to expand his power and his contacts. Within a few years, he was indeed godfather of a rapidly expanding empire. Marcello became more prominent on the national Mafia scene when "Costello [and] mob financier and adviser Meyer Lansky agreed to establish a national underworld communications center in New Orleans, and later a national clearinghouse for underworld money laundering . . . in the Crescent City," according to Davis. He said the thirty-seven-year-old Marcello "bought an eight-bedroom Italianate mansion . . . and moved his growing family—he now had a son and three daughters—into . . . surroundings worthy of some of the grand old families of New Orleans."

Marcello became more powerful, wealthier, and more influential in the Mafia—and in Louisiana politics—with each passing year. At that time, officials ranging from US Attorney General Howard McGrath to FBI Director J. Edgar Hoover publicly expressed skepticism that the Mafia even existed. However, Tennessee Democratic Senator Estes Kefauver knew the Mafia was a very real threat, so in 1950, as Chairman of the Special Committee to Investigate Organized Crime in Interstate Commerce, he began a well-publicized investigation. In addition to targeting national crime figures such as Frank Costello, Kefauver called Marcello "the evil genius of organized crime in New

Orleans" and held hearings there, on the mob boss's own turf. Kefauver possibly singled out Marcello not only because of New Orleans's long-standing reputation for vice but also because of an article by prominent muckraking newspaper columnist Drew Pearson, who described the low-public-profile Marcello as "the crime czar" of the city.

On January 25, 1951, Carlos Marcello was forced to appear before Senator Kefauver's hearings in New Orleans. In response to 152 questions, Marcello claimed Fifth Amendment protection against self-incrimination, refusing to answer such basic queries as his age, marital status, and—most important to Marcello—where he was born. The only question he even briefly answered was "'What laws have you violated?' To which he replied: 'Not being an attorney, I would not know.'" His New Orleans attorney, G. Wray Gill, was sitting right beside him, as he would continue to do for years to come, including when Marcello was in federal court the day JFK was shot.

Carlos Marcello was charged and convicted of contempt of Congress for taking the Fifth so many times, though that conviction was eventually overturned on appeal. But Davis points out that Kefauver had also "recommended to the Attorney General that deportation proceedings be initiated against Marcello as soon as possible." It took two years, but "in 1953 the federal government issued its first deportation order against Marcello," a matter that would reach a critical turning point soon after John F. Kennedy took office as president. However, that was still eight years away. In the meantime, Marcello grew even more powerful under the new Republican administration of President Dwight Eisenhower and especially his vice president, Richard Nixon.

The 1953 deportation order against Carlos Marcello didn't produce results while Nixon and Eisenhower were in office, for reasons that remain unclear. Marcello did eventually hire a powerful

Washington attorney, Jack Wasserman, to help with his deportation case, and he also retained his own Washington lobbyist. But it's possible that Marcello wasn't deported because of one or more high-level bribes, since he was so experienced at funneling money to politicians in Louisiana and, as his territory expanded, Texas.

In general, as long as Nixon was vice president, Marcello and the Mafia flourished, not just in the United States but also in countries ranging from Cuba to Guatemala. Marcello—and his closest mob ally, Florida's Santo Trafficante—was even associated with attempted hits on government officials in 1954 and 1955. Unable to take the Fifth as Marcello had done, New Orleans Sheriff Frank Clancy reluctantly testified to the Kefauver Committee about the "5,000 slot machines in his parish" and said that "New Orleans boss Carlos Marcello opened three gambling casinos." By 1955 Sheriff Clancy was reportedly "talking to federal agents about Louisiana gambling," according to one Mafia history.

In April 1955 Clancy was hospitalized for a medical condition, but the "guard outside his door" was removed on a pretext. Then the patient in the room next to Sheriff Clancy, a bank teller, had his skull smashed open "with a cleaver" while he lay in his hospital bed. It's unclear whether the hit man simply mixed up the rooms and killed the wrong person or if the murder of the man in the next room was meant to send a message to Clancy. In any event, Clancy "ceased giving information to federal agents." The same was true for "a nurses' aide who had seen the killer and provided police with a detailed description." But "three days later she suddenly recalled she had no idea what the man looked like." No one was ever arrested in the hospital murder case, and the same type of witness intimidation would occur after JFK's assassination.

Carlos Marcello became increasingly involved with Santo Trafficante and his operations as the 1950s progressed. Both men preferred to avoid publicity and to wield their growing power away from the limelight. Like Marcello, Trafficante was ruthless with his enemies; testimony given at the Kefauver Committee hearings tied Trafficante's mob family to at least fourteen murders over two decades. Among those killed was a Kefauver Committee witness, who was murdered before he could testify. Tampa's police chief did give testimony, which was later summarized thusly: Trafficante "had a standard operating procedure for murder, which included the importation of hired killers from out of town and setting up patsies to take the fall."

Unlike Marcello, Santo Trafficante had long been groomed to take over for his father, Santos Trafficante Sr., whose accomplishments included creating the American side of the French Connection heroin network. According to one mob history, that network originally extended "from Marseilles, France, through Cuba to Florida," and from its Tampa base, the Trafficante family helped supply heroin to cities ranging from New York to Chicago. In the 1950s Marcello's organization was part of that network, bringing in heroin through ports in Louisiana and Texas, as well as across the border from Mexico.

Trafficante Sr. had sent his son to Cuba in 1946 both to help with the heroin trafficking that resumed after World War II and to gain a piece of the Havana casino action. Santo Trafficante managed casinos for his father until the elder Trafficante's death in 1954, at which point Trafficante assumed control of the mob family.

Santo Trafficante spoke fluent Spanish and continued to spend time in Cuba as well as Tampa, with frequent visits to the "open" mob city of Miami. Because of his lack of a passport and US citizenship, Marcello could not easily or safely travel to Cuba, which by the

1950s was the Mafia's gambling mecca for well-heeled travelers from the United States. Trafficante was one of the two main casino owners in Havana with the other being mob financial genius Meyer Lansky. Trafficante completely controlled one casino, the Sans Souci, and had shares in three more.

For years it was thought that Marcello's inability to travel to Cuba prevented him from holding a share in the mob's Havana gambling industry, but as revealed here for the first time, that wasn't the case. Decades later, in prison, Marcello made an admission to Jack Van Laningham, who reported that "he was partners with a man that ran the Mafia in Florida, [Santo] Trafficante, [and] they were [also] partners in a casino in Cuba, and made millions before Castro took over and shut them down."

Mafia casinos in Cuba had flourished under the brutal dictatorship of Fulgencio Batista, whose regime was embraced by Vice President Richard Nixon and tolerated by President Eisenhower. Nixon reportedly had business interests on the island with his mob-connected best friend, Charles "Bebe" Rebozo. Nixon had visited the Mafia casinos and had been given honors by Batista. The repressive Cuban dictator had partnered with mob bosses like Meyer Lansky and Santo Trafficante, who gave him a lucrative piece of the growing Havana casino industry. Meanwhile, much of the Cuban populace suffered from bad nutrition, low wages, and Batista's vicious police state.

By 1957 Cubans Fidel Castro, his brother Raul, and Juan Almeida—as well as Argentinean doctor Che Guevara—were leading a small but growing guerrilla movement in Cuba's Sierra Maestra. While the charismatic Fidel got the lion's share of favorable press attention, other rebel leaders and groups also fought against the regime, putting more and more pressure on Batista's corrupt police state. When Eisenhower established an arms embargo, it didn't slow the fighting but only allowed the Mafia and the CIA to fill the void by providing weapons, and not just to Batista. Surprisingly, the CIA and Trafficante played both sides, providing small quantities of arms to Fidel Castro and his men.

However, all the fighting occurred far from the plush Havana casinos, which continued to flourish and expand in 1957. They generated so much revenue that New York mob boss Albert Anastasia wanted a big piece of the action. Frank Costello had been forced into retirement, meaning that Trafficante couldn't turn to Marcello's old mentor for help. On October 24, 1957, Trafficante met with Anastasia in the New York mob boss's suite at the Park Sheraton Hotel, but apparently the two were at an impasse. The next day two men murdered Anastasia in the hotel's barbershop. Trafficante checked out of the hotel an hour later and left New York. Even though the *Washington Post* described him as the "leading suspect" in arranging Anastasia's murder, he was never charged.

The Administration's tolerance of the Mafia was such that Trafficante felt safe to return to New York State for a meeting just two weeks later, along with almost a hundred other mob bosses from across the country. The ever-cautious Carlos Marcello didn't attend and instead sent "his most trusted brother, Joe" and his top two Dallas lieutenants, Joseph Civello and Joe Campisi Sr. Their agenda ranged from replacing Anastasia to providing assistance for Batista and Fidel Castro. The mobsters met at a secluded country estate near the small town of Apalachin, New York.

Marcello's caution proved to be justified when local officers raided the unusual meeting, arresting fifty-eight mob leaders, including Trafficante and Joe Marcello. They were detained only briefly, but the huge meeting, combined with the recent sensational front-page news of Anastasia's assassination, only served to fuel the frustration of many Americans—and some members of Congress—that the Mafia seemed to operate with near impunity under J. Edgar Hoover's FBI and the rest of the Eisenhower–Nixon Administration.

IN THE 1950S, two successful assassinations of government officials were linked to close associates of Carlos Marcello; one took place the same year as Apalachin, 1957, and the other in 1954. Though Marcello was not the driving force in either, both are important for understanding how the godfather later murdered JFK, and they show how Marcello partnered with, and learned from, his fellow mob bosses.

Marcello's partner Santo Trafficante was one of the vice lords behind the highly publicized assassination of Alabama's Attorney General–elect in 1954. The hit occurred in Phenix City, Alabama, long known as the most corrupt town in America. Just across the river from much larger Columbus, Georgia, and its huge Fort Benning US Army base, Phenix City was a cesspool of all forms of vice that preyed on servicemen: drugs, gambling, and clip joints featuring armies of B-girls and prostitutes. Prior to World War II, Franklin Roosevelt had sent General George Patton to clean up the town, but to no avail. Santo Trafficante had a major influence in Phenix City through one of his longtime lieutenants, and Marcello had criminal interests in Alabama as well. State officials either looked the other way or—in the case of Alabama's sitting Attorney General—were part of the criminal operation.

In 1954 Phenix City's Albert Patterson ran for Attorney General of Alabama on a promise to clean up the town. He won the Democratic nomination, which in 1950s Alabama made him the Attorney

General–elect, but Patterson was quickly assassinated by gunfire. The confident crime lords hadn't bothered to use any type of patsy to take the blame, so it was immediately clear that organized crime was responsible for the murder.

The assassination of Attorney General–elect Patterson generated huge headlines across the country. Though the Eisenhower–Nixon Administration, including FBI Director J. Edgar Hoover, had basically taken a hands-off approach to organized crime, National Guard General Walter Hanna pressured the Alabama Governor, who finally got Eisenhower to take action. Phenix City was placed under "Martial Rule" by the National Guard, putting the city under US military occupation. That drastic step finally ran the rackets out of Phenix City, though after a time they simply reorganized on a smaller scale across the river in Columbus, Georgia.

Bringing the assassins of Attorney General–elect Patterson to justice was another matter. Two local vice lords had immediately fled to Trafficante's territory in Florida, while the city's corrupt "night Police Chief" went to Texas, now part of Marcello's territory (along with southern Mississippi). The corrupt sitting Attorney General of Alabama, Si Garrett, was targeted by the grand jury investigating the assassination, but he entered "a psychiatric clinic in Galveston, Texas." After the court indicted Garrett, he stayed either in Texas or Mississippi until 1963, when all charges against him were inexplicably dropped. As with other hits involving Trafficante and Marcello, witness intimidation and murder kept the investigation from ever reaching the level of the two bosses. Of the four men indicted, just one was convicted of murder, eventually serving only seven years, while one was acquitted and a third was allowed to plead nolo contendere to a minor charge.

One might think the Phenix City assassination would have caused the Eisenhower–Nixon Administration to declare war on organized crime, but it didn't. J. Edgar Hoover continued to turn a blind eye toward the Mafia in general and Marcello in particular. *Time* magazine in 1975 first revealed secret meetings and friendship between Hoover and mob boss Frank Costello, which were confirmed by William Hundley, the Justice Department organized crime chief during the Kennedy Administration. Hoover's predilection for gambling on horse races is now well known, and it's also possible Hoover was blackmailed by the Mafia over his closeted homosexuality.

Carlos Marcello's partners had gotten away with murder, but they had lost the lucrative cash cow that was Phenix City. However, they learned from their mistakes, and the next time Marcello's associates assassinated a government official, a patsy would be on hand to be quickly blamed and killed to divert suspicion from organized crime.

IN ADDITION TO Trafficante, another important mob figure with whom Carlos Marcello became involved in the 1950s was Johnny Rosselli, the Mafia don who handled the Chicago mob's interests in Los Angeles and Las Vegas. Rosselli was a smooth operator who in the 1940s had hobnobbed with movie studio chiefs until he was caught running a union shakedown operation for the mob. After Rosselli's release from federal prison, he still had clout in Las Vegas, but the studio heads had to distance themselves from him. Court records show Rosselli was still influential enough to be an executive producer on three low-budget film noirs in the late 1940s, though his name couldn't be listed in the credits. One of the films, *He Walked by Night*, featured a crazed ex-serviceman who turned killer. The young ex-serviceman kept his long-barreled weapon hidden away, wrapped in a blanket, but he carried a pistol and used it to shoot a policeman in his patrol car. Rosselli later credibly confessed his role in JFK's murder, which had a similar scenario involving Lee Oswald and Officer Tippit.

Before leaving the movie business for the greener pastures of Las Vegas and Cuban casinos, Rosselli helped get his friend Frank Sinatra a dramatic role in *From Here to Eternity,* which reignited Sinatra's career. Rosselli's biographers say the pressure he applied on Sinatra's behalf inspired the famous "horse's head in the bed" scene in the first *Godfather* novel and film.

Johnny Rosselli was very active in Guatemala in the mid-1950s, and his biographers documented from two sources that "Rosselli's primary concern in Guatemala was to protect and advance the interests of" a New Orleans company with ties to Carlos Marcello. In 1956 Marcello decided that "Guatemala would be the most appropriate country" from which to obtain a fake birth certificate, since it "was easily accessible to New Orleans by air, telephone, and telegraph." President Castillo Armas ruled the country, having been installed as dictator after the Eisenhower–Nixon Administration used the CIA to overthrow the liberal government of the democratically elected Jacobo Árbenz in 1954.[*]

While President Armas reportedly did not take bribes from the Mafia, that was not true of his prime minister. Carlos Marcello paid $100,000 to Guatemala's prime minister and his former law partner for his fake birth certification and citizenship papers. There was also casino gambling in Guatemala run by Ted Lewin, Johnny Rosselli's associate from Los Angeles.

---

[*]That coup involved CIA agents E. Howard Hunt, David Atlee Phillips, and David Morales, all of whom played roles in the CIA's attempts to assassinate Fidel Castro; Morales would later make a credible confession to JFK's murder.

President Armas tried to close the casinos, and he jailed Rosselli's friend Lewin. Four days later, in July 1957, Armas was assassinated, apparently by a lone Communist assassin. The "assassin" was said by accounts to have "immediately committed suicide with the same rifle he had used to kill the President." One historian notes that even more conveniently, police "produced some leftist propaganda that had supposedly been found in his pockets and a suspicious 'diary,' but few if any Guatemalans believed the official explanation." Rosselli's biographers said "a more plausible explanation, one that gained currency in Guatemala City at the time of the shooting, was that Castillo Armas had run afoul of . . . the Mafia."

There are striking parallels between the 1957 Guatemalan patsy, Vasquez Sanchez, and Lee Oswald, the seemingly Communist former Marine who was able to get a job at the sensitive Dallas U-2 map firm at the height of the Cuban Missile Crisis, even though he had recently returned from the Soviet Union. In Guatemala, the government described the patsy "as a 'Communist fanatic' . . . expelled from the Guatemalan Army six months ago for 'Communist ideology,' but [he] had" been allowed to join "the Presidential Palace Guard." Like Oswald, the Guatemalan patsy was supposedly an ardent Communist, yet "no evidence ever turned up that [he] was a member of the . . . Communist Party."

The US government and news media, still in the thrall of the McCarthy–Nixon "Red Scare," which saw hundreds blacklisted or graylisted in Hollywood and elsewhere, quickly accepted that a seemingly lone Communist had murdered President Armas. Eisenhower's son John declared that the accused killer had been "acting under orders from Moscow." However, historians point out that a letter supposedly found on the patsy's body, said by authorities to be the bodyguard's correspondence with Moscow about his assassination assignment, was actually only a form-letter postcard from Radio Moscow.

Another US-backed right-wing dictator quickly took Armas's place, and Marcello kept his fake citizenship papers. At the time of the assassination, Marcello was involved in a business venture with Rosselli in Las Vegas, the godfather's only direct foray into that city. Rosselli helped Marcello become a partner in the new Las Vegas Tropicana hotel and casino, then the "most luxurious . . . on the strip." Vegas needed that luxury to compete with the burgeoning Mafia casinos being built in Havana. Rosselli was only a Mafia don, not a mob boss or godfather like Marcello, but he was the consummate deal-maker, and he managed the Tropicana for a time.

However, Rosselli and the Mafia were still learning how to hide mob ownership from the Nevada Gaming Commission. As Marcello later explained to Jack Van Laningham, he "tried to get into gambling in Vegas" using a front man, and "all was going good until the Nevada Gaming Commission learned that Carlos Marcello was involved. They were shut down and lost a great deal of money in the venture [and] he stayed clear of Vegas after that." Marcello always tried to stay out of the limelight and the newspapers, and he could have all the gambling he wanted in Louisiana without worrying about a state Gaming Commission. Marcello stayed out of Las Vegas after that, even in the 1970s when he had a chance to put up money for the real casino depicted in Martin Scorsese's film *Casino*. Instead, Marcello simply brokered that deal to the Kansas City mob, getting an enormous onetime (and untraceable) "finder's fee" in the process, something the FBI learned but never revealed to the public.

Even after the Tropicana problem, Marcello continued to deal with the smooth, articulate Rosselli. In addition to Sinatra, Rosselli was close to Dean Martin, Marilyn Monroe, and other celebrities. Furthermore, like Marcello, Rosselli wasn't an American citizen, having been born Filippo Sacco in Esperia, Italy, on July 4, 1905. But unlike with Marcello, the US government didn't realize Rosselli wasn't a citizen, and it wouldn't learn that until 1966, setting off a chain of events that would help trigger Watergate and lead to Rosselli's gruesome 1976 murder on Trafficante's orders, with Marcello's support. But in 1957 the fifty-two-year-old Rosselli and the forty-seven-year-old Marcello still got along well.

Marcello and Rosselli had something else in common—neither hesitated to kill those who got in his way or who incurred his wrath. By the mid-1950s, Willie Bioff—the key witness whose testimony had sent Rosselli to prison and ended his glamorous Hollywood lifestyle—was living in Phoenix and was good friends with Arizona Senator Barry Goldwater.

Despite Bioff's friendship with, and political support of, Senator Goldwater, Rosselli and the Mafia got their revenge: Bioff was killed when his truck exploded in his driveway at his Phoenix home on November 4, 1955, destroyed by "a dynamite bomb." No one was arrested for the murder. Three years later Rosselli approved the murder of another good friend of Goldwater's, Gus Greenbaum, owner of the Riviera casino and "mayor" of the Las Vegas strip.* After becoming addicted to heroin, Greenbaum refused mob orders to sell his interest in the Riviera. So on December 3, 1958, Greenbaum was almost completely "decapitated" while his wife, Bess, had "her throat slashed with a butcher knife" according to crime writer Ovid Demaris. Senator Goldwater attended Greenbaum's funeral, but there was no

---

*The Las Vegas strip is actually an unincorporated town named Paradise.

arrest. Several years later DeMaris documented the arrival of two hit men from Miami shortly before the murder. Afterward they left in a private plane. Rosselli may well have used his mutual associate with Marcello—Santo Trafficante—to provide the hit men. Employing out-of-town hit men was a technique both Trafficante and Marcello increasingly used since it was difficult to tie them to a crime and locale. Five years later all three men would employ a variation of that approach against JFK.

CARLOS MARCELLO'S EMPIRE continued to grow and would soon be bringing in "$2 billion annually from criminal operations in Louisiana, Mississippi, and Texas," according to his biographer. While much of that went to payoffs and support for a wide range of local, county, state, and federal officials, Marcello had plenty of cash to invest in land and in legitimate businesses (to which, he later boasted to Van Laningham, he gave a criminal competitive advantage). Not that Marcello necessarily bought those legitimate businesses—as Marcello later explained to Jack Van Laningham, he took what he wanted:

> by force. Anyone that got in the way of what he wanted was eliminated one way or another. He told me about the bars and liquor business in New Orleans. He never bought bars, he took them. Marcello would send men to see the owner that he wanted to do business with. The owner was told that from now on, you will be selling our liquor. If the bar owner made trouble or refused, fights were staged, furniture broken up, and the guests harassed. Whores were sent in to cause trouble. The owner of the bar either went out of business or

went into partnership with Marcello. Marcello had his own still in New Orleans and also shipped liquor in from Texas, in five-gallon cans. Since all of the police were on the payroll, it did no good to call them, he had them all in his pocket, along with the judges.

That pattern was repeated dozens, probably hundreds, of times, and not just in the bar and restaurant business but also in the companies that supplied them. Marcello also explained to Van Laningham that "the way to make and keep money was to buy ground"—in other words, land. Marcello told Van Laningham that "he owned hundreds of acres of ground that he had bought for peanuts, and now it was worth millions."

Marcello's real estate holdings in Louisiana and cities such as Dallas were extensive and growing. They included his secluded and massive sixty-four-hundred-acre Churchill Farms estate. Once mostly swamp, part of the land had been drained, and Marcello used the remote farmhouse in the middle of it for some of his most sensitive meetings—including several concerning plans for JFK's assassination.

By 1957 Marcello had set up his daily office at the nondescript Town and Country Motel, a location he would use for routine business for the next two and a half decades. Located on the equally nondescript Airline Highway connecting the city to Moisant Airport, it was an appropriate venue for the publicity-shy godfather; the road was described by his biographer as an "ugly . . . endless procession of gas stations, parking lots, billboards, striptease joints, sleazy bars, cheap motels, and neon signs"—the kind of area that could be found in most larger cities throughout America at that time.

The Town and Country Motel was the center of a multistate prostitution ring as well as the center of Marcello's gambling empire, which included his "national racing wire network." Every Sunday Marcello held court in the motel restaurant. Marcello's private office behind the motel was the site of most of his weekday meetings when he wasn't traveling through his extensive empire, where he also maintained smaller offices and mistresses. Marcello's main office had one other notable feature, "a sign on the door leading out" that according to his biographer gave visitors a chilling reminder of whom they "were dealing with":

THREE CAN KEEP

A SECRET

IF TWO ARE DEAD

When frustrated New Orleans citizens tried to bring in experienced law enforcement help from the outside, even there they were thwarted. The former FBI agent in charge of Chicago, Guy Banister, was brought in to be New Orleans's Assistant Police Superintendent, focusing on the ties between organized crime and the department. However, the extremely conservative and racist Banister seemed more interested in going after left-wingers and alleged Communists. He quit the force after pulling his gun on a waiter in a bar. The alcoholic Banister then formed a local private detective agency; by the early 1960s his clients included Carlos Marcello—who would use Banister's law-enforcement connections, his interest in white supremacy, and his undercover anti-Communist activities in the plot to kill JFK.

Carlos Marcello was free to expand his criminal empire, using murders when needed, and according to the New Orleans Crime Commission those included "the gangland-style killing of two of

Marcello's narcotics associates," according to John H. Davis. The heroin network Marcello shared with Trafficante was their most lucrative, most secret—and thus most deadly—enterprise.

Marcello continued to rely on his own brothers and extended family when possible. Of his six brothers, the youngest, Joe, was his favorite and most trusted, acting "as Carlos's right-hand man [and] immediate underboss." But each of the others—Pete, Pascal, Vincent, Tony, and Sammy—also played key roles in helping manage Marcello's ever-expanding empire.

There appeared to be no concerns for Carlos Marcello on the federal front since Richard Nixon enjoyed increasing power and respect as the 1950s advanced, due to a series of health issues plaguing President Eisenhower. Nixon had weathered the only two potential scandals he'd recently faced, aided in one case by his long-time patron, billionaire Howard Hughes. The other scandal involved exposure of the mob ties of attorney Murray Chotiner, Nixon's closest advisor.

Richard Nixon and Murray Chotiner had longtime and well-documented links to the Mafia. Los Angeles mobster Mickey Cohen admitted giving Nixon $5,000 (nearly $50,000 in today's money) in Nixon's first race for Congress in California, in 1946. Cohen upped that to $75,000 (almost $700,000 today) for Nixon's 1950 Senate run. Chotiner, Nixon's chief political aide and strategist from 1946 until the time of Watergate, had arranged those payoffs. Chotiner, an attorney, and his brother had represented 221 of Cohen's bookmakers in just one four-year period.

Chotiner wasn't the only Nixon associate tied to the Mafia. Richard Nixon's best friend from the 1950s until his death—Charles "Bebe" Rebozo—had extensive banking, real estate, and business ties to the mob, including associates of Meyer Lansky and Santo

Trafficante. Evidence, including later admissions by former government officials such as John Mitchell, shows that Rebozo often fronted businesses and shady deals for Nixon in locales ranging from Cuba to Florida to the Bahamas.

However, Chotiner's role as an advisor to Vice President Nixon had caught the eye of Democrats in Congress. As it happened, a Congressional committee probing Chotiner publicized the case before having enough evidence against him, and Chotiner avoided any charges. He did have to assume a less prominent role for the Vice President, away from the public eye, but Nixon's other Mafia ties remained unexposed.

One of the counsels on the committee investigating Chotiner was a young Robert F. Kennedy, and he learned from the mistakes he saw in that investigation. In 1957 Robert Kennedy teamed up with his brother, Senator John F. Kennedy from Massachusetts. They were investigating Teamster corruption starting with union president Dave Beck, the only major union leader to support the generally anti-union Eisenhower–Nixon ticket. After corruption charges forced Beck to step down, John and Robert Kennedy focused on his successor, Jimmy Hoffa.

The Kennedys' investigation of Hoffa would have crucial ramifications for all concerned. The corruption and Mafia ties the brothers uncovered would lead them to focus on exposing Hoffa's crimes, first through Congressional hearings and later through prosecutions that would eventually send Hoffa to prison. Their actions began a blood feud between the Kennedys and Hoffa that would last until JFK's assassination, followed five years later by Robert's. Finally, the Mafia ties uncovered in 1957 by the Kennedy brothers' Hoffa investigation soon led them to focus extensively on fighting organized crime.

Some say that effort was a way for the politically ambitious John to counter rumors about his own immensely wealthy father's ties to or friendship with members of organized crime. Others claim that JFK pursued the mob to garner publicity, and it is true that he generated huge amounts of media coverage for the anti-Mafia hearings he pushed. But from newspaper headlines alone, there was clearly a need for someone to take on the Mafia in America since J. Edgar Hoover and the Eisenhower–Nixon Administration seemed so reluctant to do so. Starting in the late 1950s, John F. Kennedy took up that fight.

The Kennedys wasted no time in going after Carlos Marcello and Santo Trafficante, both soon to be close allies with the new Teamster leader, Jimmy Hoffa. Senator Kennedy dispatched a trusted investigator, former journalist Pierre Salinger, to New Orleans to look into Marcello's criminal activities firsthand. Before his death, Salinger spoke to me about that and described the fear and intimidation he encountered in New Orleans in the late 1950s. While Salinger could document a clear paper trail, people at all levels were afraid to talk; he himself worried that he wouldn't survive the experience. However, aided by the New Orleans Crime Commission, a group of concerned local citizens headed by Aaron Kohn, Salinger helped the Kennedys put together a remarkable list of Marcello's criminal enterprises.

The Kennedys knew one thing Marcello feared was publicity, so they arranged to force him to come to Washington to testify before the Senate Select Committee on Improper Activities in Labor and Management, chaired by Arkansas Senator John McClellan. However, the Kennedys were its driving force, and they received the lion's share of the enormous radio, newspaper, and television publicity the hearings generated.

The Kennedys and Salinger knew that Marcello would simply take the Fifth, so they devised a strategy designed to convey Marcello's story to the American people anyway. First they extensively questioned Aaron Kohn of the Crime Commission, whose answers gave a detailed overview of Marcello's life and numerous crimes. Next they questioned Salinger, who provided more documentation and details about the complex web of companies controlled by Marcello.

Finally, on March 24, 1959, Carlos Marcello himself was forced to go before the glare of television lights in Washington to confront the Kennedys' Senate committee.

CHAPTER 5

Marcello, Cuba, and Jack Ruby

R OBERT F. KENNEDY personally confronted godfather Carlos Marcello for the first and only time on Tuesday, March 24, 1959, in a Senate hearing room on Capitol Hill. RFK was the brash, blunt-spoken Chief Counsel of the Senate Select Committee on Improper Activities in Labor and Management, which now focused on organized crime. But he still maintained what was often described as a boyish demeanor, and that was especially true when compared with his older brother, Senator John F. Kennedy. However, on that day both JFK and Senator Barry Goldwater had other business to attend to and were not at the hearing. That left RFK in full command of the interrogation of Carlos Marcello, the first of a series of events involving the godfather that would result in tragedy for RFK, his brother, and at times even Marcello.

Attired in a well-tailored, expensive-looking pin-striped suit, the forty-nine-year-old godfather sat at the witness table. Dark glasses concealed his eyes, and he would wear them for the entire hearing. Though Marcello tried to maintain a relaxed image in his rare pub-lic appearances, he could be quick to anger; perhaps the dark glasses were intended to make it harder for RFK and the Senators to read his reactions. Seated beside Marcello was his top Washington attorney,

Jack Wasserman, one of the country's best immigration attorneys. The fact that he chose Wasserman instead of a criminal defense attorney or a high-profile Washington power attorney showed that what Marcello feared most was his lack of citizenship. Unlike Santo Trafficante, Marcello couldn't duck the Kennedys' subpoena by traveling to another country. As a noncitizen, if Marcello ever left the United States he might be denied reentry, so Wasserman told him he had no other recourse than to report for the hearing.

With his bow tie and glasses, Wasserman looked nothing like a typical mob lawyer and more like a university professor. Next to Wasserman was one of the godfather's brothers, Vincent Marcello, who ran the slot machines for his brother's empire. In contrast to his compact, portly brother, Vincent was taller and more conventionally handsome. He looked like a well-dressed businessman, not a Mafia underboss.

Still, with his Roman profile and imperious attitude, Carlos Marcello was a commanding presence in the hearing room. But Robert Kennedy—who had already sparred with Jimmy Hoffa in earlier hearings—remained focused on his carefully prepared questions, designed to reveal to the American public the huge scope of Marcello's criminal empire. Part of that involved exposing Marcello's control of Dallas and important parts of the heroin trade. When RFK asked Marcello, "You are an associate of Joe Civello of Dallas, Texas, who attended the meeting at Apalachin?" Marcello replied, "I decline to answer on the ground it may tend to incriminate me." A later Senate report would make it clear that "Joe Civello . . . controls all rackets in Dallas and vicinity." Along with another Dallas Marcello underboss, restaurateur Joe Campisi Sr., Civello conveyed Marcello's orders to lower-level mobsters in Dallas, such as Jack Ruby.

RFK then asked if Marcello was an associate of "Sam Carolla, who was deported in 1947 as a narcotics trafficker." Marcello said only, "I decline to answer on the same ground." However, other witnesses and huge charts clearly showed the importance of Marcello and New Orleans to what would soon become known as the French Connection narcotics trade.

RFK then asked, "Have you been able to use law enforcement officials to assist you in your business, Mr. Marcello?" Once again, Marcello fell back on his right to avoid incriminating himself, as he would for almost all the questions that day. Still, by the time RFK had finished his list of questions, they—along with information provided earlier by Assistant Counsel Pierre Salinger and Aaron Kohn of the New Orleans Crime Commission—had given the America press and public their first good overview of Marcello's criminal empire: gambling, prostitution, corruption of public officials, real estate fraud, terrorizing legitimate businessmen, narcotics trafficking, and much more. Then came the time for the Senators to ask their questions. Since RFK had said that "Mr. Carlos Marcello has been under orders of deportation from the United States since about 1953," much of their questioning centered on why he was still allowed to live in the United States. Kohn had earlier testified that Marcello had "been in court some 37 times in various appellate proceedings, and in various hearings" to avoid deportation, but it's clear that some Senators felt some factor other than Jack Wasserman's legal skill accounted for the current Administration's failure to deport Marcello.

Senator Sam Ervin of North Carolina—later chairman of the famed Senate Watergate Committee—began by reminding Marcello of his two felony convictions and then asked "how a man with that kind of record can stay in the United States for five years, nine months, twenty-four days after he is found to be an undesirable alien. . . . How have you managed to stay here?" Marcello eventually answered, "I wouldn't know." Senator Ervin expressed his frustration at the current Eisenhower–Nixon Administration, saying, "[T]he American people are entitled to more protection at the hands of the law than to have an undesirable alien who has committed serious felonies remain in this country." He summed up by essentially calling Marcello a leech who preyed "upon law-abiding people [and who] ought to be removed from this country."

South Dakota's Senator Karl Mundt took up the cudgel against Marcello and the Eisenhower–Nixon Administration, commenting that Committee Chairman Senator John McClellan should "direct a letter to the Attorney General inquiring as to why this deportation has not been implemented." Even so, Marcello left the hearing unbowed, and despite all the publicity, as long as President Dwight Eisenhower and Vice President Nixon remained in office, no serious additional efforts were made to deport the godfather.

However, John and Robert Kennedy weren't through with the Mafia, and Chicago mob boss Sam Giancana was set to receive the same treatment accorded Marcello. Giancana was a former mob hit man, both ruthless and charming. (He would soon be involved in a well-publicized romance with Phyllis McGuire, one of America's most popular singers at the time.) He wasn't a godfather like Marcello but essentially ran the day-to-day operations of the Chicago mob for two elder Mafia chiefs. Giancana's influence extended beyond Chicago, to Las Vegas, Hollywood, and Reno, with the help of his Mafia don, Johnny Rosselli.

On June 9, 1959, RFK verbally sparred with Sam Giancana, trying to draw him into a revealing response. RFK asked, "Would you tell us, if you have opposition from anybody, that you dispose of them by having them stuffed in a trunk? Is that what you do, Mr. Giancana?" Giancana appeared to stifle a laugh, not taking the Committee and RFK's questions seriously, leading RFK to ask, "Is there something funny about it, Mr. Giancana?" and "Would you tell us anything about any of your operations, or will you just giggle every time I ask you a question? I thought only little girls giggled, Mr. Giancana."

RFK was unable to prod Giancana to do more than plead the Fifth, which Giancana did over three dozen times. Nevertheless, as with Marcello, RFK was still able to expose Giancana's criminal network, which included narcotics trafficking, something the Chicago Mafia for years disingenuously continued to claim it avoided. RFK also relied on questioning Pierre Salinger before the Committee to put even more of Giancana's crimes on the record.

As they sought to question additional mob leaders, Senator Kennedy and RFK were stymied on one occasion by the CIA, foreshadowing problems with the Agency that would plague the two men even after JFK become President. In a 1975 report for the *New York Times* that was confirmed by two RFK aides, Pulitzer Prize–winning journalist Seymour Hersh discovered that in 1959 the CIA had given a "free pass" to one mob boss for his help in trying to assassinate Fidel Castro for the US government. When RFK and his aides tried to question him in private, the Mafia chief replied, "You can't touch me. I've got immunity." Robert demanded to know "who gave you immunity?" The Mafia boss replied, "The CIA. I'm working for them, but I can't talk about it. Top Secret." RFK must have been stunned, but after looking into it, he found that "the CIA had made a deal with" the mob boss.

As eventually documented in the 1970s by Hoffa expert Dan Moldea, in 1959 the CIA was working with three mob bosses from the northeastern United States, trying to assassinate Fidel. Those mob bosses—James Plumeri, Russell Bufalino, and Salvatore Granello— were contacted and handled by Teamster President Jimmy Hoffa, who acted as a "cutout" for the CIA in the transaction. Hoffa was a logical choice because both new Cuban President Fidel Castro and the Mafia viewed him as an ally. Before Castro and his allies assumed power on January 1, 1959, Hoffa had been involved in CIA-sanctioned arms smuggling to Cuba. By the early summer of 1959, Hoffa was participating in a complex deal, one that John and Robert Kennedy tried to unravel using their hearings and investigators. In the deal, Hoffa's mob associates sold surplus planes to Cuba, financed by Teamster money and it also involved stolen securities. The Kennedys' investigation hit a stone wall because they couldn't locate a mysterious "Jack La Rue," apparently the alias of a Hoffa associate involved in the deal. Hoffa's complicated transaction was also likely used to provide cover for his work on the 1959 CIA– Mafia plots to kill Fidel. Those Hoffa-brokered plots would last for almost a year, but because the northeastern mobsters didn't have extensive resources in Castro's Cuba, their assassination plans made little progress.

As part of their hearings, John and Robert Kennedy wanted to question godfather Santo Trafficante about the murder of Albert Anastasia. Though Trafficante fled to Cuba to avoid testifying, in his place the Kennedys heard testimony from the Miami Crime Commission chief. Under questioning from RFK, he talked about Trafficante's heroin network and his mob's "twenty-one gang killings" in twenty years, "none of which . . . were ever solved." To show he wasn't afraid of the Kennedys or the Committee, Trafficante had ordered another mob hit the previous day, and Robert had to announce in the hearing that he had been informed "there was another one yesterday." Like the others, it would never be solved

On June 9, 1959, Fidel ordered that Trafficante be placed in a comfortable detention center in Havana, along with several of his mob associates. Historians still debate the reasons for Trafficante's detention, with some saying the godfather wanted to be detained in Cuba so he wouldn't have to return to the United States to testify about the Anastasia killing to the Kennedys or to New York City authorities. Trafficante's confinement was comfortable, and he was even allowed to attend his daughter's lavish wedding at the Habana Hilton. One account says that once the godfather was released, Trafficante continued to visit Havana for almost three months.

However, other historians cite Trafficante's later testimony—and information from some of his associates—to the effect that his detention wasn't voluntary and that at times he feared for his life. Given these conflicting views, it's probable that his detention was initially unexpected and potentially dangerous, but as time went by, a financial accommodation was gradually reached, leading to his release. His stay in Cuba lasted until the Kennedys' committee had finished its work.

When Trafficante was in detention, it was hard for him to access his considerable wealth, and he had no easy way to communicate with his most powerful ally, Carlos Marcello. The only way to get Marcello's help was to use trusted messengers who could freely travel from the United States to Cuba and back without arousing the suspicion of US or Cuban authorities.

In Marcello's organization, there was a man well suited for the role of messenger and courier between the two godfathers: Jack Ruby. Ruby's role was confirmed by a Britsh man named John Wilson Hudson who was detained with Trafficante. Unlike most of the others in detention, Hudson did not have a criminal record. Hudson caused a stir after the Kennedy assassination when he told authorities that in detention in 1959, he had met a man who "accompanied the person who brought Trafficante his meals." Hudson said the man visited the detained Trafficante "frequently" and that man was Jack Ruby.

To understand how Ruby came to be a messenger between Marcello and Trafficante in 1959—and how he came to play a critical role for both men in their 1963 murder of JFK—it's important to look closely at his background. Knowing who Jack Ruby really was, and the role he played in organized crime for decades, is crucial to understanding JFK's assassination, since Ruby's actions before, during, and after the tragedy were dictated by the Mafia.

Originally born Jack Rubenstein in Chicago on March 25, 1911, Jack Ruby dropped out of high school and began working for the mob. According to Seth Kantor—the respected journalist who saw Ruby at Parkland Hospital soon after JFK was shot—the young Ruby delivered "sealed envelopes at the rate of $1 per errand for Chicago's No. 1 racketeer, Al Capone."

Investigator Scott Malone says that "Ruby moved from Chicago to Los Angeles in 1933 and began selling handicappers' tip sheets at Santa Anita racetrack. Johnny Rosselli testified to the Kefauver Crime Committee in 1951 that he, too, had moved from Chicago to Los Angeles in 1933—to oversee gambling at Santa Anita for the Chicago mob." By 1939 Ruby was back in Chicago as a "secretary to the Waste Handlers Union" and was questioned "in connection with the murder of the secretary-treasurer of the local." Even though the victim was Ruby's friend, he gave no useful information to the police, showing those in power that he could be trusted not to talk.

The union was "described by the FBI as 'largely a shakedown operation.'" Malone points out "that murder enabled the mob, and eventually the Teamsters, to take over the union. " Years later Robert Kennedy wrote that this murder was important in helping the Mafia eventually dominate the Teamsters. Luis Kutner, a Chicago lawyer and staff attorney for the Kefauver Committee, says that Ruby "hobnobbed with Chicago mob boss Sam Giancana, and his crowd" . . . "during this period."

According to Michael Valentine, author of two recent histories of the Federal Bureau of Narcotics (FBN), some members of "the Ruby family had a long history in the illicit drug trade." One of Jack Ruby's brothers "was convicted in 1939 of buying two ounces of heroin." One high FBI official wrote that one of Ruby's brothers "had been his informant since July 1946." Ruby would soon also become involved in the narcotics trade. In 1947 Ruby worked in the Chicago Mafia's attempt to move into Dallas, "according to former Dallas sheriff Steve Guthrie." That was at a time when Marcello was just taking over control of the New Orleans Mafia. After Marcello was in firm control of the rackets in Dallas, Ruby began to perform work for his organization. The Jewish Jack Ruby could never aspire to the heights of non-Sicilian mob heavyweights like Meyer Lansky or Mickey Cohen, so the low-level mobster basically had to scramble, to do whatever he could for the local mob powers.

In 1950 Jack Ruby "briefed the Kefauver Committee about organized crime in Chicago," according to Luis Kutner. In addition, Kutner's "staff learned that Ruby was 'a syndicate lieutenant who had been sent to Dallas to serve as a liaison for Chicago mobsters.'" This was the first of many times Ruby would appear to cooperate with authorities in return for protecting his—and his superiors'—criminal activities or to find out what authorities knew.

FBN agent "Jack Cusack had informed the McClellan Committee in January 1958 that Mafioso Joseph Civello ran the heroin business in Dallas," and "Cusack linked Civello with Marcello, Trafficante, and Jimmy Hoffa," according to Valentine. Mafia expert David E. Scheim wrote that later Civello informed the FBI "that he had known Ruby casually 'for about ten years.'" An employee of Civello's told the FBI that "Ruby was 'a frequent visitor and associate of Civello.'" Investigative journalist "Ovid Demaris . . . reported that Civello told him, 'Yeah, I knew Jack—we were friends and I used to go to his club.'" Civello, as noted earlier, was Carlos Marcello's top underboss in Dallas.

Jack Ruby's close relationship to law enforcement, a major factor in the aftermath of JFK's assassination, began to develop in the 1950s. It continued to grow into the early 1960s, when—according to one Warren Commission file—Ruby "was well acquainted with virtually every officer of the Dallas Police force." Another Warren Commission document called Ruby "the pay-off man for the Dallas Police Department." If Ruby was the "pay-off man," then who was he working for? After all, Ruby was just a small-time hood. It's clear now, and confirmed by Carlos Marcello's own comments about Ruby during CAMTEX, that Ruby was Marcello's pay-off man for the Dallas Police. The police corruption wasn't just about money, since Ruby was soon involved in various nightclubs and with strippers and prostitutes. It was said that policemen never had to pay for a drink at Ruby's club and sometimes were even provided with women.

Ruby was "very close friends" with Dallas Police Captain Will Fritz, who headed the Homicide Bureau. According to the attorney for Officer J. D Tippit, "Ruby, in spite of his reputation of being a 'hood,' was allowed complete run of the Homicide Bureau." Ruby would later take advantage of that access to kill Oswald. But Ruby had even higher friends on the Dallas Police Force, and an FBI document says that Ruby "took the Chief of Police" of Dallas to "Hot Springs, Arkansas," in 1956, when it was a gambling mecca.

Jack Ruby took advantage of his law-enforcement ties whenever he could. Roselli's biographers documented that "from 1947 to 1963, Jack Ruby . . . was arrested nine times in sixteen years, but developed connections to the Dallas Police strong enough that he never faced a trial."

According to one Warren Commission document, Ruby was active in the Dallas segment of Trafficante and Marcello's French Connection heroin network, the same network that John and Robert Kennedy investigated in their 1959 hearings. The document said that in 1956, "Jack Ruby of Dallas" gave "the okay to operate" locally for a "large narcotics set-up operating between Mexico, Texas, and the East." Ruby appears to have had a small role in making sure Marcello's heroin that flowed through Dallas from Mexico and the Texas ports stayed en route to Chicago. Declassified files show that that same heroin network would play a role in JFK's murder: One female heroin courier who worked for Ruby tried to expose the plot to assassinate JFK just prior to his murder. A major French heroin trafficker—Michel Victor Mertz—would be in Dallas when JFK was shot. Mertz's associate, French Canadian heroin kingpin Lucien Rivard, was imprisoned with Trafficante in Havana in 1959.

Congressional investigator Michael Ewing wrote that "Ruby had several dozen friends, employers, associates, and acquaintances who were significantly involved in organized crime." He also noted "Ruby's close friendship" with the head of "the special Dallas Police unit charged with investigating organized crime cases as well as narcotics and vice," whom "Warren Commission testimony shows regularly (sometimes nightly) visited" one of Ruby's strip clubs.

Also in the late 1950s, FBI files—most provided to the Warren Commission—show that Ruby became involved in gunrunning to Cuba with several associates of Santo Trafficante, among them gangsters Norman Rothman and Dominick Bartone, as well as corrupt former Cuban president Carlos Prio. Los Angeles mobster Mickey Cohen was also running guns to Cuba at that time, and "Ruby told one of his business partners . . . he was a close friend of Mickey Cohen." The FBI documented numerous ties between Ruby and Cohen's girlfriend, a well-known burlesque dancer from Texas whose stage name was Candy Barr. Jack Ruby also knew Jimmy Hoffa, according to Hoffa's son. Much evidence and testimony shows that Ruby was involved in the same operations as "Jack La Rue." Unbeknownst to Robert Kennedy in 1959, when he was fruitlessly looking for the mysterious Jack La Rue, Jack Ruby was running guns to Cuba with the associates of "La Rue." Jack Ruby could have well been one of those using the La Rue alias.

In 1959 Ruby's Cuban gunrunning and arms deals with Castro's men made him an excellent candidate to be a courier/messenger between Ruby's boss Marcello and the detained Trafficante. But Ruby had an even better cover for his activities because he'd recently become an informant for the FBI. In March of 1959, Ruby had been interviewed by the Bureau and asked to become an informant. Ruby, no doubt after checking with mob superiors in Dallas such as Civello or Campisi, agreed. Such an arrangement could give him an extra degree of protection for his illegal activities and a way to find out what crimes the FBI was interested in.

In 1959 Ruby reported to the FBI "on at least eight occasions," but according to historian Gerald D. McKnight, the Warren Commission hid that fact from the American public. It was "not until twelve years after the Warren Report was published that the American people" learned that Ruby had been an FBI informant. The fact that Ruby's tenure as an informant overlapped with his trip to Cuba to visit Trafficante might explain why the Warren Commission refused to reveal Ruby's role as informant for the Bureau. Ruby met with his FBI handler on July 2, 1959, less than a month after Trafficante was detained. Ruby met with the FBI again on July 21.

Trafficante originally had another messenger he could rely on, electronics expert John Martino. According to *Vanity Fair*, "Martino said that his principal mission had been to liberate gambling cash left behind by Trafficante." Those funds were essential for any attempt to buy Trafficante's release from his Cuban detainment. But Martino was arrested in Cuba on July 23, 1959, after a flurry of trips between Miami and Cuba. Unlike Trafficante, Martino was sent to a Cuban prison, serving three years in what he considered hellish conditions. Martino's absence made someone like Ruby even more important as a potential messenger/courier.

According to Scott Malone, Congressional investigators found that those "who wanted Trafficante released included Johnny Rosselli and his boss, Sam Giancana—both of whom . . . visited Trafficante in jail in 1959." Other accounts say that "Carlos Marcello attempted to free Trafficante," so his underling Jack Ruby was apparently part of that effort.

While Trafficante was in jail in Cuba, Jack Ruby attempted arms deals to help secure Trafficante's release, according to several accounts. Scott Malone found that "Congressional investigators" noted in a "briefing memorandum" that "in 1959 Jack Ruby traveled to Cuba and visited Santo Trafficante in jail." Other reports came from the "British journalist" John Wilson mentioned earlier, who was "briefly jailed by Castro" and who "said that while in jail he 'knew a gambling-gangster type named Santo' who, he said, 'was visited frequently by another American gangster-type named Ruby.'" A close friend of both Rosselli and Giancana who "testified before the Senate Intelligence Committee" in the 1970s "says Rosselli told him, 'Ruby was hooked up with Trafficante in the rackets in Havana.'"

Ruby had many associates in common with Trafficante, but the most likely person to have taken Ruby to see Trafficante was gambling supervisor Lewis McWillie, whom Ruby described as "high class." Even after the Revolution, McWillie was one of many mobsters still operating in Cuba. While most people think that Fidel Castro shut all the Mafia casinos when he took over, that's only partially true. For economic reasons, they were quickly reopened. Frank Fiorini (who later renamed himself Frank Sturgis), a Trafficante hoodlum who'd fought alongside Fidel, was made the liaison between the Cuban government and the mob bosses who still ran—even if they no longer owned—the casinos. The former mob casinos would remain open until the fall of 1961.

Jack Ruby admitted frequently that Lewis McWillie was his "idol," someone he almost worshipped as the personification of mob power and high-level access that Ruby could only dream of. Many years later, when interviewed under oath by the House Select Committee on Assassinations, McWillie prevaricated when asked if Ruby had accompanied him on his visits to Trafficante in prison. McWillie said, "It's possible he could have . . . I don't recall it, but he could have. I don't know for sure . . . I went out there with someone but I don't recall who

it was. It may have been Ruby. I don't think so. He could have been."
McWillie testified shortly after the murders of numerous Marcello and
Trafficante associates and government witnesses—Giancana, Rosselli,
Hoffa, Nicoletti, and others. Since Marcello and Trafficante were still
alive and in power when McWillie testified—and he was still working
at casinos—his equivocation is as close to a "Yes, Ruby went with
me" as the Committee could possibly expect.

As *Rolling Stone* noted in a major investigative article, "In August
1959 Ruby visited Havana at the invitation of Lewis McWillie, the
Syndicate's manager at the Tropicana casino and a man Ruby said he
'idolized.' A friend of Ruby's recently told House investigators that
the former errand boy had been summoned to help arrange freedom
for Santo Trafficante."

Official US and Cuban records show a confusing array of several
trips by Ruby to Cuba in the late summer of 1959, with unexplained
gaps in the travel records indicating that some of his entrances and
exits were surreptitious. On August 6, 1959, Ruby met with his FBI
handler again. Two days later, on August 8, Ruby flew to Cuba from
New Orleans, listing the Capri Hotel and Casino (mostly owned by
Trafficante) as his destination. Ten days later, Trafficante was released
from detention. Trafficante's attorney, Frank Ragano, wrote that
Trafficante told him he had met with "Raul Castro (Fidel's brother).
'We worked out an arrangement,' he said cryptically." Ragano said
that "most probably the meeting with Raul was decisive in getting him
released" but that "nevertheless, there had to be a bribe at some point
in the chain of events that led to his freedom." Ruby may well have
helped with that bribe, and/or its aftermath, as his mysterious trips
to Cuba continued into September. After his Cuba visits ended, Ruby
ceased being an FBI informant on October 2, 1959.

Ruby had one more unusual role to play in Cuba, in early 1960. The Hoffa-brokered plots between the CIA and the Mafia to kill Fidel that began in 1959 were continuing in the early months of 1960, though neither Trafficante nor Ruby's boss Marcello had any documented role in those plots. However, former Cuban mob powerhouse Meyer Lansky had reportedly placed a million-dollar bounty on killing Fidel Castro, since, unlike Trafficante, Lansky had been unable to reach an accommodation with the Castro brothers.

In January 1960, Tropicana casino manager Lewis McWillie asked Jack Ruby to legally buy four Colt Cobra revolvers in Dallas and bring them to Havana. Jack Ruby was then the manager of two small Dallas nightclubs, including one he fronted for Carlos Marcello's organization. Because so much gunrunning to Cuba had been going on, the Colt revolvers could have been easily obtained by a gangster like McWillie in Havana. Likewise, Ruby—a career criminal—could have easily obtained such weapons illegally in Dallas. But for some reason McWillie needed these pistols to be easily traced back to a legal purchase in Dallas so that it was clear they weren't linked to organized crime or any illegal—or CIA—gunrunning operation.

On that occasion, Jack Ruby for some reason balked at McWillie's request to go to Cuba even though he had visited Cuba several times the previous summer. After Ruby's refusal, the Tropicana's McWillie asked Ruby to ship the four pistols to him in Havana. Records and testimony are murky about what happened next and whether or not some of the guns were shipped to Cuba. What is known definitively is that Ruby purchased at least one Colt Cobra.

A few journalists have asked if Jack Ruby was "supplying the pistols to McWillie so they could be [used in an assassination] plot against Castro." Some evidence does indicate that the episode could have been part of the continuing plots to kill Fidel brokered by Hoffa between the CIA and the Mafia. Gangster Lewis McWillie had been part of Ruby's Cuban venture with Hoffa associate Dominick Bartone the previous year, and government files show that McWillie had solid Mafia connections to Meyer Lansky, who also wanted Castro killed. When Ruby bought the pistol for McWillie, Ruby was accompanied by an ex-boxer, possibly close Hoffa associate Barney Baker, described by Robert Kennedy as one of Jimmy Hoffa's "roving emissaries of violence." Cuban authorities arrested a "gangster" and his associates for attempting to kill Fidel later in 1960, and among the weapons photographed was a pistol resembling the Colt Cobras McWillie pressed Ruby to buy.

One Colt Cobra definitely purchased by Jack Ruby in January 1960 would find greater infamy more than three years later. It was the pistol Ruby used to shoot accused assassin Lee Oswald on live television on November 24, 1963. Ruby's notorious gun at the very least came out of his involvement with the Mafia and possibly from the mob's early work with the CIA to kill Fidel.

Another important factor in Ruby's character and in JFK's assassination—the Carousel strip club that Ruby managed in Dallas, across from the posh Adolphus Hotel—also began in 1960. New information for the first time shows that Carlos Marcello and his organization actually controlled the Carousel Club, not Jack Ruby. Ruby was only the club's manager, but the timing indicates that being allowed to manage the Carousel—and to present himself as its owner—might have been Marcello's reward to Ruby for his activities in Cuba with Trafficante.

Ruby ran a string of failed clubs before the Carousel, and for decades it was assumed by authorities and historians that Ruby had at least one investor, his good friend Ralph Paul, who kept lending Ruby huge sums of money for his money-losing ventures. Ruby also owed large sums to the IRS throughout the early 1960s, first approaching $20,000 and by 1963 $40,000. In today's dollars, that's $240,000. Yet the House Select Committee on Assassinations found that Paul repeatedly loaned Ruby money, "which eventually may have totaled $15,000" plus an additional "larger sum of money (allegedly $15,000 to $17,000) to assist Ruby" with his taxes. In today's dollars, that's at least $180,000. Yet Ralph Paul was only the owner of a relatively small restaurant in Dallas, the Bull-Pen Drive-In, and it's impossible to imagine he could have come up with those sums let alone continue to loan money to a man who owed the IRS so much money.

Even more bizarre, despite the best efforts of the FBI and the Warren Commission, no one could ever determine who owned the other 50 percent of the Carousel Club. More unusual still, after Ruby became famous for shooting Oswald and the Carousel Club became known nationwide, Ralph Paul simply gave up his 50 percent ownership in the club. Instead of profiting from what could have been a must-see tourist stop (even if Dallas had pulled the club's liquor license), Ralph Paul simply walked away from his 50 percent ownership of the club and the $180,000 (in today's dollars) he'd sunk into the club and Jack Ruby. It all makes no sense.

We now know from Carlos Marcello's admission to Jack Van Laningham during CAMTEX that Marcello's organization controlled the Carousel Club. One of Marcello's underbosses in Dallas—most likely Joe Campisi Sr.—funneled the money to Ralph Paul to launder the funds for the Carousel. House Select Committee investigators were confused when Joe Campisi said in an FBI interview that "Ralph Paul [was] his partner." Campisi's Egyptian Restaurant was large and popular, and Campisi was powerful, so he certainly didn't need Ralph Paul as a partner. However, Joe Campisi's comment makes perfect sense if he was funneling Marcello money to Paul as part of Paul's fronting ownership of the Carousel for the mobsters.*

Still, by the later part of 1960, Ruby got to call the shots at the Carousel and act like a club owner, even though in reality he was simply taking a small percentage of the club's revenues as a kind of salary for managing the club on behalf of Carlos Marcello. However, this arrangement would have huge ramifications for Marcello less than three years later, when it gave the godfather leverage to get Ruby to risk his life for the godfather after JFK's murder.

---

*Reportedly, Marcello had a hidden interest in many clubs in Dallas, including some or all of the city's five gay nightclubs (a surprising number for conservative Dallas in the early 1960s and probably possible only if they were operating with Mafia protection).

CHAPTER 6

CIA vs. Castro, and The Kennedys vs. Carlos Marcello

B Y AUGUST OF 1960 a major development that would have a huge impact on JFK's murder three years later was in the works for Carlos Marcello and Santo Trafficante: new, greatly expanded plots between the CIA and the Mafia to assassinate Fidel Castro. These new CIA–Mafia plots involving Trafficante and Marcello were the dark secret in the covert war the United States was waging against Cuba. Most of those involved in JFK's assassination had some role in these new plots, so it's important to see how they originated.

In 1960 John F. Kennedy was running for President, having announced his candidacy in the same Senate hearing room where Carlos Marcello had been grilled the previous year. His opponent was the two-term Vice President, Richard Nixon. One of the few areas where President Eisenhower allowed Nixon major input on US policy was Cuba. Eisenhower had left Washington the previous year when Fidel Castro had come to the United States, leaving it to Nixon to meet with the new Cuban leader. Instead of offering US financial aid as Castro had hoped (since the former US-backed dictator, Fulgencio Batista—a friend of Nixon—had fled with much of the Cuban treasury), Nixon had lectured Castro and offered no help. Nixon had also confided to others that he felt Castro was dangerous, and soon after that the CIA began working with Jimmy Hoffa to have the three northeastern mob leaders kill Fidel. Those plots had not worked, and now the 1960 election was rapidly approaching.

Vice President Nixon apparently thought that if Castro was killed before the election, and US troops had to be sent into Cuba to protect Americans and American interests, the voting public would chose the eight-year veteran Vice President over the young and relatively inexperienced Senator Kennedy. Nixon told "a press aide [that] the toppling of Castro would be 'a real trump card'" for the election, according to Anthony Summers.

As Eisenhower, the former General in command of America's D-Day forces and now elder statesman, prepared to end his last term as President, he was cautious about Cuba. He clearly didn't want to leave office in the middle of a war with the island nation, but he delegated some aspects of Cuba policy to his Vice President, Nixon. According to many sources—including President Eisenhower—the March 1960 meeting of the National Security Council authorized neither a huge Bay of Pigs invasion force nor the CIA–Mafia plots to kill Fidel. Instead, its general resolution involved support for anti-Castro operations and the creation of a US-backed coalition of exile groups. Among those helping to coordinate that coalition were two veterans of the CIA's 1954 Guatemala coup, friends E. Howard Hunt and David Atlee Phillips.

Nixon, however, seemed to press for more direct action, and the CIA met with him dozens of times about the Cuban problem, conferences for which the notes have never been released. Even so, we do know the result of those meetings. The original CIA–Mafia plots, which began in 1959, were so cautiously structured at arm's length, using Hoffa as a cutout, that they hadn't been effective. It's also likely that President Eisenhower didn't even know about them.

Nixon apparently believed that more direct action was needed, and soon. He ordered his National Security Aide, General Robert Cushman, to meet with Hunt. Later Hunt admitted that he had written one of the first CIA memos calling for the assassination of Fidel Castro, though it—like so much other CIA information about Hunt—was withheld from Congressional investigators and has still not been released. Hunt later wrote that "Cushman had urged me to inform him of any project difficulties the Vice President might be able to resolve. For Nixon was, Cushman told me, determined that the effort should not fail." Cushman told Hunt that Nixon was the "chief architect . . . the honcho" of the US effort to topple Fidel. That was confirmed years later when President Nixon told a White House aide that he had been "deeply involved" in the Cuban operation.

E. Howard Hunt later "confirmed that his proposal that Castro be killed had been discussed at his June [1960] meeting with Nixon's aide General Cushman." Anthony Summers points out "that Cushman would have passed the information on to Nixon; it was after all his responsibility to do so." Given Hunt's positive previous meetings with Nixon and Hunt's key role in the successful Guatemala coup, it's logical that Nixon would have viewed Hunt—and his proposal—favorably. Nixon also probably knew that the United States had been trying without success to assassinate Fidel, as Hunt wanted, since the previous year. If Hunt wasn't involved in helping plan Fidel's assassination before his meeting with Nixon's aide, he almost certainly was after it.

Hunt, like Nixon, publicly denied knowing about, let alone working on, the CIA–Mafia plots to kill Fidel. Yet Hunt's mentor—and Nixon's future CIA Director—Richard Helms disagrees. Much later,

Helms testified that the CIA–Mafia plots to kill Fidel "were known 'to almost everybody in high positions in government.'"

Robert Maheu (an ex-FBI agent and former partner of Guy Banister) later admitted that Richard Nixon was personally behind the ramped-up CIA–Mafia plots to assassinate Fidel Castro and that Nixon had chosen Maheu to be the CIA's new cutout to the Mafia. Eight years later Maheu confided to his friend Pierre Salinger "that the CIA had been in touch with Nixon, who had asked them to go forward with this project. . . . It was Nixon who had him do a deal with the Mafia in Florida to kill Castro."

It was logical that Nixon would want Maheu on the project, since he'd worked with him on two previous, successful covert operations. Also, Howard Hughes, Maheu's main client, was closer to Nixon than he was to any other politician. Though Hughes had vanished from public view, a Nixon memo confirms that the reclusive billionaire had actually met with Nixon the previous year.*

In 2013 I first published information showing that Santo Trafficante himself confirmed Nixon's role in starting the new, ramped-up CIA–Mafia plots in the summer of 1960; those plots soon involved Trafficante, Johnny Rosselli, and eventually Carlos Marcello. In 1973, during the height of the Watergate investigation, Trafficante was being represented by famed attorney F. Lee Bailey, according to Daniel Sheehan, the noted activist lawyer who was then working for Bailey. Sheehan says that Trafficante explained to Bailey's Chief Investigator that in the summer of 1960, Vice President Nixon had

---

*Before turning to Maheu in late August of 1960, the CIA had run a security check on Guy Banister that same month to clear him for a sensitive operation. Instead, once Maheu was chosen, apparently by Nixon, Banister was assigned to a different Cuban operation for the CIA.

originally reached out for help to his longtime patron, the reclusive billionaire Howard Hughes. Hughes, who did extensive work for the US government, assigned his key aide, Robert Maheu, to handle the matter. Maheu, a longtime CIA asset, reached out to Mafia don Johnny Rosselli, who in turn asked Santo Trafficante to join the operation. Trafficante still maintained extensive contacts in Cuba, since his former casinos remained open.

However, Trafficante was leery of the operation, since he—of all the mob bosses who had left Cuba—had worked out a type of accommodation with the new Cuban regime. Trafficante told Rosselli and Maheu that he wanted some form of personal assurance that Vice President Nixon was actually behind the operation. At Trafficante's third meeting about the plots with Rosselli in Miami, a CIA security official joined them and confirmed to Trafficante that Vice President Nixon had personally ordered the Castro assassination operation. Trafficante agreed to join the venture and to use his men in the operation. Rosselli's boss Sam Giancana also joined the plots and, later, so did Carlos Marcello.

Nixon's September 1960 CIA–Mafia plots with Trafficante, Rosselli, and Giancana were hidden from the Warren Commission and wouldn't be officially exposed until Congressional hearings in 1975, a year after the Watergate scandal forced Nixon to resign. Those CIA–Mafia plots were never publicly linked to Watergate, even though in 2012 I first published memos showing that Senate Watergate investigators had learned of the connection eight months before Nixon resigned. However, Marcello's role in Nixon's CIA–Mafia plots remained unexposed until 1989 and is still overlooked by most historians today. The CIA–Mafia plots were first linked to JFK's assassination in 1975 and led to two Congressional investigations of the assassination. But because Marcello's role in the CIA–Mafia plots was hidden from those investigations, the full connection between those plots and JFK's murder hasn't been available until now.

ONE IMPORTANT PART of the CIA–Mafia plots that began in 1960 wasn't connected to those plots until 2012. This was the fact that the mob bosses involved in the plots—including Marcello, Trafficante, and Giancana—paid a huge bribe to Vice President Richard Nixon the same month the plots began. Nixon's background shows how that bribe came about and why Nixon turned to the Mafia to kill Castro in the first place.

As noted earlier, Richard Nixon had extensive ties to the Mafia dating to 1946 and his first run for Congress, when Mickey Cohen, as the Los Angeles mob figure later admitted, gave Nixon $5,000 (over $40,000 in today's dollars). Cohen confessed that Nixon received even more Mafia money for his races after that, while author Anthony Summers documented many additional Mafia ties that Nixon developed in the 1950s. When Nixon first ran for Vice President, with Dwight D. Eisenhower heading the ticket, "Sam Giancana, then a rising power in the national crime syndicate, [said] 'I like Ike. But I like his running mate, Nixon, even better. . . . I'm hedging my bets. We got campaign contributions to both sides: Our guys out in California are backing Nixon.'" At that time, "Our guys out in California" meant Johnny Rosselli and his associates.

Nixon also received support from his first race onward from billionaire Howard Hughes. Once Nixon became Vice President, he received even more favors and illicit money from Hughes. Twice Hughes had his top covert operative, Robert Maheu, help Nixon with difficult problems.

Marcello clearly had every reason to want to see JFK defeated and Nixon become president. Santo Trafficante also viewed Nixon favorably. "'Santo,' recalled his attorney Frank Ragano, 'viewed Nixon as a realistic, conservative politician who was not a zealot and would not be hard on him and his mob friends. The Mafia had little to fear from Nixon.'"

Marcello and Trafficante wanted to do all they could to ensure a Nixon victory, especially since their ally Jimmy Hoffa was soon expected to face a federal indictment as a result of all the attention the Kennedys' hearings had focused on him. Accordingly, Marcello began to gather money for Nixon, and in addition to Trafficante, Giancana later claimed that he had contributed, as did Tony Provenzano, a Mafia Teamster official in New Jersey who was close to Marcello.

In September 1960, Richard Nixon received a bribe of at least $500,000 from the same mob bosses who began working that month on his CIA–Mafia plot to kill Fidel. Prior to September 26, 1960, Teamster President Hoffa—facing an expected indictment for crimes exposed by the Kennedys—went to Louisiana "to meet Carlos Marcello." As first revealed by Hoffa expert Dan Moldea, a Louisiana-based Hoffa aide, Grady Edward Partin, who later "turned government informant," was with Hoffa at the meeting. Partin said, "Marcello had a suitcase filled with $500,000 cash which was going to Nixon." That was only half of a promised total payment to Nixon of $1 million (more than $6 million in today's dollars), with "the other half coming from the mob boys in New Jersey and Florida." The Florida mobster contributing was Santo Trafficante, who was at the time joining the CIA–Mafia plots. Among the "mob boys" in New Jersey was Mafia capo Tony Provenzano, who was close to Marcello. In a boast to a family member, Sam Giancana claimed that he was also part of the group "giving the Nixon campaign a million bucks."

The September 1960 Mafia–Hoffa–Nixon bribe was extensively documented by the Justice Department. The man who witnessed Hoffa accepting $500,000 from Marcello for Nixon was Louisiana Teamster official Grady Partin. Two years later Partin became a trusted informant for the Justice Department, and his testimony against Hoffa eventually sent the Teamster President to prison. Partin passed a government polygraph test about the bribe, and the Justice Department found independent "information confirming the Marcello donation" to Hoffa for Nixon. Though the 1960 Mafia–Hoffa–Nixon bribe would also be independently verified by Senate investigator Michael Ewing, the public would not learn about Nixon's bribe until 1978, long after the Watergate investigations ended.[*]

Marcello and his associates' bribe to Richard Nixon produced immediate results. "Almost coincident with the Marcello donation [to Nixon], the Eisenhower-Nixon Justice Department abruptly stopped the indictment process [against] Hoffa." However, Marcello's illicit cash for Nixon had another important goal: According to Grady Partin, Marcello said he "hoped . . . to extract a pledge that a Nixon administration would not deport him." Marcello's huge bribe to the Vice President also raises the possibility that an earlier payment to Nixon might have been the reason Marcello hadn't been deported during Nixon's Vice Presidency. The bribe given by Marcello, Trafficante, and the others produced other benefits as well. It garnered the Republican

---

[*]The link between the September 1960 Mafia–Nixon bribe and the fact that most of those contributing—Marcello, Trafficante, and Giancana—were also working at the behest of Nixon on his CIA–Mafia plot to kill Fidel was not publicly made until the publication of my book *Watergate: The Hidden History* in 2012.

Nixon some of his only union backing when the Teamsters, that same month, "gave [Nixon] the union's official support."

DECLASSIFIED CIA FILES and reports show that Nixon's CIA–Mafia plots had kicked into high gear by late September 1960, with the CIA wanting Trafficante and the others to kill Fidel Castro in classic gangland fashion. That was really a primary reason the CIA wanted to use the Mafia in the first place, to give the public an entity other than the CIA or the US government to blame for the murder. Because the mob bosses knew the Cuban people wouldn't tolerate the mob retaking control of its casinos if they blamed the Mafia for the death of the popular Cuban leader, Trafficante, Rosselli, and the others focused on low-profile types of assassination, such as poisoning. The CIA later admitted having its scientists work on developing deadly toxins to use in the plots.

Two plots to poison Fidel can be documented in the weeks leading up to the 1960 Presidential election. One involved Richard Cain, a "made" Chicago mobster who also worked in Chicago law enforcement. The other effort included Frank Fiorini, the mob associate who had fought for Fidel's forces and then become the liaison between Fidel and the mobsters who ran (and had owned) the Havana casinos. But Fiorini had since fled Cuba and was now working for the CIA. Years later Fiorini would change his name to Frank Sturgis and become infamous as one of the Watergate burglars working for E. Howard Hunt. Though Fiorini's mob and CIA ties have since been documented, those links would not become widely known during the Watergate scandal.

CIA officer E. Howard Hunt played a major role in the Agency's covert plot to eliminate Fidel in the fall of 1960. If Castro was killed by mob assassins and US military forces were deployed to protect Americans in Cuba, it would take only a small group of trained exiles to help install another US-backed strongman or dictator. Hunt was helping oversee the political side of the training of such a small force (a few hundred men at that time). Though experienced with coups, at that point Hunt had no experience with the Mafia.

To address that issue, in September 1960 longtime mob associate Bernard Barker was assigned as Hunt's assistant, a position he would maintain for years. The son of an American father, Barker had been born in Cuba and had attended school in the United States. He originally had dual American–Cuban citizenship but because of his service in Cuba's brutal and corrupt secret police, his US citizenship was revoked in the mid-1950s. Barker and Hunt say that Barker worked for the CIA for several years in the 1950s, though according to Barker's released CIA file, he began working for the Agency only in the spring of 1959, when he was forty-one. After Barker left Cuba (and possibly before), he became a longtime associate of Santo Trafficante's mob, though an FBI memo says that since "the late 1940's" Barker had been involved "in gangster activities in Cuba."

FBI Director J. Edgar Hoover got wind of the secret plots, as verified by an October 18, 1960, memo to a high CIA official overseeing the plots, in which Hoover said that "during recent conversations with several friends, [Sam] Giancana [said] the 'assassin' had arranged with a girl, not further described, to drop a 'pill' in some drink or food of Castro's." Hoover's description perfectly matches other descriptions of Frank Fiorini's part of the CIA–Mafia plot.

Nixon's plotting with the CIA and the Mafia continued right up until the 1960 election, but his effort was not successful. JFK won a narrow victory against the Vice President. Sam Giancana would later claim that he gave Kennedy his close win, but Giancana's boast has since been debunked. That the son of one of America's richest men would need Giancana's help to win in heavily Democratic Chicago, whose powerful Mayor, Richard Daley, was JFK's close ally, strains credibility. Historian Michael Beschloss found that "Daley's citywide control counted for more than the mob-run wards, which were solidly Democratic in any case." A published statistical analysis by political scientist Edmund Kallina shows "clearly that the Illinois Presidential vote was not stolen for Kennedy by the mob or anybody else." Unlike Marcello, Giancana was open to the possibility of a Kennedy presidency, and had tried—and would continue to try—to use mutual associate Frank Sinatra to influence JFK's tough stand on the Mafia. Sinatra had also introduced JFK to one of his mistresses, Judith Campbell, earlier in 1960.

However, it was to no avail, since JFK—and his new Attorney General Robert Kennedy—wasted no time in declaring war on the Mafia. Press accounts show that singled out for special attention in that war were Carlos Marcello and Santo Trafficante, who were soon targeted by RFK's hugely increased staff of Justice Department Mafia prosecutors.

Despite those stories in the press, the Agency continued the CIA–Mafia assassination plots into December of 1960 and into 1961 without telling the new President. December 1960 was an especially active time. That month New Orleans private detective Guy Banister was linked to a CIA plot to stage a fake attack on the US naval base at Guantánamo, Cuba, to provide a pretext for a US attack on Cuba. However, Cuban authorities got wind of the plot and arrested forty Cubans involved. In the press, the Cuban government "unmasked the CIA's participation" and denounced the organization involved in the fake attack, "the Anti-Communist League of the Caribbean," which was largely controlled by Banister.

The CIA also began working with a mid-level, relatively powerless Cuban official named Rolando Cubela, and a cable from December 1960 "referred to the possibility of giving a [poison] 'H capsule' to Rolando Cubela, the former [student group] leader who was now a disaffected associate of Castro." Cubela had several ties to the CIA–Mafia plots and to Trafficante associates. In addition, "in late 1960, the Agency sent a sniper rifle to Havana via diplomatic pouch," according to CIA Congressional testimony uncovered by historian David Kaiser.

That was only some of the crucial information the CIA hid from President-elect Kennedy, and the Agency would continue to deceive him after he took office. As the CIA would reluctantly admit years later in Congressional hearings, it had begun a program in 1960 to eliminate problematic foreign leaders, ominously named ZR/RIFLE. The CIA was also using ZR/RIFLE to try to assassinate another foreign leader, the charismatic Patrice Lumumba of the Congo, an attempt that succeeded shortly before JFK was sworn in. Involved in that assassination effort was a European assassin recruiter for the CIA code-named QJWIN. As detailed later, QJWIN would also be used in the plots to kill Fidel Castro and would surface in relation to JFK's murder.

CIA Director Allen Dulles, a close associate of Richard Nixon, never told JFK that he was continuing the CIA–Mafia plots. He did want JFK to continue major covert action to overthrow Fidel Castro, but the four hundred Cuban exiles then being secretly trained by the CIA in Central America clearly couldn't do the job. Dulles instead told JFK they were planning a Cuban exile invasion of Cuba, and Dulles quickly escalated the number of exiles being trained, which eventually reached two thousand.

Dulles knew that even two thousand Cuban exiles had no chance of staging a viable invasion against one hundred thousand members of the Cuban army and militia and against a Cuba populace that largely backed Fidel Castro. As a backup to the CIA–Mafia plots, he had CIA officers such as David Atlee Phillips begin a new plan that recycled the failed "fake Guantánamo attack" from December. While the vast majority of the CIA's Cuban exiles were being trained at secret camps in Guatemala, a CIA memo "routed to David Atlee Phillips" says a secret exile training base was set up eight miles from New Orleans at the "Belle Chasse training camp," located "at the US Naval Ammunition Depot." JFK was told that the exiles being trained there were for a "diversionary landing" force that would stage a decoy attack on Cuba, far from the main exile force, to draw the attention of Cuban military forces.

However, the CIA's real goal was different. After being trained at the secluded thirty-five-hundred-acre camp adjoining the Mississippi River, the exiles would sail into Cuba on their own ship, the *Santa Ana*. They were not told ahead of time the true nature of their mission. Like JFK, they believed they were going to stage a diversionary landing on the far eastern shore of Cuba to distract Fidel from the main force. Not until they neared shore would their CIA commanders break out Cuban military uniforms and explain they were to attack the US naval base at Guantánamo Bay in the guise of Castro's forces. E. Howard Hunt's associate David Atlee Phillips was handling propaganda for the whole Cuban operation and could ensure that the United States and the world quickly heard about Castro's supposed attack on Guantánamo Bay. Even if the Mafia failed to assassinate Fidel before the CIA's exile invasion, that fake attack was designed to force JFK to break his public pledge not to use US military force against Cuba.

The secret CIA exile training going on outside New Orleans gave Guy Banister and David Ferrie opportunities to become involved in the covert operation. In an unusual foreshadowing of events to come, it's well documented that one of Banister's associates even used the name "Oswald"—then in the Soviet Union—as an alias when trucks were purchased for Cuban exiles at a New Orleans Ford dealership. One of Banister's associates involved had briefly employed Oswald when he was a teenager, which is probably why the name of the well-publicized defector was used.

More important, as New Orleans became a center of covert Cuban exile activity—a role that would continue into 1963—Marcello became involved in those operations. In addition to being part of the CIA–Mafia plots, Marcello donated money to Cuban exile groups. As he developed ties to Guy Banister and David Ferrie, Marcello's access to covert US anti-Castro operations only increased. As for David Ferrie, in early 1961 he was still an Eastern Airlines pilot, but he claimed he took leave from that position to assist with the exiles' Cuban invasion plans.

E. Howard Hunt and his assistant, Bernard Barker, played two roles in those invasion plans in the early months of 1961, after JFK became President. Officially, Hunt worked with exile leaders such as Tony Varona and Manuel Artime (Hunt's best friend), who were supposed to run Cuba after Fidel was gone. However, the CIA admits that Varona was also working at the same time on the CIA–Mafia plots with his associate Santo Trafficante, as was Artime. Much evidence shows the same was true for Hunt and Barker, who were also involved in the CIA–Mafia plots since the new exile leadership of Cuba would have to be ready to take over as soon as the Mafia assassinated Fidel. Barker's work for Trafficante could help that coordination.

Confirmation of Hunt's CIA work with Rosselli in March 1961 came only in 2006, when former CIA Agent Bayard Stockton wrote that "in March 1961 [Johnny] Rosselli went to the Dominican Republic, accompanied by Howard Hunt of the CIA." Stockton became a long-time *Newsweek* bureau chief after leaving the Agency, and his 2006 book *Flawed Patriot*, which confirmed that Hunt worked with Rosselli, was reviewed and approved by the CIA. Stockton's account shows that E. Howard Hunt was working with Johnny Rosselli on assassination plotting, even as the CIA–Mafia plots were actively under way.

In early 1961 CIA Director Allen Dulles was confident that Castro would be killed by the CIA–Mafia plots or that JFK would be forced to commit US military forces because of the fake attack on Guantánamo. Allen Dulles was so sure of success that he ignored an incredible opportunity to ensure the fall of Fidel without resorting to deceiving JFK.

A CIA memo from February 20, 1961, identified "Commander Juan Almeida, who is Chief of Fidel's army, Cuba and is about to defect." On March 7, 1961, another CIA memo stated that "Major Juan Almeida, Chief of Staff of the Cuban Army, has been approaching certain Latin Ambassadors in Havana to determine whether he would be accepted" for political asylum. Both reports about Almeida's dissatisfaction with Castro went to CIA headquarters in Washington.

This was a golden opportunity for the CIA. Commander Almeida was extremely popular in Cuba and was far more powerful than Che Guevara, who wasn't even Cuban. In a population that was 70 percent of African heritage, Almeida was the highest-ranking black Cuban official. He was essentially the third-most-powerful man in the country, after Fidel and his brother Raul, and could have been an incredible covert ally for the United States.

Yet CIA Director Dulles was apparently so confident in the CIA–Mafia plots and the fake Guantánamo attack that the Agency made no approach to Commander Almeida. The CIA did not even tell President Kennedy what it had heard about Almeida. The CIA memos about Commander Almeida's offers were not revealed during investigations, later that year, into the failure of the invasion, not even to the Agency's own Inspector General. In fact, the memos were so sensitive that they weren't declassified for decades. They remained unpublished until 2005 (after I was the first to find them in the National Archives).

Even as the CIA Director ignored Commander Almeida's comments and kept them—and the CIA–Mafia plots and fake Guantánamo attack plans—secret from JFK, President Kennedy expressed his dissatisfaction with the CIA's proposed landing site near the city of Trinidad. Given what little the CIA was telling him, JFK, a combat veteran from his PT boat days, thought a more secluded landing spot made more sense. Accordingly, the CIA chose a new beachhead on Cuba's southwest coast in an area called the Bay of Pigs. In a tragic irony of history, when Fidel divided command of Cuba into thirds for defense against the anticipated invasion, Commander Almeida was given control of the portion of Cuba that included the Bay of Pigs. If the CIA had told JFK about Almeida, who could have been encouraged to remain in place and assist the United States, history could have been radically different.

Even as planning for the Bay of Pigs continued, Carlos Marcello was firmly in the sights of new Attorney General Robert Kennedy. With the start of RFK's highly publicized war on organized crime, the head of the Immigration and Naturalization Service (INS) finally began to target Carlos Marcello for strong action. RFK insisted on more aggressive action against the Tunisian-born Marcello, who wasn't a citizen and had only falsified birth records from Guatemala. Attorney General Kennedy decided to use Marcello's own forgeries against him and had the INS arrange Marcello's deportation to Guatemala.

On April 4, 1961, when Carlos Marcello went to the local INS office for what he thought was a routine visit, he was detained and then flown to Guatemala without a hearing. RFK publicly took full responsibility "for the expulsion of" Marcello and the following week had the IRS file "tax liens in excess of $835,000 against" Marcello and his wife.

Just seven months earlier, Marcello had given a half million dollars to the man he thought would be the next President, and now the enraged godfather found himself in Guatemala, the same small country where the CIA was training Cuban exiles for the upcoming Bay of Pigs invasion. The US-backed dictator of Guatemala, already under pressure from his country's press and populace for allowing the US-supported Cuban exile training, faced new scrutiny for allowing a notorious American godfather to reside in the country. He ordered Marcello and his American attorney detained and escorted to the border. From there Marcello was taken "20 miles into Honduras [and] unceremoniously dumped . . . on a forested hilltop with no signs of civilization in sight." The man who was America's most powerful godfather now had to scramble through the jungle-lined back roads of Honduras in his expensive Gucci shoes.

According to Marcello biographer John Davis, "Still wearing their city clothes and their city shoes stuffed with cash," Marcello and his associate "had little to drink or eat. . . . Marcello found breathing difficult along the mountain-top road. He collapsed three times in the dust, complaining that he could not go on any farther, that he was finished, and that it was that rich kid Bobby Kennedy who had done this to them. 'If I don't make it . . .' Carlos told [his associate] at one point as he lay exhausted in a roadside gutter, 'tell my brother when you get back, about what dat kid Bobby done to us. Tell 'em to do what dey have to do.'" Before arriving at a small airport, the exhausted Marcello plunged "down a pathless slope. They ended up in a burrow, bleeding from thorns, bruised by rocks, with Marcello complaining of a severe pain in his side" from "three broken ribs."

Carlos Marcello, a hugely wealthy godfather who commanded an empire the size of General Motors, was now forced to struggle in the sweltering heat of the Honduran jungle, battling pain, thirst, hunger, and swarms of tropical insects. As the overweight Marcello trudged the muddy, desolate jungle road, with every painful step his thoughts were no doubt consumed with the two men he saw as responsible for his plight, John and Robert Kennedy.

Years later, the searing experience still haunted Marcello, and he talked of it often in prison to Jack Van Laningham during the CAMTEX operation. Marcello told Van Laningham that "he had been kidnapped and that he hated the Kennedys." Even more, the god-father said he had been "furious" because of his ordeal "and vowed to get even with the Kennedys."

CHAPTER 7

Marcello and Trafficante: Planning JFK's Murder

A S GODFATHER CARLOS Marcello trudged the jungle roads of Honduras while swearing vengeance against the Kennedys, the CIA and President Kennedy were in the tense days leading up to the supposedly secret exile invasion of Cuba at the Bay of Pigs. Reports of the impending exile invasion were rampant in Miami and among reporters, and JFK had publicly pledged that US military forces would not be used to attack Cuba. Getting wind of the threat, Fidel Castro ordered the arrests of dissidents and suspects throughout Cuba as a precaution.

CIA Director Allen Dulles later admitted that he knew the Cuban populace—largely supportive of Fidel Castro and his regime—couldn't be expected to "rise up" against Fidel, as CIA officials had indicated to JFK. Shortly before President Kennedy took office, Eisenhower had closed the US Embassy in Havana, depriving the United States— and President Kennedy—of a valuable listening post (and spy base) in Cuba. This lack of clandestine information from observers on the scene left JFK almost completely at the mercy of CIA officials regarding the situation in Cuba.

Director Dulles still depended on the CIA–Mafia plots to kill Fidel just before the invasion. The killing was supposed to throw that country into chaos and force JFK's hand, but a communications mix-up doomed that plan. The mistake happened after right-wing CIA officer E. Howard Hunt dropped out of the Bay of Pigs operation at the last minute, to protest the inclusion of a liberal in the prospective post-Fidel government.

Even without Hunt, the CIA–Mafia plots continued, with Cuban exile leader—and Trafficante associate—Tony Varona playing a key role. A Varona contact inside Cuba agreed to place a CIA-provided poison pill in Fidel's food just before the invasion, after receiving a signal from Varona. However, the abrupt departure of Hunt—who handled exile leaders like Varona—left only a few officials who knew about the highly secret CIA–Mafia plots. Because Hunt was no longer involved, Varona was placed in a secure US military facility with the other exile leaders to await the outcome of the invasion and was unable to give the signal to poison Castro.

That still left Dulles the fake attack plan on Guantánamo, set to be staged by the exiles trained near New Orleans. Once their transport ship neared Guantánamo, the Cuban exiles were told that they were to put on the uniforms of Castro's troops and stage an attack on the American base while thus disguised. This provocation would let the CIA and US Navy press JFK, who did not know about the operation, to respond against Castro with massive US military force. However, the Cuban exiles refused to undertake the bizarre, possibly suicidal landing and attack. They were there to risk their lives fighting Castro's troops, not the US military.

The failure of those two operations, along with the lack of real secrecy about the operation and the CIA's refusal to take advantage of Cuban Army Commander Almeida's offer, primarily caused the Bay of Pigs disaster. JFK publicly took responsibility, but privately he was furious. Internal investigations followed, though they would not uncover the CIA–Mafia plots, the fake Guantánamo attack, or Commander Almeida's offers. However, CIA Director Dulles and his second-in-command were eventually forced to resign.

Even so, the CIA—and possibly Johnny Rosselli and E. Howard Hunt—did manage one success in the weeks following the Bay of Pigs disaster, though it was one the Agency couldn't boast about. On May 30, 1961, Rafael Trujillo, dictator of the Dominican Republic, died in a spectacular gangland-style slaying in his car—a hit carried out the same way the CIA had originally wanted the Mafia to kill Fidel. Years later Trujillo's security chief claimed that Hunt and Johnny Rosselli had been involved. The Church Committee would conclude in 1975 that the CIA's involvement in the actual assassination was limited to the fact that "CIA-supplied weapons may have been used." However, the earlier-noted information about Johnny Rosselli and E. Howard Hunt's joint mission to the Dominican Republic, along with other CIA information about the two, had been withheld from that Committee. Years later, after Watergate, Frank Fiorini—tired of the CIA's spin that Hunt was a minor, bumbling CIA figure—said in a published interview that "Howard [Hunt] was in charge of other CIA operations involving 'disposal' [assassination] and . . . some of them worked."

Surprisingly—or perhaps because of the success of Trujillo's assassination—the CIA–Mafia plots to assassinate Fidel continued even after the Bay of Pigs, with Trafficante, Rosselli, Varona, and others continuing their roles.

DURING THE BAY of Pigs disaster and the run-up to Trujillo's assassination, Carlos Marcello continued his ordeal in Central America. As Marcello explained to Jack Van Laningham, "the governments of these countries did not want Marcello and he was forced to move on to another country. [Marcello] said that he spent thousands as payola [to government officials], but when the money ran out he would have to move on."

In Honduras, Marcello—nursing his three broken ribs—barely managed the seventeen-mile trek to a tiny village and another slog through the jungle before finally reaching a small airport.

Carlos Marcello explained to Van Laningham that he was eventually able to buy "new papers in Guatemala and returned to the US through Florida." The FBI was fairly certain Marcello had been flown to Miami on a Dominican air force jet. An FBI memo later uncovered by John Davis suggests that "a high-ranking US government official may have intervened with the Dominican Republic on Marcello's behalf," identifying a key player as "Senator Russell Long of Louisiana, who had received financial aid from Marcello, [and who] had been very much concerned with the Marcello deportation." Long would later serve on the Warren Commission.

Marcello still had to regain the relative safety of Louisiana, and a Border Patrol report says that pilot David Ferrie was involved in Marcello's return. (The godfather's huge Churchill Farms estate reportedly had its own private airstrip.) Marcello told Van Laningham that "he hid out for a long time and moved around, so he could not get caught. He finally turned himself in and was placed in a camp in Brownsville. His attorneys fought the case in court and he was allowed to stay." Marcello returned home and resumed running his vast criminal empire from his office at the Town and Country Motel.

THROUGH THE REST of 1961 and into 1962, Carlos Marcello's associates Santo Trafficante and Johnny Rosselli continued to work for the

CIA on the Agency's plots to assassinate Fidel Castro, though President Kennedy remained unaware of them. CIA officer William Harvey was now running the Castro assassination operation. Agency files confirm that Harvey was still in charge of the CIA's broader "executive action" assassination program code-named ZR/RIFLE. That program continued to employ assets such as QJWIN, the European assassin recruiter linked to narcotics trafficking.

On November 19, 1961, JFK finally replaced CIA Director Allen Dulles with John McCone, the former head of the Atomic Energy Commission. However, when McCone joined the Agency, no one told him about the CIA–Mafia plots to kill Fidel—either that they had occurred or that they were continuing. In December 1961, within weeks of assuming office, McCone decided to make Richard Helms his new Deputy Director for Plans, though Helms did not officially assume that position until February 1, 1962. The Deputy Director for Plans was essentially the highest operational position in the CIA, with higher posts like Director being concerned more with administrative and political tasks. Richard Helms had no documented taint from the Bay of Pigs fiasco, though an unconfirmed report from noted CBS reporter Daniel Schorr linked him to the start of the 1960 CIA–Mafia plots. That may be why Helms wouldn't tell McCone about his use of the Mafia even when Helms began to expand the plots. To a later Senate committee, John McCone "testified that he was not briefed about the assassination plots by Dulles, Bissell, Helms, or anyone else," something Helms confirmed in his own testimony. Also kept in the dark about the plots' continuation were President Kennedy and Robert Kennedy.

In working with William Harvey on the plots, Helms wanted him to focus on just Johnny Rosselli, easing Trafficante, Giancana, and the others out of the operation. However, the Mafia doesn't work that way, and there are plenty of indications that the other mob bosses— including Carlos Marcello—remained active in the CIA–Mafia plots into the fall of 1963. Those plots would play a central role in helping Marcello and his partners kill JFK in a way that would force high CIA officials such as Richard Helms to cover up crucial information after JFK's assassination.

Apparently no longer involved in the CIA–Mafia plots was E. Howard Hunt, a protégé of Richard Helms. However, Bernard Barker remained Hunt's assistant—in addition to fulfilling other Miami-based CIA duties—and Barker also continued his work for Santo Trafficante.

IN 1962, A problem with the CIA–Mafia plots finally brought their existence to the attention of President Kennedy and Attorney General Robert Kennedy. However, neither man was told that the plots were continuing. An FBI memo confirms that in the spring of 1962, Robert Kennedy's Justice Department had to suppress the prosecution of an associate of Chicago mobster Richard Cain, who had been wire-tapping a Las Vegas comedian back in October 1960 to learn if the comedian was having a relationship with "Phyllis McGuire, girl friend of top hoodlum Sam Giancana." The prosecution of Cain's associate had to be suppressed to avoid exposing the CIA–Mafia plots to kill Castro, which meant that RFK would have to be told something about the plots.

On May 7, 1962, the CIA's General Counsel and the Agency's Director of Security told an angry Robert Kennedy about the CIA–Mafia plots from October 1960 to the Bay of Pigs and even into early 1962. However, the two assured RFK that the plots had been stopped. There are indications that a year earlier, RFK had learned in general terms about the CIA's use of Giancana in some capacity during the Bay of Pigs, but it's unclear whether he knew that Giancana was involved in assassinations or thought he was just helping to provide intelligence. In any event, the CIA admits that RFK was not told the plots were continuing even after he was assured they were over.

With lawyerly understatement, the CIA's General Counsel, Lawrence Houston, later testified, "If you have seen Mr. Kennedy's eyes get steely and his jaw set and his voice get low and precise, you get a definite feeling of unhappiness." A frustrated Robert Kennedy said that because of the CIA, "It would be very difficult to initiate any prosecution against Giancana, as Giancana would immediately bring out the fact the US Government had approached him to arrange for the assassination of Castro." That was a serious matter for Robert Kennedy, since the Chicago Mafia had been a particular target of his ever-increasing war against organized crime, along with Trafficante's empire in Florida and Marcello's organization in Louisiana.

As Robert Kennedy faced the two CIA men in his office on May 7, 1962, he demanded that they check with him first if the CIA ever decided to work with the Mafia again. They passed the message along to Richard Helms, who ignored it and continued to have William Harvey work with Johnny Rosselli and exile leader Tony Varona. The CIA has admitted that in June 1962 Rosselli told Harvey that Varona had sent a three-man assassination team into Cuba.

Also in the spring of 1962, Marcello and his Mafia partner lost two other potential methods of influencing or pressuring JFK to back off on his war on organized crime. The relationship between Sam Giancana and Frank Sinatra became so close that JFK decided to terminate his friendship with Sinatra. The singer had been an enthusiastic supporter of JFK. The FBI—now wire-tapping mobsters because of pressure from RFK—had even recorded one Mafioso talking about Sinatra's fruitless attempt to persuade JFK to ease up on the mob.

In 1960 Sinatra had also introduced JFK to Judith Campbell, who later became his mistress. Shortly before JFK ended his friendship with Sinatra, J. Edgar Hoover sent "a top-secret memorandum to" Robert Kennedy "that summarized Judith Campbell's telephone contact with the President as well as her association with Sam Giancana. A copy of the memo also went to a top JFK aide, with a cover note: 'I thought you would be interested in learning of the following information which was developed in connection with the investigation of John Rosselli.'"* This event led to "Hoover's lunch with the President on March 22, [1962]," which a JFK aide described as "bitter" and "which went on for no less than four hours." According to historian Richard Mahoney, "the concession the [FBI] Director sought was confirmation in his post as head of the FBI." I interviewed Courtney Evans, the FBI liaison between Hoover's FBI and RFK, and he confirmed details of the strained relationship between RFK and the FBI Director. RFK wanted Hoover to be replaced or forced to retire when he met the mandatory federal retirement age, which was rapidly approaching. But because of Campbell, JFK was in no position to force Hoover to leave. By the following year, Hoover had received from JFK the confirmation he sought, leaving him secure as FBI Director even if JFK served a second term.

The fact that President Kennedy ended his relationships with two of Johnny Rosselli's close friends was a critical blow to Marcello and Trafficante. Campbell and Sinatra had potentially represented ways

---

*It's important to note that while Campbell did have a relationship with JFK, her later claims that she was a courier between JFK and Giancana were thoroughly debunked by Johnny Rosselli's biographers.

that John or Robert Kennedy might have been pressured—or black-mailed—to back off from their massive assault on the Mafia. Now the mob bosses had few options to stop the Kennedys' ever-increasing pressure on them.

Even before RFK and JFK began to learn of the CIA–Mafia plots, the Kennedy brothers had developed their own effort to topple Fidel Castro. "Operation Mongoose" is well-known today, though its one-year existence remained largely secret for more than a decade, until Congressional investigations of the mid-1970s. Not willing to trust a CIA official to oversee the operation after the Bay of Pigs fiasco, the Kennedys instead picked General Edward Lansdale, fresh from the Vietnam conflict. Operation Mongoose was in some ways a joint CIA–U.S. military effort, though by far the lion's share of the operation fell under CIA control. By early 1962, "the CIA station in Miami [had] quickly expanded into the world's largest [with] six hundred case officers and as many as three thousand contract agents," according to Helms biographer Thomas Powers.

Operation Mongoose was a loose collection of actions directed at Cuba, including support for exile groups, sabotage, and plans for military action. As an outsider, Lansdale was not part of Richard Helms's ongoing CIA–Mafia plots, and neither was CIA Director John McCone.

In addition to the assassination team sent in by Johnny Rosselli and Tony Varona mentioned earlier, in the summer of 1962 the CIA resumed contact with Rolando Cubela, the disgruntled mid-level Cuban official the Agency had first dealt with regarding an assassination plot a year and a half earlier. Cubela made no progress in 1962, but in 1963 the CIA would once again ask for his help in assassinating Fidel. These contacts always seemed to coincide with developments in the CIA–Mafia plots, which—along with Cubela's ties to Trafficante's associates—indicates that in many ways they were simply another aspect of the CIA–Mafia plots.

In the early days of Mongoose, US military leaders proposed a bizarre array of actions the United States could take against Cuba. Declassified only in the 1990s, one proposed action was code-named Operation Northwoods. ABC News reported the Joint Chiefs' startling Northwoods operation as a proposal "to kill innocent people and commit acts of terrorism in US cities to create public support for a war against Cuba." The proposal included "blowing up a US ship and even orchestrating violent terrorism in US cities . . . to trick the American public . . . into supporting a war to oust . . . Fidel Castro." One plan in the declassified Northwoods files stated, "We could blow up a US ship in Guantánamo Bay and blame Cuba."

Operation Northwoods actually offered two options for false Guantánamo attacks, another being to "pay someone in the Castro government to attack US forces at the Guantánamo Naval Base." Neither President Kennedy, the CIA's Inspector General, nor JFK's new CIA Director had ever learned about the CIA's fake Guantánamo attack planned for the Bay of Pigs. The inclusion of a similar idea in the Joint Chiefs' Northwoods proposal in 1962 suggests that the head of the Joint Chiefs in the spring of 1962—General Lyman L. Lemnitzer, who'd had that same position in 1961—had been a witting participant in the CIA's original Guantánamo provocation. From a practical point of view this makes sense, so the fake CIA attack could have been coordinated with the US military at a high level.

The Northwoods proposals shocked President Kennedy, and he rejected them all. The plan apparently showed JFK that some of the Joint Chiefs—especially its Chairman, General Lemnitzer—were very much out of touch with JFK's view of the world. Within months, JFK replaced Lemnitzer with General Maxwell Taylor, who had headed JFK's Bay of Pigs investigation. General Taylor would remain Chairman of the Joint Chiefs throughout JFK's Presidency and was so admired by RFK that he named one of his sons after him.

The Cuban Missile Crisis, which most Americans think began in mid-October 1962, has its own complex history, too long to detail here. Still, in many ways it was the culmination of three years of US covert action against Cuba, including the CIA–Mafia plots, massive US military exercises in the Caribbean in the summer of 1962, and small raids into Cuba sponsored by Operation Mongoose. The first US official to sound the alarm about Soviet missiles in Cuba was CIA Director John McCone on August 10, 1962, even though his more experienced subordinates believed he lacked evidence. At first no one knew whether or not the Soviet missiles had nuclear warheads, but by September 19 evidence that they did had started accumulating. On September 27 the US military began preparing contingency invasion plans for Cuba. JFK was briefed on October 16 that "hard photographic evidence" from a U-2 spy plane flight confirmed that Soviet medium-range nuclear ballistic missiles were being installed in Cuba. He made plans to reveal the Crisis to the nation six days later, after having daily consultations with a full range of top military and civilian advisors.

On October 22, 1962, at 7 p.m. (eastern time), President John F. Kennedy went on national television to tell the American people the country was on the brink of nuclear war. Families across America were riveted to their television screens as Kennedy described the missiles and the blockade of Cuba he was instituting to be sure that no more "offensive military equipment" reached the island. Essentially,

JFK drew a blockade line around Cuba, one that several Soviet ships were fast approaching.

As the Cuban Missile Crisis unfolded during those tense times, it's important to remember that this is when recently returned "defector" Lee Oswald was allowed to take the job at the U-2 map firm in Dallas. The firm's sensitive work would be visible on television throughout the Crisis, which makes it incredible that Oswald would be allowed to work there unless he had US intelligence connections.

William Harvey had his own idea about how to handle the Crisis. Thomas Powers writes that "on October 21 [1962], the day before President Kennedy announced a blockade of Cuba in a televised speech, a CIA team headed by future Watergate burglar Eugenio Martinez landed two agents on the northern coast of Cuba. At least one other team made a similar landing the same night." Harvey told a subcommittee of the National Security Council that "several agents had already landed [and] there was no way to communicate with them, and thus no way to recall them." However, the *New York Daily News* later tracked down "intelligence sources" who confirmed that one of Harvey's teams was actually "an execution squad [sent] to ambush Castro near Santiago de Cuba as he drove to a memorial service . . . snipers hid among trees and bushes lining the road . . . machine guns and rifles sprayed the second jeep [of a five-jeep motorcade] with bullets, killing the driver and his passenger, who turned out to be Castro's lookalike bodyguard." Robert Kennedy was furious when he found out and wanted CIA Director McCone to immediately fire Harvey, "but Helms talked" both men out of it. The CIA, in particular Richard Helms, would take similar unauthorized action the following year in a way that inadvertently aided the plans of Marcello, Trafficante, and Rosselli to assassinate President Kennedy.

WHILE THOSE EVENTS were building and unfolding, Marcello and Trafficante were consumed by the Kennedys' war against them and the rest of the Mafia. Marcello faced an $850,000 tax assessment, as well as "indictment for illegal reentry, [new] McClellan committee hearings, [an] indictment . . . for conspiracy and perjury, and now the deportation order [was] upheld after an unsuccessful appeal," wrote John Davis. He added, "People close to the Marcellos at this time have remarked that . . . the family's hatred of Robert Kennedy knew no bounds."

The IRS busted Santo Trafficante's Orlando gambling operations and even arrested two of his family members. According to historian Richard Mahoney, "the IRS had launched an audit of Rosselli's tax records in February 1962," and an "FBI detail . . . secretly scrutinized all his banking and stock transactions." He notes that "Rosselli . . . grew openly bitter. He told one associate of Jack Ruby, 'I'm being run right into the ground—it's terrible. . . . Here I am helping the government, helping the country, and that little son of a bitch is breaking my balls.'" Rosselli's boss, Chicago godfather Sam Giancana, was also facing pressure from the FBI, at RFK's urging.

Jimmy Hoffa, who had a number of criminal activities with Marcello and Trafficante, was under such intense pressure from the Kennedys that he decided to kill Robert Kennedy. In September 1962 Edward Partin, the Justice Department informant who had witnessed Marcello's $500,000 bribe to Hoffa for Nixon, approached officials about becoming an informant after he heard Jimmy Hoffa discuss plans to assassinate Attorney General Kennedy. Partin had passed "a meticulous FBI polygraph examination" and had provided to RFK's Justice Department a stream of information about Hoffa's crimes.

Hoffa trusted Partin, a Louisiana Teamster official, and told him about two different plans he was considering to end RFK's war against him and the Mafia. One plan "involved firebombing Hickory Hill, Robert Kennedy's Virginia estate," hoping that RFK would either be killed by the blast or "would be incinerated, since 'the place will burn after it blows up.'" Jimmy Hoffa's other plan to murder Robert Kennedy was to have him "shot to death from a distance away" by a "gunman . . . without any traceable connection to Hoffa and the Teamsters [and using] a high-powered rifle with a telescopic sight." Hoffa thought the best place to do it would be "somewhere in the South [while] Kennedy" was in a "convertible." Jimmy Hoffa declared to Partin that "somebody needs to bump that son of a bitch [RFK] off." Partin said that Hoffa also badly "hated [President] Kennedy . . . he'd fly off [when JFK's] name was even mentioned."

However, by the late fall of 1962, Hoffa was no longer telling Partin about his plans to assassinate RFK. Godfathers Carlos Marcello and Santo Trafficante had apparently persuaded him that the problem of Robert Kennedy required a different solution, one that didn't involve murdering the Attorney General, despite Marcello's visceral hatred of RFK and JFK. Instead, assassinating JFK was the way to end RFK's war against the mob bosses.

BY THE FALL of 1962, Carlos Marcello had been safely back at home in Louisiana for more than a year, following his humiliating ordeal in the jungles of Central America. His organization had quickly recovered from his absence and was more profitable than ever. However, John and Robert Kennedy had only increased their pressure on Marcello and his Mafia allies and were now mounting the largest assault on organized crime America had ever seen. Attorney General Robert Kennedy had finally persuaded FBI Director J. Edgar Hoover to begin fighting the mob. Not content to depend on the aging and imperious Hoover, RFK had hired ten times more Justice Department Mafia prosecutors than were employed during the Eisenhower–Nixon Administration. The Kennedys' pressure on Marcello, and on his close partners Santo Trafficante and Jimmy Hoffa, was unrelenting. Something had to be done.

In October 1962, Marcello briefly and unexpectedly explained his solution to the Kennedys' war on the Mafia. The godfather was with two of his most trusted associates in the place he felt safest, the middle of his secluded sixty-four-hundred-acre Churchill Farms property outside New Orleans. With Marcello were his trusted long-time driver, Jack Liberto, and his favorite nephew, Carlo Roppolo. Joining the three was Ed Becker, a former public relations man for two Las Vegas casinos. Marcello felt comfortable talking to Becker not only because he'd worked for mob-run casinos but because Becker was now in business with Roppolo, who vouched for him. According to Becker, Marcello "pulled out a bottle and poured a generous round of scotch. The conversation wandered until Becker made an off-hand remark about Robert Kennedy and Marcello's deportation. The reference struck a nerve, and Carlos jumped to his feet, exclaiming the Sicilian oath, 'Livarsi na pietra di la scarpa!' (Take the stone out of my shoe!)." Marcello didn't speak Sicilian but was repeating an old saying he had heard many times from those who did.[*]

As Becker later wrote, "Reverting to English, Marcello shouted, 'Don't worry about that Bobby son-of-a-bitch. He's going to be taken care of.'"

---

[*] After the meeting, Becker checked with someone who spoke Sicilian to make sure he understood the phrase exactly.

Becker told the godfather that killing RFK would get Marcello "into a hell of a lot of trouble." In answer, "Marcello invoked an old Italian proverb: 'If you want to kill a dog, you don't cut off the tail, you cut off the head.'" Becker says the implication was that "Bobby was the tail" and "if the President were killed then Bobby would lose his bite. Marcello added that he had a plan, to use 'a nut' to take the fall for the murder . . . then Marcello abruptly changed the subject, and the Kennedys were not mentioned again."

Many people knew that Robert Kennedy and Vice President Johnson hated each other, and one of them was the politically savvy Marcello, who "owned" US Senators, members of Congress, governors, and judges. If Marcello killed President Kennedy, then RFK's status as the second-most-powerful man in America—with far more power than a typical Attorney General—would end, and with it so would RFK's extraordinary war on Marcello and the Mafia.

According to all accounts of the incident, "Becker related his encounter with Marcello to the FBI soon after the meeting, and well before the Kennedy assassination, but no action was taken by the Bureau." In addition, "former FBI agent Julian Blodgett, who was familiar with Becker at the time, corroborates Becker's account." The House Select Committee on Assassinations investigated Becker's story, took his sworn testimony, and found him and his account credible.

IN THE FALL of 1962, around the same time Marcello told Ed Becker about his plan to assassinate JFK, godfather Santo Trafficante made a similar comment to an associate named Jose Aleman. Trafficante confirmed to Congressional investigators that he knew Aleman and acknowledged having met with him on business approximately three times, although some accounts put the number much higher. Aleman's family had long-standing Mafia ties; former FBI agent William Turner notes that Jose Aleman's grandfather "had been Lucky Luciano's lawyer in Havana." Aleman's family had recently helped Jimmy Hoffa gain control of a Miami bank that Hoffa could use to launder money from his criminal activities. Also, Aleman knew Rolando Cubela, the disgruntled mid-level Cuban official and CIA asset, who had his own ties to Trafficante associates.

According to the *Washington Post*, Jose "Aleman had been a rich young revolutionary in Havana" whose "considerable wealth" involved "Miami real estate, including the Miami Stadium." But after losing "his land holdings in Cuba to the revolution" and the death of his father, Aleman "was forced to sell the Miami Stadium" and other Miami real estate, except for "the three-story . . . motel" where Aleman would meet with Trafficante in 1962. By the fall of that year, Aleman "was in debt," though his contacts and reputation could still be of use to someone like Trafficante, who was always looking for seemingly legitimate fronts for money laundering and other scams.

The *Post* notes that "Aleman . . . became involved with Trafficante in 1962 through his cousin, [a] resourceful lawyer" for Trafficante. Aleman testified under oath to the House Select Committee on Assassinations that in 1962 an associate of Trafficante "came to me and he said Santo wants to meet you." Aleman said he was initially reluctant, since he "had to testify against Santo's people in 1960" in a complex case involving Trafficante associates. Aleman had been a reluctant witness, and his testimony had not been especially damaging. Aleman said that despite his initial reluctance, he did "ultimately go to . . . meetings with Trafficante."

"Aleman said that Trafficante" made the threat against JFK as "part of a long conversation that lasted from sometime during the day until late at night." Aleman said the conversation with Trafficante "came about because" his cousin had helped get "someone out of a Cuban jail," and Trafficante "wanted to help Aleman get out of his financial difficulties in return."

To the Congressional investigators, "Aleman attempted to explain why" Trafficante "would have contact with him, much less offer him assistance, in view of the fact that Aleman had testified for the State." Aleman said he explicitly told Trafficante about his testimony, but Trafficante "laughed out loud and said not to worry about it, that it didn't matter at all." According to the *Washington Post*, Aleman had been subpoenaed by the FBI to testify, and Aleman "tried to avoid testifying, but the FBI reminded him that, if he did not cooperate, he might be subject to prosecution for illegal gunrunning."

The *Post* said that "Trafficante had offered to arrange a million-dollar loan for Aleman . . . from the Teamsters Union," which "had 'already been cleared by Jimmy Hoffa himself.' It was natural that the conversation turned to Hoffa when Trafficante met Aleman at the Cott-Bryant Hotel in Miami in September 1962." Aleman told Congressional investigators that Trafficante complained about JFK: "[H]ave you seen how his brother is hitting Hoffa . . . mark my word, this man Kennedy is in trouble and he will get what is coming to him.' When Aleman disagreed with Trafficante and said he thought . . . Kennedy would be re-elected," Trafficante said, "You don't under-stand me. Kennedy's not going to make it to the election. He is going to be hit." Aleman told the government investigators "that Trafficante 'made it clear . . . he was not guessing about the killing, rather he was giving the impression that he knew Kennedy was going to be killed.'"

According to historian Richard Mahoney, "Aleman later main-tained that he reported this comment to two Miami FBI agents."

Another historian confirmed: "Disturbed by what had transpired at that meeting, Aleman immediately began informing on Trafficante to" two FBI agents at "the FBI's Miami Field Office, but Trafficante's hints were apparently judged mere gangland braggadocio." The historian goes on to write that "thirty years later Aleman's accusations would resist positive confirmation, with Bureau records of his debriefings remaining classified." One of the Miami FBI agents, "when advised of Aleman's allegations, would affirm: 'He's a reliable individual.'" The *Washington Post* notes that after Aleman testified for the state, "Aleman's relationship with the Bureau grew very close. The FBI men came to rely on him." Declassified files I found bear that out and show that Aleman continued to provide information about Trafficante to the FBI through 1964.

The House Select Committee on Assassinations found Aleman and his story of Trafficante's threats credible: "The Committee found that Santo Trafficante's stature in the national syndicate of organized crime, notably the violent narcotics trade, and his role as the mob's chief liaison to criminal figures within the Cuban exile community, provided him with the capability of formulating an assassination conspiracy against President Kennedy." In addition, the House Select Committee found that "examination of the FBI's electronic surveillance program of the early 1960s disclosed that Santo Trafficante was the subject of minimal, in fact almost nonexistent, surveillance coverage. During one conversation in 1963, overheard in a Miami restaurant, Trafficante had bitterly attacked the Kennedy Administration's efforts against organized crime, making obscene comments about 'Kennedy's right-hand man,'" who had recently coordinated various raids on Trafficante gambling establishments. In the conversation, Trafficante stated that he was under immense pressure from federal investigators, commenting, "I know when I'm beat, you understand."

Like his partner Carlos Marcello, Santo Trafficante felt like he had been backed into a corner by the Kennedys and had nothing to lose by trying to assassinate JFK. Soon Johnny Rosselli joined them in their plotting, and new developments in the secret war between the United States and Cuba gave the three mob bosses a way to kill JFK while forcing high US officials to withhold crucial evidence from the press, the public, and each other.

Even as Marcello and Trafficante plotted their murder of President Kennedy, John and Robert Kennedy were working frantically behind the scenes to defuse the tense standoff of the Cuban Missile Crisis. Nuclear-armed Soviet missiles in Cuba were aimed at the United States, just ninety miles away, and at the height of the Cold War any miscalculation could spell disaster.

President Kennedy reached an agreement with Soviet leader Nikita Khrushchev: The United States secretly agreed to remove US Jupiter missiles in Turkey targeted at Russia while Khrushchev would remove the Soviet missiles from Cuba. However, a myth has persisted ever since that "that Kennedy had struck a secret deal with Khrushchev binding the US to a commitment not to invade Cuba," even though historians from the nonprofit National Security Archive at George Washington University first documented twenty years ago that that was not the case. Files declassified thirty years after the Missile Crisis revealed "that no such deal was ever made." They explained that "President Kennedy's pledge not to invade Cuba . . . was conditioned on the implementation of adequate inspection and verification pro- cedures." As JFK wrote to Khrushchev, only "upon the establish- ment of adequate arrangements through the United Nations to ensure [that all the missiles had been removed would the United States] give assurances against an invasion of Cuba." But as the National Security Archive historians documented, "Cuba did not allow on-site inspection" by the United Nations to verify the removal of the Russian missiles, so the pledge never took effect.

JFK's Secretary of State at the time, Dean Rusk, confirmed that to me in a 1990 interview, explaining that Fidel Castro had been angry that he wasn't consulted before Khrushchev made the deal with JFK and therefore refused to allow UN weapons inspectors into Cuba. In JFK's November 20, 1962, prime-time press conference, he reaffirmed the need for UN inspections before putting a "no invasion pledge" into effect. In response to the question, "If we wanted to invade Cuba . . . could we do so without the approval of the United Nations?" JFK gave a carefully worded reply, saying that the United States reserved the right to act against Cuba "on our own if that situation was necessary to protect our survival or integrity or other vital interests." Just over a year later, the specter of the Cuban Missile Crisis—and a secret Cuba plan begun by JFK six months after the Crisis apparently ended—would loom large over the secrecy surrounding his own assassination.

Central to understanding all that secrecy was a man who grew close to Robert Kennedy in the days after the Crisis appeared to have passed: Cuban exile Enrique "Harry" Ruiz-Williams. Harry Williams, as he liked to be called, was a wounded survivor of the Bay of Pigs. He was one of sixty injured men Castro had released seven months earlier to spur US efforts to ransom the remaining prisoners, an effort that had been constantly thwarted by Richard Nixon and other conservatives. Before Williams and the others were released, Cuban authorities told the men they had to return to prison in Cuba by the end of 1962 if the United States did not ransom the remaining prisoners. Worse, they were told that one Bay of Pigs prisoner would be shot for each released prisoner who didn't return.

At forty, Williams was older than most of the other exile fighters. He had been a mining engineer raising a family in Cuba before the Revolution. After his release in 1962, Williams took a leading role in trying to win the release of his comrades who remained in prison. The Kennedys were sympathetic, and Harry developed a working relationship with Robert Kennedy while trying to find some way to free the prisoners. Both JFK and RFK admired Williams because of his courage, which he had demonstrated on two notable occasions during and immediately after the Bay of Pigs disaster. Once ashore in Cuba, Williams "fought bravely" and was "blown into the air by an enemy shell . . . and hit by more than seventy pieces of shrapnel. Both of his feet were smashed and he had a hole near his heart and a large one in his neck," according to one Cuban exile historian.

Williams was near death when Castro's army brought him to a makeshift field hospital. What happened next became the stuff of legend among Cuban exiles. As Pulitzer Prize–winning journalist Haynes Johnson wrote, Williams and the other wounded men in a makeshift field hospital "were suddenly confronted by the person of Fidel Castro." The badly wounded "Williams . . . recognized him at once. He groped under his thin mattress and tried to reach a .45 pistol he had concealed there earlier in the afternoon." As Williams told me, and as other exiles confirmed to Haynes, Williams gathered enough strength to point the weapon at Castro and—at almost point-blank range—to pull the trigger.

But the weapon only clicked—it was empty. Earlier, William's compatriots had worried that he might be in such pain from his wounds and so depressed over the failure of the invasion and their capture that he might use the gun on himself, so they removed the bullets while Williams was unconscious. Castro's men quickly set upon Williams, but Fidel ordered them not to harm the gravely injured man and instead ordered that Williams and the other wounded men be taken to a hospital in a nearby city. There, an old friend, Cuban Army Commander Juan Almeida, visited Williams. Almeida was no doubt frustrated that the United States had never acted on his clear signals of dissatisfaction with Castro. Commander Almeida told Williams that the time for action against Fidel was not right, that he was too powerful in the wake of his victory at the Bay of Pigs. Almeida could not have known it then, but that situation would finally change six months after the Cuban Missile Crisis.

The Missile Crisis put on hold Williams's efforts to persuade John and Robert Kennedy to ransom the remaining Bay of Pigs prisoners. Robert Kennedy was impressed when Williams volunteered to guide US troops on a mission to rescue the remaining prisoners if the United States had to attack Cuba during the Crisis, to take out the Soviet missiles.

After the Missile Crisis, as Castro's end-of-the-year deadline approached, Robert Kennedy was shocked when Williams began making preparations to return to Cuba. Castro had given Williams and the others only until the end of the year to ransom the remaining prisoners. If the ransom was not paid, they had to return, and one prisoner would be shot for each man who did not. So Williams felt he had no choice but to go back to Cuba. John and Robert Kennedy felt great sympathy for the prisoners' plight, but freeing them now became a personal matter for RFK. As documented by Haynes Johnson, Robert Kennedy moved heaven and earth in December 1962 to try to win the prisoners' release, searching for a ransom acceptable to both Fidel Castro and JFK's Republican opponents.

JFK, RFK, their aides, and Williams were successful, and $53 million in food and medicine was transferred to Cuba. On Christmas Eve, the 1,113 prisoners returned to Miami. The Orange Bowl hosted a lavish ceremony for all the freed prisoners and their families, during which JFK made an impromptu pledge, promising to return the brigade's flag to them "in a free Havana." For President Kennedy, those weren't just words. Operation Mongoose was officially over, but six months later, JFK, RFK, and Williams would have a new plan to topple Fidel, one that would trigger much of the secrecy that still surrounds JFK's assassination.

CHAPTER 8

Marcello Meets with Ruby and Oswald

B Y EARLY 1963, Carlos Marcello appears to have been working with well-connected New Orleans private detective Guy Banister and pilot David Ferrie to set up Lee Oswald in relation to JFK's assassination. US covert operations against Cuba would give Banister and Ferrie a way to accomplish that task. Though Operation Mongoose had ended, small-scale US covert actions against Cuba continued, and JMWAVE, the huge Miami CIA station, remained active. The United States also continued to distribute hundreds of thousands of dollars a month to a variety of Cuban exile organizations and leaders, including Tony Varona. According to the CIA's Deputy Chief in New Orleans, Hunter A. Leake, both Banister and Ferrie continued to work for the CIA, and Cuba seems to have been their main focus. According to historian Michael Kurtz, Leake had admitted to him that Banister "served as a key CIA liaison with many anti-Castro Cuban refugees in southern Louisiana. Banister often handled details of the training and supplying of various anti-Castro organizations. Typically, Hunter Leake or another CIA agent from the New Orleans office would meet Banister in Mancuso's Restaurant, located in the infamous 544 Camp Street Building." The reasons for that building's infamy were noted in Chapter Two and are explained later.

Kurtz wrote that the CIA's Leake "provided Banister with substantial sums of cash, and Banister would use the money to purchase needed supplies and to pay the salaries of the men working in certain anti-Castro operations." As for Ferrie, Leake told Kurtz that the pilot "performed a series of tasks for the CIA," which included "conducting propaganda sessions among refugee units, thus reinforcing their hatred of the Castro regime; and serving as an intermediary between the CIA and organized crime." The latter would have been easy for Ferrie in 1963 since he—like Banister—was working for Carlos Marcello.

Even though the official record shows that Oswald moved to New Orleans on April 24, 1963, he had made at least one trip to the city well before that date, according to Congressional testimony cited in Chapter Two. The testimony was first obtained in 1975, meaning that critical information was not available to the Warren Commission. Oswald's visit had occurred in March, February, or perhaps as early as January. His trip there involved some sort of Cuba-related activity, resulting in his being jailed in New Orleans and claiming to the INS to be a Cuban exile, even though he couldn't speak Spanish. Within a few months, numerous witnesses would place Oswald as working with Guy Banister and David Ferrie. However, Oswald's unusual visit to New Orleans in early 1963—missing from Warren Commission records—suggests that he'd had contact with them well before that, which might even explain his later move to New Orleans.

In early 1963, Oswald engaged in several unusual activities that provoked controversy for decades. However, when viewed through the lens of the intelligence connections of Banister and Ferrie—and their work for Carlos Marcello—Oswald's actions make perfect sense.

Oswald's suspicious activities in the space of less than two months included apparently using an alias to order a pistol and a rifle through the mail; photographing himself holding both weapons and two Communist newspapers (of opposing views); being linked to a shooting at the home of far-right, racist, retired General Edwin Walker; and writing letters to the head of the pro-Castro Fair Play for Cuba Committee.

Some of those activities are consistent with simply maintaining and building his cover as a Communist/Marxist while continuing to avoid meeting or talking to any real American Communists or Socialists. Other actions appear to have been undertaken in cooperation with—or on the orders of—someone else.

First, it seems odd that Oswald would order guns through the mail when cheaper and more reliable weapons were easily available in Dallas. Likewise, it seems strange for Oswald to suddenly develop a great interest in Cuba and to begin a phony one-man chapter of a small organization called the Fair Play for Cuba Committee when both Dallas and New Orleans had legitimate far-left and Socialist organizations that he could have joined. In early 1963—as Marcello and Trafficante were making plans to assassinate JFK—two related Congressional committees were looking into the Fair Play for Cuba Committee and into mail-order gun sales by the very firms from which Oswald ordered. Not only were both hearings in the newspapers of the time—making it easy to see where Banister or his associates got the idea to take advantage of them—but members of both Congressional committees had ties to Trafficante operatives Frank Fiorini and John Martino. Martino, who had finally been released from his Cuban prison the previous fall, was very bitter over his experience, blaming the Kennedy Administration for not securing his release sooner. In addition to his work for Trafficante, in 1963 Martino also became close to Johnny Rosselli, and the CIA admits that Martino—like

Rosselli—became a CIA asset. Also like Rosselli (and Marcello and Trafficante), late in life Martino admitted his involvement in the JFK assassination plot.

As explained in Chapter Two, it's also important to keep in mind that Oswald was still under "tight" surveillance by Naval Intelligence, with the assistance of the CIA. Both during Oswald's early 1963 trip to New Orleans and after he moved there in late April, Banister and Ferrie were well positioned to assist the CIA and Naval Intelligence with that surveillance.

Oswald was probably encouraged first to write and then to join the Fair Play for Cuba Committee to further legitimate US intelligence objectives for the CIA and Naval Intelligence. These include making him more attractive for KGB recruitment, laying the groundwork for involving Oswald in anti-Castro operations, and making him part of CIA officer David Atlee Phillips's efforts to penetrate and compromise the Fair Play for Cuba Committee. Oswald probably ordered the weapons at the behest of someone working for the Mafia, such as Banister or Ferrie. Given their work for Marcello at the time, it was all too easy for them to manipulate Oswald under the guise of furthering some US intelligence activity.

As for the shooting at General Walker's home, Banister belonged to the same white supremacist circles as General Walker, and associates of the two had been at a white supremacist conference in New Orleans just four days before someone shot into Walker's home. Any role Oswald had in that incident was probably at Banister's behest, an effort to plant evidence that would make Oswald look murderously violent after he was arrested for JFK's assassination.

A closer look at the timing of all these events shows just how intertwined they were and reveals other links to the Mafia's role in

JFK's assassination. First, here's a brief summary: Someone using the alias Alek Hidell and Oswald's post office box in Dallas ordered a .38-caliber pistol on January 28 from a Los Angeles company and ordered a Mannlicher-Carcano rifle from a Chicago firm on March 12, 1963; both weapons were shipped the same day, March 20. On March 31 Oswald's wife, Marina, photographed him in his backyard holding both weapons and the two Communist newspapers.* In the first week of April, Oswald was fired from his job at the U-2 map firm in Dallas, and he wrote his first letter to the head of the Fair Play for Cuba Committee. On April 10 a bullet was fired into the Dallas home of General Walker. On April 24 Oswald moved to New Orleans, where he initially lived with his uncle, a bookie for Carlos Marcello.

As for the guns, journalist Henry Hurt wrote that the theory "that Oswald chose to acquire his guns by mail order has never made much sense. Its only value is to the official version of events" by creating a "chain of documentary evidence to link Oswald to the weapons supposedly responsible for the murders of President Kennedy and Officer Tippit," even though "the same make of rifle and revolver could have been purchased by Oswald at stores only a few blocks from where he worked in Dallas." Hurt points out that under the laws at the time, "there would have been no record of his purchase and ownership" had he bought the guns at a store, as there would be for mail-order guns. By using the mails, Oswald appears to have deliberately left much more of a trail than if he had made the same purchase by spending a few minutes at a busy gun shop's counter.

The mail-order guns also tied Oswald's actions to a Senate committee investigating mail-order weapons; some of the committee's

---

*The House Select Committee on Assassinations analyzed both photos and found them to be genuine.

members were at the same time investigating the Fair Play for Cuba Committee. Guy Banister had worked for racist Mississippi Senator James O. Eastland, Chairman of the Senate committee investigating Fair Play for Cuba. Eastland would soon be working on a covert CIA operation involving John Martino, Johnny Rosselli, and Santo Trafficante. Trafficante operative Frank Fiorini "later admitted to having intelligence connections to" Eastland's Senate committee.

Those connections and the newspaper headlines the hearings generated would have made it possible for Guy Banister to manipulate Oswald into thinking he was assisting those committees by ordering the guns and writing to the Fair Play for Cuba Committee. Historian George Michael Evica notes that between Oswald's conveniently timed mail-order gun purchases and his contact with the Fair Play for Cuba Committee, "Oswald could not have set up a more consistent pattern had he been working (whether directly or indirectly) for" the Senate committees. That may be exactly what Oswald thought he was doing. Oswald may well have thought that if he followed the orders of Banister and Ferrie, he might someday be testifying before Congress like his boyhood hero from *I Led Three Lives*. Under that scenario, Oswald would think he was assisting the committees—by showing that a former Russian defector and a Fair Play for Cuba Committee member could easily order a rifle and pistol through the mail—when in actuality he was being set up.

In addition, John Newman, historian and retired Army Intelligence major, discovered that the Chicago FBI office launched a major "investigation of the [Fair Play for Cuba Committee] on March 8 [1963], four days before Oswald" seems to have "ordered the rifle from Chicago." (Recall that Banister was a former FBI chief in Chicago.) Newman also notes that word of the FBI investigation of the FPCC "was transmitted to the CIA" for some reason, something that was not always the case. There were more Fair Play for Cuba Committee hearings on March 13, 1963—the same day Oswald appears to have ordered his rifle. On March 31 Lee Oswald wrote his first letter to the head of the Fair Play for Cuba Committee. That was also the day Oswald had his wife, Marina, take the famous photos of him holding his recently arrived mail-order rifle. More Senate Fair Play for Cuba Committee hearings were held on April 3, 1963, and just over two weeks later Oswald wrote another letter to the head of that organization. In the meantime, someone had fired a shot into General Walker's home on April 10. Oswald moved to New Orleans on April 24, 1963, after surreptitiously visiting the city earlier that year.

The shooting at General Walker's was termed "an assassination attempt" by Walker and the Warren Commission, and when word of it emerged soon after JFK's assassination, it seemed to some to clinch the case against the deceased Oswald. However, Walker's background, the evidence, and the actions of Marcello associates such as Oswald and Ruby suggest a different interpretation of the shooting.

General Walker became controversial in 1961 when JFK removed him from command of the Twenty-fourth Infantry Division in Germany for indoctrinating his soldiers with inflammatory material from the John Birch Society. That material made ridiculous claims, such as saying that former President Dwight Eisenhower was "consciously serving the Communist conspiracy, for all his adult life."

General Walker resigned, and in September 1962, when James Meredith tried to become the first black student to enroll at the University of Mississippi, Walker went to the campus and delivered incendiary racist remarks, full of blatant lies and distortions. Walker's opposition march erupted into a riot that left two dead and seventy injured. The Kennedys had Walker arrested and placed under psychological observation, but after his release he returned to his home in Dallas and ran for Governor of Texas. Following his defeat, Walker continued making outrageous claims in speeches as he railed against the Kennedys, civil rights, and Castro.

Walker flew the Confederate flag in front of his home and later made a well-publicized visit of support to Byron de la Beckwith, Medgar Evers's assassin. Walker moved in the same far-right, racist circles as Guy Banister (whose close friend wrote a book praising Walker).

Walker also apparently knew another Marcello subordinate, Jack Ruby. According to an FBI memo, Walker's handyman said he saw "Jack Ruby visiting General Walker on several occasions. . . . Ruby called at the Walker residence on a monthly basis from December 1962 through March 1963. . . . Ruby stayed approximately one hour at Walker's home and talked with Walker behind closed doors." The Walker shooting occurred soon after Ruby's last visit to Walker's house.*

For the April 10 shooting at Walker's, we have only the word of Walker that he was even in the room where the shot was fired. Otherwise, a shot fired into an empty room would be little more than a case of serious vandalism. Walker's long-standing pattern of public lies and exaggerations in regard to civil rights and minorities calls into question his overly dramatic story of lowering his head just as the bullet was fired into the room.

The Warren Commission and others have tried to pin the Walker shooting exclusively on Oswald to show a propensity for murderous

---

*The Walker–Ruby connection made by the handyman is interesting because both men were closeted gays, something not known by the public at the time. For Ruby, that fact was shown by numerous FBI memos and for Walker by his later arrest in Dallas for soliciting gay sex from an undercover officer.

violence that is otherwise missing in Oswald's background. But numerous journalists and authors have pointed out serious problems with that theory. Witnesses saw at least two people at the shooting, and at least two cars were involved in suspicious activity around Walker's house. None of the witnesses said any of the men looked like Oswald, and Walker's night watchman said the driver of a suspicious 1957 Chevrolet he spotted casing the house a few days earlier looked "Cuban."

In addition, Oswald couldn't drive and didn't own a car, raising the ludicrous spectacle of Oswald walking along the sidewalk or suspiciously skulking through suburban alleys with his rifle, or else taking his rifle on the bus to Walker's home. Even disassembled, the rifle would have been so long as to provoke the suspicions of those he encountered, at least the following day when they learned about the shooting and recalled seeing a young man in the area with an unusually long package.

While others were involved in the incident, Lee Oswald's statements to Marina and to his CIA monitor George DeMohrenschildt make it clear that Oswald was as well. Since others were involved in the Walker incident with Oswald—meaning it was a conspiracy—that's a strong indication that others were involved in what happened to JFK. In addition, research by Dick Russell and Anthony Summers strongly indicates that the Walker shooting was not an assassination attempt at all. Instead, it was a stunt to publicize General Walker, who faced a fading career as a reactionary extremist. Walker's breathless story to reporters that he was almost killed—and would have been shot in the head if he hadn't bent down at just the right moment—generated tremendous regional and national publicity.

Guy Banister got what he wanted: publicity for a white supremacist ally, a test of whether he could manipulate Oswald into dealing with firearms, and several actions on Oswald's part that would incriminate him after JFK's death. Since Oswald had begun the Cuban phase of his covert activity just ten days before the Walker incident—with a letter to the national chairman of the small Fair Play for Cuba Committee—his actions in relation to Walker were probably designed to test his abilities for his new assignment. Unlike Oswald's previous "defect and return" Russian assignment, anti-Castro operations demanded a new set of skills, from surreptitiously arranging and attending meetings (and keeping them secret from his wife) to dealing with firearms in a covert way. The Walker incident was a chance to see if Oswald, who had never served in combat, could handle that type of assignment. Given Oswald's dramatic increase in Cuban activity in the months after the Walker incident, he obviously passed the test, whether he fired the shot or was involved in some other capacity. By late April 1963, Oswald was living with his uncle Dutz Murret, a bookie for Carlos Marcello, and he would do so for two weeks, until Marina Oswald joined him in New Orleans and they got their own apartment.

WHEN OSWALD MOVED in with Carlos Marcello's bookie, the godfather himself was waiting on word about his appeal to the Supreme Court regarding a new deportation order, which had been spearheaded by Attorney General Robert Kennedy. Soon after, John Davis said that Marcello received word that the "Supreme Court . . . declined to review the Marcello deportation action." The decision was "prominently reported in the New Orleans papers" and "meant that all Carlos's appeals were exhausted." With that defeat, "the pressure increased many times over" on Marcello to take action against the Kennedys in order to preserve his freedom and his empire.

As 1963 wore on, Marcello's allies in the plot to murder JFK faced similar pressure from the Kennedys. Santo Trafficante came under

ever-increasing scrutiny from the Kennedys, who busted his operations and made increasing use of IRS tax liens against him. RFK also
made the very private and reclusive Trafficante the focus of major
Congressional hearings. Finally, by subpoenaing Trafficante's wife, the
Kennedys had broken what Trafficante considered an unwritten law.
Trafficante did plenty of philandering, as did Marcello, but the godfathers liked to maintain the image of being traditional family men, and
their wives had been considered off-limits during the previous decade.

The FBI also still dogged Johnny Rosselli, except when he was working on the CIA–Mafia plots to kill Castro. His boss, Sam Giancana, was
put under "lockstep" surveillance by the FBI at the urging of Robert
Kennedy, crippling Giancana's ability to function (and preventing him
from having an active role in JFK's assassination). Rosselli's power in
Las Vegas and Hollywood flowed from Sam Giancana's high position
with the Chicago mob, so unless Rosselli could eliminate RFK's pressure on Giancana, Rosselli's own future looked dim.

Remarkably, even as the Kennedy brothers increased their attacks
on the mob bosses, the crime families still conducted their deadly business as usual, even assassinating a government official in the United
States. A Chicago mobster who was a "close friend of Ruby" was
"credited by law enforcement officials with the murder of [Chicago
alderman] Benjamin F. Lewis," as documented by investigative journalist Dan Moldea. The Chicago official was found dead on "February
28, 1963 . . . face down in a four-foot-wide pool of blood" after "the
back of his head had been shot off by three bullets." His assassination was "the 977th unsolved underworld hit in Chicago since the
early 1900s." While law-enforcement officials knew who did the killing, no one was ever tried and convicted for the crime. Such killings
showed why Rosselli, Marcello, and Trafficante viewed a much more

carefully planned hit on a much higher official as a viable solution to their mutual problems with the Kennedys.

IN THE SPRING of 1963, Carlos Marcello made more documented remarks about assassinating President Kennedy, only this time his comments were not to Ed Becker. They were made to a much closer associate and were not disclosed until the publication of John Davis's biography of Marcello in 1989. At that time, Marcello had been carefully planning JFK's murder with his allies for about six months. Davis wrote that one spring weekend in 1963, Marcello was "at his [fishing] lodge" at Grand Isle, Louisiana, with "close friends from the old Sicilian families of New Orleans."

"While having a scotch with one of them in the kitchen," a friend of Marcello's friend "made a casual reference to an article he had read . . . about the Supreme Court upholding" Marcello's deportation order. "At the mention of Robert Kennedy's name, Carlos suddenly seemed to choke, spitting out his scotch on the floor. Recovering quickly, he formed the southern Italian symbol of . . . 'the horn,' with this left hand." . . . "Holding the ancient symbol of hatred and revenge above his head, he shouted: 'Don't worry, man, 'bout dat Bobby. We goin' to take care a dat sonofabitch.'"

The friend asked if Marcello was going to "give it to Bobby," but Marcello replied, "What good dat do? You hit dat man and his brother calls out the National Guard. No, you gotta hit de top man and what happen with de next top man? He don't like de brother." Marcello declared to his friend, "Sure as I stand here somethin' awful is gonna happen to dat man."

Marcello knew that if he killed the Attorney General, JFK would simply order the National Guard or the Army into Marcello's strongholds, much as had happened in 1954 in Phenix City, Alabama, after Trafficante's associates killed the Alabama Attorney General–elect. That would render powerless the political figures in Louisiana and elsewhere that Marcello had corrupted and relied on for protection. For Marcello and his associates, that meant the answer was to kill JFK, not RFK. The animosity between RFK and Vice President Lyndon Johnson—who would be the new president—was well known, and Johnson had never made prosecuting the Mafia any sort of priority. History would prove Marcello's reasoning to be largely correct.

Confirmation of Marcello's spring 1963 remarks about assassinating JFK comes from Atlanta businessman John Knight Sr., who grew up in Louisiana. Knight's father, a merchant in Lafayette, owned one-third interest in a forty-five-foot boat docked at Grand Isle, a popular fishing area on the Gulf of Mexico, a hundred miles southwest of New Orleans. After one of the boat's other owners sold his fishing camp at Grand Isle to Carlos Marcello, the teenaged Knight was introduced to Marcello by Felix Kiger, forty-three years old, who cooked and looked after the camp.

Later that spring, Knight's father was angry when he heard that Marcello was going to be using his boat. Knight and his father raced to the dock, but the vessel was already pulling away. They were told that a Los Angeles mobster was also on the boat with Marcello and Kiger.*

Many days later, Knight was talking to Kiger, and after a couple glasses of wine, Kiger became emotional when speaking about Marcello. Kiger said, "Something bad is going to happen to our

---

*When Knight heard about the Los Angeles mobster, the man was assumed to be LA mob boss Mickey Cohen, since he was the most famous gangster in America at the time. But Cohen was in prison then, so the LA mobster was likely someone like Johnny Rosselli.

President." The distraught cook said that he had been cooking while Marcello and the Los Angeles mobster were talking. "They don't think Kiger hears 'em"—but the man gleaned from their conversation that JFK was going to be the target of an attack planned by Marcello.

Knight asked Kiger why Marcello would want to do such a thing to President Kennedy. Kiger replied that it was because of Robert Kennedy's sudden deportation of Marcello and the harrowing ordeal Marcello had to endure. Not long after Marcello managed to sneak back into the United States, Kiger saw the godfather and said his hands and knees were still raw from injuries he had suffered in Central America.

Marcello wasn't linked to JFK's assassination in the press until the late 1970s, so Knight didn't fully appreciate the ramifications of what Kiger had told him for years. Knight's account appears credible and is full of additional specific names and details. Jack Ruby's good friend Joe Campisi, a Marcello underboss, later testified to Congressional investigators that Marcello "goes to Grand Isle every year" since "he has a camp there." Campisi admitted meeting with Marcello at the camp, showing that the godfather felt secure conducting mob business there.

IN 1963 CARLOS Marcello actually had at least one face-to-face meeting with Lee Oswald. Marcello's meeting with the nephew of his longtime bookie, Dutz Murret, was revealed by the godfather to Jack Van Laningham twenty-two years later, during the CAMTEX undercover FBI operation. Van Laningham later explained to me how Marcello's admission came about, but he prepared a written account three years after Marcello's remarks that can be found in the FBI's declassified CAMTEX file. In addition, a remarkable amount of independent evidence supports Marcello's Oswald admission.

Jack Van Laningham explained that there was only one other inmate at the federal prison that Marcello felt comfortable talking to about his New Orleans activities. Van Laningham said, "I had another friend at Texarkana that had worked for Marcello's brother, as a bartender. The 'little man' would let him come to our room and they would talk about New Orleans for hours. One night, Marcello was talking about the Kennedys. He told me and my friend about a meeting with Oswald. He had been introduced to Oswald by a man named Ferris [Ferrie], who was Marcello's pilot. He said that the [meeting] had taken place in his brother's restaurant. He said that he thought that Oswald [was] crazy. They had several meetings with Oswald before he left town."

Additional confirmation of an Oswald–Marcello connection comes from another FBI informant. When the CAMTEX operation began targeting Marcello in 1985, he was in federal prison after being convicted of charges arising from a 1970s FBI undercover operation code-named BRILAB (for "bribery and labor"). BRILAB had grown out of the FBI investigation of a Teamster insurance scam involving Santo Trafficante. As a result of that investigation, a business-man named Joe Hauser agreed to become an informant for the FBI against Carlos Marcello. He wore a wire into Marcello's office in the late 1970s, yielding the undercover BRILAB tapes that eventually sent Marcello to prison in the 1980s.

According to FBI informant Hauser, Marcello told him that he and some of his men did indeed know Oswald: "I used to know his fuckin' family. His uncle he work for me. Dat kid work for me, too." Marcello indicated that Oswald had worked for a time as a runner for his gambling network, the same one that involved Oswald's uncle.

There are only two time periods when Oswald could have worked for Marcello as a runner: one in late April and early May 1963, while he was living with Dutz Murret, and the other in late July, August, and early to mid-September 1963, when Oswald was not officially employed but when several witnesses saw him working with Guy Banister and David Ferrie. However, starting in early August, Oswald gained a high profile in the New Orleans media for his unusually well publicized pro-Castro activities, making it unlikely Oswald would have been used as a runner in politically conservative New Orleans at that time.

As for the meeting with Oswald that Marcello described to Van Laningham, the godfather may have ostensibly been talking to Oswald about gambling business while checking out for himself the person who would later take the blame for JFK's murder. It's clear from other accounts that mobsters sometimes conducted Mafia business at restaurants in both New Orleans and Dallas. Since the meeting place was his brother's restaurant, Carlos Marcello would have felt secure there, especially since he could have had a private dining room and private entrance to avoid being seen with Oswald. Besides, meeting with an associate's nephew and giving him a temporary job would appear even to the restaurant's trusted staff to simply be routine business.

Marcello almost certainly did not discuss the assassination of John F. Kennedy with Oswald. It's highly unlikely that an experienced godfather like Marcello would spend a year carefully planning JFK's assassination only to entrust the shooting to an inexperienced young man who was out of practice with a rifle and was not a very good shot the last time he was tested in the Marines. In addition, Marcello told Van Laningham that he had brought two hit men over from Europe to shoot JFK, as mentioned in Chapter One and detailed in Chapter Twelve. Marcello's admission about the two hit men was recorded on FBI undercover audiotape.

Carlos Marcello's account to Van Laningham about meeting Oswald fits with much information that would only become public knowledge years later with the 1989 publication of *Mafia Kingfish*, Marcello's biography by John H. Davis. (Van Laningham's account of the Marcello–Oswald meeting in the FBI files was written the year BEFORE Davis's book came out.) Long-overlooked FBI files from the days, weeks, and months after JFK's assassination, including files that had not been published or cited in any book when Van Laningham's written account for the FBI was prepared, also furnish collaboration for the meeting.

FBI memos first published in Davis's Marcello biography describe Oswald getting money from one of Marcello's men at the restaurant of the Town and Country Motel. The nondescript motel on Airline Highway—far from the tawdry glitz of the French Quarter—served as Marcello's headquarters. The meeting occurred in late February or early March 1963. That fits the time frame when Oswald was briefly in New Orleans, where he was interviewed in jail by the INS agent and claimed to be Cuban. According to the FBI memos, Oswald was sitting in the mostly empty dining room when the FBI's source saw the restaurant's "owner remove [a] wad of bills from his pocket, which he passed under the table to the man sitting at the table," whom the source identified as Oswald.

The FBI's source was a businessman from Darien, Georgia, named Gene Sumner. His brother-in-law was a police lieutenant in the area, and several days after JFK's murder, Sumner told him what he had seen the previous winter. Sumner's brother-in-law then contacted the FBI, as recorded in a November 26, 1963, memo. As with all the dozen-plus associates of Carlos Marcello that J. Edgar Hoover's FBI interviewed following JFK's assassination, the investigation of this incident was cursory and routine. (Hoover had stated publicly that Oswald had acted alone, and agents knew that crossing Hoover would end their careers.) Sumner described the man he thought was the owner of the restaurant—the man he saw giving Oswald money—as being six feet tall, which means he wasn't Carlos Marcello. One of Marcello's brothers was the legal owner of the Town and Country, while a top lieutenant for Marcello—Joseph Poretto—managed the restaurant. The FBI interviewed both, and of course they denied knowing Oswald. Davis notes a variety of logical avenues of investigation that the FBI did not pursue: interviewing Sumner's companions that night, checking the records of the hotel where Sumner stayed to establish the exact date, and showing Sumner a photo of the restaurant's manager.

When the FBI sent the information to the Warren Commission, it excluded important details about the Mafia from the report. These included the facts that the man who gave Oswald money admitted involvement "in the rackets," that Sumner's associate that night had a father who "was formerly a racketeer and was known to the restaurant's owner," and that the Town and Country was "a known hangout for the hoodlum element." This fits the pattern—noted by Congressional investigators and Hoover expert Anthony Summers—of Hoover's FBI downplaying the organized crime ties of Marcello and his associates. Hoover also withheld FBI field reports like this one from Attorney General Robert Kennedy, who would have immediately grasped its significance.

John H. Davis was also the first to report that Marcello briefly mentioned the FBI interviews of his brother and Poretto to the FBI's BRILAB informant, Joe Hauser. Carlos Marcello told Hauser, "The Feds came up to de motel askin' about him, but my people didn't tell 'em nuttin'. Like we never heard of the guy, y'know?" Hauser's credibility on this point is enhanced because at the time he heard the remarks, the Sumner incident had never been mentioned in any book. Shortly after the payoff Sumner witnessed, Oswald moved to New Orleans to stay with his bookie uncle, Dutz Murret.

Murret, Banister, and Ferrie weren't the only links between Marcello and Oswald. The House Select Committee on Assassinations uncovered other ties between Oswald, his family, and the Marcello organization. As summarized in *Vanity Fair*, Oswald's "childhood and youth had been spent in New Orleans [where] Oswald's mother's friends included a corrupt lawyer linked to Marcello's crime operation and a man who served Marcello as bodyguard and chauffeur." In the summer of 1963, Oswald was bailed out of jail by a man close to "one of Marcello's oldest friends, Nofio Pecora," the same man who was "called three weeks before the assassination by Jack Ruby."

Lending further credence to Marcello's remarks about Oswald is that fact that FBI files contain other accurate information that Van Laningham had written down that Marcello told him about Ferrie. The godfather said that Ferrie "was an ex-airline pilot. It seems that he flew to Guatemala to pick up some new papers that Marcello needed to fight the INS in a court case." Ferrie admitted to authorities soon after JFK's assassination that shortly before JFK was murdered, he had flown to Guatemala twice for Marcello regarding his deportation case. At the time Van Laningham reported Marcello's account to the FBI, Ferrie's work for Marcello was not well known by the general public or even most historians.

CARLOS MARCELLO ALSO told Jack Van Laningham about his control of Jack Ruby, including an important meeting that took place in 1963, more than five months before JFK's murder. Marcello's 1985 remarks about Ruby are briefly summarized in the CAMTEX FBI file, but Van Laningham added more important information in our talks.

By the spring of 1963, Jack Ruby owed a small fortune to the IRS—almost $160,000 in today's dollars—and was desperate for money. The IRS filed tax liens against Ruby on March 13, 1963, and Ruby faced ruin unless he could find another source of money to pay his bills.

According to Carlos Marcello, Ruby found the money he needed by taking it from cash that flowed through the Carousel Club. As Marcello explained to Jack Van Laningham years later, his organization actually controlled the Carousel strip club; Ruby merely managed it. Since the club was across the street from Dallas's most distinguished hotel, the Adolphus, whenever conventions or company meetings were held at the hotel, business at the Carousel was especially brisk, and Ruby probably figured it would be easy to skim some of the proceeds for his own pressing financial needs. Marcello had hidden ownership of several clubs in Dallas, and his financial operatives would have known what all the clubs should be making at particular times of the year. When the Carousel came up short compared to in previous years or other clubs, it wouldn't have been hard for Marcello's people to confirm Jack's ongoing theft. Marcello would have been furious that a longtime mobster like Ruby would take such action, knowing the deadly consequences if caught.

However, just as in 1959, Jack Ruby was once again the right person in the right situation at the right time to help Carlos Marcello and Santo Trafficante. Beginning in late April 1963, Ruby became of great interest to Marcello, and not just for his skimming. The former director of the House Select Committee on Assassinations wrote that "though the [Warren] Commission apparently believed that press speculation about the President's trip [to Dallas] did not begin until September 13, 1963 . . . a story in the *Dallas Times Herald* on April 24, 1963 . . . quoted Vice President Johnson as saying that President Kennedy might 'visit Dallas and other major Texas cities [that] . . . summer.'" Starting the following month, the HSCA "discovered a pattern of [Ruby] telephone calls to individuals with criminal affiliations, calls that could only be described as suspicious."

Jack Ruby's well-documented long-distance phone calls provide a clear record that he was becoming involved in something quite unusual by May 1963. After making fewer than ten long-distance calls in April 1963, Ruby suddenly more than doubled that total to twenty-five in May and more than thirty in June. He continued on that approximate pace through September, but after JFK's trip to Dallas began firming up for November, Ruby's total skyrocketed to more than 80 long-distance calls in October 1963 and more than 110 in just the first three weeks of November. Even in those calls, Ruby would have relied on coded words and phrases common in transacting Mafia business, often going through one or more intermediaries to get information to its ultimate destination.

Carlos Marcello gave Jack Van Laningham the godfather's own unvarnished view of Jack Ruby. According to the FBI file, in talking "about Jack Ruby," Marcello said he "had met him in Dallas, Texas. He set him up in the bar business there. He said that Ruby was a homo son-of-a-bitch but good to have around to report to him what was happening in town. Marcello told us that all the police were on the take, and as long as he kept the money flowing they let him operate anything in Dallas that he wanted to. Ruby would come to Churchill Farms to report to Marcello, so the little man knew what was happening all the time."

Marcello's admission about Ruby goes beyond anything known previously but makes sense in light of information uncovered by Congressional investigators and the FBI. It's important to remember that Ruby's ties to the Mafia were completely unknown to the general public until the late 1970s, and even then most writers overlooked Ruby's connections to several of Marcello's close associates. Even the landmark biography of Ruby by Seth Kantor, 1978's *Who Was Jack Ruby?*, doesn't mention Marcello, though it was the first book to outline Ruby's ties to numerous other mobsters. Dallas reporter Earl Golz was one of the first to clearly make the connection between Ruby and Marcello's organization and Marcello's control of vice in Dallas, a link soon confirmed by the 1979 House Select Committee on Assassinations report. However, it was not until the extensive print and television coverage that accompanied the twenty-fifth anniversary of JFK's murder in November 1988—and publication of Marcello's biography by John Davis in January 1989—that the general public really began to learn about Ruby's ties to the mob. It's important to note that Van Laningham's report on Marcello's remarks about Ruby was written up and in FBI files well before that.

In contrast to the way the FBI presented Ruby to the public and the Warren Commission, the Bureau's own files—from 1963 and earlier—confirmed Ruby's close ties to the Mafia. A formerly secret "FBI Damage Control" memo, first published by historian Gerald D. McKnight in 2005, was actually prepared by the Bureau in the late 1970s in case it had to defend "its investigation into the Kennedy assassination." This was a type of tickler memo, highlighting problems and information the FBI knew it had withheld from the public and press. The FBI Damage Control memo regarding "Jack Ruby" admits that the Bureau had "extensive teletypes and reports on [his] organized crime connections." In contrast to that secret, internal admission, the FBI essentially used statements from several of Ruby's mob associates to claim to the Commission that Ruby had no mob associates.

Other statements Marcello made to Van Laningham are easily confirmed. Even today, most people are unaware that Jack Ruby was gay (or bisexual), even though such information comes up almost forty times in Warren Commission documents and Ruby's roommate at the time of JFK's murder described himself as Ruby's "boyfriend."

FBI files also back up Marcello's remark that in Dallas, "all the police were on the take, and as long as he kept the money flowing they let him operate anything in Dallas that he wanted to." FBI memos mentioned earlier—and made available to the Warren Commission but not mentioned in its widely published *Report*—say that Ruby "was well acquainted with virtually every officer of the Dallas Police force" and was "the pay-off man for the Dallas Police Department."

With the FBI holding such information close to its vest, journalists and historians had to ferret out the details of Ruby's involvement with the mob and Marcello's men bit by bit. Almost four years after Marcello's 1985 admission to Jack Van Laningham—which was withheld from the public at the time and for the next twenty years—John H. Davis detailed tantalizing connections between Ruby and several Marcello associates. These included Marcello's Dallas mob lieutenants Joe Civello and Joe Campisi Sr. Campisi was the first person to visit Ruby in prison after he shot Oswald; he also met with Ruby the night before JFK's murder. Davis documented that in the months and weeks leading up to JFK's assassination, Ruby visited or made calls to five people in Marcello's organization. In addition to those five, Davis writes, "It appears that Jack Ruby knew at least two of Carlos Marcello's brothers" via the slot machine and strip club businesses.

The most startling admission about Ruby that Carlos Marcello made to Van Laningham concerned a dramatic meeting that Ruby was summoned to, where the godfather confronted Ruby about stealing his money—and made him an offer he couldn't refuse. Van Laningham is a large man with a deep voice, and he is normally good natured. However, when he first related to me what Marcello told him about that meeting, he took on the menacing tone that Marcello conveyed to Ruby at that meeting.

Marcello confronted Ruby in the old farmhouse in the middle of his sixty-four-hundred-acre Churchill Farms property. Most of it had once been swampland, and some of it still was. Marcello disposed of the bodies of men who crossed him at Churchill Farms, a fact not lost on any member of the godfather's organization summoned there for a meeting. Recall Marcello's murder of Thomas Siracusa described in Chapter Four; his body, according to the FBI, was "thrown into a tub of lye and after decomposition, the partially liquefied remains were poured into the swamp."

Ruby, knowing he was stealing money from Marcello, was probably already nervous when he arrived at the isolated farmhouse. One can only imagine his fear and pleading when Marcello confronted him about his thievery, and the fury Marcello unleashed on him.

As Marcello described the scene to Van Laningham, Ruby was trembling and begging, willing to do anything to keep from paying the ultimate price for stealing from the godfather. If it eventually meant going into a crowded police basement full of well-armed cops, pulling out his gun, and shooting a prisoner, Ruby had no choice but to do it. As indicated by Ruby's later remarks, it was likely not just Ruby's life that was on the line but those of his family (two brothers, a sister, nieces, and nephews) as well. An undoubtedly grateful Ruby left the meeting with his life but would become increasingly involved in the dangerous JFK plot. As with any sensitive Mafia operation, Ruby's participation would be on a need-to-know basis, getting only limited amounts of information about the plot when he needed to know it.

The FBI has released files with Marcello's remarks about Ruby written in the 1980s, and we also have Jack Van Laningham's videotaped oral history with additional details about Marcello's Ruby comments. Marcello's revelations were also recorded by the FBI's secret CAMTEX taping system. However, none of the CAMTEX tapes or transcripts have been released as the 1992 JFK Act requires, and they should be so that the public can hear Marcello's own words about the matter.

Using information compiled by the House Select Committee on Assassinations, it's possible to pinpoint the likely time of Marcello's confrontation with Ruby. Committee investigators compiled detailed information on Ruby's many calls and visits to New Orleans in 1963, usually to people or places connected to Marcello. But they were unable to find out where Ruby stayed during his visit to New Orleans from June 5 to June 8, 1963. One journalist has suggested that Ruby may have stayed at Churchill Farms during that time, which would account for the lack of any record. Ruby had called a Marcello associate several times before that visit, and Ruby called a club run by one of Marcello's brothers two days after he returned to Dallas.

FBI files show that "on June 22, 1963"—two weeks after Ruby's visit to New Orleans—a horse trainer for one of Carlos Marcello's brothers said he was in "a bookie joint" in New Orleans, where he worked part-time. The horse trainer told the FBI that another one of Marcello's brothers came in and spoke to the owner. The trainer overheard Marcello's brother say, "[T]he word is out to get the Kennedy family."

In 1963 as in 1959, Jack Ruby was not a major player but had been given an offer he couldn't refuse because he knew the right people in the right places. Ruby worked in a city controlled by Carlos Marcello, a city that was expected to be visited by JFK. In Cuba, Ruby had met and tried to help Santo Trafficante, and he was familiar with Tampa, having once lived there and sometimes visiting the city while scouting strip acts. Ruby had worked for Johnny Rosselli's Chicago Mafia and knew that city well. Jimmy Hoffa's son admits that his father knew Jack Ruby. The mob bosses and Hoffa had more than a dozen associates in common with Ruby, making it easy to communicate with Ruby through intermediaries, as Ruby's phone records confirm. Ruby was also a small part of Marcello and Trafficante's drug network, which would also figure into the JFK plot. Finally, Ruby had the connections with the Dallas Police to arrange for anyone blamed for the assassination in Dallas to be quickly killed. If that didn't happen, Ruby would have to do the job himself, and the same would likely be true if the assassination occurred in a city besides Dallas.

In preparation for Ruby's help with the JFK plot, and to provide cover for his activities, he may have been given a small role in the CIA–Mafia Castro assassination plots. By the fall of 1963, Jack Ruby would be having face-to-face meetings with Johnny Rosselli in Miami while the CIA–Mafia plots to kill Castro were continuing.

Carlos Marcello had also apparently given Ruby a substantial financial incentive for producing results in his work on the JFK plot. Several months after the Marcello meeting, and shortly before JFK's trip to Dallas, Ruby began to make plans to move away from the lower-middle-class Oak Cliff neighborhood. He planned for a new home in the most expensive and exclusive part of Dallas, Turtle Creek, where prominent citizens such as General Edwin Walker lived. Also around that same time, Ruby talked to his tax attorney, claiming "he had a connection who would supply him money to settle his long-standing" and huge IRS debt. In a few months, Ruby had gone from being desperate for money to being afraid of being killed to feeling like he was finally ready to hit the financial big time.

Ruby had one more set of skills that made him valuable to Marcello and Trafficante in their JFK plot: his experience with Cuba and gunrunning. Cuba would provide the godfathers the key they needed to kill JFK in a way that would prevent high US officials from conducting a truly thorough investigation to avoid exposing secrets that could trigger—in the words of one memo—"World War III."

CHAPTER 9

Marcello and Trafficante Infiltrate JFK's Secret Cuba Plan

B Y THE SPRING of 1963, Carlos Marcello, Santo Trafficante, and Johnny Rosselli had the motive to assassinate President Kennedy—and in many ways the CIA–Mafia plots to kill Castro provided the means. CIA Deputy Director for Plans Richard Helms was still hiding those plots from John and Robert Kennedy and his own CIA Director. By using people linked to those operations in their still-developing plan to assassinate JFK, the Mafia chiefs could employ people and equipment for what appeared to be CIA operations—but later some would seem to be linked to JFK's assassination, forcing CIA officials such as Helms to cover up or destroy much crucial information. After all, in 1963 high US government officials could not afford to let the world know they were trying to topple or kill a foreign leader such as Castro only months after the Cuban Missile Crisis—especially using dangerous criminals.

However, Marcello and the other mob bosses needed something more than the CIA–Mafia plots to trigger a truly widespread cover-up, one that would ensure there could be no thorough and complete investigation of JFK's murder. Fear of revealing any possible link between the CIA–Mafia plots and JFK's assassination would cause Helms and his close subordinates to hide important information from investigators. However, the godfathers also needed a way to force CIA Director John McCone, Attorney General Robert Kennedy, and new President Lyndon Johnson to withhold crucial information from the press and public, to prevent a potential nuclear confrontation with the Soviet Union at the height of the Cold War.

THE CIA AND the Mafia worked together on two well-documented attempts to kill Fidel Castro in the spring of 1963, efforts that would later be linked to JFK's assassination by the Mafia. These two attempts aren't well known and are missing from the CIA's later accounts of the CIA–Mafia plots. However, Cuban authorities extensively documented the two attempts, having captured many of the Cuban participants and much of their CIA-supplied armaments and communications equipment. The Cubans photographed both men and material at the time, and the full details reached the American press a decade later.

Both of these attempts involved Mafia don Johnny Rosselli, operating under the supervision of CIA officer William Harvey. Harvey, a hard-drinking, rotund agent sometimes called America's James Bond, was becoming close friends with Rosselli, who was an expert at manipulating people for his own ends. The first of the two attempts was on March 13, 1963, and was described in Cuban accounts as involving "a plan to assassinate [Castro] from a house near the University of Havana shooting with a mortar" and other weapons. Cuban forces captured and photographed "[b]azookas, mortars, and machine guns," along with an assassination team of five men, including one named as a CIA agent. According to the account, "the instructions" for the attempted assassination "were given by the CIA through Guantánamo Naval Base."

Naval War College historian David Kaiser documented that Johnny "Rosselli identified the team as his own" twice in later years. Four years after the attempt, Rosselli and his attorney spread provocative stories to select journalists, accounts that reached President Lyndon Johnson and other high-ranking US officials. Rosselli's later story claimed "that the team had been tortured and captured and had confessed that they were on an official mission for the US government; and that this led to Castro's decision to arrange the assassination of Kennedy." Rosselli would leak the story again in 1971, adding even more details, including William Harvey's name.

In planting those and similar fake stories blaming JFK's murder on Fidel, Rosselli, Trafficante, and Marcello not only diverted blame for JFK's murder away from themselves but also ensured that it couldn't be fully investigated without exposing dark secrets the CIA and other high officials didn't want revealed.

According to a 1975 *Miami Herald* article, an even larger CIA attempt to kill Fidel occurred "at the Latin American Stadium on April 7, 1963." It involved "sixteen men armed with pistols and fragmentation grenades." At least three of the men were captured and photographed, along with a large array of weapons, including sniper rifles, machine guns, assault rifles, and pistols. Based on Rosselli's later remarks, that attempt was also part of his CIA–Mafia plotting.

However, those two attempts wouldn't have provided enough cover for Marcello, Trafficante, and Rosselli. Because Robert Kennedy and the CIA Director didn't know about US backing for the attempts, they wouldn't have had the same motivation as Richard Helms to cover up information if they were linked to JFK's murder. So an embittered John Martino—an associate of Marcello, Trafficante, and Rosselli—helped concoct a plot designed to secure the backing of the

CIA Director and the Kennedys, a plot that was really about providing the Mafia cover for its planned assassination of JFK.

Martino found some powerful allies for his planned operation, including wealthy and influential William Pawley, a friend of former Vice President Richard Nixon, and Senator James O. Eastland, who was investigating the Fair Play for Cuba Committee at the time. The CIA officially authorized Martino's plan—put together with the help of Rosselli and Trafficante—and code-named it Operation TILT.

Martino's story was designed to appeal to the CIA and to JFK and was compelling though far-fetched. The plan's stated goal was to send a ten-man Cuban exile team into Cuba to bring back three Soviet technicians, who were supposedly ready to defect and reveal that Soviet nuclear missiles remained hidden in caves in Cuba. The scenario sounded plausible to CIA officials because thousands of Soviet technicians and troops remained in Cuba. Fidel had never allowed the UN weapons inspections, so there was no way to prove with absolute certainty that some missiles weren't hidden in caves or underground, beyond the view of American U-2 spy plane flights.

For President Kennedy, if Cuba still held on to Soviet missiles, he wanted to be the first to know, before his political enemies used the information to attack him. However, JFK, RFK, and their aides were skeptical of the story and didn't become involved in the operation. Martino and his mobster bosses pressed ahead with the plan, hoping one or more JFK aides might decide to support the operation. The story did appeal to the nation's most popular weekly news-photo magazine, *Life*, which "promised [to give] each of the three Soviet defectors $2,500 in return for their stories."

However, Dr. Kaiser found that "Rosselli and Trafficante were using Martino [as a cutout] to enlist the help of the CIA" for the operation. Historian Richard Mahoney documented that Operation TILT was actually an early attempt to lay the groundwork for the Mafia's plot to assassinate JFK. Mahoney wrote that it "fit nicely with Rosselli's later claim that President Kennedy was assassinated by an anti-Castro sniper team sent in to murder Castro, captured by the Cubans, tortured, and redeployed in Dallas."

Martino's ten-man exile team to be sent into Cuba was originally going to include Loran Hall, a US mercenary who had earlier spent time in detention with Santo Trafficante in Cuba. Kaiser wrote that John "Martino . . . asked Hall if he might be interested in something bigger than a raid, backed by 'people' from Chicago and Miami." Hall was then taken to meetings in Miami in April 1963, first with "Trafficante [and then with] Giancana and Rosselli." Martino explained "that the assassination of Castro was the real object of the raid." Hall, smelling something fishy, wisely stayed out of the operation.

Eventually a team of ten armed Cuban exiles headed off toward Cuba, watched by a photographer from *Life* magazine, two CIA agents, and John Martino. The team never returned, and Cuban government officials claim the ten never landed in Cuba. In reality, no Soviet technicians waited, ready to defect—the entire story had been a ruse by Rosselli and Trafficante, spread by Martino to CIA officials. Kaiser points out that "ample evidence, however, shows that the raid was actually just another mob plot against Castro's life, having nothing to do with Soviet technicians," and that it was "sold to the Agency under a false cover." As noted by historian Mahoney, the mob bosses' real goal was to provide cover for JFK's assassination.

It's important to note that by the spring of 1963, Trafficante, Rosselli, and Marcello would have no longer seen killing Fidel as their highest priority. The pressure on the mob chiefs from JFK and RFK had increased by that time. Carlos Marcello faced federal charges later in the year and knew he would be personally prosecuted by RFK's men. Trafficante's operations were under increasing assault, and their ally Jimmy Hoffa faced three trials for various crimes. Rosselli's boss, Sam Giancana, was severely impacted by the FBI's "lockstep" surveillance. Killing Fidel Castro while JFK and RFK were still in power would do the mob bosses little good, which meant that murdering JFK was much more important—and time sensitive—for the Mafia chiefs.

Ultimately, there was a major problem with Rosselli and Trafficante's plan: John and Robert Kennedy never supported Operation TILT. Because they also knew nothing about the CIA–Mafia plots in March and April 1963, RFK would have no incentive to protect those operations if they appeared linked to his brother's murder. Fortuitously for the mobsters, by the time Operation TILT ended in early summer 1963, a new US operation against Cuba had evolved. It was one the Kennedys fully supported and directed and that the three Mafia leaders would soon infiltrate. In pentrating this operation, the mob bosses would gain access to sensitive information that could compromise various branches of government, stifling any real investigation of JFK's murder until at least the late 1970s.

BY APRIL 1963, Kennedy Administration policy about Cuba had become muddled, according to accounts from the various subcommittees of the National Security Council dealing with Cuba. Some officials pressed for strong action while others called for a more cautious approach. JFK didn't want Cuba to dominate the headlines as it had during the Cuban Missile Crisis. That's why he and his officials were careful not to remind the public that there was not yet a "no invasion pledge" because Fidel had not yet allowed UN weapons inspectors into Cuba. Yet the secret war against Cuba, run out of Miami's huge JMWAVE station, continued, with extravagant sums being spread among dozens of exile groups, large and small.

By the early spring of 1963, JFK had approved small exile raids against Cuban ships, but ships of other countries were not supposed to be attacked. However, Richard Helms appears to have taken a harder line against Cuba on his own, again without telling JFK or CIA Director McCone, which caused problems for President Kennedy.

For example, one CIA-backed Cuban exile group that Helms supported made an unauthorized attack in Cuba that violated JFK's guidelines. On March 18, 1963, a group named Alpha 66, run by exile Antonio Veciana, "announced that it had [attacked] a Russian ship and a Russian training area" in Cuba. According to E. Howard Hunt, Alpha 66 and Veciana were handled for the Agency by his good friend CIA officer David Atlee Phillips. Veciana milked the operation for maximum publicity, Phillips's specialty. Outraged at the unauthorized and dangerous attack on a Russian ship, JFK had the US State Department immediately condemn the raid. It's highly unlikely that Phillips would have ordered Veciana to undertake the attack, which could have led to a new confrontation between the United States and the Soviets, without Helms's approval. While the Kennedys wanted Alpha 66 and Veciana to receive no CIA assistance, Helms—without informing JFK or RFK—told Phillips to continue supervising Veciana and his group.

Also in 1963 Richard Helms approved an even more outrageous provocation, one that endangered the lives of three imprisoned CIA agents as well as JFK's personal emissary, who was then trying to negotiate their release. The three agents were among the last twenty-seven US citizens still held in Cuban prisons. From January through

April 1963, JFK had prominent New York attorney James Donovan working to secure their release. Donovan had helped Robert Kennedy negotiate the release of the Bay of Pigs prisoners, and his rapport with the Cuban government soon translated to a working relationship with Fidel, which included accompanying the Cuban leader on skin-diving trips.

The CIA developed two plans to assassinate Fidel while he was skin diving with Donovan, something the Agency admitted both in internal reports and in Congressional testimony. One plan involved devising "an exotic seashell" to attract Fidel's attention "in an area where Castro commonly went skin diving." However, the shell would actually be "rigged to explode underwater," killing Castro and anyone who might be with him. CIA Technical Services—the same group that created the poison pills for the Mafia to use against Fidel—"explored" the idea but found too many problems.

The "second plan involved having James Donovan . . . present Castro with a contaminated diving suit" as a gift. CIA Technical Services actually "bought a diving suit, dusted the inside with a [deadly] fungus . . . and contaminated the breathing apparatus with [tuberculosis bacteria]." The only reason "the plan was abandoned [was] because Donovan gave Castro a different diving suit on his own initiative" and "Helms [later] testified that the [poisoned] diving suit never left the [CIA]." The lethal plans approved by Helms were never revealed to Donovan, CIA Director McCone, JFK, or RFK. Donovan was already in some danger, since the CIA's March 1963 and April 1963 assassination operations (about which Donovan knew nothing) were being planned while he was in Cuba, negotiating with Fidel. Ironically, Castro actually talked with Donovan about the CIA's attempts to kill him while the men were on a skin-diving excursion.

For decades, and even today, former CIA personnel—in books and interviews—give the impression that the CIA undertook efforts to assassinate Fidel Castro only because President Kennedy and Robert Kennedy pressed it to do so. However, the facts show a different story. The CIA fully admits to many well-documented Castro assassination attempts that were not authorized by JFK, RFK, even CIA Director John McCone. More importantly, the CIA's attempts to assassinate Fidel began before JFK became President and continued long after he was dead.

IN A PRIVATE meeting with President Kennedy on April 15, 1963, CIA Director McCone advised him to either "establish relations with Castro" or "to overthrow him." Surprisingly, JFK "suggested that both options might simultaneously be pursued"—a dual strategy that would become a reality by the fall. McCone followed up his meeting with a memo saying that "a military coup in Cuba [was] the United States' only hope" to resolve the Cuba situation. Two days before McCone's memo, Defense Secretary Robert McNamara told a National Security Council subcommittee "that Castro must be overthrown, preferably by provoking an internal revolt that would allow the United States [military] to intervene."

US officials made two attempts to identify Cuban military leaders willing to lead a revolt: a CIA operation named AMTRUNK (which involved *New York Times* journalist Tad Szulc) and a CIA task force with the recently created Defense Intelligence Agency, an umbrella agency designed to coordinate the intelligence services of all US military branches. Neither was producing results, especially since most of the power in Cuba was concentrated in the hands of a relatively small number of officials that Fidel trusted.

Frustrated by the lack of progress, having no clear strategy, and lacking time to give the difficult situation the attention it needed, JFK delegated Cuba to Robert Kennedy. However, the constant bickering and never-ending requests for money by Cuban exile groups receiving CIA support quickly frustrated RFK. In addition, the extensive attention RFK gave to Cuban matters was on top of an already full plate of activities he had to oversee as Attorney General, issues ranging from civil rights matters to the war on organized crime.

Robert Kennedy turned to his exile friend Harry Williams, telling him he didn't want any more Cuban exile leaders coming to RFK for money. Instead, the exiles were to go through Williams, who would then identify for RFK the select few he thought were serious and deserved US backing. By using Williams, RFK also established his own channel into the exile community so he wouldn't be completely dependent on the CIA. RFK turned to Williams because they had grown increasingly close since the Bay of Pigs prisoner release. A frequent visitor at RFK's Hickory Hill estate, Williams even stayed at RFK's New York apartment on visits to Manhattan. The fact that Williams was close to—and trusted by—RFK has been confirmed in accounts by Pulitzer Prize–winning journalist Haynes Johnson, *Newsweek* editor Evan Thomas, and historian Richard Mahoney. Thomas wrote, "Increasingly through 1963, RFK relied on [Harry] Williams, organizing and motivating the others to keep the pressure on Castro." Years later Haynes Johnson wrote in the *Washington Post* that of all "the Cuban leaders of the Bay of Pigs invasion," Williams "was the closest such person to the [JFK] administration" in 1963.

Word soon spread in the exile community—and even in Cuba— that Williams was essentially the gatekeeper for RFK and JFK. Those wanting the support of either man would have to go through Williams.

Marcello, Trafficante, and Rosselli took notice as well. Rosselli used mob money to fund a phony Cuban exile group, the JGCE (Junta of the Government of Cuba in Exile), run by Paulino Sierra. CIA agent Bernard Barker, also working for Trafficante, helped spread the word about the new group. The mob bosses wanted Sierra's group to get Williams's—and the Kennedys'—blessing, in which case it could be used as cover for the plot to kill JFK. However, a journalist raised suspicions about Sierra's Mafia funding in May 1963, and my interview with Sierra's daughter confirmed Sierra's ties to the mob. Sierra's group lingered for several months, but it never received the backing of Williams or the Kennedys and thus was of no real use in the JFK plot.

A MAY 10, 1963, Associated Press report that would have a huge impact on the secrecy surrounding JFK's assassination appeared in the *New York Times* and other newspapers. Long overlooked, the article gave surprising details about Harry Williams's work for Robert Kennedy, information that both men had hoped to keep out of the press:

> A new all-out drive to unify Cuban refugees into a single, powerful organization to topple the Fidel Castro regime was disclosed today by exile sources. The plan calls for formation of a junta in exile to mount a three-pronged thrust consisting of sabotage, infiltration, and ultimate invasion. The exile sources said the plan had been discussed with Cuban leaders by US Central Intelligence agents. Seeking to put together the junta was Enrique [Harry] Ruiz Williams, a Bay of Pigs invasion veteran and friend of US Attorney General Robert F. Kennedy. . . . [Tony] Varona, former Premier [of Cuba], said he had told Mr. Ruiz Williams he would cooperate in plans to unify the exiles.

RFK and Harry Williams were furious when they saw the article revealing information about their secret plans. The information was probably leaked by Tony Varona, who had volunteered to become the first exile leader to join Williams's operation, no doubt at the urging of Santo Trafficante. Varona had worked on the CIA–Mafia plots with Trafficante and Rosselli, and he was still working for Trafficante in 1963. That Varona was working on behalf of Trafficante and the Mafia was confirmed soon after Varona began working with Williams when the CIA received a report that Rosselli's associates had paid a bribe of $200,000 to Varona. Neither RFK nor Williams knew about Varona's work for Trafficante and Rosselli or about the ongoing CIA–Mafia plots, and the CIA never informed RFK about Varona's bribe from the Mafia. Thus the Kennedys' covert plans for Cuba were penetrated by Trafficante almost from the start.

However, the May 10, 1963, AP article quickly caught the attention of Commander Juan Almeida, Williams's old friend in Cuba, still head of the Cuban army. Commander Almeida reached out to Williams within forty-eight hours of seeing the article, getting a message to him to call a certain number in Cuba, a line that was safe from wiretaps. (Almeida helped oversee some of Cuba's electronic surveillance operations.) At that time Almeida was in many ways the third most powerful official in Cuba, behind only Fidel and his brother Raul Castro, and he wielded far more authority and men than Che Guevara.

Commander Almeida told Williams that Fidel was becoming nothing more than a dictator, betraying the very Revolution they had all fought so hard for. Then Almeida surprised Williams by offering to stage a coup against Fidel—if JFK would back him. As soon as he got off the phone, Williams immediately called Robert Kennedy about Almeida's offer. Williams and RFK were in near daily contact by May

1963, and Williams appears often in RFK's official Justice Department phone logs. Williams also made many calls and visits to RFK's Virginia home, Hickory Hill, and to his New York City apartment.

Robert Kennedy wasted no time in discussing Almeida's offer with President Kennedy, since this appeared to be the big break regarding Cuba they'd been hoping for. RFK's official phone logs at the National Archives indicate some of the timing. The logs show that on May 13, 1963, at 5:50 p.m., RFK took a call from President Kennedy. The very next call RFK accepted, at 6:05 p.m., was from Harry Williams. RFK told Williams that JFK had decided to accept Almeida's offer to stage a coup to overthrow Fidel and that the US government would give Almeida its full backing for the attempt.

That was the start of the JFK–Almeida coup plan, one of the most secret covert US operations since D-Day. In fact, that very term was used on May 29, 1963—just over two weeks after Almeida contacted the Kennedys via Williams—when Joint Chiefs of Staff Chairman General Maxwell Taylor wrote a memo saying that it was "a matter of priority" to examine the possibility "of an invasion of Cuba at a time controlled by the United States in order to overthrow the Castro government"; the memo included "a proposed date for D-Day." Select officials at the Pentagon later played major roles in the JFK–Almeida coup plan, with the CIA relegated to supporting status.

Williams and other aides to John and Robert Kennedy, including Secretary of State Dean Rusk (who also gave an on-the-record confirmation to *Vanity Fair*), verified the JFK–Almeida coup plan to me. Though the vast majority of files about the plan are still classified, a surprising number have slipped through. They include a 1963 CIA report to the Agency's Director, with information from Bernard Barker about an "operation including Juan Almeida" designed to "overthrow"

Fidel, who would be replaced by a new Cuban government to "be recognized immediately" by JFK's administration. Another CIA dispatch discusses a plan for "an internal uprising" in Cuba by "Cuban military figures, who are conspiring against Fidel Castro. Among the key figures in the plot [is] Juan Almeida." Hundreds of pages of files about the US military side of the operation have been declassified.

The JFK–Almeida coup plan was designed to avoid the main problems that befell the Bay of Pigs operation, which had been a relatively open secret known to dozens of officials, aides, agents, and military officers in the US government, as well as to numerous journalists and even partially to Fidel. This time, any knowledge of the coup plan would be tightly held. Only about a dozen people—including JFK, RFK, CIA Director John McCone, and CIA Deputy Director for Plans Richard Helms—would know the full scope of the plan. The leading US role in the coup plan was never supposed to be revealed, even after the coup succeeded—and not even years later, since US officials hoped Almeida and trusted exiles might play roles in Cuba's new government for decades to come. If things worked as JFK and RFK hoped, it would simply appear as though JFK had responded well to the unexpected situation of Fidel's "elimination" (the term the Kennedys used with their aides).

In the five months of strategizing about Cuba before Almeida's offer in May 1963, General Maxwell Taylor and other top officials had approved three drafts of a purely hypothetical "Plan for a Coup in Cuba." After Almeida's offer was relayed to the Kennedys, the planning took on a new sense of urgency. In just the next four months, ten drafts were completed, some growing to more than eighty pages. Officials at the CIA and State Department reviewed and approved them all. At that point no one at State knew about Almeida, and Dean Rusk would be told about him only after JFK's death. Thus most—but not all—of those working on these drafts thought they were only contingency plans, just in case a ranking Cuban official could be found to lead a coup. Only about a dozen officials knew the plans were not just a contingency—they were for real, and one of the highest officials in Cuba was already working with JFK. However, these drafts still give a surprisingly accurate overview of the coup plan. None of those files were declassified for over three decades, until the mid-1990s, partially as a result of information I provided to the staff of the JFK Assassination Records Review Board.

According to the plans, the Cuban leader of the coup had to "have some power base in the Cuban army," and the United States would also "seek the cooperation of selected Cuban exile leaders." The point of the plan was to stage a seemingly internal "palace coup in Cuba [that would] neutralize the top echelon of Cuban leadership." The plan stresses that "it is important [that] the revolt appear genuine and not open to the charge of being a façade for a forcible US overthrow of Castro [since] a well-planned and successful 'rescue' of a revolt could be made politically acceptable" to US allies and the Soviets. After Castro's death, President Kennedy would "warn [the] Soviets not to intervene." The leaders of the coup "would have announced via radio and other means the . . . establishment of a Provisional Government. They would have appealed to the US for recognition and support, particularly for air cover and a naval blockade, ostensibly to make certain that the Soviets do not intervene but actually, by prearrangement, to immobilize the Cuban Air Force and Navy." That was important, since "twelve to thirteen thousand Soviet military personnel of all kinds remain [in Cuba]." After "completion of such initial air attacks as may be necessary, provision will be made for the rapid, incremental introduction of balanced forces, to include full-scale invasion."

However, it's important to point out that "full-scale invasion" was a worst-case scenario that JFK and others hoped wouldn't happen. It was possible that Commander Almeida could stage the coup without US military forces. A multiracial group of Cuban American Bay of Pigs veterans—commanded by a black exile officer—was soon training at Fort Benning and Fort Jackson. They would be the first US troops into Cuba if US military forces were needed on the ground. In fact, Commander Almeida could actually ask for the intervention of US forces to help prevent a Soviet takeover of Cuba. A careful reading of all the declassified files and of exclusive interviews with participants in the coup plan shows it was even possible that US military forces could wind up fighting side by side with Commander Almeida's Cuban troops against forces backing Raul Castro or old-line Cuban Communists.

JFK's "Plan for a Coup in Cuba" with Almeida was vastly different from the CIA–Mafia plots. The United States wanted support from its allies, and the Kennedys' ultimate goal was a free and democratic Cuba. According to the plans, "The OAS [Organization of American States] will send representatives to the island to assist the Provisional Government in preparing for and conduct of free elections." The "Provisional Government" would include the Cuban America exile troops and the leaders of four exile groups, who would secure bases outside the United States prior to the coup. The four exile leaders would represent a broad spectrum of politics, from the ultraconservative Manuel Artime, E. Howard Hunt's best friend, to the extremely liberal Manolo Ray (and his group JURE) and Eloy Menoyo (and his SNFE). Among them, unfortunately, was Tony Varona, who was working for the Mafia.

Within several months, CIA memos began to describe those disparate groups as working on a major plot to overthrow Castro. As mentioned, one CIA memo noted that Manolo Ray's "JURE was currently sponsoring a plan to assassinate Fidel Castro and other high ranking Cuban government officials as part of an operation designed to incite an internal rebellion in Cuba." The same memo says, "This plan involves an internal uprising with the support of certain Cuban military figures . . . among the key figures in the plot are Juan Almeida."

The American public knew nothing about the JFK–Almeida coup plan for decades. Finally, some documents were declassified in the 1990s, but the few mentioning Almeida were separate from the files about the "Plan for a Coup in Cuba," so most historians thought the plans were only a what-if contingency. The JFK–Almeida coup plan didn't start to become fully exposed until 2006, after the US government sent me a written determination that some files describing Commander Almeida's secret work for JFK could be released.

The secrecy surrounding the JFK–Almeida coup plan helps explain why so much related to JFK's assassination stayed secret for so long. Nonetheless, a surprising number of documents slipped through over the years, though some of their significance is clear to historians only now, in hindsight. Among those documents are files about Tony Varona's summer of 1963 $200,000 bribe from the Mafia. Other memos, such as two from June 1963, outline the goals of John and Robert Kennedy: "The ultimate objective [was for] dissident elements in the military . . . of the Cuban regime to bring about the eventual liquidation of [Fidel] Castro [and] the elimination of the Soviet presence from Cuba." The handful of exile leaders who were willing to help do that, chosen by Harry Williams and approved by RFK, would receive major funding from the Kennedy Administration to base their operations "outside the territory of the United States." Those exiles had to be dedicated "to the idea that the overthrow of

[Castro] must be accomplished by Cubans inside and outside Cuba working in concert." In addition, "an experienced [CIA] liaison officer would be assigned to each group to provide general advice, funds, and material support." Although the groups would be called autonomous, RFK made it clear they were really working for the United States, but "if ever charged with complicity, the US Government would publicly deny any participation in the groups' activities."

The goals of the Kennedy brothers were both noble and politically pragmatic: to bring democracy to Cuba while also keeping the volatile issue of Cuba—and whether all the Soviet missiles had really been removed—out of the 1964 elections. Kennedy aides told me something later confirmed by a declassified memo: JFK wanted to keep Cuba from becoming a "political football" during the 1964 campaign, which would begin in January 1964. That meant they had to take action before the end of 1963, preferably at least a month before the Christmas holidays.

It's critical to point out that for the JFK–Almeida coup plan to have worked, Commander Almeida could not take public responsibility for Fidel's death and neither could Williams or the other Cuban exiles. The Cuban populace could hardly be expected to rally around new leaders who boasted of having killed Fidel, whom the CIA admitted was still admired by many on the island. Thus, Williams told me, someone else would "take the fall" for Fidel's death. Williams said he had no involvement with finding the "fall guy," that Robert Kennedy was handling that with the CIA.

Evidence gleaned from CIA memos and coup plan files indicates that Fidel's death would have been blamed on a Russian or a Russian sympathizer, a way to help neutralize the thousands of Soviet personnel still in Cuba. Many newspaper accounts noted increasing tension between Fidel and the Soviets in the second half of 1963. As head of the army, Almeida knew the locations of all Soviet forces in Cuba, as well as Fidel's security plans. Almeida had enough personal prestige that if he went on Cuban TV and announced that their beloved Fidel had been killed by a Russian or Russian sympathizer, the Cuban people would accept his word, the same way most US citizens at that time would accept a pronouncement by a trusted figure such as J. Edgar Hoover. In addition, Commander Almeida was the highest black official in a country estimated to be 70 percent of African descent, so it was felt the populace would more easily rally around him than someone like the Argentinean Che Guevara (struggling as an economic bureaucrat in 1963) or one of the white Cuban officials the Russians might back.

It's important to stress that as the months progressed, the Kennedys constantly looked for a peaceful alternative to what one memo called a potentially "bloody coup." Yet they also continued to make increasingly detailed plans to overthrow Fidel. As discussed in later chapters, by fall the Kennedys were pursuing two different, secret "peace feelers," trying to jump-start peace talks with Castro. When Secretary of State Dean Rusk confirmed the existence of the coup plan to *Vanity Fair* in 1994, the article's authors asked Rusk about the Kennedys' attempts to negotiate with Castro at the same time they were planning a coup against him. In pursuing the two strategies at the same time, "Rusk admits that the Kennedys were 'playing with fire.'" Rusk told *Vanity Fair*, "Oh, there's no particular contradiction there . . . it was just an either/or situation. That went on frequently."

JFK's earlier-noted comments to John McCone reflect this dual strategy, as does Robert Kennedy's Oral History at Boston's John F. Kennedy Presidential Library. RFK said, "There were some tentative [peace] feelers that were put out by [Castro] which were accepted by us." But in the very next sentence, RFK adds that at the same time "we were also making more of an effort [against Castro] through espionage . . . in . . . August, September, October [1963]. It was better organized than it had been before and was having quite an effect." In what may be an oblique reference to the coup, RFK says that one of his goals was "internal uprisings" and that "we were more [than just] assisting" because of his "contact with some of those people." Pursuing peace and war at the same time also reflected the indecisiveness of the American public about Cuba. JFK biographer Richard Reeves notes that 60 percent of Americans in 1963 thought Castro "was a serious threat to world peace," yet a slightly higher percentage "were against sending United States troops to invade Castro's island."

GIVEN THE DECADES of secrecy surrounding the JFK–Almeida coup plan, it's shocking that a dozen associates of Carlos Marcello, Trafficante, or Rosselli knew about—and in seven cases actually worked on—the top-secret operation. Learning about the coup plan gave Marcello's group the deadly secret it needed to prevent a full and public investigation of JFK's murder, if the effort to overthrow Fidel could be linked to JFK's murder. In addition, as plans for the coup and invasion progressed, there was also a chance that phony evidence implicating Fidel in JFK's death could trigger a US invasion of Cuba, one that the US military had been preparing for months.

John and Robert Kennedy tried to bar the Mafia from any participation in the coup plan. That included keeping the Mafia out of Cuba after the coup's hoped-for success, when the mob would not be allowed to reopen their casinos. Unfortunately, declassified files show that several associates of Carlos Marcello not only knew about the secret plan, but made documented comments about this otherwise top-secret operation.

An FBI report written just weeks after JFK's assassination quotes Jack Ruby as talking about something he must have learned before being jailed for shooting Oswald. According to the memo, Ruby talked about "an invasion of Cuba [that] was being sponsored by the United States Government."

That long-overlooked remark wasn't in the *Warren Report*, but it was included in the twenty-six volumes of supporting evidence and documents that the Warren Commission issued. To most in the Bureau and on the Warren Commission, and later to the relative few who read the twenty-six volumes, such a claim undoubtedly seemed absurd. But they didn't realize that JFK's "no invasion pledge" regarding Cuba had never taken effect and that "the United States Government" really had been planning "an invasion of Cuba." Those plans were withheld not only from the Warren Commission but also from the House Select Committee on Assassinations and all other Congressional investigating committees.

Remarkably, as detailed in the next chapter, Ruby was just one of twelve associates of Carlos Marcello, Trafficante, or Rosselli who knew important information about the JFK–Almeida coup plan. Even more remarkable, seven associates of the Mafia chiefs were actually working on parts of the coup/invasion plan, even though John and Robert Kennedy had banned the Mafia from having anything to do with the operation.

FBI files show that Marcello's pilot, David Ferrie, knew about the "second invasion" planned for Cuba (the Bay of Pigs being the first). According to an FBI memo, a close associate of Ferrie told the FBI about Ferrie's "dealings with the late Attorney General Robert

Kennedy [and] plans for a Cuban second invasion." Guy Banister, Marcello's private detective, knew about the coup plan as well. A close friend of Banister—likely using information from the detective—even wrote an account in the summer of 1963 that described secret "Kennedy Administration planning" for Cuba in which Castro "would be the fall guy in a complete reorganization for the [Cuban] regime which will [then] be free of Soviet influence." Banister's friend wrote that following Castro's removal, "a new government [for Cuba would be] set up with such men as . . . Manolo Ray," who was one of five exile leaders chosen by RFK and Harry Williams to be part of the coup plan.

According to new witnesses uncovered by Dr. Michael L. Kurtz, John Martino—Santo Trafficante's technician—also worked with Carlos Marcello and Guy Banister in the summer of 1963. Kurtz cites the former Superintendent of the New Orleans Police Department as saying that Martino "met with Marcello himself at the Town and Country Motel." FBI files cite several accurate descriptions Martino gave of the JFK–Almeida coup plan after JFK's murder as he taunted the FBI with his knowledge that "President Kennedy was engaged in a plot to overthrow the Castro regime by preparing another invasion attempt against Cuba."

Martino elaborated on the secret Kennedy scheme in an obscure newspaper article contained in an FBI file not released until 1998. In it Martino is quoted as saying—two months after JFK's death—that when he died "Kennedy was embarked on a plan to get rid of Castro. There was to be another invasion and uprising in Cuba." Martino accurately noted that "since the death of Kennedy the work on an invasion has virtually stopped." He even mentioned that according to Kennedy's plan, after the coup, "the Organization of American States [would be involved] until an election could be set up." The OAS role, as detailed in several of the fourteen drafts of the top-secret "Plan for a Coup in Cuba," drawn up under Robert Kennedy's direction in the summer and fall of 1963, wasn't declassified until 1997. Yet Marcello's associate Martino knew about that—and more—decades earlier.

Even Lee Oswald, who had connections to Marcello documented earlier, made an interesting remark about "an invasion of Cuba" by "the United States" at a time when almost no one was publicly speculating about such an operation. A long-overlooked *New York Times* article even quotes a Cuban exile—who had contact with Oswald in New Orleans in August 1963 and who knew David Ferrie—as saying that "Lee H. Oswald had boasted [about what he would do] if the United States attempted an invasion of Cuba." In the summer of 1963, Oswald—accompanied by David Ferrie—reportedly visited a training camp near New Orleans that was affiliated with Manuel Artime, one of the key exile leaders for the JFK–Almeida coup plan.

CIA memos I first published in 2005 confirm that in the early 1960s, Manuel Artime was also working on the CIA–Mafia plots, which also involved Trafficante, Rosselli, and Marcello. Artime, E. Howard Hunt's best friend, would soon become part of Trafficante's drug trafficking network. Artime was one of seven associates of the three mob bosses who were actually working on the JFK–Almeida coup plan. The same is true for Tony Varona, the first Cuban exile leader to join Harry Williams's operation, all while he was still working with Santo Trafficante and Johnny Rosselli on the CIA–Mafia plots. It was their work on those unauthorized plots that allowed some of the mob bosses' men to infiltrate the Kennedy brothers' authorized operation, the JFK–Almeida coup plan.

E. Howard Hunt has long been the subject of speculation and Congressional investigations regarding his possible involvement in JFK's murder, though evidence remains elusive, as explained in the book's final chapter. Even Hunt's taped "confession" isn't really a confession at all but an account full of recycled (and debunked) theories, speculation, and important omissions—such as the Mafia ties of his best friend, Artime, and his longtime assistant Bernard Barker. However, Barker was definitely involved in JFK's murder, according to Harry Williams, RFK's friend and aide for the JFK–Almeida coup plan. Long before files linking Barker to organized crime were declassified, Williams told me and my research associate that Barker had worked for Trafficante and was doing so in 1963—at the same time Barker was working on the JFK–Almeida coup plan.

As Williams explained to me, E. Howard Hunt was one of two prominent CIA officers assigned to assist Harry Williams. Kennedy aides, former FBI agent William Turner, and *Vanity Fair* all confirmed Hunt's work with Williams. Williams detailed to me and to William Turner the important role Barker played as Hunt's assistant in 1963, something Barker himself indicated in published interviews. Many of Barker's 1963 CIA files, including all those involving his admitted work as Hunt's assistant that year, remain unreleased. However, quoted earlier was a Barker CIA memo that slipped through. It mentioned a coup plot against Fidel involving Commander Almeida. In a 1970s TV documentary, Barker said, "At the time [of] the Kennedy assassination . . . President Kennedy's government had reached its 'peak' in its efforts to overthrow Castro," something not reflected in any history books or government reports at the time Barker made his comments.

Harry Williams said there were "dozens [of meetings] from May to November [1963]" with E. Howard Hunt and a CIA security officer assigned to the operation. Bernard Barker arranged those meetings, most of them held away from Miami. "Barker was Hunt's assistant, very close to Hunt," Williams explained.

As the JFK–Almeida coup plan progressed, Barker assisted Hunt with two of the most sensitive parts of the plan. Barker helped Hunt with the covert payment of $50,000 to Commander Almeida through a foreign bank, the initial installment of an agreed-upon total sum of $500,000 (more than $3 million today). Robert Kennedy had authorized the money in the event the coup was unsuccessful and Almeida had to flee Cuba; if he was killed, the money would alternatively provide for his wife and two children. Barker was well suited for such a financial role, since one of his jobs before the Bay of Pigs invasion "was to deliver CIA cash laundered through foreign banks."

Secondly, Barker and Hunt were also part of a covert operation in which Almeida's wife and two children left Cuba on a seemingly innocent pretext prior to the date set for the coup. The plan was for Almeida's family to wait out the coup safely in another country, under secret CIA surveillance. RFK had also authorized Williams and the CIA to assure Almeida that if anything happened to him and his family couldn't return to Cuba, his family would be taken care of. In addition to providing for their safety, having the family in another country, under the watchful eye of the CIA, also ensured that Almeida didn't double-cross the CIA and the Kennedys.

Even Barker's routine CIA reports from the summer and fall of 1963 that have been declassified—the ones that don't mention Hunt— show him submitting a stream of information linked either to the mob or the coup plan. For example, Barker filed reports about a meeting between Manuel Artime and Tony Varona to discuss unity and noting Artime's meeting with Trafficante "bagman" Frank Fiorini in Dallas to buy an airplane. Barker's CIA reports also mention Eloy Menoyo's plan to overthrow Fidel and the operations of Manolo Ray. Barker also reported on the efforts of Sam Benton, another private detective working for Carlos Marcello, to recruit an American mercenary, part of the CIA–Mafia plots to kill Fidel. The mercenary backed out when he learned that an associate of Johnny Rosselli was involved in the plot.

In 1963 Harry Williams—and Robert Kennedy—didn't know that "Barker was connected to [Santo Trafficante]," as he later learned. Williams was not privy to FBI and CIA files (released decades later) tying Barker to the mob; nor did he realize that his associates Tony Varona and Manuel Artime also had ties to Trafficante.

The JFK–Almeida coup plan gave Marcello and Trafficante the opportunity they needed to kill JFK in a way that would prevent even Robert Kennedy—as well as Lyndon Johnson and J. Edgar Hoover— from pursuing a full or public investigation of the murder. Though the Kennedys had tried to bar the Mafia from any knowledge of or participation in the coup plan, the network of Marcello and Trafficante surrounding the CIA–Mafia Castro plots allowed the mob bosses to use Barker, Varona, and others to infiltrate the coup plan and ultimately link it to JFK's assassination.

TWELVE YEARS AFTER JFK's murder, Richard Helms tried to explain to Congressional investigators why he continued the CIA–Mafia plots in 1963 without telling President Kennedy, Robert Kennedy, or CIA Director John McCone. In his long-secret testimony to the Senate Church Committee in 1975, Helms hinted at the JFK–Almeida coup plan (which the CIA withheld from the Committee), saying that "President Kennedy . . . mentioned the desire to have the military of some force inside [Cuba] rise up against Castro, some internal revolt."

Helms went off the record with the Committee Counsel, who then summarized, "In June of 1963, President Kennedy approved [a] program [that] also involved the promoting [of] disaffection among [the] Cuban military hierarchy."

Helms indicated then—and in later testimony—that he saw no difference between that effort and hiring the Mafia to assassinate Fidel. To Helms, having mobsters shoot Fidel so he could be replaced by a right-wing dictator—perhaps someone like Manuel Artime, best friend of his protégé Hunt—was no different from, and perhaps even preferable to, helping an internal coup that would be followed by a coalition government, free elections, and democracy. Kennedy aides and officials—including Secretary of State Rusk—told me they totally disagree with Helms's view. Historian Gerald McKnight talked about the CIA's "culture of arrogance, assumed privileged insights, and special understanding," in which the Agency believed it "knew the requirements of national security better than the transient elected officials to whom the CIA was nominally accountable." McKnight was writing about CIA officer William Harvey, but his description also applies to Richard Helms, whom history now shows withheld crucial information from JFK, LBJ (who made Helms CIA Director), and Richard Nixon (who finally fired Helms after he refused for years to show Nixon the CIA files he wanted). That arrogant attitude is apparently why Helms continued the CIA–Mafia plots even after the JFK–Almeida coup plan was far along.

William Harvey was replaced as head of Cuban operations after his unauthorized raids into Cuba during the Cuban Missile Crisis. Officially, his replacement early in 1963 was Desmond FitzGerald, a patrician figure from a family even wealthier and more blue-blooded than that of Richard Helms. FitzGerald was brought over from Far

Eastern operations and had no previous experience in Cuban affairs. Perhaps for that reason, William Harvey continued to work with Johnny Rosselli on the CIA–Mafia plots; Harvey had also grown close to Rosselli. But his role with the Mafia don had to end in June 1963, when the FBI learned that Rosselli was visiting Harvey.

However, after the FBI learned of the June meeting between Rosselli and Harvey, the CIA assigned Rosselli to a new contact: David Morales, the Miami Operations Chief. A gruff, powerful, and forceful man of southwestern Native American descent, Morales had headed covert operations for the CIA in Havana before the closing of the US Embassy, where he had supervised David Atlee Phillips. Morales also had a role in the Bay of Pigs operation and was extremely bitter at its tragic outcome, which he blamed exclusively on President Kennedy. The number-two official at the Miami CIA station bluntly described Morales: "If the US government . . . needed someone or something neutralized, Dave would do it, including things that were repugnant to a lot of people." Former US diplomat Wayne Smith, who worked with Morales at the US Embassy in Havana, said that "if [Morales] were in the mob, he'd be called a hit man."

Johnny Rosselli, always looking for an advantage to exploit, soon turned the hard-drinking David Morales into a close friend; they even took a trip to Las Vegas together. For Rosselli, Morales was just another CIA agent he could use for his own ends—in this case, the JFK assassination. While Barker was helpful, he was only a CIA agent. But Morales was a high-ranking CIA officer who could control operations, who could order weapons shipped, and who was also working on the JFK–Almeida coup plan.

Like Rosselli, David Morales would eventually confess late in life to having a role in the murder of JFK. Morales made his confession to his attorney and also to a lifelong friend after going on a tirade about JFK's sole responsibility for the failure of the Bay of Pigs. Morales said he had "to watch all the men he had recruited and trained get wiped out because of Kennedy." Morales then told his friends that "we took care of that son of a bitch" JFK. Congressional investigator Gaeton Fonzi, who worked for both the Senate Church Committee and the House Select Committee on Assassinations, uncovered Morales's JFK confession and found it credible.

In the fall of 1963, Morales and Rosselli were observed working closely together. An Army Ranger assigned to the CIA in the summer and fall of 1963 later wrote an account of his time in South Florida training Cuban exiles. He wrote about a "Col. Rosselli," who also worked with one of the exile groups, saying that Rosselli's team included "a sharpshooter" who "did daily marksmanship practice . . . rehearsing for the day when he could center the crosshairs of this telescopic sight on Fidel." Rosselli's "sharpshooter" was able to kill "three cormorants at a range of nearly five hundred yards." Apparently, the CIA was preparing to have shooters available to kill Fidel if Almeida had problems finding someone to eliminate the Cuban leader. The Army Ranger also documented Rosselli's work with David Morales at the time; given the JFK confessions of Rosselli and Morales, some researchers have wondered if their sharpshooter and advanced sniper weapons were intended only for Fidel Castro.

CARLOS MARCELLO'S ACCESS to the highly secret CIA–Mafia plots and those working on the JFK–Almeida coup plan gave the godfather, and his allies Trafficante and Rosselli, the connections he needed to create grave concerns at the highest levels of the US government— if those plans appeared linked to JFK's murder. From August to

November, Marcello and his men would move to compromise more key elements of the coup plan—and other covert CIA operations—as part of their plot to kill JFK.

CHAPTER 10

Plans to Assassinate Fidel Castro and President Kennedy

T HROUGHOUT THE SUMMER and fall of 1963, CIA Deputy
Director for Plans Richard Helms juggled an array of authorized and unauthorized covert attempts to "eliminate" Fidel Castro;
all of them would impact JFK's assassination.* The authorized operations included JFK's coup plan with Cuban Army Commander Juan
Almeida and two far less successful efforts to identify Cuban military
officers willing to lead a coup against Fidel: a CIA operation named
AMTRUNK and a joint CIA–Defense Intelligence Agency (DIA) Task
Force. In addition, several exile leaders in the JFK–Almeida coup plan
continued to attempt tiny raids into Cuba or against Cuban ships, minor
efforts designed to "keep the pot boiling," in the words of one official,
until the day for Almeida's coup arrived. Those raids also kept up the
morale of Cuban exiles still receiving US funding, since only a handful
of their leaders knew about Commander Almeida and the coup.

---

*According to the Kennedy aides and officials I interviewed, "eliminate" was the term used by John
and Robert Kennedy with the dozen aides and officials who knew about the JFK–Almeida coup plan,
as well as when discussing AMTRUNK or the CIA–DIA Task Force. Even then, they usually spoke of
"eliminating Castro's regime" as opposed to eliminating an individual.

In addition to all those efforts, in the remaining months of 1963, Richard Helms actually increased his use of unauthorized operations designed to simply assassinate Fidel Castro. All his unauthorized assassination plots involved Mafia associates, so Helms may have viewed them as simply different aspects of one operation, the same CIA–Mafia plots that had been running for three years. Also, based on his later Congressional testimony, Helms apparently saw no real distinction between his CIA–Mafia plots and the Kennedys' authorized efforts to stage a coup against Fidel. As Helms would testify to Senate investigators in 1975, "I believe it was the policy at the time to get rid of Castro, and if killing him was one of the things that was to be done in this connection, that was within what was expected." If true, that belief doesn't explain why Helms kept President Kennedy, CIA Director McCone, and Attorney General Robert Kennedy in the dark about his unauthorized operations—or why he used mobsters the Attorney General was trying to prosecute.

The most generous view of the actions of Richard Helms—and a handful of his subordinates—in deceiving his superiors would be that Helms viewed the CIA–Mafia plots as a kind of backup plan in case something happened to Commander Almeida before he launched the coup. Helms might have seen the CIA–Mafia plots as a way of salvaging the operation in the event that Commander Almeida lost his position; was injured, imprisoned, or killed; or decided to flee prior to the coup. Helms might have thought that even if Almeida could initiate the coup, it would still be helpful to have Mafia or exile sharpshooters on hand to finish the job, just in case anything went wrong. While the CIA had only a supporting role in the JFK–Almeida coup plan, the CIA–Mafia plots were something that Helms could fully control—or at least he thought he could.

Rolando Cubela, an old element of the CIA–Mafia plots, took on new prominence in the summer of 1963. Cubela, a physician, had headed the Directo Revolucionario (DR), a student group that had helped win the Revolution. However, Cubela quickly grew disaffected with Castro rule, and by December 1960 he was working with the CIA on plots to kill Fidel. In many ways, Cubela was simply another part of the CIA–Mafia plots since he'd met Santo Trafficante in Cuba and knew at least two associates of the godfather who were also involved in the CIA–Mafia plots. Cubela had been briefly in touch with the CIA in 1962. In June 1963 the CIA contacted Cubela again, just as David Morales was taking over the supervision of Johnny Rosselli from William Harvey.

Although Cubela had no real power within the Cuban government, he received a generous travel budget as the former head of the DR, and he frequently flew to Europe and Communist-bloc countries. According to Cuban reports, David Morales actually met with Cubela in Paris in September 1963, and the CIA acknowledges that a series of meetings between Cubela and CIA personnel followed. Cubela says the CIA kept pressuring him to assassinate Fidel, while the CIA claims assassination was Cubela's idea.

Rolando Cubela wasn't part of the JFK–Almeida coup plan. As JFK's Secretary of State Dean Rusk told me—and as CIA files clearly show—he had no following inside Cuba that would have allowed him to stage a coup on his own. For decades it was thought that Cubela's contacts with the CIA were known only inside the Agency, where he was identified as a potential assassin code-named AMLASH. However, Rusk and another committee member told me that Cubela was discussed by name in some of RFK's Cuba subcommittees of the National Security Council, though not as a possible assassin. Richard Helms and Desmond FitzGerald mentioned Cubela to some subcommittee members only as someone who might help them find a higher-ranking, more powerful official who could stage a coup.

To an official like Rusk, who didn't yet know about Almeida, that sounded reasonable. Twelve years later, when Rusk found out that the CIA was actually using Cubela as a potential assassin, he was livid at Helms's deceit, with an anger that the usually calm statesman demonstrated in my interview with him. Only a mid-level official at best, Rolando Cubela played an even smaller role in Cuban affairs as fall 1963 progressed. CIA files establish that Cubela lost his ceremonial military title after he "resigned from the Army after difficulties with Raul Castro," and an October 18, 1963, CIA memo confirms "that Cubela has no official position in the government." Yet Richard Helms and Desmond FitzGerald increased CIA pressure on Cubela to assassinate Fidel, with FitzGerald even flying to Paris to confer with Cubela that same month. Though FitzGerald claimed to be the personal emissary of Robert Kennedy, Helms later admitted that RFK was never told about the meeting or the assassination aspect of the CIA's dealings with Cubela.

The CIA admits it tried to persuade Cubela to poison Fidel, but CIA files also show that the Miami CIA station, where David Morales ran operations, was prepared to provide rifles to him. Cubela owned a house next to Fidel's home at Varadero Beach, the resort to which Fidel drove on many weekends in an open jeep in a sort of re-creation of his triumphant drive across Cuba after the Revolution. AMWORLD files indicate that at one point the CIA planned to use snipers to assassinate Fidel as he drove toward his beach house. Clearly, having Fidel's neighbor Cubela as part of that plot would be very advantageous: The CIA could use his house as the sniper's nest and/or even blame him for Fidel's murder. Cubela was both a disgruntled official and one who—because of his extensive travels—came in contact with Russians overseas more often than most Cuban officials. Blaming Cubela for Fidel's murder might also let the CIA implicate Russia in Fidel's assassination.

Someone in the CIA, most likely David Morales, arranged for Cubela to be in a meeting with his case officer in Paris on November 22, 1963, at the exact time JFK was scheduled to be riding in an open car through Dallas. If Morales arranged that as part of his work with Johnny Rosselli, it was the perfect way to force Helms to hide a great deal of information from internal CIA investigators and other high US officials, which is exactly what happened. Americans would not learn about the Cubela operation until twelve years after JFK's murder, and it was never revealed to the Warren Commission.

Richard Helms also approved keeping the CIA's European assassin recruiter, QJWIN, on the payroll throughout 1963, despite his released files showing a complete lack of results. William Harvey originally supervised QJWIN, but after David Morales took over Harvey's supervision of Johnny Rosselli in June 1963, it's likely that Morales had some role with QJWIN as well. The mysterious QJWIN was part of the CIA's ZR/RIFLE assassination program. CIA files indicate that ZR/RIFLE had been applied to the Castro problem and that QJWIN made a 1963 trip to Florida for an operation involving Johnny Rosselli. However, the ZR/RIFLE program then disappears from the CIA files that have been released, and William Harvey later admitted in Senate testimony that some of his "notes" about ZR/RIFLE were "missing [and] had been destroyed." As a result, the true identity of QJWIN remains unresolved, with various CIA memos and sources giving different names.* Files and testimony say that QJWIN's job was to recruit assassins from the underworld and that he was involved in narcotics trafficking in Europe in the early 1960s.

The CIA files of the European criminal assassins that QJWIN tried to recruit—especially those with last names beginning with "M"—are all heavily censored. Santo Trafficante's French Connection heroin associate Michel Victor Mertz has two dozen parallels with QJWIN. Mertz could have been recruited by QJWIN, and/or it would have been easy for Mertz to have assumed QJWIN's role or clandestine identity. As detailed in an upcoming chapter, declassified files show that Mertz was deported from Dallas soon after JFK's murder, and other evidence implicates him in the crime.

Michel Victor Mertz is a little-known but important figure in the JFK plot due to his long ties to Trafficante and Marcello's heroin network. It was Mertz who perfected the technique of smuggling heroin hidden in cars on ocean liners, as depicted in the award-winning film *The French Connection*. Though Mertz was a deadly assassin, he also had ties to French intelligence (the SDECE) and had saved the life of French President Charles de Gaulle in 1961 after infiltrating an anti–de Gaulle group by getting into a fistfight while pretending to be against de Gaulle. Mertz was considered "untouchable" by French authorities, and he often visited America. He made a trip to Louisiana in 1963 using the alias of an anti–de Gaulle activist who'd had contact with the CIA.

---

*Released files about QJWIN are still censored, though William Harvey's notes identify him as José Marie Mankel. But Harvey's notes also say that his ZR/RIFLE files should be "forged and backdated." Other notes indicate that Mankel was only QJWIN-1 and that assassins he recruited were also called QJWIN. Other people identified by historians as QJWIN include Moses Maschkivitzan, Jean Voignier, and Michel Mancuso.

In addition to QJWIN and the Cubela portions of the CIA–Mafia plots, Carlos Marcello, Santo Trafficante, and Johnny Rosselli continued their connections to the Castro assassination plots, though only Rosselli was supposed to be involved. Historians have questioned how much of the mob bosses' efforts were really directed at Fidel—and how much those same efforts were part of their plan to kill JFK remains a question. For example, historian Richard Mahoney concluded that "under the CIA penumbra, Rosselli could move guns and assassins in relative secrecy. All experienced murderers seek cover. By putting the Agency's fingerprints on [Mafia] operations, the mob could anticipate that the CIA would [be forced to] cooperate in the cover-up" of crucial information related to JFK's assassination.

Marcello, Trafficante, and Rosselli could meet to discuss their plan to assassinate JFK, safe from law-enforcement surveillance. While Marcello was under pressure from RFK's Justice Department, the New Orleans FBI agent in charge of Marcello claimed the godfather was merely a lowly "tomato salesman" who was not involved in organized crime.* Marcello was not bugged or wiretapped—or closely monitored by the local FBI—so Trafficante felt comfortable visiting him in New Orleans. In 1963 Johnny Rosselli visited New Orleans and met with Guy Banister, according to one of Banister's secretaries. Mafia protocol makes it almost certain that Mafia don Rosselli also met with Marcello. In addition, Marcello, Trafficante, and Rosselli sometimes met at a secluded resort outside Tampa, the Safety Harbor Spa, whose exclusive clientele and distinctive staff freed the mob bosses from any possibility of law-enforcement surveillance.

---

*The FBI's hands-off approach to Marcello might be explained by Johnny Rosselli's boasts to Jimmy "The Weasel" Fratianno that Hoover was once arrested for homosexual acts in New Orleans.

As a corollary to RFK's pressure on Rosselli's boss Sam Giancana, the FBI monitored Rosselli's movements—except when he was on CIA business in Florida. While FBI surveillance reports for Rosselli exist for other times and places, no surveillance reports for his time in Florida in 1963 have yet been released—if they still exist.

One reason for the missing records might be Johnny Rosselli's meetings with Jack Ruby in Miami in late September and early October 1963. Investigative journalist Scott Malone confirmed that "Ruby met secretly with Johnny Rosselli in Miami" on two occasions in that time span. Malone says that "Rosselli was under FBI surveillance" part of the time, and "an FBI agent familiar with the case says that Rosselli was indeed in Miami when the meetings with Ruby are supposed to have occurred" and that "investigators were able to identify the exact motel rooms [where] the meetings occurred." When Congressional investigator Michael Ewing wrote a meticulously detailed nine-page analysis of Scott Malone's six-page article after it was released—noting anything even slightly in error—he pointed out no problems with the article's description of the fall 1963 Ruby–Rosselli meetings in Miami.

Notorious Chicago hit man Charles Nicoletti, another member of Rosselli's Mafia family, also joined the CIA–Mafia plots in the fall of 1963, according to the *Miami Herald* and United Press International. A Senate hearing had exposed Nicoletti's 1962 arrest in a specially modified vehicle that the press called a "hit car" and that had "a hidden compartment [behind] the front seat [that was] fitted with brackets to hold shotguns and rifles [and was so large] that a machine gun could be secreted in the compartment." Cuban officials and unconfirmed US accounts say that Nicoletti also became part of the mob's plan to kill JFK, as did Herminio Diaz, another mob hit man who worked for Santo Trafficante.*

Diaz had recently left Cuba to join Trafficante in Florida. Cuban authorities described him as "a hit man" since the 1940s who had tried to assassinate the President of Costa Rica in 1956. In 1963 Diaz began working on the CIA–Mafia plots for Trafficante and was also of great interest to David Morales's supervisor, Miami CIA Station Chief Ted Shackley. The CIA was especially interested in Diaz because in his first interview in the United States with David Morales's Cuban exile agents, Diaz mentioned Juan Almeida and Rolando Cubela as part of a group of disgruntled Cuban officials who wanted to act against Castro. Diaz had probably acquired the information second- or third-hand from Trafficante (or Bernard Barker), but even though Diaz got some of the details wrong, his mention of Almeida and Cubela was enough to get the CIA's attention. Despite another CIA asset's comment that Diaz was "fond of gambling and capable of committing any crime for money," the CIA considered using Diaz as an "agent candidate or . . . asset."

It was important for the success of the mob bosses' plot to kill JFK that the trusted men they brought into the plan—Diaz, Charles Nicoletti, Michel Victor Mertz, and John Martino—all had intelligence ties. That gave them cover for their work on the plot, plus ways to feed disinformation to the agencies they worked for, before and after JFK's murder. The bosses knew that the agencies might also be reluctant to investigate their own assets, especially when there was someone else who could be blamed.

---

*Also known as Herminio Diaz Garcia.

Carlos Marcello was also still involved in the CIA–Mafia plots in the summer and fall of 1963. Historian Dr. David Kaiser wrote that "Marcello had been involved in the CIA–mafia plot against Castro from the very beginning" and was still working on it into the summer of 1963. At that time, another detective working for Marcello, Sam Benton, assisted in the CIA–Mafia plots in both Louisiana and Miami.

Marcello was also backing Cuban exile groups. The main exile group the godfather supported was the New Orleans branch of Tony Varona's Cuban Revolutionary Council, which also involved David Ferrie. The Cuban Revolutionary Council had originally been organized by E. Howard Hunt with the assistance of Bernard Barker.

Varona, Hunt, and Barker were now working on the JFK–Almeida coup plan with Harry Williams while also continuing to work on the CIA–Mafia plots. It's easy to see how the lines become blurred between the covert Cuban operations that JFK and the CIA Director had authorized and the unauthorized operations Richard Helms was hiding from them. Helms may not have minded the crossover—he might have even welcomed it—since it gave him cover if problems arose with his unauthorized operations. It was probably also easier for him to manage the operations by using some of the same personnel, such as Morales, FitzGerald, Barker, Artime, and Cubela, on both the authorized and unauthorized activities.

Unfortunately, that also gave the mob bosses access to potentially compromise each exile component of the JFK–Almeida coup plan. In addition to Harry Williams, the exiles leaders the Kennedys wanted for their operation were Artime, Varona, Manolo Ray, and Eloy Menoyo.* The mob bosses attempted to link each to either the CIA–Mafia plots or to Lee Oswald in the summer and fall of 1963, and they often succeeded.

---

*His full name is Eloy Gutiérrez Menoyo.

The Mafia's effort to intimidate, buy off, or kill Harry Williams began in the summer of 1963. Kennedy aides and Robert Kennedy's phone logs agree that Harry Williams sometimes stayed at Robert Kennedy's New York apartment, as Williams undertook extensive travels for RFK. On one occasion in 1963, former death squad leader Rolando Masferrer—accompanied by two thugs described as looking like Mafia "torpedoes"—confronted Williams there. Masferrer was an associate of both Santo Trafficante and John Martino. Masferrer insisted on joining Williams's operation, but knowing the Kennedys had banned Masferrer from receiving US backing, Williams refused to be intimidated. Masferrer left.

Next Trafficante tried to bribe Williams. Bernard Barker had apparently arranged for Williams to meet with the CIA security officer for the JFK–Almeida coup plan at a Miami restaurant. During the meeting, the CIA officer excused himself and Williams was called over to the table of Santo Trafficante, who offered Williams a bribe. Williams declined, and when the CIA officer returned, the Agency man made no mention of Trafficante or the bribe.

Since Williams resisted intimidation and bribery, Trafficante tried one final approach. Later in the summer of 1963, Williams traveled to Guatemala City to confer with Manuel Artime, a trip that Barker had also likely helped arrange. While Williams dined at a restaurant the night before the scheduled meeting, two gunmen attacked him. He barely escaped after shooting one of them. Back in his hotel, Williams immediately called RFK. The Attorney General told him to leave the country as soon as possible. It's important to note that Williams was in touch with the FBI before and after the incident (Bureau agents had warned Williams to be careful, which is why he was carrying a pistol), but Williams's FBI file—like his CIA file—has never been released. The few memos about Williams released in other documents prove that his FBI and CIA files in 1963 alone would have been quite extensive given the high-profile people he met with.

As mentioned earlier, a summer 1963 CIA memo says that exile leader Tony Varona was bribed with $200,000 (more than $1 million today) from Rosselli's boss Giancana. The CIA learned of the bribe from Mafia member Richard Cain, who had been involved in the CIA–Mafia plots since 1960. After bugging a Communist embassy in Mexico City the previous year, Cain began working for the CIA as an asset in the summer of 1963, while he was also Chief Investigator for the Chicago/Cook County Sheriff. CIA memos later withheld from Congressional investigators show that Cain's information about Tony Varona traveled via an unusually secure channel directly to Desmond FitzGerald, the CIA official working closely with Richard Helms. That secure channel to FitzGerald and Helms would also soon be used to convey troubling information about Lee Oswald.

However, at the time of Varona's bribe, perhaps CIA officials like Helms saw nothing wrong with the payment, since Varona, Giancana, and Cain had all been working for the CIA on the CIA–Mafia plots. But after JFK's murder, Varona's Mafia bribe would be yet another explosive piece of information that Helms would have to hide from his own CIA Director. The Agency also had in its files incriminating remarks Varona made to former death squad leader Rolando Masferrer just weeks after Varona received his $200,000 bribe. In the late summer of 1963, Varona ominously told Masferrer that he would help remove certain "obstacles" preventing Masferrer from getting US backing, something possible only if JFK was no longer President.

Manuel Artime, E. Howard Hunt's good friend, was called by some exiles the CIA's "golden boy." His part of the JFK–Almeida coup plan was so important that the CIA assigned it a separate code-name, AMWORLD, and its own supersecure communications network at the Miami CIA station. Congressional investigators later documented the lavish support the CIA gave Artime: "four bases, two in Costa Rica and two in Nicaragua," with "two large ships, eight small vessels, two speed boats, three planes, and more than 200 tons of weapons and armaments and about $250,000 in electronic equipment."

Unlike Varona, Artime was probably not a knowing participant in the plan to kill JFK. In the late 1970s, shortly before Artime's death, Congressional investigator Gaeton Fonzi received information that Artime had "guilty knowledge" of the crime, but that could have come after JFK's murder. Artime received so much support from the CIA and the Kennedys—and was slated for such a major role in Cuba if the coup succeeded—that he would seem to have nothing to gain by helping kill JFK before the coup. However, CIA files withheld from Congress make it clear that not only was Artime working on the CIA–Mafia plots but the CIA looked at using the Mafia to provide cover for all the weapons it was providing to Artime. Those Agency memos also show that the CIA was well aware of the talk of Mafia activity that swirled around Artime.

Artime's operations were further compromised when they were linked to Lee Oswald. In the summer of 1963, David Ferrie reportedly took Oswald to a small training camp outside of New Orleans that supplied recruits for Artime's camps in Central America.

The Mafia would also try to compromise liberal exile leader Manolo Ray, whose reputation for integrity seemed to render him incorruptible. Trafficante and Marcello's men thus took an indirect approach to tie Lee Oswald to Ray and his exile group. In the late summer of 1963, Oswald appears to have made an unusual visit to

Silvia Odio, a female member of Ray's group in Dallas. Odio's father was in prison in Cuba because of a Castro assassination attempt by Alpha 66's Antonio Veciana. With no advance notice, an American and two Cuban exiles appeared at the door of Odio's Dallas apartment. The American was introduced to her as "Leon Oswald." Both Odio and her sister saw the three men. The day after the unusual visit, one of the exiles phoned Odio to make the provocative claim that Oswald was a former Marine, an expert marksman who said the exiles "should have assassinated Kennedy after the Bay of Pigs."

More than two months later, after the JFK assassination, both Silvia Odio and her sister recognized Oswald during TV coverage. Gaeton Fonzi extensively investigated and documented the Oswald–Odio meeting, finding Odio and her sister's account very credible. The provocative visit appears to have been engineered with the assistance of two Trafficante associates: John Martino, who'd met Odio's sister in Dallas, and Rolando Masferrer, whose brother lived in Odio's apartment complex. It was another example of explosive information— information that would cause problems for investigators and intelligence agencies when it surfaced—being planted months before JFK's murder. Indeed, Odio's story would cause major last-minute problems for the Warren Commission, until an associate of Trafficante—Loran Hall—indicated that it was he and his friends who made the visit, not Oswald. However, after the *Warren Report* was published, Hall denied making the visit.

One by one, Marcello, Trafficante, and their men attempted to compromise or link to JFK's upcoming murder the handful of Cuban exile leaders and groups involved in the JFK–Almeida coup plan. What they did to link exile leader Eloy Menoyo's group to Oswald is described later in this book.

As for Trafficante and Marcello, their motivation to kill JFK only increased during the summer and early fall of 1963. New developments in their cases help explain their extensive and careful plans to assassinate the President. Trafficante was fighting the IRS—the same organization that had sent Al Capone to prison—and three of his brothers were also named in the IRS complaint. Marcello faced an upcoming federal trial in New Orleans. The Justice Department attorney presenting the case against him would be one of RFK's own Mafia prosecutors, meaning this was one trial that Marcello couldn't buy his way out of with bribes to local or state authorities. Any conviction could result in another deportation, and Marcello was still scarred with the memory of that traumatic experience.

Marcello was not alone among mob bosses in his hatred of John and Robert Kennedy. Though the FBI had not wiretapped Marcello's phones and had placed only one minor wiretap on Trafficante, RFK's pressure had resulted in the FBI's wiretapping other mob leaders, who vented their rage at the Kennedys. Bureau agents heard one Philadelphia mobster complain, "With Kennedy, a guy should take a knife . . . and stab and kill that fucker, I mean it." The mob chief of Buffalo went even further, saying of the Kennedys, "They should kill the whole family." Marcello differed from them in two ways: He had more to lose, more quickly, from the Kennedys' assault. And because Marcello headed America's oldest Mafia family, he didn't need approval from the other bosses on the national Mafia "commission" before pursuing major hits, like killing JFK.

Jimmy Hoffa appears to have been aware of Marcello and Trafficante's plan to kill JFK, but he couldn't take an active role because of the intense scrutiny he was under from Robert Kennedy's Justice Department. Hoffa was being investigated (and eventually charged)

on three fronts, basically—in the words of historian David Kaiser—
"involving his use of union funds—particularly pension funds—to
enrich himself and others." Recipients of Teamster pension fund loans
included Marcello and Trafficante, and the latter shared an attorney—
Frank Ragano—with Hoffa. Kaiser points out that Ragano later said
that on July 23, "he met Hoffa in Washington" before leaving to see
Marcello and Trafficante. Hoffa gave him a message to take to the godfathers. Hoffa wanted Ragano to tell them, "Something has to be done.
The time has come for your friend [Trafficante] and Carlos to get rid of
him, kill that son-of-a-bitch John Kennedy. This has got to be done. Be
sure to tell them what I said . . . we're running out of time—something
has to be done."

According to Ragano, he delivered the message, and "the two men
looked at one another in icy silence and did not respond." Of course,
by that time Marcello and Trafficante had already been carefully planning JFK's murder for at least nine months. Ragano later wrote that he
didn't take Hoffa's demand seriously. But Ragano's behavior in the fall
of 1963—including publicly toasting JFK's murder with Trafficante on
the night of the assassination and, as reported in an FBI file, handling a
huge sum of cash for the assassination—indicates that Ragano played
a larger role in JFK's murder than the attorney ever admitted.

Johnny Rosselli was also feeling pressure from Robert Kennedy in
the summer of 1963 since RFK had targeted his boss Sam Giancana;
the Attorney General "pushed to get Giancana at any cost," according to Mafia prosecutor William Hundley (who would later learn
of Rosselli's confession to JFK's murder). In the summer of 1963,
Hundley represented the Justice Department at the Chicago hearing
on Sam Giancana's lawsuit to end the devastating "lockstep" surveillance the FBI had him under.

To stall the government's questioning of him, Giancana apparently helped leak a story to a reporter with the *Chicago Sun-Times*, which ran an article stating that "Sam Giancana had done work for the CIA," helping the Agency with intelligence related to Cuba in 1960. The newspaper item didn't mention assassination, but it did reveal the October 1960 bugging incident with Giancana and singer Phyllis McGuire that had involved the CIA. The article produced two major results: First, Hundley had to back off from questioning Giancana during the court hearing for fear he might reveal the CIA–Mafia plots, which RFK had been told had ended the previous year. Giancana won the suit; the ruling forced the FBI to stay farther away from him. Even so, RFK didn't let up the pressure and soon began working on a plan to drive the Mafia out of Las Vegas, threatening to eliminate a major source of revenue for Giancana, the Chicago Mafia, and especially Johnny Rosselli.

The second major result of the *Chicago Sun-Times* article was that it caught the attention of CIA Director John McCone, leading to another fateful decision for Richard Helms. Instead of giving McCone the full story of the CIA–Mafia plots to kill Fidel, Helms instead told McCone that the plots had lasted only from 1960 to May 1962 and had ended. Helms didn't inform the CIA Director that he was continuing the plots into 1963 without authorization. He couldn't do so without losing his position.

The CIA–Mafia plots were a deep secret even within the CIA, with only a handful of trusted officials like Desmond FitzGerald, Helms's protégé E. Howard Hunt, David Morales, and William Harvey still working on them. Helms must have felt confident that his dark secret would never leak, even within the Agency.

CHAPTER 11

Oswald in New Orleans, Dallas, and Mexico City

K ENNEDY AIDES EXPLAINED to me—and declassified files confirm—that ultimate control for the JFK–Almeida coup plan rested
with Robert Kennedy, acting on behalf of President Kennedy. They delegated the leading role in the coup plan to Army Secretary Cyrus Vance,
named as the "Executive Agent of the Department of Defense for Policy
toward Cuba"; Joint Chiefs Chairman Maxwell Taylor; and General
Joseph Carroll, head of the Defense Intelligence Agency. Secretary of
State Dean Rusk told me why he and Defense Secretary McNamara
couldn't have had a knowing role in the JFK–Almeida coup plan while
it was being developed: They had far too many aides and staff and met
too frequently with the press—so it would have been impossible to
maintain the coup plan's tight secrecy. Rusk said he understood that
and wasn't angry when he found out soon after JFK's death that the
extensive plans that he, McNamara, and other officials had been making over the summer and fall were not "just in case" contingency plans
but were for a real coup that was just days away when JFK died.

Harry Williams told me that E. Howard Hunt resented the fact
that the CIA had only a supporting role in the JFK–Almeida coup
plan. That was probably also true for Hunt's mentor Richard Helms

and may have been one reason Helms kept pursuing the unauthorized CIA–Mafia plots.

One of the most important of the CIA's "supporting operations" for the upcoming coup to topple Castro was "the introduction by CIA as soon as practicable of assets into Cuba for the development of intelligence . . . and the development of a suitable cover plan," according to long-secret declassified files from 1963—never shown to the Warren Commission or the House Select Committee—that I was the first to quote in 2005. This important CIA attempt to move "assets into Cuba" would accelerate through the summer and into the fall and would include several men linked to JFK's assassination, including Lee Oswald.

The CIA allies of Marcello, Trafficante, and Rosselli working on the JFK–Almeida coup plan—including David Morales, Bernard Barker, and David Ferrie—would use the Agency's efforts to put "assets into Cuba" as part of their plot to kill JFK. In that regard, Rosselli's friend David Morales was in a position to influence the actions of CIA officer David Atlee Phillips, while Trafficante's man Barker could impact the actions of E. Howard Hunt—all without Phillips or Hunt being aware that Morales and Barker were really acting on behalf of the mob bosses.

Marcello's men David Ferrie and Guy Banister had the important task of using the CIA's plan for getting "assets into Cuba" to make Lee Oswald look guilty after JFK was murdered. Oswald's covert activities appear to have been largely controlled by Banister and Ferrie during at least the first nine months of 1963. On one hand, Ferrie and Banister were acting for US intelligence, as later described by New Orleans Deputy CIA Chief Hunter Leake and Victor Marchetti, former Special Assistant to Richard Helms, both quoted in earlier chapters. (Since their main CIA files remain unreleased, it's not clear whom in the CIA Ferrie and Banister were reporting to, though David Atlee Phillips was involved by the summer of 1963.) However, at the same time, Banister and Ferrie were also acting on behalf of their employer, Carlos Marcello, making sure many of Oswald's activities would later make him look guilty of JFK's murder. Banister and Ferrie both hated Fidel, and aside from whatever Marcello was paying them, they no doubt hoped that blaming JFK's death on a seemingly pro-Castro Communist would trigger the US invasion of Cuba that both men knew was being planned.

Lee Oswald's public activities in New Orleans in August 1963 are incredibly well documented because of extensive media coverage of them at the time, which resurfaced quickly on television and radio after he was accused of shooting JFK. Oswald first tried to join the local chapter of the DRE, an American anti-Castro group that grew out of Cubela's old DR group in Cuba. While meeting with the head of the tiny New Orleans DRE chapter, Oswald claimed that he wanted to overthrow Fidel. Shortly after that, Oswald presented a completely opposite impression by very publicly passing out pro-Castro Fair Play for Cuba Committee leaflets on the street in New Orleans, an act that provoked an attack by the same DRE official and two of his associates. Oswald's arrest led to newspaper coverage as well as radio and TV appearances, in which he handled himself remarkably well. How could Oswald—or any lone left-winger in the conservative South—generate so much publicity? Court records indicate that a "Mr. Phillips [with US intelligence] from Washington" met with Banister at his office in New Orleans and that they discussed an anti-Castro TV appeal. Dr. Gerald McKnight later confirmed that it was indeed CIA propaganda specialist David Atlee Phillips who'd met with Banister the previous year. Recall that earlier Phillips had run an operation against the Fair Play for Cuba Committee, and according to E. Howard Hunt's sworn testimony to Congressional investigators, David Phillips also ran the DRE for the CIA. Thus in 1963 Oswald was dealing with two organizations involving Phillips, the DRE, and the Fair Play for Cuba Committee.

CIA files confirm that at the same time Oswald was generating remarkable publicity, David Atlee Phillips was working on Manuel Artime's AMWORLD portion of the JFK–Almeida coup plan. The actions of Phillips and Oswald reveal that Oswald's unusual pro-Castro publicity blitz was part of the CIA's efforts to place US intelligence assets in Cuba. That would include a face-to-face meeting with Oswald within weeks of Oswald's publicity blitz, followed by Oswald's trip to Mexico City as he attempted to leverage that publicity into permission to fly to Cuba.

Before looking more closely into those activities, it's important to focus on aspects of Oswald's New Orleans street fight incident that the Warren Commission didn't know about—or chose to ignore. Gerald McKnight observed that during Oswald's "five months in New Orleans all his known activities were consistent with what is called in the intelligence game 'building a cover.'" On May 26, 1963, Oswald had "founded" a New Orleans chapter of the Fair Play for Cuba Committee entirely by mail, and it had exactly one member—Lee Oswald. Moreover, he never made a serious effort to recruit anyone else; he continued to avoid real American Communists and Socialists who might have been sympathetic to Cuba.

Dr. McKnight points out that instead, before the leaflet incident that led to Oswald's arrest, he took the unlikely recruiting step of first passing out pro-Castro "'Hands off Cuba' flyers to Navy personnel attached to the aircraft carrier USS Wasp, at New Orleans' Dumaine Street Wharf on June 15, 1963." Only nine months after the tense naval action during the Cuban Missile Crisis, it would be hard to find a group less likely to favorably respond to pro-Castro flyers than US Navy personnel. Clearly, Oswald hoped to provoke a reaction from them, preferably in the form of a punch or other physical altercation that he could leverage into an arrest record and publicity. However, the Wasp's crew only complained, and "Oswald was peacefully sent on his way," notes McKnight.

Oswald's first leafleting incident, on June 15, occurred when he was working for the Reilly Coffee Company, run by William Reilly, a staunch anti-Communist who hated Castro. David Kaiser writes that Reilly "was deeply involved in" INCA, "a private propaganda organization attempting to combat Communist influence in Latin America and the United States." Oswald was officially "fired" from his job there on July 19, but four weeks later he debated the director of INCA on live radio in New Orleans.

After leaving the Reilly Coffee Company, Oswald held no job—officially at least—for the next three months. Unofficially witnesses—including a CIA asset—saw him working for and with Guy Banister and David Ferrie. Oswald would have earned little money, since he was still under "tight" surveillance by Naval Intelligence, in hopes that the KGB would try to contact either him or Marina, so he couldn't appear to have significant, unexplained sums of money. In addition, keeping Oswald low on funds was a way for Banister and CIA officers like David Phillips to ensure that he had little choice but to do what they asked in hopes of a large payday down the road.

As Oswald prepared for his second attempt to get himself arrested for passing out leaflets, one building, with two addresses, became important. Dr. Kaiser points out that some of Oswald's pro-Castro Fair Play for Cuba Committee leaflets were stamped with the address "FPCC 544 Camp St." Kaiser writes, "This was one of two addresses used by a corner building, the other being 532 Lafayette Street, where Guy Banister Associates had [their] offices." Banister was of course staunchly anti-Castro, and the addresses are simply one more indication that Oswald was working for Banister in the leaflet operation.

As noted earlier, historian Richard Mahoney documented that six witnesses saw Oswald with Ferrie or Banister in the summer of 1963; two of them said that Oswald was working for Banister at that time. Declassified files and Michael Kurtz later revealed additional witnesses. One uncovered by Kurtz, Consuela Martin, provides a new explanation of why Banister's office address appeared on the pro-Castro leaflets. Kurtz writes that Martin's office was next to Banister's and that "she saw Oswald in Banister's office at least half a dozen times in the late spring and summer of 1963. . . . On every one of these occasions, Oswald and Banister were together." Oswald sometimes asked her to do translating work for him by typing documents into Spanish. Martin believes that the 544 Camp Street address was used in hopes of luring unsuspecting pro-Castro leftists to Banister's office, thus yielding more information for Banister's voluminous files on leftists, all of whom he viewed as Communists.

Though no one would suggest that Oswald was as far right or anti-Communist as Banister, in the Cold War environment of the early 1960s, many liberals—most notably John and Robert Kennedy—were also anti-Communist. David Kaiser points out that far from being a "sincere" member of the far left, Oswald "only embarrassed the [Fair Play for Cuba Committee] and the Castro cause in the New Orleans area, and his behavior throughout resembled that of an agent provocateur rather than a genuine" Communist, Marxist, or other member of the far left, no matter what Oswald claimed in his media appearances.

Aside from Oswald's using the address for Banister's building on some of his pamphlets, there is one other curious fact about them. Oswald handed out copies of the first printing of *The Crime against Cuba*, a pro-Castro pamphlet printed in the United States in 1961. One copy wound up as FBI evidence after the assassination. However, Oswald was in Russia in 1961, when the first printing sold out. Only the fourth printing of the pamphlet was available when Oswald returned to the United States and in the summer of 1963. Oswald would have needed help in obtaining dozens of copies of the long-sold-out first printing. It's possible that Banister ordered one or two copies for his files in 1961, but he had no reason to order dozens of copies. The pamphlet's author was ninety years old when researcher James DiEugenio located him, but he had saved a copy of the three-dollar "28 June 1961" purchase order he had received for forty-five copies from the "Central Intelligence Agency, Mailroom Library, Washington 25, D.C." Those first-printing pamphlets had been ordered when David Atlee Phillips was running operations targeting the Fair Play for Cuba Committee, making Phillips a possible source of pro-Castro literature for Oswald's PR efforts.

Though Oswald wouldn't succeed in provoking a fight by handing out leaflets until August 9, 1963, five days BEFORE that—in a letter postmarked August 4—Oswald had written to the New York office of the Fair Play for Cuba Committee. In the letter Oswald says that his "street demonstration was attacked" by "some Cuban-exile(s)" and that he was "officially cautioned by police." Clearly, Oswald was writing about what he planned to have happen six days later. In addition, Dick Russell notes that despite Oswald's repeated writing to the Fair Play for Cuba Committee—whose mail the FBI closely monitored—and other Communist organizations, Oswald's name "was never included on either part of the [FBI's] Security Index, not even after he went on to set up his highly visible Fair Play for Cuba chapter." Oswald's absence from the list was especially odd since he was a former defector to the Soviet Union, so Russell asks, "[H]ad the FBI received word from someone to keep a relative distance from Oswald . . . because he was considered part of another intelligence operation?" The Warren Commission was never able to satisfactorily answer that question because if Oswald had been on the Security Index, he would certainly have been subject to law-enforcement attention on the day of JFK's motorcade in Dallas.

The local DRE chapter in New Orleans was run by a Cuban exile named Carlos Bringuier. While the DRE was a real organization managed by the CIA, the New Orleans chapter was tiny. FBI files indicate that it had only one delegate, Bringuier, and that its activities "were limited to propaganda-type efforts . . . in any available channel of the news media." Oswald first approached Bringuier on August 5, in his clothing store, offering to help train "anti-Castro guerilla fighters." Bringuier, an acquaintance of David Ferrie, was suspicious of Oswald and declined his offer.

Four days later, on August 9, Oswald returned to the area to promote himself publicly as proudly pro-Castro. As Dr. McKnight points out, "Oswald had noted in his address book the concentration of Cuban exile stores" in the area of his demonstration, and "if he wanted to make sure to attract Bringuier's attention, he was in the very heart of New Orleans' [exile] community." Oswald was handing out "Hands off Cuba" flyers "and wearing a placard round his waist with 'Viva Fidel' written in large black block letters." Oswald soon engaged in a confrontation with Bringuier and two friends. Oswald provoked Bringuier by dropping his hands and putting "his face close to the enraged, burly Cuban, and taunt[ing], 'OK, Carlos, if you want to hit me, hit me.' At that point in the confrontation the police arrived and arrested all four men for creating a public disturbance."

A New Orleans police lieutenant who talked to Oswald after his arrest later testified to the Warren Commission that Oswald "seemed to have set them [the exiles] up, so to speak, to create an incident." The police lieutenant also said that Oswald "liked the President," a sentiment shared by most people who ever heard Oswald mention JFK. A police sergeant observed that Oswald "knows very little about [the Fair Play for Cuba Committee] that he belongs to and its ultimate purpose or goal." A New Orleans attorney later testified to the Warren Commission that "Oswald had told him he was being paid to hand out pro-Castro leaflets on the streets of New Orleans."

However, Oswald's arrest and subsequent trial were "prominently reported in the New Orleans papers" and on TV, which seems to have been the goal for both David Atlee Phillips—who was trying to build Oswald's pro-Castro credentials so he could get into Cuba— and Banister, who wanted to make Oswald look like a pro-Castro Communist.

In addition to Guy Banister, two other Marcello connections are evident upon close inspection of Oswald's August 1963 incident. John Martino's son told a former Congressional investigator that in August 1963, Martino "saw Lee Harvey Oswald passing out pro-Castro leaflets in New Orleans." That is around the time that witnesses place Martino with Carlos Marcello and Guy Banister. Historian Kurtz cites the former Superintendent of the New Orleans Police Department as saying that Martino "met with Marcello himself at the Town and Country Motel," where Marcello had his office.

A close associate of Carlos Marcello's lieutenant Nofio Pecora arranged Oswald's release from jail, as documented by the Director of the House Select Committee on Assassinations. It's interesting that Jack Ruby had called Pecora just six days earlier.

According to historian Dr. John Newman, Oswald's August 12 trial "was well attended by local television and newspaper reporters." Only four days later, evidently unworried about being attacked or arrested again, Oswald once more passed out pro-Castro leaflets on a New Orleans street. Though unemployed, Oswald "reportedly hired two helpers, paying them $2 apiece to help pass out his pro-Castro leaflets." One of the men, who appeared Hispanic, has never been identified. Oswald passed out leaflets "for only a few minutes, yet the demonstration was filmed by WDSU-TV."

On August 17, 1963, a WDSU radio host contacted Oswald and invited him to be interviewed on a weekly radio show. The radio personality "admits he had been briefed by the FBI on Oswald's background." Oswald came across as very intelligent and well informed. On August 21, the WDSU radio host moderated a radio debate between Oswald, Carlos Bringuier, and Ed Butler, who worked with the anti-Communist propaganda group INCA (which included Oswald's former employer at the Reilly Coffee Company). Oswald was again articulate and did well in the debate—until he was confronted on the air about his defection to Russia, which he had not mentioned. Oswald was apparently not prepared for that, which seems odd since his defection was well publicized. However, the subject had the effect of discrediting the Fair Play for Cuba Committee to the listening public, which is what David Atlee Phillips had been trying to do for more than two years. According to author Dick Russell, "after the taping, Oswald popped into the WDSU-TV studio for a quick interview" and said "on film that he was a Marxist." That was good for helping Phillips build Oswald's pro-Castro persona, but that footage would be played endlessly after JFK's murder, cementing in much of the public's mind that Oswald was a dangerous Communist.

CIA OFFICER DAVID Atlee Phillips met with Oswald in Dallas in late August or early September 1963, apparently to debrief him after his New Orleans media appearances. Oswald had built a public and documented record as firmly pro-Castro and had handled a variety of situations well. Phillips was ready to prepare him for his next assignment: to be one of the US assets going to Mexico City to obtain Cuban permission to fly to Havana. While the United States could use speedboats to sneak assets and agents into Cuba at night, those people couldn't travel freely or openly talk to lower-level officials and the public and thus could not gauge the level of public support for the coup. Since the United States had no embassy or diplomatic relations with Cuba, and since travel to the island was severely restricted, the United States needed a number of assets who could travel openly. As a former defector to Russia, someone like Oswald was especially valuable because if he ever got into trouble, the United States could claim that the Russians were behind his activities.

Phillips's meeting with Oswald was unusual for two reasons: It occurred openly, in a public place in Dallas, and it involved Cuban exile leader Antonio Veciana of the CIA-backed exile group Alpha 66. Veciana and his Alpha 66 group were barred from the JFK–Almeida coup plan because of their earlier attack on a Russian ship in Cuban waters. However, Veciana was also very close partners with Eloy

Menoyo, one of the exile leaders the Kennedys and Harry Williams wanted to participate in the JFK–Almeida coup plan.

Veciana's story of meeting Oswald and Phillips in the lobby of the new Southland Building in Dallas has been controversial, though Congressional investigator Gaeton Fonzi concluded that such a meeting did take place. Veciana hinted that Phillips used the name Maurice Bishop, and CIA official Ross Crozier later confirmed that to Congressional investigators. Kurtz found new confirmation, saying that "Hunter Leake told me that David Atlee Phillips . . . used the alias [Maurice Bishop]." Veciana revealed to my researcher, Thom Hartmann, that he originally named his group Alpha 66 after the Phillips 66 gas stations that were common in the early 1960s.

David Atlee Phillips came from nearby Fort Worth, and by meeting Oswald in public—in the lobby of Dallas's newest glittering office tower—Phillips must have realized he could have been seen with Oswald by someone who knew him. Such behavior seems illogical and inconsistent with Phillips's long intelligence experience, unless Oswald was being used as an intelligence asset for an operation far from Dallas. In addition, it's hard to believe a veteran CIA officer like Phillips would be in public with Oswald in Dallas if he knew that Oswald was going to be an assassin or a patsy for JFK's assassination in that same city.

The Phillips–Oswald–Veciana meeting makes sense if Phillips was using Oswald in the CIA's anti-Castro operations as one of the US assets the Agency planned to move into Cuba before the coup. Apparently, Phillips hoped Oswald's pro-Castro media blitz would help him get into Cuba via Mexico City. Phillips was based in Mexico City, where he headed anti-Castro operations. In addition, Phillips played a major role in the CIA's Cuban operations based in the United States, ranging from being a part of the JFK–Almeida coup plan to handling Cuban exile groups like the DRE and Alpha 66, as well as generating anti-Castro propaganda and working against the Fair Play for Cuba Committee. Some of Phillips's most sensitive anti-Castro operations—for Washington CIA officials Richard Helms and Desmond FitzGerald—were kept secret from most others in the CIA, including Winston "Win" Scott, the CIA Chief of Station in Mexico City.

Antonio Veciana said that Phillips had summoned him from Miami to the Dallas meeting so they could "discuss plans . . . to kill Castro." Veciana also claimed that at the Dallas meeting, Oswald and Phillips were "talking about something that we can do to kill Castro." Gaeton Fonzi notes that David Morales also worked closely with Phillips. He wrote that "Morales was away from the [Miami CIA] Station a lot" in 1963, "usually . . . on trips to Mexico City." That close relationship between Morales and Phillips also meant that Johnny Rosselli could learn from his close friend Morales what Phillips was working on. In 1963 David Morales—who admitted helping to assassinate JFK— still outranked David Atlee Phillips and could easily have proposed to Phillips that he meet Oswald in public and that Veciana be allowed to see Oswald for some reason.

Years later Phillips wrote a never-published autobiographical manuscript, part fact and part fiction, which has been quoted in *Vanity Fair* and other publications. In it Phillips confirmed that Oswald was part of the CIA's effort to assassinate Fidel Castro. He added that President Kennedy was shot using "precisely the plan we had devised against Castro." Phillips wrote that the plan involved using "a sniper's rifle from an upper floor window of a building on the route where Castro often drove in an open jeep." In some ways, that confirms something indicated in later AMWORLD memos: The CIA planned to have Fidel shot in his open jeep as he drove into Varadero Beach.

On the other hand, Phillips built a long and decorated CIA career as a propagandist using half-truths, distortions, and lies, so what he wrote must be taken with a grain of salt. It was also probably designed as damage control in case files or testimony emerged that could harm the reputation of Phillips or the CIA. While there is probably some truth in what he wrote, Oswald was not an experienced assassin, and the CIA would have no more trusted him to murder Fidel than the Mafia would have used the inexperienced Oswald to shoot JFK. However, as with JFK's murder, Oswald did have the proper background to be an excellent patsy to take the blame for Castro's death. If Phillips had no knowing role in JFK's murder, it's also possible that someone like David Morales manipulated things so that Phillips—and Richard Helms—believed Oswald was a "bad apple" who used "the plan we had devised against Castro" to kill JFK. The result would have been—and was—that Helms and Phillips would withhold substantial amounts of crucial information from the press, the public, their superiors, and other agencies.

Based on the statements of both Phillips and Veciana, Oswald appears to have been involved in the CIA's attempts to kill Fidel Castro. That perhaps casts the meeting between Oswald and Marcello in a different light, since the godfather was also part of the CIA–Mafia plots to kill Fidel. Essentially, they were on the same side and doing work for the same agency.

AS FOR OSWALD, his recent flurry of activity and upcoming attempt to get to Cuba through Mexico City no doubt made him think his years of undercover toil were about to pay off in a big way. The FBI found telling notes that Oswald wrote and that the Warren Commission left out of its Report because they clashed with the Commission's view of

Oswald as an ardent Communist. Instead, they were included only in the Warren Commission's rarely seen twenty-six volumes of supporting material. In the notes, Oswald wrote that the United States and Russia "have too much to offer to each other to be tearing at each other's throats in an endless cold war. Both countries have major shortcomings and advantages, but only in ours is the voice of dissent allowed opportunity of expression."

Oswald makes it clear in these notes that he still hates Communism, writing, "[T]here are possibly few other Americans born in the US who [have] as many personal reasons to know—and therefore hate and mistrust—Communism." According to the Warren Commission, Oswald wrote these "Notes for a speech by Lee Harvey Oswald" but never delivered the speech. It was the kind of oration Oswald could have given only after he was no longer undercover and had been revealed as a US asset, perhaps scoring a lucrative book and television deal like his childhood idol from *I Led Three Lives*.

After meeting Phillips, but before going to Mexico City, Oswald apparently traveled from New Orleans to Dallas. There, someone—most likely someone working with the Mafia such as Martino, Banister, or Morales—manipulated Oswald into visiting Silvia Odio, thus linking him to both JFK's assassination and another of the exile groups in the JFK–Almeida coup plan. Oswald's Odio visit and the exile's follow-up phone call don't appear to have involved David Atlee Phillips because they seem to undermine what he was trying to do with Oswald. By connecting Oswald to several parts of the JFK–Almeida coup plan, those working for Marcello, Trafficante, and Rosselli could ensure that when Oswald surfaced as the main suspect, the CIA and other agencies would have to cover up much information to protect the coup plan—which is exactly what happened.

HISTORIAN JOHN NEWMAN, a twenty-year veteran of military intelligence, posed the question, "Why did Oswald come into contact with so many people with CIA connections in August and September 1963?" He named five individuals, but more have since emerged, including John Martino (whom the CIA admits was a CIA asset), David Ferrie, and David Atlee Phillips. One of those Newman named was William Gaudet, a CIA asset who worked for INCA's founder. It's now clear that Gaudet was part of the "tight" surveillance of Oswald mentioned earlier.

A former Senate investigator wrote that "before his death in 1981, Gaudet admitted witnessing Oswald's distribution of pro-Castro leaflets in" New Orleans. Historian Richard Mahoney says that when "Oswald applied for and received a Mexican tourist card (FM 824085) in New Orleans on September 17 (1963), the individual who received the tourist card with the previous number (FM 824084) was William George Gaudet . . . who had close ties to the local office of the CIA. Gaudet later admitted under oath that he had seen Oswald one day 'in deep conversation with [Banister] on Camp Street . . . they were leaning over and talking and it was an earnest conversation.' Gaudet said his impression was that Banister was asking Oswald to do something for him."

William Gaudet later saw Oswald in Mexico City, as he explained to Michael Kurtz. Gaudet's testimony is further proof that Oswald was involved in US intelligence activity in 1963. It also helps explain why he was never placed on the FBI's Security Index before Dallas. Yet Gaudet's observations are further proof that Oswald was working with Guy Banister, who was part of Carlos Marcello's plot to kill JFK.

WHOLE BOOKS AND a massive Congressional report have been written about the unusual aspects of Oswald's trip to Mexico City in late September 1963, when he apparently visited both the Cuban and Soviet embassies. However, for JFK's assassination, only a few facts are key. First is that Oswald visited the Cuban Embassy on the same day as two other unusual young men, and all three tried to get Cuban entry visas. One turned out later to be working for intelligence in Nicaragua, one of the countries where Manuel Artime had an AMWORLD base and worked with the intelligence service. Summers says the third young man "behaved as though he was on some sort of undercover mission in Mexico, and [his] movements ran parallel to Oswald's." This young man worked for intelligence in Costa Rica, which was the other country where Artime had an AMWORLD base. Thus all three young men appear linked to Manuel Artime. The CIA was clearly attempting to slip multiple assets into Cuba through Mexico City at the same time in the hope that some might get through.

Oswald was under surveillance by US intelligence in Mexico City, according to Win Scott, the CIA's Mexico City Station Chief. Scott said the CIA's hidden cameras photographed Oswald at the embassy, and he saw photos of Oswald there. The House Select Committee on Assassinations found additional evidence of the existence of photos of Oswald in Mexico City. However, only unrelated photos of someone else (who looked nothing like Oswald) would be furnished to the Warren Commission and eventually made public. That's probably because the CIA's photo surveillance operation in Mexico City was under the control of David Atlee Phillips, who was no doubt acting on orders from Richard Helms. One reason for withholding the Oswald–Mexico photos—and denying the CIA had known Oswald was in Mexico—would be that Oswald was involved in a highly sensitive, covert operation run by Phillips and Helms.

It was important for JFK's murder that someone didn't want Oswald to actually get to Cuba. We know that because five phony calls claiming to be from Oswald were made to the Russian and Cuban embassies while the real Oswald was in Mexico City. We know these calls, monitored for the CIA, weren't really from Oswald because the person (or persons) making them spoke broken Russian (in which Oswald was fluent) and excellent Spanish (a language Oswald didn't speak). The Mafia had the connections to ensure that he never got to Cuba. A Mexican police agency involved with Trafficante's heroin network monitored the Cuban and Russian embassy calls for the CIA while mobster (and active CIA asset) Richard Cain had formerly bugged a Communist embassy in Mexico City.

At the time of Oswald's visit, a flurry of odd cables flowed between the Mexico City CIA station and CIA headquarters in Washington along two different paths. One path carried accurate information about Oswald to Desmond FitzGerald and Richard Helms, while the other conveyed inaccurate information about him. *Washington Post* reporter Jefferson Morley interviewed a former CIA official who told him that "CIA records suggested that members of [FitzGerald's staff] seemed to be carefully guarding information about Oswald in the weeks before Kennedy was killed." The person managing both the accurate and the inaccurate information about Oswald was Richard Helms's assistant. After JFK's murder, and for almost three decades later, Helms maintained that before the assassination the CIA hadn't even noticed Oswald's embassy visits. Declassified files now show that claim to be completely false, as documented by historian and retired Major John Newman.

The actions of Oswald and the CIA are consistent with Oswald's being one of several US intelligence assets the CIA was trying to get into Cuba openly. In fact, a Warren Commission memo, left out of its Final Report, showed exactly how Oswald could have been planning to travel to Mexico City again, and on to Cuba, on November 22, 1963. As an American with a pro-Castro persona, Oswald could have openly walked the streets of Havana or Varadero Beach talking to Cubans and low-level officials.

Additionally, Oswald's time in Russia would have made it possible to blame any problem he had in Cuba on the Russians, something CIA notes by William Harvey indicate was always essential for an assassination mission. After analyzing many recently declassified files, Naval War College professor and historian David Kaiser concluded in 2008 that "in all probability, Oswald's attempt to reach Cuba via Mexico City . . . was designed to give him an opportunity to assassinate Castro." I agree with Kaiser that Oswald was trying to get into Cuba as part of an effort to eliminate Castro. But I disagree that Oswald intended "to assassinate Castro." He didn't have the experience necessary for such a task, and he'd never killed anyone. But he could have had a supporting role in a Castro elimination plot, and he would have made an excellent fall guy. Oswald had been part of an operation against Fidel when he was in Mexico City, and after his failure to get into Cuba, Oswald had probably been told—likely by Banister, Ferrie, or Martino—that he still was part of such an operation.

Even as Lee Oswald prepared to return to Dallas from Mexico City in early October 1963, one more important link was being forged between Oswald, JFK's assassination, and the JFK–Almeida coup plan. The training camp outside New Orleans where David Ferrie reportedly took Oswald was a sort of minor-league training camp for Manual Artime's AMWORLD portion of the JFK–Almeida coup plan. The camp's owner later said that "he bought arms from Ferrie, who in turn got them from US Army personnel who had stolen them." Declassified files show that some arms reported stolen from National Guard armories in the Texas area were actually being supplied to Cuban exile leaders like Manolo Ray's JURE group, which JFK and RFK wanted for their coup plan. Other military personnel were taking advantage of that situation by stealing and selling arms and keeping the money.

In October 1963 the Treasury Department tried to stop the trafficking in stolen arms with an undercover sting. Surprisingly, FBI and Treasury Department memos from that operation quote a Dallas gun dealer as giving a fairly accurate description of the upcoming JFK–Almeida coup plan. The Dallas gun dealer said that in "the last week of November 1963 . . . a large scale amphibious operation would take place against the Cuba mainland" and "United States military forces or government agencies would possibly be involved in this operation [which] involved an attack by rebel Cuban forces." Writers for the *Washington Post* linked longtime gunrunner Jack Ruby to that same stolen-military-arms ring. As for the gun dealer who accurately described the upcoming US action against Cuba, the *Washington Post* said he was the gun dealer who sold the bullets used in Oswald's rifle on November 22, 1963. That means even the bullet found in Oswald's rifle after JFK's assassination had been connected to the JFK–Almeida coup plan.

BY OCTOBER 1963, Carlos Marcello faced losing his empire, his freedom, and even the ability to stay in America—unless he ended Robert Kennedy's extraordinary power by killing JFK. Two dates in particular now loomed large for Marcello. He was scheduled to be tried in New Orleans on federal charges on November 1, 1963, with one of RFK's own Mafia prosecutors—John Diuguid—handling the trial. Anxious to avoid the deportation a conviction could bring, Marcello would soon begin efforts to bribe a key juror. However, that was at best only a temporary solution, since the godfather knew that even if he was not convicted, RFK would launch a new investigation as soon as that trial ended. (Indeed, the Justice Department would later prosecute him for bribing the juror.) RFK was already focusing on serious tax charges against Marcello, and the Mafia chief knew he would have no respite while JFK was alive.

Carlos Marcello knew he had to act before the coup took place and removed his only opportunity to force a cover-up by top US officials. Marcello had nothing to gain, and everything to lose, by allowing the JFK–Almeida coup plan to go forward. Robert Kennedy and aides such as Harry Williams had made it clear that as long as JFK was President, Cuba would never be a safe haven for Marcello, Trafficante, or any other Mafia boss.

The date for the coup was firming up to be sometime in early December 1963, something Marcello, Trafficante, and Rosselli could have learned from their CIA allies in the JFK plot, like David Morales and Bernard Barker. If Marcello killed JFK before the coup, it would force Robert Kennedy, CIA Director McCone, military leaders like General Maxwell Taylor, and others to withhold critical information from investigators, the press, and the public to prevent a confrontation with the Soviets that could go nuclear.

With the coup date looming, Marcello and the others organized attempts to kill JFK in November 1963 during motorcades in three different cities: Chicago, Tampa, and Dallas. Marcello relied on his trusted associates—the Chicago mob's Rosselli and Trafficante in Tampa—to help him oversee the plot.

First they would try to kill JFK during his long Chicago motorcade on November 2, 1963, the day after Marcello's trial was set to begin. The mob bosses' year of careful planning meant that even their backup plan (Tampa during JFK's November 18 motorcade) had a backup (Dallas on November 22) and that each city's Mafia family equally shared the risk. That risk would be minimized by the mob bosses' using only experienced men they knew they could trust.

The Mafiosi had come up with one basic plan that could be applied in each of the three cities. Because the opportunities were so close together, the bosses could use most of the same personnel for each attempt. Each of the three target cities had a key Mafia operative close to law enforcement who would monitor any leaks about—or investigations into—the JFK hit.

In Chicago, the mob's top "made" man in law enforcement was Richard Cain, who was also chief investigator for the Cook County Sheriff. The CIA continued to deal with Cain in the fall of 1963, giving him a pipeline not only into law enforcement but into intelligence as well. In Tampa, Trafficante's man was Sergeant Jack de la Llana, who had formed and become director of the Tampa Police Department's first criminal intelligence unit. As revealed in Senate hearings in October 1963, when de la Llana testified while posing as an honest cop, he was also "chairman of the Florida Intelligence Unit, a statewide agency which coordinates information . . . throughout the State of Florida." This cooperation even extended to other states, as shown when Sergeant de la Llana exchanged information with the New Orleans Police Department about the Fair Play for Cuba Committee. As described to me by Chief Mullins and others (who didn't realize de la Llana was working for Trafficante in 1963), de la Llana was the perfect man for the Tampa godfather to have on the force.

▲ Attorney General Robert Kennedy and President John F. Kennedy waged the largest war against the Mafia that America has ever seen. They especially targeted Louisiana-Texas godfather Carlos Marcello.

◀ In 1985, Carlos Marcello—for decades the most powerful godfather in America—confessed to an undercover FBI informant that he ordered the assassination of President Kennedy.

▲ The FBI obtained Marcello's JFK confession as part of a two-year undercover operation, code-named CAMTEX. In addition to his confession, Marcello talked on undercover FBI audio tapes about his meetings with Lee Oswald and Jack Ruby.

▲ Marcello's partner in JFK's murder was Tampa godfather Santo Trafficante (right), seen here with Marcello (left) in 1966. In 1979, the House Select Committee on Assassinations concluded JFK was likely murdered by a conspiracy and "found that Trafficante, like Marcello, had the motive, means, and opportunity to assassinate President Kennedy." Shortly before his death, Trafficante confessed his role in JFK's assassination to his attorney.

▲ Guy Banister, the former FBI Special Agent in charge of Chicago, worked as Marcello's private detective in 1963.

▲ David Ferrie, a pilot, also worked for Marcello in 1963.

```
OSWALD, LEE HARVEY
201-289248                          100-300-017
SEX M DOB ?                         DBC -12878
                                    09 APR 68
CIT ?                               FBI
OCC ?                               P10
MOREOVER, UNTIL THEN, THERE HAD BEEN NO
SECRET AS FAR AS ANYONE WAS CONCERNED IN
REGARD TO THE FACT THAT BANISTER DAVID
WILLIAM FERRIE AND SUBJ MAY HAVE KNOWN OR
BEEN ACQUAINTED WITH ONE ANOTHER.



WAS  DEFERRED
                                    R 6805270089
```

▲ The Assistant Chief of the New Orleans CIA office said that Banister, Ferrie, and Oswald performed work for the CIA in 1963. Numerous witnesses saw Oswald with Banister and Ferrie in the summer of 1963, and this CIA card shows the Agency was aware of their connections.

GARNER EXHIBIT 1

▲ In the summer of 1963, Lee Oswald got a significant amount of TV, radio, and newspaper publicity for his phony, one-man chapter of the Fair Play for Cuba Committee in New Orleans. Here, he passes out pro-Castro leaflets.

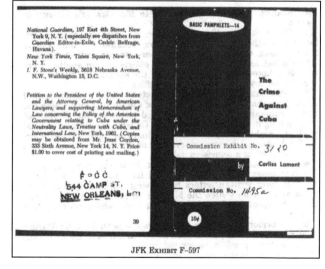

National Guardian, 197 East 4th Street, New York 9, N. Y. (especially see dispatches from Guardian Editor-in-Exile, Cedric Belfrage, Havana).
New York Times, Times Square, New York, N. Y.
I. F. Stone's Weekly, 5618 Nebraska Avenue, N.W., Washington 15, D.C.

Petition to the President of the United States and the Attorney General, by American Lawyers, and supporting Memorandum of Law concerning the Policy of the American Government relating to Cuba under the Neutrality Laws, Treaties with Cuba, and International Law, New York, 1961. (Copies may be obtained from Mr. Jesse Gordon, 333 Sixth Avenue, New York 14, N. Y. Price $1.00 to cover cost of printing and mailing.)

F·O·C·C
544 CAMP ST.
NEW ORLEANS, LA.

39

BASIC PAMPHLETS—14

The Crime Against Cuba

Commission Exhibit No. 3110

by   Corliss Lamont

Commission No. 1495a

10¢

JFK Exhibit F-597

▲ Some of Oswald's leaflets were stamped with the address "544 Camp Street," which was the building where the staunchly anti-Communist Banister had his office.

PLOT ON KENNEDY IN CHICAGO TOLD

Lawyers Quote Imprisoned Ex-Secret Service Agent

SPRINGFIELD, Mo., Dec. 5 (AP)—Three lawyers said today that a former United States Secret Service agent, now a prisoner at the Federal medical center here, had told them that the agency had known before President Kennedy's assassination that an attempt to kill him had been planned.

An attorney representing the former agent, Abraham W. Bolden, 32 years old, asserted that his client had told him he had been sent to prison after having been refused permission to tell the Warren commission about the alleged information.

The charges were made in a

Accused Agent Says JFK Guards Were Lax

CHICAGO, May 21 (UPI) — A Secret Service agent charged with trying to sell a government report said yesterday he is being framed because he intended to reveal details of heavy drinking and "general laxity" among agents assigned to President Kennedy.

Abraham Bolden, 29, who in 1961 became the first Negro assigned to the Secret Service detail guarding the President, outlined his charges in a news conference at his home here.

FILE SALE

He is charged with trying to sell a confidential file to a man indicted in the alleged counterfeiting of $5000,000 in bonds and checks.

Mr. Bolden said he told another agent two weeks ago: "I'm going before the Warren Commission and tell about the drinking and disappearance of the (Secret Service) agents from

—UPI PHOTO
ABRAHAM BOLDEN

what happened in Dallas, but I intend to tell the Warren Commission what I know."

HSCA

▲ Helping Marcello and Trafficante implement their plan to kill JFK was Johnny Rosselli, the Mafia don who represented Sam Giancana and the Chicago mob in Las Vegas and Hollywood. Shortly before he was murdered on Trafficante's orders, Rosselli confessed his role in JFK's assassination to his attorney.

◀◀ Three weeks before Dallas, JFK had to cancel his Chicago trip and motorcade because of an assassination plot involving four men. An ex-Marine, not Oswald, who worked at a warehouse overlooking JFK's motorcade route was arrested. JFK kept word of the threat out of the press at the time, for national security reasons. Before Abraham Bolden, the first black presidential Secret Service agent, could tell Warren Commission staff about the Chicago plot, he was arrested and sent to prison on false charges.

◂▸ On November 18, 1963, four days before Dallas, JFK was almost assassinated during his long motorcade through Tampa, Florida. This plot was kept hidden from the press at the time by JFK, and this small article only slipped out the day after he died. The Warren Commission—and the five government committees that later investigated parts of the JFK assassination—were never told about it. Tampa's police chief told me they were most worried JFK would be shot from the Floridan Hotel, which looks like a larger version of the Texas School Book Depository.

◂ Tampa godfather Santo Trafficante (left), and his attorney Frank Ragano (right)—seen here in 1966—toasted JFK's murder the night he died, at the same Tampa hotel where JFK had spoken just four days earlier.

◄ Three months before JFK was elected President, Vice President Richard Nixon had ordered the CIA to work with Trafficante, Rosselli, and other mobsters to assassinate Fidel Castro. Carlos Marcello also joined those CIA-Mafia plots, which CIA official Richard Helms continued into 1963 without telling JFK or even CIA Director McCone.

▲ Robert Kennedy, seen here with the released leaders of the failed Bay of Pigs invasion, and JFK had their own plan to topple Fidel Castro, if they couldn't reach a negotiated settlement with him. Robert Kennedy's top Cuban exile aide was Enrique "Harry" Ruiz-Williams (right), and they were assisted by exile Manuel Artime (far left).

ii. Q. Who is "B-1" and what is the name of the anti-Castro group both of which are mentioned on page 89 of the (SSC) Report.

A. This is Manuel Artime, and his group was known as the Democratic Revolutionary Front.

(Comment. Artime and his group were supported by CIA. He also was used by the Mafia in the Castro operation, This information should not be released)

▲ The Kennedys had banned the Mafia from their coup plan, or from reopening their casinos after the coup. Unknown to JFK, Robert Kennedy, or Ruiz-Williams, the CIA was using exile leader Manuel Artime in the CIA-Mafia plots with Trafficante and Rosselli in 1963. This fact was also hidden from the Warren Commission and the House Select Committee on Assassinations.

AP IMAGES

▲ In contrast to the CIA, the Kennedys' plan in 1963 involved working with Commander Juan Almeida (right), the head and founder of the Cuban Army, and the third most powerful man in Cuba, to stage a "palace coup" against Fidel that would lead to free elections.

c. US intervention would be based on:

                             a Provisional Government set up by

    (1) A pre-arranged call for help from the insurrectionists (preferably to the OAS, although US action would not await formal OAS approval), or

    (2) A call for help from the insurrectionists after a coup had started without prior US concurrence, if the US determined that the insurgents met generally the criteria for support, or

    (3) Intervention by local Soviet forces.

d. A coup would:

    (1) Have some power base in the Cuban army or militia in order to survive.

                    Provisional Government,

    (2) Establish a however rudimentary, with some sort of public claim to political viability to provide an adequate political basis (unless Soviet troops were clearly fighting Cuban patriots) for overt US action.

    (3) Neutralize the top echelon of Cuban leadership.

▲ The JFK-Almeida coup plan was completely withheld from the Warren Commission and the House Select Committee on Assassinations. Above is one of hundreds of pages of files about the JFK-Almeida coup plan declassified in the 1990s. Fidel's death would likely be blamed on a Russian or Russian sympathizer.

NATIONAL ARCHIVES

▲ JFK's Secretary of State, Dean Rusk, first revealed the existence of the coup plan to the author. He later confirmed to Vanity Fair that JFK was pursuing the coup plan at the same time he was trying to negotiate a peaceful settlement with Fidel Castro.

▸ Richard Helms was the Deputy Director for Plans in 1963, essentially the top operational official in the CIA. He decided to continue the CIA-Mafia plots with Rosselli and the others, without telling President Kennedy, CIA Director John McCone, or Robert Kennedy.

▲ Helms was the mentor of CIA official E. Howard Hunt (left). Hunt had originally been involved in the CIA-Mafia plots, but in 1963 he was a key liaison between Ruiz-Williams and the CIA. Hunt's assistant, CIA agent Bernard Barker (right), was also working for Santo Trafficante at the time, and sold out the JFK-Almeida coup plan to the godfather. Barker was one of a dozen associates of Trafficante, Marcello, or Rosselli who knew about—or actually worked on—the top secret coup plan.

◀ CIA officer David Atlee Phillips, a close friend of Hunt's, was a publicity specialist who had targeted both Fidel Castro and the Fair Play for Cuba Committee. In the summer of 1963, after Oswald's amazing run of publicity, Phillips reportedly met with Oswald to discuss an operation targeting Castro.

▸ David Morales was Operations Chief for the huge Miami CIA Station, JMWAVE. Like Phillips, Morales also worked on the top secret JFK-Almeida coup plan in 1963. But Morales hated JFK because of the Bay of Pigs, and in the fall of 1963, he worked closely with Johnny Rosselli, supposedly on the CIA-Mafia plots. Morales later confessed being part of JFK's assassination to two close associates.

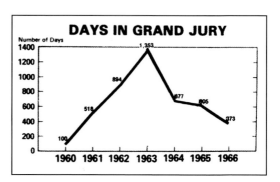

▸ This chart graphically depicts Attorney General Robert Kennedy's war against Marcello, Trafficante, and other mob leaders. He hired ten times the number of Mafia prosecutors as the Eisenhower-Nixon administration, and they spent 13 times more days presenting Mafia cases to grand juries.

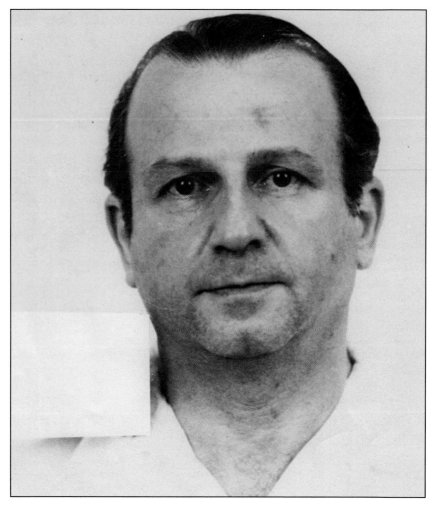

▲ Jack Ruby was a low-level mobster in the Dallas arm of Carlos Marcello's organization. Marcello told the CAMTEX FBI informant that his group secretly owned Ruby's Carousel strip club—along with many other clubs in Dallas—and when Ruby was caught stealing from the till, Marcello summoned him for a confrontation.

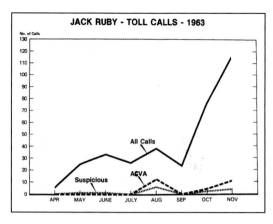

JACK RUBY - TOLL CALLS - 1963

◄ Ruby's long-distance phone calls went up markedly when word was first published about a possible JFK trip to Texas, and they skyrocketed once the trip was officially announced. Ruby, Marcello's "payoff man" for the Dallas Police, had to either find a police officer to silence the person accused of killing JFK, or do the job himself.

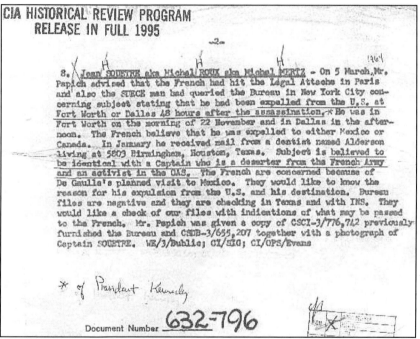

CIA HISTORICAL REVIEW PROGRAM RELEASE IN FULL 1995

8. Jean SOUETRE aka Michel ROUX aka Michel MERTZ - On 5 March, Mr. Papich advised that the French had hit the Legal Attache in Paris and also the STECE man had queried the Bureau in New York City concerning subject stating that he had been expelled from the U.S. at Fort Worth or Dallas 48 hours after the assassination.* He was in Fort Worth on the morning of 22 November and in Dallas in the afternoon. The French believe that he was expelled to either Mexico or Canada. In January he received mail from a dentist named Alderson living at 5803 Birmingham, Houston, Texas. Subject is believed to be identical with a Captain who is a deserter from the French Army and an activist in the OAS. The French are concerned because of De Gaulle's planned visit to Mexico. They would like to know the reason for his expulsion from the U.S. and his destination. Bureau files are negative and they are checking in Texas and with INS. They would like a check of our files with indications of what may be passed to the French. Mr. Papich was given a copy of CSCI-3/776,742 previously furnished the Bureau and CSDB-3/655,207 together with a photograph of Captain SOUETRE. WE/3/Public; CI/SIG; CI/OPS/Evans

* of President Kennedy

Document Number 632-796

▲ This CIA document, and other information from French authorities, shows that assassin Michel Victor Mertz, a French Connection heroin trafficker who worked with Trafficante, was deported from Dallas shortly after JFK's assassination, an important fact kept from the Warren Commission. In addition, Marcello told the FBI's CAMTEX informant that he imported two shooters from Europe for the JFK hit.

‣ The Warren Commission claimed that all the shots that hit JFK came from the Texas School Book Depository. But witnesses saw more than one man on that floor, and most said neither resembled Oswald, who had recently started working there.

‣ But some witnesses saw shots from the Grassy Knoll, including JFK's two closest aides in the limo directly behind JFK's. Several Dallas deputies encountered men behind the knoll and behind the Book Depository who claimed to be Secret Service agents, but no real agents were on the ground in Dealey Plaza.

CE 399
FBI C1

National Archives

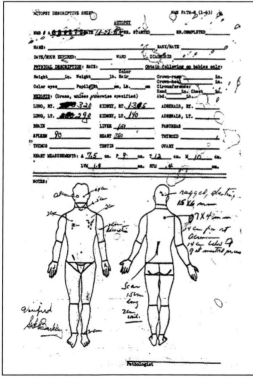

▲ This almost pristine slug is called by some the "magic bullet." For the "single bullet theory" to work, and for Oswald to have fired all the shots that hit JFK and Governor John Connally, this bullet had to hit JFK in the back, supposedly exit his throat, then dive down and shatter four inches of Connally's rib before smashing into his wrist bones and plowing into his thigh.

◀ In addition to the improbability of the "magic bullet," this autopsy sheet—and JFK's shirt and suit coat—all show that JFK was shot in the back almost six inches below the top of his collar, as you can see in the figure on the right. Yet, for the "magic bullet" theory of the Warren Commission to work, that same bullet had to emerge from JFK's throat, just below his Adam's Apple, which is higher than the back wound—which would have made it impossible for the bullet to then dive down and hit Governor Connally.

▲ One of the six government investigating committees to look into aspects of JFK's assassination was the Senate Church Committee, in 1975. Before former Chicago mob boss Sam Giancana (left) could testify about the CIA-Mafia plots, he was murdered on June 19, 1975. Jimmy Hoffa (right) had been leaking information to the Committee, and he was murdered on July 30, 1975. Santo Trafficante was linked to both murders.

▲ Johnny Rosselli (left) kept being forced to testify to the Church Committee, and shortly after his last meeting with Trafficante, Rosselli's body was found dismembered and floating in an oil drum near Miami. Chicago hitman Charles Nicoletti (right)was murdered on March 29, 1977, the same day Oswald's best friend in Dallas, the anti-Communist George DeMohrenschildt, committed suicide. Both died before they could testify to the House Select Committee on Assassinations.

In Dallas, Jack Ruby could serve a similar function. Though Ruby wasn't a member of law enforcement, his friendly contacts with Dallas Police were long-standing and ran deep. According to government files, Ruby knew at least seven hundred of the twelve hundred Dallas policemen; several officers and Ruby associates claimed that Ruby actually knew EVERY Dallas policeman. Ruby was particularly close to several corrupt cops, and as noted earlier, one Warren Commission document called Ruby "the pay-off man for the Dallas Police Department."

One key requirement of the assassination plan was the same for Chicago, Tampa, and Dallas: JFK would be killed in public in a moving car. Shooting JFK in a moving car gave the Mafia several advantages. The mob bosses knew from earlier motorcades—like JFK's spring 1963 trip to Chicago—that Secret Service agents rode with the motorcade and were not on the ground except at the beginning and end of the route. This meant that if JFK was shot en route, no Secret Service would be stationed at the site of the shooting. Even better for them, shooting JFK in a car—as opposed to blowing it up—would take the Secret Service agents away from the crime scene, since they would have to stay with the motorcade to protect the President on the way to the hospital.

The Mafia's plan to kill JFK was very similar to the CIA's plan to kill Castro in the CIA–Mafia plots, and likely to Almeida's part of the coup plan. For top US officials who knew about the coup or the CIA–Mafia plots, hearing how JFK had been shot would be an additional shock that would make maintaining the secrecy surrounding the coup plan a top priority. That cloak of secrecy would also help obscure the Mafia's role in JFK's death.

We noted earlier David Atlee Phillips's autobiographical manuscript about the CIA's decision to have Fidel shot "with a sniper's rifle from an upper floor window of a building on the route where Castro [was riding] in an open jeep." The sad irony is that the Mafia may have taken the very plan the CIA had intended to use against Castro in his jeep and adapted it to kill JFK in an open limousine.

More confirmation for the CIA's approach to killing Castro comes from declassified CIA files and from Manuel Artime's top lieutenant from AMWORLD, Cuban exile Rafael "Chi Chi" Quintero. Speaking of a later version of an AMWORLD plot to kill Fidel, Quintero said the plan was to shoot Castro at Varadero Beach. Still another, later CIA AMWORLD document, which mentions Commander Almeida, says "the assassination [of Fidel] is to take place in public so that everyone can see that the leaders have been killed."

Killing JFK in public, in a car, would ensure that the CIA, Robert Kennedy, and other high officials recognized immediately on hearing the first reports of the tragedy the similarity between JFK's death and the plans to eliminate Castro.

How the mob could have applied the CIA's Castro plan to instead assassinate JFK becomes clear when we consider the October 1963 Senate testimony of Neil G. Brown, who was stepping down as Tampa Police Chief at the end of the month, to be replaced by J. P. Mullins. Chief Brown provided the Senators, and the press, with a remarkable summary of how Tampa's Trafficante conducted and got away with mob hits; much of it reads almost like a script for what happened in Dallas the following month. Brown's Senate testimony makes it clear that Trafficante—as well as Marcello and Rosselli—would do on a larger scale with JFK's assassination what they had already done successfully in the past.

Brown testified about Trafficante's ties to Rosselli's boss, Giancana, and to a French Connection heroin partner Michel Victor

Mertz. Next came his accounts of Trafficante's direct links to several murders, in addition to many others he had ordered.

After noting Trafficante's role in the still officially unsolved barbershop slaying of New York mob boss Albert Anastasia, Brown explained that Trafficante had "been picked up by the police for questioning about the gangland slayings of three [other] men" over the years, but authorities were unable to prosecute Trafficante for those hits because the godfather took care to insulate himself from mob executions, using intermediaries and professional hit men to carry out his dirty work.

Brown pointed out the "relative infrequency with which such professional murders are successfully prosecuted" and explained why. He said that police had solved only one of twenty-three Mafia murders in Tampa, and the lone exception was not a typical Mafia hit. Brown said it was very "difficult to obtain evidence sufficient for successful prosecution of Mafia members, because the witnesses who might offer such evidence have always been reluctant to do so [due to] fear of Mafia reprisals, since it is common knowledge in Tampa that the Mafia does not hesitate to murder" those who talk to the authorities or testify.

One of the Trafficante hits described by Brown in his testimony is very similar to what happened to JFK and Oswald. Brown said Trafficante targeted a victim whose "head was blown off [while he] was seated in his automobile." Then the main "suspect in this murder was himself murdered," as happened with Oswald.

CHAPTER 12

Carlos Marcello and the Hit Men for JFK's Murder

E VEN AS JFK'S plan with Almeida proceeded in the fall of 1963, he and Robert Kennedy looked for a way to find a peaceful solution to the problem of Cuba that wouldn't involve what one memo called "a bloody coup." Historians have long known that the Kennedys initiated two separate back-channel attempts to negotiate with Fidel in the fall of 1963, one using pioneering TV journalist Lisa Howard and special UN envoy William Attwood, and the other through French journalist Jean Daniel. The JFK–Almeida coup plan helps explain the urgency of those efforts at that particular time.

However, neither of the Kennedys' secret peace efforts had produced any breakthroughs, and that would continue to be the case up until JFK's assassination on November 22, 1963. To maintain deniability in case the secret talks were exposed, JFK had to work through William Attwood, who in turn talked to Fidel's doctor, who dealt with Fidel. The parties were wary of each other, and the negotiations slow. Fidel also had to deal with factions within his own regime, with one Attwood memo to JFK noting that Fidel didn't want Che Guevara to find out about the secret talks because "there was a rift between Castro and the Guevara [and] Almeida group on the question of Cuba's future course." JFK kept his own secrets from Attwood, not telling him that, barring some dramatic breakthrough in the secret talks, JFK and Bobby planned to allow Almeida to overthrow Fidel in December 1963.

Frustrated by the slow pace of the Attwood negotiations yet anxious to avoid a violent coup if possible, in late October 1963 JFK asked French journalist Jean Daniel to talk to Fidel on his behalf. But Fidel had kept Daniel cooling his heels in Havana for weeks. Daniel would not get to see Fidel until November 21, the day before JFK's trip to Dallas. No real progress was made in their talk, but Fidel was intrigued enough by Daniel's message from JFK that he invited the journalist to a follow-up lunch on November 22 at Castro's villa at Varadero Beach. However, Daniel could not securely communicate directly with JFK or Bobby about his talks with Castro, so the Kennedys would have no way to know that Daniel was finally speaking with the Cuban leader.

John and Robert Kennedy had basically one overall goal for Cuba by late October 1963: to resolve the situation so that the United States could peacefully coexist with Cuba. That could come about with a peacefully negotiated settlement if possible, but if not, they would try to bring it about by supporting Commander Almeida and the Cuban exile leaders with their coup, hopefully leading to eventual free elections and democracy in Cuba.

President Kennedy, RFK, and other key officials in the Kennedy Administration were very concerned about Cuba and the 1964 election. William Attwood said in a memo that they needed to "remove the Cuban issue from the 1964 campaign." Talks with other Kennedy aides show that John and Robert Kennedy shared that opinion, and it was one factor in scheduling the JFK–Almeida coup plan for December

1, 1963, a date confirmed in a memo by CIA Director John McCone and by RFK's top exile aide, Harry Williams. That way, the Cuba situation would be resolved—one way or the other—before the official start of the campaign in January 1964. In addition, CIA files and Harry Williams said that after December 1, Cuban officials planned to institute a draft, which would dilute the loyalty of Commander Almeida's army, allowing Cuban intelligence and other rival factions in the Cuban government to infiltrate his ranks. As Dean Rusk and a Kennedy aide explained to me, having the coup by December 1 was also necessary so that US troops wouldn't be fighting in Cuba during the Christmas holidays and any US air support for the coup would be over before the Pearl Harbor anniversary on December 7.

What would happen if Fidel found out about the JFK–Almeida coup plan, or one of the less advanced efforts like AMTRUNK, and decided to retaliate against the United States in some way? That question was obviously on the minds of John and Robert Kennedy, who took steps to deal with just such a situation. Today, even most historians have no idea that in the days and weeks before JFK's murder, Robert Kennedy had a secret subcommittee developing plans for what to do if a US official was assassinated.

The development of "contingency plans" for dealing with the possible "assassination of American officials" grew out of planning for the coup and involved many of the same officials, such as Colonel Alexander Haig, who worked for Army Secretary Cyrus Vance and his aide Joseph Califano. This planning had begun in September 1963, but since some of the officials working on these Cuba Contingency plans didn't know about Almeida, they no doubt viewed the issue far differently, and with far less urgency, than the few who did. Only three of the many files this subcommittee generated have been declassified, though I also spoke with two members of the Kennedy Administration who were familiar with the plans.

One of my sources was John H. Crimmins, Coordinator of Cuban Affairs for the US State Department. Crimmins worked on developing and writing the Cuba Contingency Plans but, like his boss Dean Rusk, had not been told about Commander Almeida. The other source was a Kennedy aide, who wishes to remain confidential, who saw the plans after they were drafted and who did know about Almeida and the imminent coup. While declassified plans show that the subcommittee believed the "assassination of American officials" to be "likely" in the fall of 1963, the subcommittee considered assassination attempts "unlikely in the US." Members believed that if Fidel found out about US plans and decided to retaliate, he would risk assassinating an American official only outside the United States—for example, in a Latin American country.

RFK and the officials working on the plans, especially those who knew about Almeida, were considering how the United States should react if, for example, the US ambassador to Panama was assassinated and his murder appeared to be linked somehow to Cuba and the upcoming coup. One of Cyrus Vance's memos about the coup stresses the importance of having certain types of "information . . . to enable the President to make" viable decisions so they could avoid any situation where the President "would lack essential, evaluated information . . . but would at the same time be under heavy pressure to respond quickly." Robert Kennedy and the other officials didn't want JFK to be under pressure from the public, the press, or Congress to take hasty action against Cuba if early reports pointed toward Cuban involvement in the death of a US official in Latin America. A quick US military attack against Cuba could provoke devastating retaliation from

Russia. Also, imagine the disaster if the United States started bombing Havana only to have evidence emerge proving the US official had been killed not by Fidel but in a routine crime.

To avoid those problems, the Kennedy aide cautiously indicated some of the conditions necessary for JFK to make an informed, reasoned response to the apparent assassination of a US official in Latin America. First, the United States would need to control and limit initial publicity to keep the news media from generating an outcry for an immediate military response against Cuba. To protect Almeida, any possible links between the assassination and the coup plan would have to be hidden from the press. US investigating agencies would need to take control of the investigation from local authorities as soon as possible, including gaining possession of important evidence. The autopsy would have to be conducted at a secure US military facility to ensure that information couldn't be leaked to the press. All of this would give JFK the time and information needed to make an appropriate response.

Some aspects of what many call the cover-up regarding JFK's assassination—from controlling news accounts to his controversial military autopsy—were thus actually planned weeks and months before JFK's murder but were intended to manage a completely different situation. The thinking behind the Cuba Contingency plans, and the need to protect the secrecy of Almeida's coup plan to preserve his life and to prevent a possible nuclear confrontation with the Soviet Union, is responsible for much of the secrecy that surrounds JFK's murder, even today. In addition, because officials like Alexander Haig had spent months working on scenarios involving possible retaliation by Fidel against US officials, they would be extremely receptive to the Mafia's fake "Castro did it" information after JFK's murder.

Those inside and outside the CIA who would press the "Castro did it" line often point to remarks Fidel made to Associated Press reporter Daniel Harker in September 1963. In a talk with Harker in Havana, Castro condemned the exile raids against Cuba, which, despite denials to the press, were really backed by JFK. Harker wrote that Castro then said, "We are prepared to fight them and answer in kind. United States leaders should think that if they are aiding terrorist plans to eliminate Cuban leaders, they themselves would not be safe." Soon after Kennedy's death—and even today—some claim that Castro's remark was a threat to assassinate JFK, although the comment was not noted as such when the article first appeared.

Years later, Anthony Summers wrote that Castro told Congressional investigators that "he never intended his words to be taken as a physical threat against [any] individuals in the United States." Instead, Fidel said "he probably meant to warn Washington that he knew of the plots against his own life and that it was 'a very bad precedent' which might 'boomerang' against its authors." Fidel's former head of State Security, Fabian Escalante, says that what Castro really said was, "American leaders should be careful because the [anti-Castro operations] were something nobody could control." Given that some men involved in the Castro assassination plots, such as Morales and Rosselli, confessed to killing JFK, the Cuban dictator's explanation makes sense, especially since those admissions weren't revealed until years after Castro talked to the Congressional delegation. As several historians have pointed out, it would have made little sense for Fidel to do something that would risk having his country invaded in retaliation, just to make Lyndon Johnson President. While Summers notes that Fidel said that "any successor to President Kennedy was likely to be even tougher toward Cuba," he also points out an even more obvious argument that Castro did not make: "If Castro had really intended harm to President Kennedy, he would hardly have announced it to the [American] press two months in advance."

Given the September 1963 timing of Fidel's remarks, it's important to reiterate that State Department official John Crimmins, who was working on the Cuba Contingency Plans soon after Fidel's remarks, told me that he and the others on the subcommittee didn't see Fidel's remarks as a threat against JFK. He said Fidel's comment had nothing to do with sparking the Cuba Contingency planning and that he felt Castro had no role in JFK's death.

EVERYTHING WAS ALMOST set for the Kennedys' exile leaders and groups involved in the coup plan: The Cuban American troops at Fort Benning were trained and ready, and one of the leaders of that group had been told about Commander Almeida. CIA memos confirm Harry Williams's accounts of meeting with liberal exile leaders Manolo Ray and Eloy Menoyo to get them to fully commit to his operation. Until they did, they couldn't be completely informed about Commander Almeida, though the CIA memo about Williams's meeting with Ray contains a cryptic reference to Almeida.

Exile leaders Manuel Artime and Tony Varona did know about Commander Almeida, but both men were proving problematic. Artime increasingly tried to bypass Williams and go directly to Robert Kennedy, causing gradually escalating friction between Artime and Williams. Unknown to Williams, Artime was working on the CIA–Mafia plots, and key CIA officials were not only aware of Artime's Mafia involvement, they also looked at using it as "cover" for the CIA supplying him weapons. At the same time, Tony Varona was leaking information about the coup to another Trafficante associate, former

Cuban President Carlos Prio. CIA memos show that Prio resented the fact that Williams—and not he—was leading the coup plan.

Yet another Trafficante associate, Bernard Barker, had helped CIA officer E. Howard Hunt with the initial payment of $50,000 to Almeida (out of a promised $500,000—almost $3 million in today's dollars), to help get Almeida's wife and children out of Cuba on a seemingly innocent pretext.

Rosselli had his own pipeline to information about the coup plan, via his increasingly close friend David Morales. Morales was also involved in the CIA–Mafia plots and the related Castro assassination plotting with disgruntled Cuban official Rolando Cubela.

With all those connections in place, Marcello, Trafficante, and Rosselli were ready for their first attempt to kill President Kennedy, during his upcoming motorcade through Chicago. The other elements they would need to put their plan into effect were experienced hit men, someone to be quickly blamed for the hit, and someone to make sure the fall guy was swiftly eliminated.

REVEALED HERE FOR the first time is how Carlos Marcello arranged for two of the hit men he used to kill President Kennedy. In 1985 Marcello confided to his cellmate, FBI informant Jack Van Laningham, that "two dagos came from Italy" to act as gunmen in JFK's assassination. Marcello explained that the gunmen first came to Canada, then into Michigan. The godfather made that revelation in the cell he shared with Van Laningham while the FBI secretly recorded Marcello's remarks via a bugged transistor radio that Van Laningham had given Marcello.

Van Laningham's revelation from Marcello has never been published or revealed anywhere before its appearance in this book. It's important to note that six years before Van Laningham told me about Marcello's claim, author Charles Brandt published a book that helps support what Van Laningham said. Brandt's book was about a mob assassin and Teamster associate of Jimmy Hoffa named Frank Sheeran. It was titled *I Heard You Paint Houses: Frank "The Irishman" Sheeran and the Inside Story of the Mafia, the Teamsters, and the Last Ride of Jimmy Hoffa*. In the 2004 book, Sheeran talked about:

> how Carlos Marcello liked to send to Sicily for war orphans with no families. They would get smuggled in from Canada, like through Windsor, right across the water from Detroit. The Sicilian war orphans would think they had to take care of a matter and then they could stay in America . . . they would [kill someone] and then they would get in the getaway car and be taken somewhere and [they would be killed] and nobody back in Sicily would miss them. Because they were orphans and had no family there would be no vendettas.

Marcello told Van Laningham that the two gunmen came into the United States through "Selfridge" but provided no other information about that locale. There is only one Selfridge in Michigan. It is an Air National Guard station just north of Detroit and across the bay from Canada. It's interesting to note that Selfridge is only a few dozen miles from the restaurant where Jimmy Hoffa would later disappear. It is also not far from the Windsor border crossing that Sheeran said Marcello used for his hit men from Italy.

Bringing the gunmen into the United States through Canada and then Michigan is significant for two reasons. First, that was part of a heroin smuggling route through Montreal used by Marcello's French Connection associates. The Montreal heroin ring also ran an

immigration and illegal-identity racket for "supplying false papers"—
what would be called identity theft today. In addition to smuggling,
the ring was also used for new Mafia recruits, immigrants fresh from
Italy and Sicily who needed cover identities. The illegal-identity part
of the heroin ring was run by three Mafiosi, including two longtime
associates of Michel Victor Mertz, Marcello's heroin partner. By
bringing the two gunmen in through that route, they could easily be
supplied with hard-to-trace cover identities. Second, it's possible they
were brought into the United States via Canada—instead of someplace
closer to Marcello's territory—because they were going to be used in
the attempt to assassinate JFK in Chicago.

Years before Van Laningham and Frank Sheeran made their
revelations, Marcello biographer John H. Davis described a similar
scenario based on his extensive research into Marcello's method of
operating. In 1989 he wrote that "the individuals who actually performed the assassination [for Marcello] would have come from out
of state or from outside the country . . . they would have accomplished their mission and quickly left the country."

Carlos Marcello didn't tell Van Laningham exactly when the hit
men came into the United States, so it's unclear if they made it to
Chicago or if they went straight to New Orleans after the Chicago
attempt was called off. It's also likely they weren't the only shooters but simply the ones provided by Marcello. There were three cities planned for the assassination—Chicago, Tampa, and Dallas—and
three fall guys to take the blame: Vallee, Lopez, and Oswald, one for
each of the mob bosses (Rosselli, Trafficante, and Marcello). Given
the long period of careful planning, and making sure that even backup
plans had backups, it's likely the same was true for the gunmen. It
would have made sense to have at least two teams of two shooters

in case something unexpected happened to one or two of the shooters before JFK's assassination. Over the years, seriously suggested or rumored shooters have included Trafficante's enforcer Herminio Diaz, his heroin partner and acknowledged assassin Michel Victor Mertz, Chicago hit man Charles Nicoletti, and one or two of Rosselli's highly trained Cuban exile sharpshooters.

It's important to stress that, as with any successful intelligence or criminal operation, the participants would have been informed on a need-to-know basis. Few aside from Marcello, Trafficante, and Rosselli would have known the whole plan. Other participants would have been told only what they needed to know, when they needed to know it, to prevent leaks in case any of them were arrested.

ON OCTOBER 3, 1963, Lee Oswald returned to Dallas from Mexico City, but even that trip was anything but routine, indicating that Oswald's legitimate work for a US intelligence agency continued. After Oswald's death, the *New York Herald-Tribune* revealed that "US Customs official, Oran Pugh, had said that . . . 'US Immigration has a folder on Oswald's trip'" and that the way "Oswald had been checked by US Immigration officials on entering and leaving Mexico . . . was not the usual procedure." Around the same time, the *New York Times* discovered that when Oswald first crossed the border from Texas into Mexico, his "movements were watched at the request of a 'Federal agency at Washington,'" according to "William M. Kline, assistant United States Customs Agent-in-Charge of the Bureau's Investigative Service" at Laredo, Texas. The following day, the *Times* reported from Mexico City that "there were reports here also that [Oswald's] movements were followed in Mexico by an unidentified United States agency." In addition, Warren Commission transcripts show Senator Richard Russell saying that Oswald "came back in a car" from Mexico, although Oswald didn't drive or even own a car and the official story in the *Warren Report* was that he returned by bus. All those reports are consistent with Oswald's being under surveillance by Naval Intelligence while he was also involved in an ongoing CIA operation.

In Dallas, Oswald's pregnant wife and young daughter lived with a family friend, Ruth Paine. The Oswalds had been introduced to Paine earlier in the year by Lee's friend George DeMohrenschildt, the staunch anti-Communist and admitted CIA asset.

When Oswald arrived in Dallas, he moved into the YMCA on October 3, 1963. The former Marine soon moved to a rooming house and attempted, without success, to get a job at a printing company. Oswald was asked to leave his first Dallas rooming house, and he briefly returned to the YMCA. Using an assumed name—O. H. Lee—Oswald then moved to another rooming house, in the Oak Cliff section of Dallas.

On October 15, Oswald applied for a job at the Texas School Book Depository, an eight-story warehouse for textbooks in downtown Dallas. Marina's friend Ruth Paine had heard about an opening there from a neighbor whose brother worked there. Oswald began work at the Depository the following day. However, Paine also received a call for Oswald, offering him a position at another firm at a much higher salary. It's unclear if Paine passed the message along to Oswald or if Oswald preferred the Book Depository job for some reason. Keep in mind that JFK's motorcade route through Dallas—and the fact that it would pass in front of the Book Depository—wouldn't be announced until November 19. However, it was tradition for Presidential motorcades to pass through Dealey Plaza, which was true for Franklin Roosevelt and for candidate John F. Kennedy in 1960. However, those motorcades had gone opposite the direction JFK would be traveling on November 22 and hadn't taken the dogleg from Main Street—which bisected Dealey Plaza—to Houston and Elm Street, where the Book Depository was. As far as the plotters knew in October 1963, JFK's motorcade would likely get close to the Book Depository, so Oswald was probably encouraged by his handlers— most likely still Banister and Ferrie—to take the position and not look for or take a more lucrative position.

Four days after Oswald began work at the Book Depository, Marina had their second daughter. They named her Audrey Marina Rachel. But Oswald and Marina continued to live apart, with Oswald visiting the Paine home weekends, sometimes riding there with Wesley Buell Frazier, who also worked at the Book Depository.

Oswald's activities on weekday evenings and weekends that he did not visit the Paine home are largely undocumented, so it would have been easy for him to talk with individuals related to his intelligence work or his ongoing "tight" Naval Intelligence surveillance. One of Oswald's coworkers at the Book Depository told police that "during the lunch breaks, Oswald usually made several phone calls, which were usually short in length." However, Oswald's only close friend in Dallas, George DeMohrenschildt, had left the country almost seven months earlier, so outside of Marina, it is not known who else Oswald could have been calling.

Oswald's intelligence status had to be very closely held to remain secret, meaning that few federal agents in the field could be told about it. Even though at times the FBI assisted with the Naval Intelligence surveillance of Oswald, field agents would have been told little or nothing about where their routine reports about Oswald were going after they were filed with FBI superiors. Oswald was apparently worried that a local Dallas FBI agent was going to blow his cover, which he had worked so hard to maintain for so many years, hoping he could make it pay off.

Dallas FBI agent James Hosty had visited Marina Oswald on November 1 and again on November 5. After Oswald heard about it, he wrote a note to Hosty warning him away; Oswald personally dropped it off at the Dallas FBI office on November 12. Shortly after Oswald's death, Hoover ordered the Dallas FBI office to destroy Oswald's note. The note and its destruction were kept secret from the Warren Commission and the American public. The contents of the note and the circumstances of Oswald's visit were the subject of three conflicting stories when Congress finally investigated the note in the mid-1970s. The essence of Oswald's note was that Agent Hosty should "stop bothering my wife [and] talk to me if you need to." The secretary in the Dallas office testified that she recalled a phrase about "blowing up" the FBI office. However, surely a written threat to blow up the Dallas FBI office, delivered in person by a former defector to Russia, would have provoked a swift response in 1963, as it would today. Agent Hosty and his supervisor told different stories, with Hosty minimizing any threat or concern about the note. Based on all the evidence, it's likely that Oswald was simply trying to keep the local FBI agent from "blowing" the deep cover Oswald had carefully maintained for so long.

Several odd sightings of someone later reported to be Oswald surfaced after JFK's murder. These range from Oswald causing a disruption at a firing range to Oswald visiting a car dealership, where he (with no license or money to buy a car) drove a demonstration vehicle at a high rate of speed. The incidents usually had Oswald doing something that called attention to himself. Some of those incidents could have involved the real Oswald, either doing something Ferrie or Banister had asked him to do or—in the case of the car—looking ahead to the money he hoped to make after his "big reveal" following his mission to Cuba. Some of the incidents might have involved someone posing as Oswald; others might have simply involved mistaken identities. The incidents have been investigated and written about for decades, with few definitive conclusions, so they are not detailed here.

SEVERAL OF OSWALD'S activities during the summer and fall of 1963 bore a remarkable similarity to those of another ex-Marine, Thomas Arthur Vallee—so much so that the Secret Service noted a few of them in a secret memo just three days after JFK's murder. The Secret Service didn't know about other similarities between the two men: In the summer, Oswald had visited a CIA-backed exile training camp and had met with a CIA official about killing Castro. Before moving to a new city in the fall, Oswald initially stayed at the YMCA before moving to a rooming house and getting a job at a large downtown warehouse that would overlook JFK's motorcade route. Over the same time span, ex-Marine Thomas Vallee had done almost all the same things. Vallee was at a CIA-backed exile training camp and met with a CIA contact about killing Castro. Vallee then moved to a new city, got a room at the YMCA, and then moved to a rooming house. Like Oswald, Vallee then found a job at a large downtown warehouse overlooking a motorcade route for JFK—only in Vallee's case it was JFK's planned November 2, 1963, motorcade through Chicago.

There were other interesting similarities between Oswald and Vallee that could have made both men subject to the same type of manipulation. Like Oswald, a teenaged Thomas Vallee wanted so desperately to join the Marines that he lied about his age. In Vallee's case, he succeeded and served seven years, winning "the Purple Heart and oak leaf cluster for wounds suffered in the Korean War," according to the *Chicago Daily News*.

Like Oswald, Vallee was often depicted by authorities as a troubled loner. Also like Oswald, that image might have served to hide covert activities that he didn't want to share with his family. According to investigative journalist Edwin Black, Vallee later told him that he had spent part of his time in the Marines in Japan at the Camp Otsu U-2 base, one of several U-2 bases used by the CIA operation. Recall that Oswald had served at a U-2 base at Atsugi, Japan. Like Oswald—whose outrageously pro-Russian remarks were never reprimanded by his Marine superiors—Vallee appears to have gotten special treatment in the Marines. At a time when homosexuals were rarely given honorable discharges, Vallee was given an honorable discharge even though he was diagnosed by a Marine psychiatrist as "schizophrenic reaction, paranoid type . . . manifested by preoccupations with homosexuality and femininity."

The thirty-year-old Vallee spent part of the summer of 1963 helping train CIA-backed Cuban exiles in Long Island for "the assassination of Castro." That evokes Oswald's visit to Manuel Artime's exile training camp and his meeting with David Atlee Phillips and exile Antonio Veciana, where the assassination of Castro was discussed.

In the fall of 1963, both ex-Marines moved to new cities, with Oswald returning to Dallas and Vallee returning to his hometown of Chicago. As the Secret Service noted, both men lived at the local YMCA before moving to a rooming house. Both men first tried to get jobs at printing companies. Vallee succeeded and began working at IPP Litho-Plate on West Jackson Boulevard in Chicago. Vallee's job was at a seven-story building that overlooked what has been described as a "slow turn" for JFK's upcoming November 2 motorcade through Chicago. As with the Texas School Book Depository, JFK's motorcade would pass directly in front of Vallee's workplace. Also like Oswald, Vallee would be arrested on the day of JFK's motorcade through his city, and he would have a weapon and ammunition with him.

It's clear that Thomas Vallee would have made an excellent fall guy if the mob bosses had assassinated JFK during the President's visit to Chicago. Just as Oswald worked for the far-right racist Guy Banister, Vallee also had a far-right connection. The *Chicago Daily News* said that Vallee's "apartment contained John Birch Society literature" and that Vallee claimed "he is a 'disaffiliated' member of the John Birch Society." In the fall of 1963, Trafficante and Marcello associate John Martino was a member of the John Birch Society's speakers' bureau. He was featured in the society's September 1963 newsletter as he toured the country promoting his book, *I Was Castro's Prisoner*. Martino later confessed his role in JFK's murder and told associates what Oswald had been instructed to do on November 22. Martino could have had a similar role with Vallee.

How Vallee came to be working for the CIA, training Cuban exiles to assassinate Fidel Castro, has never been explained. However, when confirming that Vallee had lived on Long Island in the summer of 1963, researcher Bill Adams discovered that Vallee had a former housemate who had been arrested for gun dealing. Given the numerous ties between gunrunning, mobsters, and Cuban exiles, ex-Marine Vallee might have come to the attention of the exiles or their CIA handlers that way. Exiles known to have operated in the New York City area include CIA asset Tony Varona and Rolando Masferrer, both Trafficante associates. Vallee himself recognized that he had undertaken activities that would have made him look guilty if JFK had been killed in Chicago. According to Edwin Black, "Vallee claimed he was framed by someone with special knowledge about him, such as his 'CIA assignment to train exiles to assassinate Castro.'"

Vallee didn't have the seeming pro-Castro connections that distinguished Oswald, but there was an attempt to link Oswald to Chicago via reports of a little-known trip that he—or someone pretending to be Oswald—made prior to the attempt to kill JFK in that city. The apparent trip to Chicago, in the weeks after Oswald's well-publicized New Orleans incident, is supported by evidence from several independent sources. The trip seemed designed to ensure that several people would remember him; it would also link him to the Chicago assassination attempt and make it appear as if he had been stalking JFK.

The head of the Ku Klux Klan told veteran newspaper reporter and editor Patsy Sims that he had met with Oswald in Atlanta. In her definitive history of the Klan, Sims writes that "one of her sources told her that Oswald, in the summer of 1963, had called on [Klan] Imperial Wizard James Venable in his office in Atlanta seeking the names of right-wing associates. Venable confirmed [to Sims] that he was fairly sure that Oswald had been there for that purpose." Oswald indicated to Venable that he was on his way to Chicago. Klan leader Venable made his statement to Sims in the 1980s, and it's difficult to see why Venable would make up an Oswald encounter since it tended to link Oswald with Venable's "right-wing associates," thus potentially giving the FBI reason to interview or investigate them.

In the 1960s, Klan leader Venable was close to an associate of Guy Banister, white supremacist Joseph Milteer, who lived in Georgia and visited Atlanta frequently. As detailed later, shortly after the Chicago attempt, almost two weeks BEFORE President Kennedy was murdered in Dallas, Milteer accurately described JFK's assassination to an informant on a Miami police undercover tape. Milteer had been seen meeting with Banister in New Orleans in the summer of 1963, when Oswald was reportedly working for Banister and with David Ferrie.

David Ferrie's long-distance phone records show several collect calls placed to Ferrie from the Atlanta suburb of Marietta from August 16 to August 20; these calls might be related to Oswald's trips. The FBI received reports of Oswald's brief stopover in Atlanta from several individuals, including Hal Suit, the highly respected news director of Atlanta's largest TV station. Some reports to the FBI mentioned Oswald leaving behind a pistol at the Holiday Inn in Marietta after he checked out. Oswald—or the person posing as Oswald—soon retrieved the pistol, but such an incident would tend to incriminate Oswald after JFK's assassination. It might also be relevant that President Kennedy had originally planned to visit Atlanta, hold a motorcade, and give a major speech in the late summer of 1963—but local Democrats had urged him to cancel or scale back the appearance because of concerns about JFK's stance on civil rights. Apparently, plans had already been made for Oswald to visit Atlanta en route to Chicago before JFK altered his plans.

Oswald apparently continued on to Chicago but first stopped at the University of Illinois at Urbana. An FBI memo says that Oswald reportedly inquired at the office of the Assistant Dean of Students about Cuban student organizations and asked the secretary "if . . . she had ever seen him on TV in New Orleans." That helps date the visit after Oswald's flurry of New Orleans publicity in mid-August. The FBI memo says that Oswald "expressed interest in any campus organization advocating humanist views." Oswald seems to have made sure that he would be remembered as being very interested in leftist causes. Oswald's actions at the University of Illinois echo those observed at what is now the University of New Orleans. Historian Michael L. Kurtz, as a student in 1963, witnessed Guy Banister with Oswald there, both at various times debating students about integration.

Oswald's trip north to Illinois might have included a visit to Canada. A report sent to the US Secret Service a week after JFK's assassination from the "Senior Customs Representative, US Treasury Department Bureau of Customs, Montreal, Canada" said that "several persons have contacted this office recently and advised that Lee Oswald, suspected of assassinating the late President Kennedy, was seen distributing pamphlets entitled 'Fair Play for Cuba,' on St. Jacques and McGill Streets, Montreal, during the summer of 1963. Mr. Jean Paul Tremblay, Investigator, Customs and Excise, Montreal stated on November 27, 1963 that he received one of the abovementioned pamphlets from a man on St. Jacques Street, Montreal, believed to be in August 1963, and he is positive that this person was Oswald. Mr. Tremblay also stated that . . . the reason for paying special attention to [Oswald] was because he was working on cases involving Cuba at the time." Canada, like Mexico, was a route for Americans to get into Cuba.

The point of the trip north by Oswald—or someone pretending to be him—was apparently to tie him to Vallee, thus linking Vallee to a seemingly pro-Castro, Communist radical. Oswald was already in the public record as having tried to infiltrate Bringuier's anti-Castro group, so the plan might have been to link Oswald to the anti-Castro, anti-Kennedy Vallee to make it look as if Oswald had put Vallee up to shooting JFK. Of course, that link would need to be made public— with the help of Martino, Milteer, and Banister—only if Vallee were arrested for JFK's assassination in Chicago.

The many parallels between Oswald and Vallee cited earlier, especially those from August to November 1963, indicate that whoever was manipulating Oswald's movements was likely doing the same with Vallee. However, there was yet another young man—this time in Tampa—who had even more parallels to Oswald from August to November 1963: Gilberto Policarpo Lopez. Government files and sources show nineteen parallels in all, which indicate that Lopez was being manipulated as the perfect fall guy if the JFK assassination was in Tampa or if an additional patsy was needed for Dallas.

Oswald and Gilberto Lopez were both former defectors with a Russian connection in their background. Each had returned to the United States in 1962 from a Communist country. Both men had an unusual involvement with the small pro-Castro Fair Play for Cuba Committee in 1963, after it became the subject of Congressional hearings and newspaper accounts. Both got into fistfights over seemingly pro-Castro statements, though at other times they made anti-Castro statements. Neither joined the Communist Party or regularly associated with American Communists. Both men were persons of interest to Naval Intelligence in 1963, and both were alleged by officials to be informants for a US government agency. Oswald and Lopez were about the same age, and both had left their wives a few months earlier, when each man had moved to a new city. Both lived in a city with much anti-Castro activity and a strong mob presence.

Both Oswald and Lopez attempted to get into Cuba in the fall of 1963 by going to Texas, crossing the border at Nuevo Laredo, and proceeding to Mexico City, where they hoped to make an air connection to Cuba. (CIA files show that undercover US intelligence agents also used this route.) Officials said that both Oswald and Lopez went at least part of the way by car, though neither man owned a car or had a driver's license or a known associate who drove him. CIA files show that each man was under Agency surveillance for at least part of his Mexico trip. And by November 1963, each would have a job in the vicinity of an upcoming JFK motorcade.*

FBI and government files confirm that Lopez left Tampa shortly after the attempt to assassinate JFK during his motorcade there. He went to Texas, where an unconfirmed newspaper account places him in Dallas on November 22, 1963. CIA and FBI files show that Lopez then crossed the border when it was reopened after JFK's assassination and went to Mexico City. From there, unlike Oswald, Lopez would be successful in getting into Cuba.

Those parallels show that in the months before JFK's murder, Oswald and Lopez were probably being manipulated by the same people, for the same purposes. Each man appeared to have some intelligence role, while neither realized that he was also subject to manipulation by the Mafia. By having Oswald visit Tampa shortly before the assassination—or at least planting information that he had—the Mafia also managed to link the two potential fall guys. This meant that much of the activity that seemed to incriminate one of the men could also be used to incriminate the other. The fact that both men seemed like troubled loners with no close friends would make it easy for the public to believe the two apparent malcontents had somehow conspired to vent their frustrations against JFK.

The Warren Commission got only fragments of information about Gilberto Lopez, though it did learn enough to write in one memo that Lopez was on a "mission" of some sort at the time of JFK's

---

*The complete list of all eighteen parallels between Oswald and Lopez will be posted on thehidden historyofjfksassassination.com.

assassination. However, the Warren Commission was never told about the attempt to assassinate JFK in Tampa, so it apparently considered Lopez of only minor interest. The CIA, FBI, and military intelligence also withheld important information about Lopez from Congressional investigators in the 1970s. Memos from the House Select Committee on Assassinations show they knew they were being stonewalled by officials regarding Lopez, and they were unable to get the information they wanted before their terms expired.

Gilberto Policarpo Lopez was a young Cuban exile. In early 1963 Lopez lived south of Miami in the Florida Keys, but by the fall of 1963, he had moved to Tampa. Both areas were under the sway of godfather Santo Trafficante. Whereas most of the setting up of Oswald took place in Marcello's territory, the unusual actions that appeared to link Lopez to JFK's assassination were likely the result of manipulation by someone working for Trafficante. A likely candidate would be David Ferrie's close associate in Florida named Eladio del Valle. Del Valle was a businessman and a Cuban exile involved in running narcotics for Santo Trafficante and was partners with Rolando Masferrer. (In 1967 del Valle was brutally murdered on the same night David Ferrie died.)

Trafficante surely knew the hysteria that would be generated if a Cuban exile was paraded in front of TV cameras as the supposed assassin of JFK had the President been killed during his Tampa motorcade. The same would be true if Lopez was found dead, either as a "suicide" after supposedly killing JFK or if shot by someone like Jack Ruby. The pressure on US officials to invade Cuba in retaliation would have been overwhelming—and Trafficante knew that the United States was poised and ready to do just that because so many of his associates had penetrated the JFK–Almeida coup plan.

IT'S IMPORTANT TO point out that while the massive weight of the evidence shows that Oswald was knowingly involved with US intelligence, the same is not necessarily true for Gilberto Lopez. A former chief of the Florida (Police) Intelligence Unit told me that Lopez was an informant for a US agency. But he might have been so unwittingly and not have known that a friend or associate was reporting his information to the agency. A friend or associate could have manipulated Lopez by playing on his hopes of getting a valid passport or for other reasons. Just as Oswald's prospects were limited by his undesirable discharge (in case he ever decided to quit his covert activities before completing his mission), Lopez needed a valid US passport to freely travel between the United States and Cuba (where his family still lived, except for a brother who was in Russia).

From all the evidence I have seen—which includes every file on Lopez that has been released, material regarding attempts to get more of his files released, and an exclusive interview with his wife—I do not think Lopez had any knowing involvement in JFK's assassination or Trafficante's criminal activities. But he was the right person in the right place at the right time to be the perfect patsy for an attempt to kill JFK during his motorcade in Tampa.

Since it was just a year after the Cuban Missile Crisis, CIA assets Trafficante, Marcello, and Rosselli knew that if JFK was murdered in public and it quickly emerged that his killer had connections to Cuba and even Russia, high US officials could wind up facing two difficult choices, either of which would be good for the mob bosses. US officials could give in to a public outcry to retaliate against Cuba, which would serve to limit the murder investigation of JFK at a crucial time as the United States went to war. Or US officials could tamp down such speculation and limit a true, full investigation of JFK's murder to prevent calls for retaliation that could lead to World War III.

Historian and intelligence expert Dr. John Newman said, "It is now apparent that the World War III pretext for a national security cover-up was built into the fabric of the plot to assassinate President Kennedy." If blamed for JFK's murder, Oswald and Lopez would have been especially good at triggering "the World War III pretext for a national security cover-up," but Vallee less so. However, the mob bosses—in particular Rosselli's good friend and coconspirator David Morales—had one more potential "fall guy" who would at least appear to be in place in Chicago and in Dallas shortly before the attempts to kill JFK in those cities.

CIA documents say that a mysterious man from Cuba was reported in the Chicago area just prior to JFK's planned motorcade there. The Cuban was named Miguel Casas Saez, aka Angel Dominguez Martinez, and he always seemed to be one tantalizing step ahead of the authorities. He was conveniently reported to be in Florida in the weeks before JFK's Tampa motorcade. More ominously, CIA reports said that Saez was in Dallas when JFK was shot. He then fled to Mexico City, where a Cubana Airlines plane was held for him for five hours. Saez supposedly rode in the cockpit so the passengers wouldn't see him. Thirdhand accounts by David Morales's Cuban exile informants (code-named AMOTs) said the formerly poor Saez suddenly had money and American clothes after he returned to Cuba from Dallas. Like Oswald and Lopez, Saez also had a Russian connection: He had taken a Russian-language course and "speak[s] Russian quite well," according to a CIA memo. That would have made it easy for Saez to talk with any of the thousands of Russian advisors and technicians still in Cuba in 1963.

The mysterious Cuban Saez was always reported to be in just the right place at the right time to trigger Newman's "World War III pretext for a national security cover-up." Later accounts show that the possibility that Saez and Lopez were Castro agents was a huge concern for the CIA's powerful Chief of Counterintelligence, James Angleton.

It's unclear now whether Saez was a real person or simply a creation of David Morales's informants, but in 1963 and 1964, the CIA, the FBI, and other agencies thought he was real. However, though the Saez allegations concerned US officials in the crucial early period after JFK's death, they eventually fell apart. When the initial report of the Cubana plane being held was finally declassified, it didn't mention Saez at all. The most incriminating information in CIA reports was all thirdhand, from sources of questionable reliability whose names are still withheld today. But those sources worked for David Morales, who—by running covert operations at the huge Miami CIA station—was in the perfect position to feed the alarming reports into the CIA's massive data collection system. Morales would have known how high US officials with access to the secret Saez reports would react after JFK's murder.

If Saez was a real person, he might have simply been a Cuban on a low-level smuggling mission to the United States who was manipulated by David Morales or his associates so that his travels later looked suspicious. Having someone like Saez (or at least reports about such a person) and Lopez in Dallas would have been necessary for the mob bosses if evidence emerged soon after JFK's murder that the President had been shot by more than one person or if something had happened to Oswald before the assassination.

Still more information falsely implicating Fidel in JFK's murder—almost all of it linked to associates of Trafficante, David Morales,

Johnny Rosselli, or Bernard Barker—would emerge in the days, weeks, and months after the assassination. The Mafia chiefs knew those allegations were crucial to maintaining "the World War III pretext for a national security cover-up" that would protect Marcello, Trafficante, and Rosselli from close scrutiny.

JACK RUBY HAD ties to all three cities in the JFK plot—Chicago, Tampa, and Dallas—and probably had the same role in Chicago that he had in Dallas: making sure the fall guy was quickly rubbed out. Ruby had grown up in Chicago, had moved back for a time in the early 1950s, and had close relatives and many friends in the city. Journalist Seth Kantor says that just two months before the Chicago attempt, Ruby had "met in Dallas with two Chicago detectives to provide them information," thus beginning an informant relationship with Chicago law enforcement that could prove useful.

Ruby had other contacts with people connected to Chicago in the weeks and months prior to the Chicago assassination attempt. On October 7, 1963—just three weeks before the Chicago attempt— Ruby had met in Dallas with Chicago businessman Lawrence Meyers, whom David Ferrie had called on September 24. Meyers would be in Dallas meeting with Ruby the night before JFK's assassination, at the restaurant of Joe Campisi, Marcello's Dallas lieutenant.

In preparation for the attempt to kill JFK in Chicago, Ruby received an envelope with approximately $7,000 from an associate of Jimmy Hoffa in October 1963. The payoff occurred in Chicago just weeks after Ruby met with Johnny Rosselli in Miami. I interviewed Jim Allison, who witnessed the payoff, along with his wife.

Jim Allison was a respected businessman who in 1963 was in the public relations field. Allison was friends with Pierre Salinger,

JFK's Press Secretary, but his work also brought him into contact with "lots of colorful characters, including mob types." One of those was A. Gordon Hardy, who introduced Allison to Jimmy Hoffa in Chicago, in Hoffa's large suite at the Bismarck Hotel. Allison came to realize that Hardy also had Mafia ties, but Hardy came to view Allison as someone he could trust.

Jim Allison was in Chicago on business on the weekend of October 27, 1963, and Hardy told Allison he could get him tickets to see the Chicago Bears play the Philadelphia Eagles. He told Allison to meet him on Sunday morning at the coffee shop at the Bismarck Hotel. Allison was having a late breakfast at the coffee shop when Hardy showed up with the football tickets. While Allison was talking with Hardy, "a little guy came in" to the coffee shop and caught Hardy's eye. Hardy asked Allison to excuse him, saying he had to give the guy money to pay for his breakfast. Hardy smiled as he pulled out a number-10 business envelope and—feeling Allison was a friend he could trust—gave Allison a look at the inch-thick stack of $100 bills inside. Hardy then went over to the "little guy" and gave him the envelope. Allison soon left the coffee shop, went to the football game, and didn't think anything more about the payoff in the coffee shop until three weeks later.

On November 24, 1963, Allison watched the transfer of Oswald from the police station to the county jail on NBC. When he saw Ruby shoot Oswald live on TV and the ensuing coverage, Allison realized "it was the man at the coffee shop" he had seen receiving the envelope stuffed with money from the Hoffa associate. However, Allison was reluctant to tell the authorities, because he'd just seen someone murdered on live TV in a police station—by someone his friend Hardy apparently knew. "Two or three months after JFK's assassination"

Allison went to see Hardy in Chicago for the first time since the coffee shop incident, but Hardy's secretary told him that her boss—though only in his late thirties and in good health—had died of a sudden heart attack.

It is unlikely that Hardy had any idea what the money he had given Ruby was for or that Ruby would soon become so notorious; otherwise, he wouldn't have met Ruby in front of witnesses. Hardy had probably simply been asked by Hoffa or one of Hoffa's men to give this man Ruby from Dallas an envelope stuffed with money. From the mob standpoint, that was all Hardy needed to know.

Neither the Warren Commission nor the House Select Committee on Assassinations could find any record of Ruby's being in Dallas on October 27, 1963, one of the few days in the months before JFK's assassination they could not account for. Ruby had called a number in Chicago the previous day, after he had called Los Angeles—Johnny Rosselli's home base. The Chicago number belonged to an associate of Allen Dorfman, a corrupt Teamster official and mobster. Ruby kept late hours, and it would have been easy for him to take a commercial flight under an assumed name to Chicago early in the morning after his club had closed. Or he could have been flown by a private pilot like David Ferrie. The FBI and Justice Department would get reports about a rumored payoff to Jack Ruby prior to JFK's death, and those reports linked Teamster official Allen Dorfman to the money.

When Ruby returned to Dallas, he bought a safe for his office, perhaps to keep the money, because he didn't put it in his bank account. A simple test of putting an inch-thick stack of bills into a number-10 business envelope shows it would have held about $7,000 in $100 bills. According to Seth Kantor, on the afternoon of JFK's assassination, Ruby was seen by "the loan officer at" his Dallas bank. The loan officer "vividly remembers Ruby standing in line" at the bank "on the afternoon of November 22, after President Kennedy was slain." According to the loan officer, "Jack was standing there crying and he had about $7,000 in cash on him the day of the assassination. . . . I warned him that he'd be knocked in the head one day, carrying all that cash on him." Ruby didn't put the money in the bank, however; bank records show that Ruby's only bank transaction that day was a withdrawal for $31.87.

CARLOS MARCELLO'S FEDERAL trial in New Orleans could result in his deportation again, a nightmare that Marcello would do almost anything to avoid. Marcello was clearly guilty of the charges Robert Kennedy had brought against him, so, according to biographer John Davis, "Marcello's principal strategy was to terrorize and possibly eliminate" the key witness against him and to "bribe as many jurors as" possible. But Marcello knew that even if he was successful in using that strategy for the trial, Robert would keep bringing new charges against him as long as JFK remained president.

By Friday, November 1, David Ferrie and Carlos Marcello were no doubt ready to see JFK killed the following day, cutting off the major source of Bobby Kennedy's power. Marcello's biographer writes that "on the morning of November 1, 1963, in a federal courtroom in New Orleans, the final showdown began in Carlos Marcello's ten-year battle to avoid deportation." Bobby had sent his own Justice Department lawyers to prosecute Marcello, who was charged with "'conspiracy to defraud the United States government by obtaining a false Guatemalan birth certificate' and 'conspiracy to obstruct the United States government in the exercise of its right to deport Carlos Marcello.'"

Carlos Marcello was joined in the courtroom by David Ferrie, who had just returned from Guatemala. Marcello had been plotting JFK's death for just over a year at that point, and now his goal was just one day away. For John F. Kennedy to die the day after Marcello's trial started would no doubt be sweet revenge for all the prosecutions—which he viewed as persecutions—and the harrowing ordeal of his humiliating deportation.

CHAPTER 13

Targeting JFK in Chicago and Tampa in November 1963

E VEN AS CHICAGO residents started to line President Kennedy's
planned motorcade route on November 2, 1963, JFK abruptly
canceled his entire trip. The Secret Service had learned of an assassination threat in the city; his visit to Chicago was cancelled on such short
notice that agents were already at the airport to meet the President.
According to Chicago Secret Service agent Abraham Bolden, whose
account was confirmed by other law-enforcement sources uncovered by journalist Edwin Black, the plot involved four men, two of
whom were briefly detained and released and two who were never
apprehended.

Because two of the men had never been caught, there was still
an active threat involving potential Presidential assassins on the
loose. Two of the suspects had Hispanic names—"Rodriguez" and
"Gonzales"—indicating a possible Cuban connection. Combined with
Immigration and Naturalization Service and CIA reports of a Cuban
agent in the Chicago area, the situation looked like the worst-case
scenario of the Cuba Contingency Plans: possible Castro retaliation
for the coup plan by the "assassination of an American official"—but
on American soil, something the officials had considered "unlikely."

Five years later, former Senate investigator Bud Fensterwald found several newsmen at the *Chicago Daily News* who knew about the four-man threat in Chicago, even though they did not write about it at the time. One of the newsmen said, "At the time of JFK's scheduled visit to Chicago [on November 2, 1963] there were four men in town who planned an assassination attempt from one of the overpasses from O'Hare into town. They were seized but apparently not arrested." The assistant city editor also recalled "a disassembled rifle in the story." However, as Fensterwald's memo of the interview with the newsmen puts it, "For some reason" the story about the assassination attempt "did not get in the paper."

A fifth man, ex-Marine Thomas Vallee, whose job overlooked JFK's motorcade route, was arrested at 9 a.m., two hours before JFK was scheduled to arrive in the city. In his car he had an M-1 rifle and three thousand rounds of ammunition. Knowing of at least two potential assassins still at large, JFK and Bobby apparently decided to cancel JFK's entire trip. They also decided to keep any mention of the assassination threat out of the press—and the press complied, even though several newsmen had heard about the four-man threat.

If the threat was made public, and the four men turned out to be Cuban agents retaliating for the JFK–Almeida coup plan, then the plan—and Almeida—could be exposed. That could have resulted in a dangerous confrontation with the Soviets just a year after the Cuban Missile Crisis. Remarkably, there is no evidence that those making the Cuba Contingency Plans, like my State Department source John Crimmins, were told about the Chicago threat. Information about the Chicago (and Tampa) threat appears to have been limited to higher officials, especially those in the Secret Service and FBI—two agencies not directly involved in the Cuban Contingency planning.

As JFK'S Press Secretary Pierre Salinger explained to me, just after he assured the press that JFK would NOT cancel the motorcade because of a crisis in Vietnam, he had to quickly issue two different phony excuses for the cancellation. The initial reason given for JFK's sudden cancellation was a cold, although that was quickly changed to the need for JFK to stay in Washington to deal with the aftermath of the assassination of Vietnamese President Diem. While Diem's death probably was a factor in JFK's decision, news services had already run a story from Salinger saying that special equipment had been installed in Chicago so that JFK could monitor the tragic events in Vietnam during his visit.

The Kennedys had done this kind of news management on a smaller scale in the past, involving incidents as diverse as leaks about the Bay of Pigs and reports of JFK's sexual indiscretions. The CIA had suppressed news stories related to Cuban operations, such as a Florida incident in September 1963, when the Agency made sure "two local newspapers suppressed" and turned over photos of several covert Cuban exile operatives after their boat had problems.

Suppressing a news story on the scale of the Chicago threat against JFK took a new level of coordination among Robert Kennedy and several agencies, but the Cuban aspects of the threat seemed to justify it. Not until years later would the public learn that Vallee had recent ties to a Cuban exile group training to assassinate Fidel Castro. Vallee also had ties to the John Birch Society, widely known at the time for its extreme stance against civil rights, Martin Luther King Jr., and JFK, especially his seemingly soft stance on Cuba.

As mentioned earlier, the CIA and INS had also received reports of a possible Cuban agent named Miguel Casas Saez in Chicago, but they were unable to track him down. In addition, two of the men sought in the Chicago incident had Hispanic names, and a later CIA memo says the plot allegedly involved "Cuban dissidents," which meant exiles. (The suspects also had a possible family connection to Tampa fall guy Gilberto Lopez.) Those Cuban connections are why Bobby and JFK kept any mention of the four-man Chicago plot, and the real reason for JFK's sudden cancellation, out of the press.

Former Chicago Secret Service Agent Abraham Bolden confirmed the four-man Chicago threat and told Congressional investigators and Fensterwald that it was handled differently from any other threat against the President. Bolden said that when Chicago Secret Service chief Maurice Martineau first learned of the threat shortly before JFK's scheduled visit, he told Bolden and the other agents, "There were to be no written reports; any information was to be given to him orally." The chief would "report only by phone to" the head of the Secret Service, "[James] Rowley, personally." Bolden testified that instead of the usual file number, any written information was put into a COS file; COS stood for "Central Office" and "Secret." COS "files were kept separate from all others" and the Secret Service "could say they had nothing in their files on a subject when in fact a 'COS' file existed." After the last-minute cancellation of JFK's trip to Chicago due to the threat, said Bolden, "the memos were then taken to O'Hare airport and given to a crew member of a commercial flight to Washington." He believes a Secret Service "employee met the flight and delivered the material to [Secret Service] headquarters."

But that wasn't the end of the secrecy about the four-man threat. Bolden said that "shortly after the [JFK] assassination," the Chicago Secret Service Chief "called all agents into his office and showed them a memo from Washington to the effect that the Secret Service was to discuss no aspect of the assassination and investigation with anyone from any other federal agency now or any time in the future. Every agent . . . was made to initial this memo." Bolden thought this memo was directed at the FBI, who "wanted to get the role of Presidential protection away from" the Secret Service. Decades later, former Chicago FBI agent Thomas B. Coll recalled, "Some people were picked up. And I'm telling you it wasn't ours. That was strictly a Secret Service affair . . . you'll get no more out of me."

Author Vince Palamara wrote that "Abraham Bolden was adamant that [Chicago Secret Service Chief] Martineau knew about" the four-man plot to kill JFK. In 1993 Martineau himself confirmed the existence of the plot to Palamara and said "he assumed everyone knew about it." Martineau also added that he believed JFK was killed as a result of a conspiracy and that there was "more than one assassin."

The investigation of the Chicago assassination threat went along two paths that began more than forty-eight hours before JFK was set to arrive. One investigative path, sparked in part by a tip the FBI passed along to the Chicago Secret Service, was about a four-man assassin team in the city. Several Chicago Secret Service agents kept watch on two of the four-man assassin team. But, as Agent Bolden later told Congressional investigators, "through a series of blunders, the surveillance" of the two assassins "was 'blown.'"

According to investigative journalist Edwin Black, the agents had been able to pick up the trail of only two of the four men and had been watching the rooming house where they were staying. When the two men left, one Secret Service agent followed them in an unmarked car. However, the car with the two men suddenly reversed direction on a narrow street and began doubling back, so the two men wound up going past the Secret Service agent's car. They overheard the agent's radio and realized they were under surveillance. With its surreptitious surveillance blown, the Secret Service felt it had no choice but to go ahead and detain the men, so "the two subjects were apprehended and brought to the Chicago Secret Service office," Bolden told investigators. Black writes that "the two men were taken into custody (but not actually arrested or booked) in the very early Friday hours and brought to the Secret Service headquarters. There are no records that any weapons were found in their possession or back at the rooming house."

The lack of any weapons—and the premature ending of the surveillance before the two men had committed any crime—presented a problem for the Chicago agents. Threatening the President was not a federal crime at the time. The only information about the two men being a threat came from the FBI, which was loath to share informants with other federal agencies. Without knowing the source or circumstances of the original information about the four-man threat, the Chicago Secret Service faced two problems: how to find out where the other two men were, and how long they could justify detaining the two men they did have in custody. Once the two men were detained by the Secret Service, no doubt various checks on them—or at least on the aliases they were using—were run in an attempt to find an outstanding warrant or other reason to hold them.

Richard Cain—Chief Investigator for the Chicago/Cook County Sheriff's Department—was in a perfect position to monitor or even influence law enforcement's reaction to the Chicago plot. A "made" member of the Mafia, Cain had also worked on the CIA–Mafia plots for Rosselli, Trafficante, and Marcello. Cain would have known about the two suspects detained and lookouts for the two still at large, showing that the secrecy of the assassination plot had been blown. The plan was no doubt called off by Cain's mob superiors. Cain's position also would have allowed him to follow a second important part of the Chicago plot.

The second path of the Chicago investigation focused on ex-Marine Thomas Vallee. The report of the House Select Committee on Assassinations confirms that "on October 30, 1963, the Secret Service learned that an individual named Thomas Arthur Vallee, a Chicago resident who was outspokenly opposed to President Kennedy's foreign policy, was in possession of several weapons." That same day, according to an FBI report, two Secret Service agents conducted a "pretext interview of Vallee . . . and noted that he had two M-1 rifles in his possession, along with [a] .22 caliber revolver and an estimated 1,000 rounds" of ammunition. Unlike the other ex-Marine fall guy, Oswald, Vallee was serious about guns. The Secret Service agents returned to the office and reported their concerns to Martineau.

On or about Thursday, October 31, 1963—one day after the Chicago agents' pretext interview of Vallee—"Vallee's landlady called the [Secret] Service office and said that Vallee was not going to work on Saturday," according to the testimony of Agent Edward Tucker to Congressional investigators. The agent testified that because Saturday was "the day of JFK's visit to Chicago," this information "resulted in the [Secret] Service having the Chicago Police Department surveil Vallee." A later FBI report says that as a result of the Secret Service request to the Chicago police, "a 24-hour surveillance was placed on Vallee and his activities by the Chicago Police Department."

On the morning of November 2, before JFK's motorcade was canceled, Thomas Vallee was heading into the city. According to Congressional investigators, he had put one of his M-1 rifles and his pistol in the trunk of his car, where he also had three thousand rounds of ammunition. Vallee wore a shirt with an open collar and a jacket—similar to what at least one member of the four-man assassin team was wearing.

According to Edwin Black, police records show that Vallee was arrested around 9 a.m., about two hours before JFK's scheduled touchdown at O'Hare. The two police officers following Vallee pulled him over for "left turn without a proper signal" and found a "hunting knife in [his] front seat." That was all the pretext the Chicago police needed to search his car, where they found the M-1 rifle and three thousand rounds of ammunition. An FBI file says a subsequent "search of Vallee's home" by Chicago police "discovered an M-1 rifle, a carbine rifle and about 2,500 rounds of ammunition." A different FBI file says that Chicago police "charged him with an 'assault with a deadly weapon' charge."

By Saturday night, November 2, 1963, all the suspects who were in custody—Vallee and the two who were part of the four-man team— had been released. As Abraham Bolden told Congressional investigators, "The two suspects in Chicago were turned over to the Chicago police who took them away in a patrol wagon." According to Edwin Black, who had several Chicago police sources, when no evidence had been found to justify holding the men, they were released. As for the heavily armed Vallee, the HSCA report says that he was "released from [Chicago Police] custody on the evening of November 2." Vallee was apparently never even brought to the Secret Service office for an interview, then or in the coming weeks. The Secret Service didn't even talk to ex-Marine Vallee in the days and weeks after the Dallas assassination was blamed on fellow ex-Marine Oswald, even though Secret Service records—some of which are still classified—show that the agency maintained an interest in Vallee for at least the next seven years. Clearly there was more to Vallee and the Chicago attempt than the records released so far reveal.

AFTER THE CANCELLATION of the Chicago portion of the plot, Marcello's two shooters from Europe headed south. As Marcello explained to his cellmate Jack Van Laningham, in a conversation secretly recorded on FBI undercover audiotape, the two hit men left Michigan and came to his huge, sixty-four-hundred-acre Churchill Farms estate. The estate had its own airfield, so they could have been flown directly there, perhaps by pilot David Ferrie. It's long been documented that Marcello and Ferrie spent the weekend of November 9 and 10 working on strategy at the secluded farmhouse in the middle of the vast Churchill Farms property. Marcello's federal trial continued in New Orleans, so the two later claimed to government investigators that they were working on trial strategy. However, Marcello had top attorneys to handle that, and Marcello's main strategy involved bribing a key juror to ensure his acquittal, or at the very least a hung jury, and Ferrie was not involved with that. Their meetings at Churchill Farms were also unusual because Ferrie usually met with Marcello in the godfather's office at the Town and Country Motel, as he had done several times in October.

Marcello admitted to Van Laningham that two rifles were obtained from a New Orleans gunsmith so the two European hit men could conduct target practice, safe from the view of law enforcement. Because of the ongoing trial, the government had to be careful not to intrude on Marcello's privacy or talks with his attorneys or their representatives. (Ferrie officially worked for one of Marcello's attorneys.) That created the perfect situation for Marcello and Ferrie to help prepare the two hit men for the upcoming hit against JFK, ironically at the same secluded house where one year earlier Marcello had revealed his intention to kill JFK to FBI informant Ed Becker.

Investigators for the New Orleans District Attorney later found "notations in the margins of one of [Ferrie's] books, a reference manual on high-powered rifles," showing "that Ferrie had measured exactly how many feet an empty cartridge flew when ejected from that rifle and at what angle." Also, shortly before his weekend planning session with Marcello, David Ferrie admitted that he'd purchased a .38 pistol and that he'd deposited the $7,000 mentioned earlier into his bank account.

On November 7 and 8, 1963, Jack Ruby talked to two of Hoffa's associates in lengthy telephone conversations. Earlier, on November 1, Ruby had called Chicago, and on November 9 Ruby's recent visitor from Chicago—Lawrence Meyers—was in New Orleans; Ferrie had called Meyers just over a month earlier. It seems unlikely that Meyers was anything more than a low-level message courier who knew nothing about the overall operation.

Jack Ruby's volume of long-distance phone calls continued to explode in November. His usual number of calls per month was fewer than 10, but that number had risen to almost 30 in September, and in November there would be at least 110 phone calls. Ruby's cover story—at the time and later accepted by the Warren Commission—was that the calls were simply about a union problem involving his performers. However, many of his calls were to an incredible number of Mafia and Hoffa associates. They served as intermediaries and cutouts, as no doubt coded phrases were passed from Ruby to eventually reach others involved in the plot, with those in the middle knowing nothing of the assassination plans. Ruby could be helpful to Marcello not just if the President was killed in Dallas but also if the hit was in Tampa. Ruby had been stationed in Tampa during World War II and in recent years had reportedly made trips there to recruit strippers for his club.

ON NOVEMBER 9, 1963, undercover Miami Police tapes recorded white supremacist Joseph Milteer talking about JFK's murder less than two weeks before the assassination in Dallas. Milteer told Miami Police informant William Somersett about a plan "to assassinate the President with a high-powered rifle from a tall building." On the police tape, Milteer accurately states that authorities "will pick up somebody within hours afterwards . . . just to throw the public off." Milteer said the assassination had been arranged in such a way as to "drop the responsibility right into the laps of the Communists . . . or Castro."

Somersett also told authorities that Milteer had indicated "this conspiracy originated in New Orleans, and probably some in Miami." Milteer said "there was a lot of money" involved in the plot, not only from far-right extremists "but from men who could afford to contribute," though the only one he mentioned by name was a Louisiana political boss who was tied to both Carlos Marcello and Guy Banister. The Miami Police told the Secret Service and FBI about the tapes and plot. The FBI assigned Atlanta agent Don Adams to the case on November 13, and he went to the southern Georgia town of Quitman, where Milteer lived, to quietly investigate him. However, Adams told me that his FBI superiors never told him about the Miami police tapes of Milteer; he later learned they withheld other relevant information from him as well. Milteer was not arrested before JFK's Tampa motorcade, before Dallas, or even after JFK's murder.

While parts of the Milteer story and the audiotapes have been known to investigators for decades, it was only in 2006 that Michael L. Kurtz published accounts of reliable witnesses who could tie Milteer directly to Guy Banister and other associates of Carlos Marcello. He wrote that on one occasion a noted architect saw Banister and "Milteer conversing with some of Marcello's people in the French

Quarter." Aside from sharing racist views and hatred of the Kennedys, Banister, Milteer, and Marcello also shared a connection to the illegal arms trade, since in 1963 the major buyers of illegal weapons from organized crime included Cuban exile groups and white supremacists. Milteer traveled extensively and was in touch with the most violent racist groups active in 1963, as well as those trafficking in arms. Kurtz also noted that "Milteer had close connections to Santos Trafficante," since Milteer was also involved in "illegal arms and narcotics trafficking." Milteer would continue to make accurate remarks to Somersett about JFK's murder in the coming days, showing he was aware of—and possibly involved in—the plot. Milteer had inherited $200,000 from his father (over a million in today's dollars), and his determination to kill JFK appears to have been motivated by his racist ideology more than money.

John and Robert Kennedy were told about Milteer's threat before JFK made his trip to Florida. However, by mid-November 1963, JFK and RFK were dealing with pressing Cuban issues on several important fronts, in addition to an array of foreign crises and domestic problems. A November 8, 1963, *Los Angeles Times* article—headlined "Kennedy Ducking Cuba Problem, GOP Says" and picked up by other newspapers—slammed JFK for doing nothing about Cuba. The article reported "Republican Party [claims] that the Kennedy administration had 'swept Cuban affairs under the rug' since the Missile Crisis of October, 1962." A review of articles in the *New York Times* from May to November 1963 shows a constant stream of charges that JFK was soft on Cuba from Republican Presidential hopefuls Richard Nixon, Nelson Rockefeller, and Barry Goldwater. Senator Barry Goldwater (the eventual Republican nominee) was especially vocal, accusing JFK—his former colleague on the Senate Crime

Committee—of "doing everything in his power" to keep the flag of Cuban exiles "from ever flying over Cuba again."

President Kennedy was doing a great deal regarding Cuba, but none of it was in the public eye. Even while JFK was making his final attempts to reach a peaceful solution with Castro, he continued his efforts to overthrow the Cuban leader. As the December 1, 1963, date for the coup approached, Commander Almeida indicated to Harry Williams that he wanted JFK's personal assurance that the President would fully support the coup once it began. The plan was that on November 18, 1963, following JFK's long motorcade in Tampa, the President would go to Miami to deliver a speech, several lines of which would specifically reassure Commander Almeida that he had JFK's personal backing.

A CIA report from 1963, uncovered years later by Congressional investigators, confirms that in "Kennedy's speech of November 18, 1963 [in Miami], the CIA intended President Kennedy's speech to serve as a signal to dissident elements in Cuba that the US would support a coup." The CIA report states the wording was intended for "dissident elements in the Cuban Armed Forces [who] must have solemn assurances from high-level US spokesmen, especially the President, that the United States will exert its decisive influence during and immediately after the coup." Years later, Pulitzer Prize–winning journalist Sy Hersh wrote that CIA officer Seymour Bolten—an aide to Cuban Operations Chief Desmond FitzGerald—told a Congressional investigator that he had personally delivered the key paragraph written for JFK's speech. Declassified files withheld from Congress and not seen by Hersh confirm that Bolten's supervisor, FitzGerald, was a key participant of AMWORLD and the JFK–Almeida coup plan.

The last memo declassified from the Cuban Contingency planning shows that on November 12, 1963, the subcommittee was still working on "the preparation of contingency plans to counter the following possible actions by Castro," including the attempted "assassination of American officials." However, apparently John and Robert Kennedy—still digesting the political and security fallout from the canceled Chicago motorcade—decided against sharing information about the Chicago threat with the entire subcommittee. Telling all the subcommittee members would have meant their supervisors, aides, and secretaries could also find out, which could compromise the security of the impending coup plan. So most of those working on the Cuba Contingency planning, and other key personnel, hadn't been told crucial information about the assassination threat in Chicago. Declassified files show that Robert Kennedy was set to meet with coup plan exile leaders Harry Williams and Manuel Artime in Washington on November 17, 1963, the day before JFK's important speech for Almeida. But neither Williams nor Artime was told about the Chicago threat.

The stakes were incredibly high for JFK and RFK, since just five days after the Chicago attempt, American newspapers reported that Soviet leader Nikita Khrushchev had publicly warned the "US that attack on Cuba will lead to war." That made it all the more crucial that no hint of the coup plan could emerge from any investigation of the Chicago threat, or any threats that might emerge during JFK's upcoming trips to Tampa and Miami on November 18, 1963.

On November 17, in Florida, President Kennedy and his aides were putting the finishing touches on the image that JFK wanted to project to assure Commander Almeida of his support. That weekend, JFK had been at the Kennedy Palm Beach estate with Richard Goodwin and other aides, creating the final draft of his important Miami speech. JFK already had the passage the CIA had carefully crafted for Commander Almeida. The aides working on the speech didn't know about Almeida or that the CIA had written a small portion of JFK's remarks, as Goodwin confirmed to me. JFK's recent activities had been orchestrated to send a show of strength to Almeida and his allies in Cuba. That day, Florida newspapers featured major front-page coverage of JFK viewing the launch of a Polaris missile from a submarine. In Tampa JFK was scheduled to have a private—though widely publicized—meeting with the head of Strike Force Command (now Central Command) and other military brass, including some brought in from Washington. Coupled with the special lines in JFK's speech, all this was designed to reassure Almeida that JFK would back him and the coup all the way, even with US military force.

THE PLOT TO kill JFK was also proceeding on November 17, 1963. In Tampa, Gilberto Lopez was waiting on a very important phone call. According to the Senate Church Committee, Lopez "was at a get-together at the home of a member of the Tampa Chapter of the Fair Play for Cuba Committee [where he was] for some time waiting for a telephone call from Cuba which was very important. It was understood that it all depended on his getting the 'go ahead order' for him to leave the United States."

The released records give so many different reasons why Lopez claimed he wanted to return to Cuba that it's hard to pin down the real reason. Congressional investigators wrote that "Lopez told his wife he had received financial assistance for his trip to Cuba from an organization in Tampa [and] he would not have been able to pay for the trip without help." Lopez's trip would be unusual because he didn't own a car or drive—yet after JFK's Tampa motorcade, Lopez would embark on a long journey by car to Texas. Lopez would then be driven by a still-unidentified person to Mexico City, where he would catch a flight to Havana.

Declassified files say that Lopez had a brother "studying in the Soviet Union" at the time, which could have made Lopez useful to US intelligence, even though an FBI report says that Lopez "spoke very little English." In addition to not being able to drive, Lopez also had no passport and little money, so someone who could help him get to Cuba could have used that as a way to manipulate him. That could have been a US intelligence agency, the Mafia, or—as in the case of Oswald—both. A 2003 newspaper report pointed out how Lopez might have come to the attention of the Mafia, concluding that "Gilberto Policarpo Lopez['s] movements and activities suggest that he was a possible participant in Trafficante's activities," though on a very low level.* As for the call Lopez was waiting on from Cuba, that could have been from any number of Mafia or US intelligence assets who traveled to Cuba, including some who worked for David Morales.

In her first interview with a journalist, Lopez's wife (they never divorced, even after he returned to Cuba) told me Lopez was "a painter by trade" and that when she "left him in Tampa, he was working painting a big building . . . across from where they lived in Ybor City." The small Ybor City enclave in Tampa was frequented by Santo Trafficante, since it was home to his favorite restaurant.

A high Florida law-enforcement official I spoke with identified the full name of a man linked to Gilberto Lopez and the Fair Play for Cuba Committee who "was watched closely in conjunction with JFK's visit." The man's last name was Rodriguez, one of the names that had

---

*My own review of all the evidence shows that if Lopez did have contact with organized crime associates, he was being manipulated and was not knowingly working for the Mafia.

surfaced in the Chicago threat investigation. However, neither that official nor Tampa Police Chief Mullins—who had recently taken over from Chief Brown—was ever told about the Chicago threat.

According to one account, Lopez had another suspicious associate. The *Tampa Tribune* later reported that "on Nov. 17, 1963 [when] Lopez attended a meeting in the home of a member of the Tampa chapter of the Fair Play for Cuba Committee [also] thought to have been at that meeting was Lee Harvey Oswald." The article goes on to say that "recently declassified FBI files quote 'operatives' as saying Oswald met with a member of the Fair Play for Cuba Committee in Tampa on that date [though] that information was never confirmed."

My high Florida law-enforcement source stated that an "informant said that he'd met Oswald at an FPCC meeting in Tampa with several other people present, just before JFK's motorcade. The informant remembered Oswald's appearance, but not his name, so if it was Oswald, he may have been using an alias. This informant was different from the one cited by the *Tampa Tribune,* Joe Burton, who was known to our source as someone who "helped the FBI."

According to John H. Davis, "over the weekend of November 16, 17 [1963], the real Oswald disappeared entirely from view and his whereabouts on those two days still remain unknown." For the Tampa assassination attempt, the point is not whether the real Oswald was in Tampa or not on November 17, 1963; what is important is that someone wanted authorities to think he was, or might have been. Before JFK's Tampa motorcade, officials there would issue a lookout describing a potential assassin that actually matched Oswald much more closely than the first description issued after JFK's murder in Dallas.

THREE WEEKS AFTER Chicago, the Kennedys faced a shocking development at a critical time when officials discovered another plot to assassinate JFK, this time during his long Tampa motorcade on November 18. Officials uncovered the plot less than twenty-four hours before JFK's arrival and advised him to cancel his visit, since at least two potential assassins were on the loose. Tampa Police Chief Mullins told me that he also advised the President and his staff to cancel JFK's visit. However, another sudden cancellation was not a viable option for President Kennedy. While he and RFK had been able to keep the real reason for the Chicago cancellation out of the press, another major motorcade cancelled at the last minute would surely raise questions they couldn't answer.

In addition, JFK was set to give his important speech that night in Miami, with the important lines of assurance for Commander Almeida. How could President Kennedy ask Almeida to risk his life to stage a coup if word leaked that JFK had been too afraid to travel in his own motorcade? Despite the warnings, JFK decided to go ahead with the motorcade. Jackie wasn't with him on this trip, so the risk would be his alone.

The Tampa threat was verified not only by Chief Mullins and a former head of the Florida Intelligence Unit (who wishes to remain confidential because of his efforts against Santo Trafficante and his crime family) but also from newspaper accounts—which appeared the day after JFK's murder—and several official files. The threat involved at least two men, one of whom threatened to "use a gun" and was described by the Secret Service as "white, male, 20, slender build." (That description could fit Oswald or Lopez, who were just a few years older; though Hispanic, Lopez had a light complexion.) According to Congressional investigators, "Secret Service memos" say "the threat on Nov. 18, 1963 was posed by a mobile, unidentified rifleman shooting from a window in a tall building with a high power rifle fitted with a scope." That was the same basic scenario as Chicago and Dallas; however, those Congressional investigators weren't told the threat was active in Tampa. Chief Mullins confirmed that the police were told about the threat by the Secret Service prior to JFK's motorcade through Tampa, and they had their own source as well. The threat triggered even more security precautions. One motorcade participant recalls commenting at the time that "at every overpass there were police officers with rifles on alert."

Secret Service agent Sam Kinney said he learned later that "organized crime" was behind the threat. The former head of the Florida Intelligence Unit—who worked closely with the Tampa Police at the time—said that he was certain there was going to be a hit on JFK in Tampa. He later confirmed that Tampa mob boss Santo Trafficante was involved.

The official accompanied the Presidential party and said that the strain of dealing with the threat was why Kennedy appeared "handsome, tan, and smiling" in front of the crowds but appeared "tired and ill" backstage. Nevertheless, JFK went out of his way to present a fearless image in Tampa in spite of the threat. After finishing one of his speeches, JFK "surged out into the crowd, which immediately engulfed him. The Secret Service men with him went crazy," according to a report in a local newspaper. The article also noted a motorcade participant's recollection of "how concerned everyone was when" JFK "stood up in the car as he rode through the streets of Tampa after his talk." We'll never know whether he did so because of his ongoing back problems or, in case word of the threat leaked to the public, to show he wasn't afraid.

Chief Mullins and other officials were especially concerned about Tampa's tallest building, the Floridan Hotel, which overlooked a hard left turn for JFK's motorcade. The redbrick Floridan looks similar to the Texas School Book Depository, only much taller and with more windows; almost a hundred had a clear view of JFK's motorcade. The hotel was full that day and impossible to secure. In 1963 one could easily register under a false name—at that time, many travelers paid with cash—and every guest room window in the Floridan could be opened. The hotel was just one short block away from the intersection where JFK's limo would have to come to almost a full stop to make its turn. For a sniper perched in one of the hotel windows, sitting back in the shadows, assassinating the President would have been all too easy.

Chief Mullins and the Secret Service didn't know if the two suspects at large were southern white supremacists, disgruntled anti-Castro exiles, pro-Castro exiles, or Cuban agents. (The shadowy Cuban Miguel Casas Saez, who was reported near Chicago just before JFK's motorcade there, had also been reported in Florida.) Even without knowing about Marcello's two hit men from Europe, officials in Tampa had plenty of reasons to urge JFK to cancel his entire motorcade.

But JFK disregarded their warnings and insisted on going ahead. The clear "bubble top" for JFK's limo wasn't used. It wasn't bulletproof anyway, and using it would send the wrong message to Commander Almeida. The Lincoln in which JFK rode in Tampa was the same one he would later use in Dallas. Just as in Chicago, a complete press blackout about the threat was informally ordered. A tight lid of secrecy was clamped down on all information about the threat. Two small articles appeared right after JFK's death, but even then the story was quickly suppressed, and they received no follow-up. Chief Mullins was quoted in those articles—at first openly talking about the threat but by the following day saying nothing—and he didn't speak for publication about the threat again until I interviewed him in the mid-1990s.

The attempt to kill JFK in Tampa was withheld from the Warren Commission and all later government investigating committees—until I told the JFK Assassination Records Review Board about it, in writing, on November 24, 1994. According to the Review Board's Final Report, just two months later, "January 1995, the Secret Service destroyed Presidential protection survey reports for some of President Kennedy's trips in the fall of 1963," including Tampa. The Secret Service informed the Board a week after it destroyed the records, "when the Board was drafting its request for additional information." That destruction apparently broke the law, since the 1992 JFK Act that created the Review Board had required agencies to preserve all relevant records. However, when the Secret Service destroyed records for JFK's Tampa trip in 1995, Commander Almeida was still alive in Cuba—and his secret work for JFK not been publicly exposed—giving the Secret Service a possible national security reason for its actions.

After JFK's death, the Tampa threat still could not be exposed to the general public since there was still the chance that Oswald or other suspects might prove to have connections to Castro or the coup plan. The public's faith in the Secret Service, already at a low ebb after Dallas, would have been shaken to the core if weeks or months after JFK's death it was revealed that the agency had covered up an assassination attempt in Tampa that had so many parallels with Dallas.

JFK GAVE SEVERAL speeches in Tampa, including one at the International Inn, where—four days later—Santo Trafficante would publicly toast JFK's death. After JFK concluded his Tampa trip, a member of the Tampa Police motorcycle detail told the *St. Petersburg Times* that "Chief of Police J. P. Mullins introduced each of us to the President," who was no doubt grateful that he had survived the motorcade unharmed.

The ex-chief of the Florida Intelligence Unit told me that Santo Trafficante had called off the attempt to kill JFK shortly before the President's arrival. He explained that Trafficante's man in the Tampa Police Department, Sergeant Jack de la Llana, "was in the motorcade meetings and was feeding information to Trafficante at the time." The official source, who also helped with JFK's security, said it was "likely that de la Llana could have tipped off Trafficante about the [security] plans" and, once the plot became known, about the "threat alerts."

Chief Mullins said his department provided much information to the FBI at the time of the Tampa threat. However, those documents have never surfaced in declassified FBI files. In fact, the declassified Tampa field office FBI file from the time of JFK's trip at the National Archives makes hardly any mention of JFK's trip to Tampa, indicating that Bureau files related to the threat were considered highly sensitive and filed separately.

The sheriff of a county adjacent to Tampa confirmed to the *Tampa Tribune*—in the small article that slipped out the day after JFK's murder—that officers had been "warned about 'a young man' who had threatened to kill the President during that trip." In the article, Chief Mullins mentioned another man at large, identified as a threat, and wondered "if the . . . two may have followed the Presidential caravan to Dallas." Chief Mullins didn't know at the time that Gilberto Lopez had indeed headed to Texas, reportedly Dallas, or that two more men investigated for JFK's murder—involved with Trafficante's drug network and described shortly—were also headed from Florida to Dallas in the coming days.

ON THE EVENING of November 18, the President flew to Miami and gave his most important speech, with lines directed at Commander Almeida and his allies in Cuba. Those carefully crafted sentences were also designed so they would not upset JFK's back-channel negotiations with Fidel. In his speech, JFK proclaimed:

> What now divides Cuba from my country . . . is the fact that a small band of conspirators has stripped the Cuban people of their freedom and handed over the independence and sovereignty of the Cuban nation to forces beyond the hemisphere. They have made Cuba a victim of foreign imperialism. . . . This, and this alone, divides us. As long as this is true, nothing is possible. Without it, everything is possible. Once this barrier is removed, we will be ready and anxious to work with the Cuban people.

The following day several newspapers trumpeted those lines almost too clearly. The *Dallas Times Herald* said, "Kennedy Virtually Invites Cuban Coup"; the *Miami Herald* said, "Kennedy Invites Coup"; and the *New York Times* proclaimed, "Kennedy says US will aid Cuba once Cuban sovereignty is restored under a non-communist government."

Commander Almeida was satisfied with JFK's remarks in Miami and communicated that to Harry Williams. Declassified files show that in the days following Almeida's response to JFK's speech, Robert Kennedy had his final meetings in Washington with Manuel Artime and Harry Williams before the coup. Robert Kennedy arranged for Harry Williams to have a crucial meeting with CIA officials on the morning of November 22, 1963, as later confirmed by the *Washington Post*.

After JFK returned to Washington, he expressed his relief at surviving the trip to his close aide David Powers. According to Kennedy biographer Ralph Martin, JFK told Powers, "Thank God nobody wanted to kill me today!" JFK explained that an assassination "would be tried by someone with a high-power rifle and a telescopic sight during a downtown parade when there would be so much noise and confetti that nobody would even be able to point and say, 'It came from that window.'"

After JFK's Tampa motorcade and Miami speech, John and Robert Kennedy could breathe a sigh of relief as they looked ahead to JFK's upcoming trip to Texas. They knew of no active threat in Texas as there had been in Chicago and Tampa. Moreover, Dallas didn't have a large Cuban exile population to worry about, as did Tampa and Chicago.

CHIEF MULLINS WONDERED if "two [of the Tampa suspects] may have followed the Presidential caravan to Dallas," and there is a well-documented account of two men and a woman doing just that. The woman was Rose Cheramie (one of many aliases used by Melba Christine Marcades), a member of the lowest rung of the Mertz–Marcello–Trafficante heroin network. Cheramie was a sometime B-girl, prostitute, and heroin courier for Ruby.

On November 21, 1963, Rose Cheramie had been dumped on the side of the road by two men she was riding with from Florida. She was eventually taken into custody by Louisiana State Police Lieutenant Francis Fruge, who drove her to East Louisiana State Hospital to be treated for heroin withdrawal. Cheramie told Fruge that she and her two male companions had been on their way to Dallas, where the men were going to "kill Kennedy." Her remarks were also heard by physicians at the hospital, including Victor Weiss, head of the hospital's Psychiatry Department, who said that on Thursday, November 21, "Cheramie was absolutely sure Kennedy was going to be assassinated in Dallas on Friday and kept insisting on it over and over again to the doctors and nurses who were attending her." According to Dr. Weiss, Cheramie said that "word was out in the New Orleans underworld that the contract on Kennedy had been let," and Dr. Weiss assumed she was referring to Carlos Marcello's organization. Cheramie would later be proven an accurate informant regarding Marcello's part in the French Connection ring, but at this time no one was taking her seriously. It's ironic that a woman who was one of the lowest members of Marcello's crime empire came so close to exposing part of the godfather's plot, which could have saved JFK's life.

The man at the highest levels of that heroin network, Michel Victor Mertz, had been traveling in America in 1963, sometimes under his own name—most recently in October—and sometimes under the name of "Jean Souetre," an old associate from a mission that Mertz had undertaken for French Intelligence several years earlier. Mertz, who won the French Legion of Honor for killing twenty Nazis for the French Resistance in World War II, sometimes did work for French Intelligence to avoid prosecution for his crimes.

Jean Souetre, the alias Mertz used in Dallas on November 22, 1963, and in the days before, was the name of a fugitive French officer who in 1962 had participated in the attempted assassination of French President Charles de Gaulle. This attempt was more serious than the one Mertz had foiled a year earlier, since Souetre's group was able to hit de Gaulle's car with numerous bullets. The French President survived, and the incident inspired Frederick Forsyth's novel *The Day of the Jackal*. Souetre was one of several men imprisoned for the attempt, though he later escaped.

Jean Souetre himself did not travel to America in the 1960s, and on November 22, 1963, the real Souetre was in Barcelona, Spain, and has witnesses to prove it. On the other hand, INS records provided to the French government show that Mertz traveled frequently to America in 1963 and before as part of his heroin-smuggling activities.

"Souetre" was a loaded name for Mertz to use as his own, since the real Souetre had met with—and sought support from—the CIA in May 1963 in Europe. Souetre had even been the subject of a memo by Richard Helms in the summer of 1963. Former Senate investigator Bud Fensterwald found that "the FBI had traced [the man they thought was] Souetre to Dallas a day before the assassination and then lost him." The fact that Mertz was using the identity of a wanted French Presidential assassin, recently tied to the CIA, was sure to generate fireworks when his alias surfaced as being in Dallas when JFK was shot.

CHAPTER 14

JFK Is Assassinated in Dallas

I N THE DAYS before the President's trip to Dallas, John and Robert Kennedy were dealing with matters related to their upcoming coup in Cuba. Richard Helms had shown RFK and JFK a Cuban rifle from a "three-ton Cuban arms cache left by terrorists on a Venezuelan beach, as well as blueprints for a coup [by Castro] against" the president of Venezuela, according to historian Michael Beschloss. Helms was no fan of JFK and RFK's secret peace feelers with Castro, so this was probably his attempt to short-circuit any peace negotiations and to cover himself if his unauthorized CIA–Mafia plots to kill Fidel were uncovered. A later US military investigation by Lt. Col. Alexander Haig and Joseph Califano—both working for Army Secretary Cyrus Vance—concluded that "many of the items found were in fact of US origin." Even veteran CIA officer Joseph B. Smith would write in his memoirs that he "was not too impressed with this evidence of the Venezuelan guerrillas' intended use of the arms. It sounded to me as though we might have manufactured it."

Smith's memoirs—written decades before the JFK–Almeida coup plan was first exposed—also contained an interesting remark he heard in 1964 from CIA official Desmond FitzGerald. Without providing any details about how it would have been accomplished, FitzGerald told him, "If Jack Kennedy had lived . . . I can assure you we would have gotten rid of Castro by last Christmas [1963]." Even within the CIA, little more than a handful of people knew about Commander Almeida, but FitzGerald was one of them.

Robert Kennedy celebrated his thirty-eighth birthday on November 20, 1963, and shortly after that had his last meeting with Harry Williams. RFK had arranged for Williams to meet on Friday, November 22, with a group of CIA officials for a final planning meeting for the Almeida coup. After a session that would stretch from morning to afternoon, Williams would leave for Miami that night. From there, he would be flown to the US Naval Base at Guantánamo on November 23, and from there slip into Castro's Cuba, to meet personally with Almeida and await the coup on December 1. The ten days from November 22 to December 1 would essentially be the countdown for the JFK–Almeida coup plan. Once Harry Williams was inside Cuba around November 26, there might be no turning back for JFK and RFK, since secure communication with Williams at that point might be impossible.

RFK appears to have been close to finally telling some Cabinet officials—including Dean Rusk—about Commander Almeida, letting them know that the coup plans they'd been working on for months were about to be put into effect. Responding to a still classified memo RFK had written on November 20 about Cuba, JFK's National Security advisor McGeorge Bundy replied to RFK by saying, "The Cuban problem is ready for discussion now . . . so we will call a meeting as soon as we can find a day when the right people are in town." JFK was getting ready to leave for Texas the next day, while Rusk and several other cabinet members would be flying to the Far East on the same day. Early the following week, around November 25, would be the soonest all the administration's top officials could be gathered. That may well have been the meeting at which officials like Rusk and McNamara would finally be told about Almeida, since at that point the coup would have been less than a week away.

JFK and RFK had been hoping for a breakthrough with their peace feelers, but progress was slow. A November 19, 1963, White House memo says that Special UN envoy William Attwood was dealing with Fidel's doctor, who'd wanted Attwood "to come to Cuba" but Attwood had "replied this was impossible for the present." He wanted Castro's doctor to come to New York, but the doctor couldn't make the trip. Instead he proposed having Attwood talk to Cuba's envoy at the UN. Even this was just to have "preliminary talks . . . for the discussion of an agenda" for actual negotiations. The ball was left "in Castro's court," but the slow pace must have frustrated JFK and RFK, especially with the December 1 coup date looming.

The Kennedy brothers had no way of knowing that their other secret peace initiative was finally starting to produce results. In Cuba, French journalist Jean Daniel finally had the meeting with Castro he'd been waiting for since late October. According to Arthur Schlesinger, after "spending three fruitless weeks in Havana," Daniel was surprised by a visit from Fidel Castro at 10:00 p.m., the night before the journalist was scheduled to leave Cuba. Daniel and Castro talked until 4:00 a.m., and Daniel conveyed Kennedy's wishes from late October about his desire for dialogue. The two men arranged to have lunch again, to continue their discussion—on November 22, 1963. Not only is the date ironic, but the location of their lunch was to be Castro's "villa at the beach," at Varadero— the very place one later AMWORLD document identifies as a good place to assassinate Castro, since it was near the home of CIA asset

Rolando Cubela.* However, with no US embassy in Cuba or other secure way to communicate, JFK and RFK had no way of learning that Daniel had met with Fidel or that he was scheduled to meet with him again.

ROBERT KENNEDY WAS continuing his unrelenting attack on organized crime, not just in the courts but also in the press. During the week of November 18 through 22, the *New York Times* ran an impressive five-part series about ties between the Mafia, Hoffa's Teamsters, and Las Vegas. RFK had supported the *Times* investigation by providing crucial information and quotes. The articles revealed that RFK was getting ready to run the Mafia out of Las Vegas, the mob's relatively secure stronghold. A separate *Times* story that week would have also pleased RFK, as it spotlighted the Mafia ties of one of JFK's potential rivals, when it reported that "Sen. Goldwater admits association with Willie Bioff, labor racketeer slain in 1955 and Gus Greenbaum, gambler slain in 1958." The publicity-shy Johnny Rosselli had ties to both murders.

RFK's *Times* series capped an autumn full of anti-Mafia publicity, which had begun with the nation being riveted by a new series of televised crime hearings that for the first time truly exposed the inner workings of the Mafia. Mobster Joe Valachi, the star of those hearings, had cooperated with authorities only because he was facing a death sentence. RFK's goal was to galvanize the public against the Mafia using the Valachi Hearings, held by the Kennedys' old friend Senator John McClellan. The focus of the hearings was "Organized Crime and

---

*It's ironic that before the Cuban Revolution, Castro's villa had belonged to the family of Ethel Kennedy, Robert Kennedy's wife.

Illicit Traffic in Narcotics," striking at the heart of Trafficante and Marcello's lucrative French Connection.

On November 20, RFK had been briefed "on the progress of the Marcello trial" in New Orleans, according to John H. Davis, who says RFK was told "a favorable verdict was expected in a couple of days. For Friday [November] 22, [Robert] Kennedy had scheduled a top-level meeting on organized crime to be attended by his personal staff and US attorneys from all over the nation. He was looking forward to giving them the good news from New Orleans as soon as it came in. On Thursday, November 21, the defense rested" in the Marcello case.

However, as Davis and a later court case extensively documented, Carlos Marcello had bribed a key juror and already knew he would be acquitted on Friday. Being in court that day would not only give Marcello an ironclad alibi for JFK's murder; it would also allow him to plan a celebration for that evening, ostensibly to celebrate his acquittal.

RICHARD HELMS WAS busy with the CIA's portion of the JFK–Almeida coup plan, which included the Agency's efforts to get US "assets into Cuba" prior to the coup. However, Helms had still not given up on his own unauthorized Castro assassination operations, the CIA–Mafia plots to kill Fidel, and the related operation with Rolando Cubela, code-named AMLASH. According to the Senate Church Committee's later investigation, "on November 19, AMLASH told a CIA officer that he planned to return to Cuba immediately." But on that same date, a CIA memo says "[Desmond] FitzGerald approved telling Cubela he would be given a [weapons] cache inside Cuba. Cache could, if he requested it, include . . . high power rifles w/ scopes." So, on November 20, 1963, a CIA officer telephoned Cubela and asked him to postpone his return to Cuba in order to attend a meeting on November 22 in Paris.

It's well documented that the CIA set the tragic timing of the November 22 meeting, not Cubela (something ignored by those who try to blame JFK's murder on Castro, by claiming Cubela was a double agent). Cubela would be meeting with his CIA case officer at the very time JFK was assassinated, while the CIA man was trying to give the reluctant Cubela a CIA-devised poison pen to use to kill Fidel. David Morales could have orchestrated that fateful timing, knowing the cover-ups it would generate within the Agency after JFK's murder.

IT'S IMPORTANT TO point out that JFK's motorcade route was first announced and published in the Dallas newspapers only on November 19, 1963. A myth has grown up that somehow the motorcade route was mysteriously changed, to bring it closer to the Texas School Book Depository. The House Select Committee on Assassinations looked into that story and found it to be false. Simply looking at all the articles published that day bears them out—the dog-leg turn toward the Book Depository was there from the start. It was necessary to keep the entire motorcade from having to drive across a concrete median to reach the Stemmons Freeway.* Prior to that announcement, the Mafia's plotters could have assumed the motorcade would pass somewhere through Dealey Plaza, and the dog-leg turn simply made their job easier.

Yet another myth about JFK's murder in Dallas is that somehow, the Secret Service was negligent or complicit, because they didn't search

---

*There's also a myth that JFK had to cancel his motorcade in Miami on November 18, where he gave a speech after his visit to Tampa. But the House Select Committee looked into that as well and found there was not a motorcade planned for Miami.

all the buildings along the motorcade route. It is true that Secret Service agent Forrest Sorrels would later testify to the Warren Commission that "while making a security survey of the route" in Dallas "with some Dallas Police Department officers, he remarked to those present that shooting JFK with a high-powered rifle with a scope would not be difficult." As we now know, Sorrells would have been worried about that because of the recent threats in Chicago and Tampa.

However, in Dallas, unlike in those cities, the Secret Service had learned of no specific threat or plot to assassinate JFK. The extraordinary security in Tampa, which involved police searching key buildings along the motorcade route, wasn't typical, as is borne out by the Secret Service's own regulations: "In general, the Secret Service does not inspect buildings along a moving [motorcade] route except under three circumstances: 1. Presidential inaugurations, 2. Visits by a king or president of a foreign country, or 3. When the motorcade route has been known for years," and not just a few days.

AFTER CALLING OFF their attempts to kill JFK in Tampa and Chicago, Carlos Marcello and Santo Trafficante had one last chance to implement their plan to assassinate JFK. After JFK's November 22, 1963, motorcade in Dallas, there would not be another opportunity to apply their plan before JFK's upcoming coup in Cuba on December 1, 1963. Without the intense secrecy surrounding the impending coup, whose exposure could trigger "World War III," they might not be able to trigger a national security cover-up by high US officials. The fact that the press secrecy surrounding the Tampa and Chicago attempts had held meant that local officials in Dallas would likely have little idea about the close calls JFK had experienced in recent weeks, making the job of the mob bosses easier.

The two European shooters—who had been training at Marcello's huge, secluded Churchill Farms estate outside New Orleans—had likely never been sent to Tampa. The gunmen were taken to Dallas by Joe Campisi, Sr., Marcello's number-two underboss in that city. Twenty-two years later, Marcello explained to his cellmate Jack Van Laningham the key role Campisi played in his plot. Campisi hid the two hitmen at his restaurant until it was time for them to go to Dealey Plaza, before JFK's motorcade was scheduled to pass through that park-like part of downtown Dallas.

The shooters' presence in Dallas prior to JFK's arrival in the city might help explain an unusual police incident that the FBI withheld from the Warren Commission. Marcello's biographer, John H. Davis, wrote that on the morning of Wednesday, November 20, 1963, two police officers on routine patrol entered Dealey Plaza . . . and noticed several men standing behind a wooden fence on the grassy knoll over-looking the plaza. The men were engaged in what appeared to be mock target practice, aiming rifles over the fence in the direction of the Plaza. The two police officers immediately made for the fence, but by the time they got there the riflemen had disappeared, having departed in a car that had been parked nearby. The two patrol officers did not give much thought to the incident at the time, but after the assassination . . . they reported the incident to the FBI, which issued a report of it on November 26. For reasons that have never been satisfactorily explained, the substance of the report was never mentioned in the FBI's investigation of the assassination, and the report itself disappeared until 1978.

While the incident sounds alarming by today's standards, the area behind the picket fence was the parking lot for the Dallas deputy sheriffs and nearby was the parking lot for the Texas School Book

Depository. It was not that unusual in Dallas at that time for men to bring rifles to work in such areas, to show, trade, or sell.

One reason Bureau officials like J. Edgar Hoover withheld that report from the Warren Commission was probably that the FBI had lost track of French assassin and heroin trafficker Michel Victor Mertz—using the name of another French assassin, Jean Souetre—in Dallas shortly before JFK's murder. Even worse, the FBI hadn't informed the Secret Service about the matter prior to JFK's arrival. Just over three months after JFK's murder, on March 5, 1964, an FBI memo sent to the CIA would state that the Bureau had learned from French authorities that using the Souetre alias, "Michel Mertz . . . was in Fort Worth on the morning of 22 November and in Dallas in the afternoon." Mertz was apparently stalking JFK, who was in Fort Worth the morning of November 22, before heading to Dallas for his afternoon visit.

ON THURSDAY, NOVEMBER 21, 1963, in Dallas at the Texas School Book Depository, Lee Harvey Oswald asked his co-worker Wesley Frazier for a ride home after work. Oswald was living in a rooming house in the Oak Cliff section of Dallas, while his wife, Marina, and their children still lived with Ruth Paine. Oswald usually went home to Marina only on weekends (though he hadn't on the previous weekend), but he told Frazier that he wanted a ride to visit Marina that evening. According to Frazier, Oswald told him he wanted to get some curtain rods. Oswald planned to spend the night at Ruth Paine's and then ride to work with Frazier on Friday.

Based on all the evidence, it appears that Oswald was planning to leave work the following day, in order—he thought—to go meet his contact at the Texas Theatre, just as confessed conspirator John

Martino said. Oswald's goal was to get to Mexico City, and then on to Cuba, as part of a mission for a US intelligence agency (either the CIA or Naval Intelligence, or both). Warren Commission counsel David Belin outlined in a memo (not in the *Warren Report*) how Oswald could have traveled to Mexico on November 22, using bus connections and the amount of money he had. While that makes sense from the perspective of Oswald's maintaining his lowly, far-left cover for a mission, it would be ludicrous for someone to try to escape on public transportation after having shot the President of the United States.

The following morning, Oswald would leave his wedding ring in a cup on the dresser and $170 in a wallet in a dresser drawer. Clearly, Oswald knew he was leaving Dallas and wouldn't be back any time soon. Oswald would bring a package with him that morning, wrapped in brown paper, but it probably wasn't curtain rods. However, it was physically impossible for the package to have contained the Mannlicher-Carcano rifle later identified as the murder weapon, that Oswald is said to have kept wrapped in a blanket in Ruth Paine's garage.

When Oswald went to work the following morning, Wesley Frazier's sister saw Oswald walking across the lawn toward Wesley's car, carrying something in a long paper bag. However, the bag could not have contained the Mannlicher-Carcano rifle that would be found later that day on the sixth floor of the Texas School Book Depository. She later testified that Oswald was holding the top of the package, which didn't touch the ground. However, even a disassembled Mannlicher-Carcano was too long at 34.8 inches to hold in that fashion without actually dragging the ground.

Her account of the length of the package was backed up by Wesley Frazier, who testified to the Warren Commission that after they arrived at the Book Depository, he saw Oswald holding the package cupped in his hand and tucked under into his armpit, under his shoulder. It's impossible for a normal human to hold a package like that, which is as long as a disassembled Mannlicher. That is easy to demonstrate with an ordinary yardstick, which is only 1.2 inches longer than a disassembled Mannlicher. You simply can't cup it in your hand, and tuck it under your shoulder, as Oswald did with the package. For Oswald's body, the maximum length the package could have been was about 23 inches, not the 34.8 inches of the disassembled Mannlicher.

The sworn accounts of Frazier and his sister are important, since that means Oswald didn't take the Mannlicher-Carcano to the Depository that day. Also critical is the fact that no one saw Oswald take any package—or any object—into the Texas School Book Depository on November 22. After they arrived, Oswald walked ahead of Frazier, who didn't see Oswald enter the building. No one in the building saw Oswald with the package. No one saw Oswald enter the building except for Jack Dougherty, who remembered Oswald but said he wasn't holding a package. This raises the possibility that Oswald's package was passed off to someone waiting near the Book Depository or the parking lot.

What was in the package? There is an unconfirmed report from a mob associate that some type of demonstration or incident relating to Cuba was planned for Dealey Plaza that day. Oswald may have been told that a pro-Cuba banner would be unfurled from a Depository window, or otherwise displayed, that would embarrass JFK with a pro-Castro message. It would have been easy for Banister or Ferrie to tell Oswald such an incident would create news stories like he'd had in New Orleans that would supposedly cause the Cuban Embassy in

Mexico City to welcome him when he tried to get into Cuba. Whatever Oswald brought in his package that morning, he could have thought it was to help with such a banner or demonstration. However, the most important thing to remember is that whatever was in the package, it wasn't the Mannlicher-Carcano rifle.

Finally, as events unfold over the coming days, it's important to keep in mind that authors such as Anthony Summers have documented that "nobody has ever made the flimsiest allegation that the authentic Lee Oswald had anything but good to say about John Kennedy." This was true in Oswald's interrogations, his media appearances, and his private talks. Three months before JFK's murder, Oswald had been interviewed by a New Orleans police lieutenant who later said that Oswald "seemed to favor President Kennedy [and] in no way demonstrated any animosity or ill feeling toward President Kennedy . . . he liked the President."

THE FBI RECEIVED numerous credible reports from witnesses that Jack Ruby was in Houston on the afternoon of November 21, a couple of hours before JFK was scheduled to arrive there. Ruby was sighted one block from the Rice Hotel, where President Kennedy would deliver a speech, before flying to Fort Worth, where JFK and Jackie Kennedy would spend the night. Ruby also called a Houston booking agent while he was in town. According to one account, Ruby didn't leave Houston until after JFK's arrival. If Ruby was in Houston, he might have been there to observe security preparations for JFK, or to meet someone else involved in the plot, or both. Just two days earlier, Ruby had seen his tax attorney and Ruby "said he had a connection who would supply him money to settle his long-standing government tax problems," which totaled $40,000 (almost $300,000 today).

On that same day, Seth Kantor notes that "Ruby's Carousel checking account" had $246.65 in it, about the usual amount.

Back in Dallas on Thursday evening, November 21, Ruby had dinner at Campisi's Egyptian Restaurant with one of his friends and business associates, Ralph Paul. It was Paul who apparently fronted the money from Marcello's organization to Ruby and who theoretically owned 50% of the Carousel Club. According to Anthony Summers, Paul was "associated with Austin's Bar-B-Cue," where one of the part-time security guards was Dallas Police officer J. D. Tippit. Congressional investigators determined that the married Tippit had been carrying on a long-term affair with a waitress at Austin's. Author Henry Hurt talked to the woman, who confirmed that, at the time, she thought she was pregnant by Tippit. This would have made Tippit subject to pressure or blackmail by one of Paul's associates—like Ruby. It could have simply been a matter of Tippit's being told to be in the right place at the right time on November 22 to make a big arrest, with no advance indication to Tippit of what was going to happen to JFK.

Joe Campisi Sr. verified Ruby's presence at his restaurant that night, though he later claimed to Congressional investigators he had not been there that day. Given the fact that Marcello has stated that Campisi was hiding the shooters at his restaurant that night, it's clear why Campisi would deny having been there. It also puts Ruby's visit to Campisi's in a whole new light, since it would have given Ruby an opportunity to make plans with Campisi for the following day, in one of the restaurant's secure back offices. Ruby would later call Campisi one of his "three best friends," but theirs was much more of a business relationship, with Campisi calling the shots. Campisi, on the other hand, was very close to Carlos Marcello.

After leaving Campisi's, Ruby spent time at the Carousel Club and the Bon Vivant Room restaurant in the Teamster-financed Cabana Hotel with Lawrence Meyers, from Chicago. As noted earlier, Meyers—who also had contact with David Ferrie—appears to have been a low-level mob messenger or courier.

AFTER JFK AND Jackie arrived at their Fort Worth hotel, many in their Secret Service detail took time to relax. After the Fort Worth Press Club closed, at least six off-duty Secret Service agents showed up at Fort Worth's Cellar Club, which Warren Commission files describe as a "night spot that poses as a beatnik place," a coffee shop where customers could bring their own liquor or drink what the Commission called "fruit drinks" (Kool-Aid spiked with high-proof alcohol). After the recent stress of the Chicago and Tampa threats, it's not surprising that the agents would be ready for some relaxation, especially since no threat or warning had emerged for the next day's Dallas visit. According to CBS anchor Bob Schieffer—then a reporter for a Fort Worth newspaper—a major attraction for the club was that its waitresses wore only "underwear" while serving drinks, though another report says they wore bikinis.

The owner of the Cellar club, Pat Kirkwood, knew both Jack Ruby and mob associate Lewis McWillie. Kirkwood claimed in a filmed interview for Jack Anderson in 1988 that several strippers who worked for Jack Ruby had come to the club late that night, and he indicated that Jack Ruby might have sent them over on purpose. Kirkwood also claimed that some of the agents "were drinking pure Everclear [alcohol]." Warren Commission documents confirm that some of Ruby's strippers knew Kirkwood. Whether or not the women were sent by Ruby on purpose, the fact that Secret Service agents were out so late the night before Kennedy's visit was important information for someone like Ruby. Their presence indicated that the Mafia's plan for Dallas hadn't leaked, as it had in Chicago and Tampa. None of the Secret Service limo drivers were involved, though several high-profile agents from the next day's events were. The agents' recent accounts of their exploits in Dallas usually leave out or gloss over this well-documented incident. Though the agents' names are all listed in the Warren Commission volumes, along with their time spent at the club and the drinks they say they consumed, I've decided not to name them here.

The agents left at various times, but the last agent didn't leave until 5 a.m., even though they had to report for duty at 8 a.m.

NOVEMBER 22, MORNING, WASHINGTON, DC

Harry Williams began his RFK-arranged meeting with CIA officials in Washington, DC, at an Agency safe house. Writing about that meeting twenty years later in the *Washington Post*, Pulitzer Prize–winning journalist Haynes Johnson said that Williams's work for the Kennedys about "the problem of Cuba . . . had reached an important point." As a result, on that day Williams "participated in the most crucial of a series of secret meetings with top-level CIA and government people." Haynes confirmed in his article that Williams was the Cuban exile leader closest to JFK's administration.

As reported by *Vanity Fair* and former FBI agent William Turner, those at the meeting included Harry Williams, E. Howard Hunt, James McCord,* and CIA Executive Director Lyman Kirkpatrick (the number-three official in the Agency, who outranked Richard Helms).

---

*James McCord was a CIA Security Officer at the time. After retiring from the CIA, he would later be convicted as one of the Watergate burglars. In contrast to Hunt, Kennedy aides like Harry Williams had only positive things to say about McCord.

Helms and Desmond FitzGerald have also been reported as having attended at least a brief part of the long meeting.

Harry Williams said that Lyman Kirkpatrick asked many probing questions about the coup plan with Almeida. Apparently, Kirkpatrick was anxious to make sure the operation didn't become another Bay of Pigs disaster for the United States. However, no problems surfaced and the plan looked ready to go forward. They would break for lunch around noon, Eastern time, with Williams eating separately from the CIA men.

That same morning, at CIA headquarters, Director John McCone sent a memo to the head of the Miami CIA Station, Ted Shackley, confirming that the "general uprising scheduled for 1 Dec" 1963 was "planned as [a] result of [the] Mil[itary] Service Act" because "in [the] opinion of" the coup "Leaders [the Cuban draft] would tremendously" impact the "clandestine movement in Cuba." McCone's memo was withheld from the Warren Commission and from all of the government investigating committees of the 1970s. It wasn't declassified until 1993, when it slipped through in a mass release of files, and wasn't published until 2005.

AT THE JUSTICE Department, Robert Kennedy was in a meeting about organized crime with forty of his attorneys from the Racketeering division. According to John H. Davis, "major items on the agenda were the investigations of" Rosselli's boss "Sam Giancana, Santo Trafficante, Jimmy Hoffa, and Carlos Marcello." RFK was told that the verdict in the Marcello case in New Orleans could come as early as that day. The last subject before they broke for lunch was Sam Giancana and corruption in Chicago. RFK would go home for lunch, to his Hickory Hill estate in Virginia.

To cover as many important facts as possible on this critical day, I will describe brief passages in approximate chronological order. Where times are given, they should be considered approximate, as are dates when events happened very late at night or very early in the morning. Since most of the key events occurred in Texas, Central time is used unless otherwise indicated. JFK's assassination occurred at 12:30 p.m. CST. Some meetings or incidents that we've covered extensively in earlier chapters are mentioned only briefly here, to place them in the context of other important events.

Most witness accounts in Dealey Plaza are from early, official Dallas Police, FBI, and Secret Service reports, supplemented by interviews conducted by noted journalists. I've chosen to focus on reliable accounts that the Warren Commission largely overlooked or ignored, because they ran counter to the Commission's conclusions. There are far more such accounts that can be noted here, but the Annotated Bibliography provides numerous sources to find them.

NOVEMBER 22, FORT WORTH AND DALLAS

7:30 a.m.: JFK woke up in the Hotel Texas in Fort Worth. JFK told Jackie and aide Lawrence O'Donnell, "If somebody wants to shoot me from a window with a rifle, nobody can stop it, so why worry about it?" JFK added, "Last night would have been a hell of a night to assassinate a president. I mean it—the rain and the night and we were all getting jostled," as JFK acted out the shooting scenario for Jackie. It's now clear that JFK was talking about assassination because of the recent threats he dealt with in Tampa and that made him cancel his Chicago trip.

After giving a breakfast speech to the Fort Worth Chamber of Commerce, and greeting crowds outside the hotel, JFK and Jackie flew from Forth Worth to Love Field, in Dallas.

11:38 a.m.: Air Force One landed at Love Field with JFK and Jackie aboard. On the presidential wavelength of the Secret Service radio net, JFK and Jackie were referred to by their code names, Lancer and Lace. An open limo driven by Secret Service Agent Bill Greer—age fifty-four, with thity-five years of experience—was waiting to take them through Dallas.

11:40-11:45 a.m.: Oswald asked another employee why a crowd was gathering outside, and when told the President was visiting, Oswald replied, "Oh, I see." When his co-workers went to lunch, Oswald remained on the upper floor, where he was working.

11:50 a.m.: A foreman "saw Oswald near the telephone on the first floor" at ten or fifteen minutes before noon (just thirty minutes before JFK was shot). It's not known what calls Oswald might have made or received that day.

11:50 a.m.: JFK's motorcade left Love Field.

12:00 p.m.: Four witnesses say that Oswald was downstairs, around the lunch room, at this time. Book Depository employee Bonnie Ray Williams returned to the sixth floor to eat his lunch.

AT THIS POINT, it's important to describe the area around the Book Depository. Dealey Plaza is a funnel-shaped area composed of Houston Street at the top (the wide part of the funnel), with Elm Street as the left of the funnel, and Commerce Street as the right side. Main Street runs through the middle of the funnel, and all three streets converge at the bottom of the funnel, going under a railroad bridge that is called the "triple underpass."

The Book Depository sits at the top left of the funnel, near the corner of Elm and Houston. Just in front of the Depository is the Elm Street extension, which runs straight into a parking lot and railroad tracks that flow into a railroad yard. Between the parking lot and Elm Street is a park-like area which includes a picket fence, a concrete monument, and the "grassy knoll." The "grassy knoll" area is at the lower left of the funnel.

11:55–12:25 a.m.: At 11:55, an important witness named Lee Bowers was in the tower in the railroad yard behind the grassy knoll. He saw a dirty 1959 Oldsmobile station wagon enter the parking lot behind the picket fence. The driver, a middle-aged white male with partially gray hair, drove around slowly, then left. The car had out-of-state plates and a sticker touting Republican Senator Barry Goldwater in the rear window.

According to his statement to police, completed on November 22 and in Warren Commission Volume 24, "at about 12:15 another car came into the area with a white man about 25 to 35 years old driving. This car was a 1957 Ford, black, 2-door with Texas license. This man appeared to have a mike or telephone in the car. Just a few minutes after this car left at 12:20 p.m., another car pulled in. This car was a 1961 Chevrolet Impala . . . color white, and dirty up to the windows. This car also had a Goldwater . . . sticker. This car was driven by a white male about 25 to 35 years old with long blond hair . . . he left the area about 12:25 p.m."

12:15 p.m.: A witness saw a man—dark-haired, maybe Caucasian or a Latin with a fair complexion—with a rifle and scope on the westernmost end of the sixth floor of the Depository (toward the grassy knoll). A dark-skinned man was visible at the easternmost end (near the apparent "sniper's nest" found after the shooting). One of the men was described as wearing a very light-colored shirt, white or a light blue, open at the collar, unbuttoned about halfway, with a regular T-shirt beneath it. (Oswald said he was wearing a red or reddish shirt at work that day; a neighbor described his shirt that day as "tan.") At 12:23, another witness saw "two men standing back from a window on one of the upper floors of the Book Depository," and she noticed that "one of the men had dark hair . . . a darker complexion than the other." At the time, she felt the man "might have been a Mexican," and "she had the impression the men were looking out, as if 'in antici-pation of the motorcade.'"

12:15 p.m.: Mrs. R. E. Arnold, a Book Depository secretary, saw Oswald standing in the hallway between the front doors leading to the warehouse, on the first floor. She puts the time at 12:15 or a little later. Oswald claims he ate his lunch in the first-floor lunch room, alone, except for a black man named Junior who walked through with a short black man. Both of the men were later identified, and were in the lunch room at times between noon and 12:25. The short man, Harold Norman, later said "there was someone else in there," but he couldn't remember who.

Oswald made a point of eating his lunch in the first floor lunch room, which was used by minority and disabled employees in that time of segregation. Such an act helped to burnish his reputation as having far-left sympathies in a very conservative city.

Also, by witness statements and his own admission, Oswald remained in close proximity to the first-floor pay telephone around lunch time, as JFK's motorcade drew closer to Dealey Plaza. Recall that one of

Oswald's co-workers at the Book Depository told police that "during the lunch breaks, Oswald usually made several phone calls, which were usually short in length." But according to the Warren Report, Oswald had no one to call but Marina, which raises the question of who else Oswald was calling. Oswald might well have been waiting to make or receive one or more phone calls that day, regarding what he thought was his "mission" to Mexico City and on to Cuba, in the same way that Gilberto Lopez had been waiting for a phone call about going to Cuba on November 17. Guy Banister's associate Joseph Milteer told William Somersett that Oswald "was downstairs in the Book Depository rather than on the upper floor" when the shots were fired at JFK.

As noted earlier, confessed conspirator John Martino admitted shortly before his death in 1975 that "the anti-Castro people put Oswald together [and] Oswald was to meet his contact at the Texas Theatre [who would] get him out of the country." However, Martino also admitted to his business partner and to a *Newsday* reporter that "Oswald didn't know who he was [really] working for—he was just ignorant of who was really putting him together." Martino said that after they got Oswald "out of the country," the plotters would "then eliminate him."

Oswald himself later said that when he finished his lunch, he went up to the second floor, to get a Coke. He would be seen near the Coke machine there less than a minute after 12:30 p.m.

12:15–12:20 p.m.: Book Depository employee Bonnie Ray Williams finished his lunch on the sixth floor and left, leaving behind the scraps of his lunch, which police later initially assumed were Oswald's. The FBI later reported that it takes six minutes to assemble a Mannlicher-Carcano, using a dime (since no tools were found)—so that left four to nine minutes for Oswald alone to supposedly move all the fifty-pound boxes into position in the "sniper's nest" on that floor, which the *Warren Report* claims he constructed.

12:15–12:20 p.m.: Jack Ruby was at the *Dallas Morning News* building, where he had been since approximately 11:45 a.m. Ruby was seen sitting on the second floor, in the only chair from which he could see the site where Kennedy would be killed. However, both shortly before and after the shooting, Ruby was not seen in the offices, meaning that he could have slipped away for a time. An FBI report says that "Ruby . . . was missed for a period of about 20 to 25 minutes" and none of the employees knew "where Ruby had gone." That was the time when JFK's motorcade was passing by the *Dallas Morning News* offices—grabbing the attention of most of the workers there—and going through Dealey Plaza.

Only two people said they saw Ruby during the time he was missing from the newspaper offices. One, a police officer, is discussed shortly, but the other was television reporter Wes Wise, who said he had seen Jack Ruby near the Book Depository "moments after the shooting." Wise was a credible reporter, who later became mayor of Dallas. If Ruby was that close to the Book Depository "moments after the shooting," he was almost certainly in the vicinity during the shooting. It's documented that within a short time of the shooting, Ruby would admit that he had his pistol with him, and he was seen by his banker with the $7,000 mentioned earlier, so he may well have had both with him when he was near the Book Depository.*

---

*It's interesting to speculate what could have happened if Oswald had run into Ruby, when Oswald left the Book Depository: It would have been easy for Ruby to claim he'd shot a would-be thief, only to be proclaimed a hero because the man he killed had apparently shot JFK.

12:20 p.m.: Two men who worked for the city and county saw a man in the sixth-floor window, but he was staring and "transfixed" at the area of the grassy knoll, not at the motorcade. One of the men remarked to the other that the man in the window looked "uncomfortable," like he "must be hiding or something." The man in the window was wearing an "open neck . . . sport shirt or a T-shirt [that was] light in color, probably white" and they mentioned a "sport shirt [that was] yellow." One of them later said "he did not think the man in the window was Oswald, insisting that the man in the window had 'light-colored hair.'"

12:20 p.m.: Huge, enthusiastic crowds greeted JFK's motorcade. John Connally later said "the crowds were extremely thick . . . there were at least a quarter of a million people on the parade route that day." He recalled that even with the throng, "there was this little girl—I guess she was about eight years old—who had a placard that said, 'President Kennedy . . . will you shake hands with me?' . . . Well, he immediately stopped the car and shook hands with this little girl, and of course, the car was mobbed." Later, "there was a nun, a sister, with a bunch of school-children . . . right by the car. And he stopped and spoke to them," too.

12:24 p.m.: Prisoners in the Dallas County Jail—which overlooks Dealey Plaza—saw two men, at least one of whom had a dark complexion, on the sixth floor of the Book Depository, adjusting the scope on a rifle.

12:27 p.m.: Twenty-two-year-old soldier Gordon Arnold was walking behind the picket fence on the grassy knoll, in the parking lot, when he was confronted by someone who "showed me a badge and said he was with the Secret Service and that he didn't want anybody up there." Arnold then went on the other side of the fence, on the grassy side of the knoll. Warren Commission files confirm that no Secret Service agents were on the knoll, or in Dealey Plaza at all. They were all either with the motorcade, or miles away at the site of JFK's scheduled speech at the Dallas Trade Mart.

12:28 p.m.: Lee Bowers, in the railroad tower overlooking the parking lot behind the grassy knoll's fence, told attorney Mark Lane that he noticed two men behind the stockade fence, looking up toward Main and Houston. One of the men was "middle-aged" and "fairly heavy-set," wearing a white shirt and dark trousers. The other, about ten to fifteen feet away from the first man, was in his "mid-twenties" and wearing "either a plaid shirt or plaid coat."

12:29 p.m.: JFK's limo turned onto Houston Street and was heading toward the Book Depository. JFK's driver, Secret Service agent William Greer, testified that "when they got to Houston from Main Street, he felt relieved. He felt they were in the clear, the crowds were thinning and . . . he did begin to feel relieved. . . ." However, the limo was moving closer and closer to the Book Depository and the alleged "sniper's nest" at the easternmost window on the sixth floor of the building, closest to Houston Street.

For almost a minute, anyone in that perch would have a totally unobstructed shot at a slow-moving car, with the target getting larger with each passing second. The limo had to slow even more as it made the 120-degree turn onto Elm, passing directly underneath the "sniper's nest," still with no trees or obstructions of any kind. As JFK's limo continued down Elm, away from the Depository, the view from the "sniper's nest"—or any of the sixth-floor windows, for that matter—would have been obscured by the branches of a large tree in the small park that includes the grassy knoll.

12:30 p.m.: Mrs. Nellie Connally, riding in the limo with JFK, Jackie, and Nellie's husband, John Connally, told JFK, "Mr. Kennedy, you can't say Dallas doesn't love you." JFK, impressed by the huge, enthusiastic throngs, which were only now starting to thin out, replied, "That is very obvious."

12:30:12 p.m.: One shot was fired at the President's limousine. JFK raised his hands to his neck. One of the emergency-room physicians, Dr. Carrico, would later describe the small wound in JFK's throat as an entrance wound. Secret Service agent Sam Kinney, in the limo directly behind JFK's, would later say that "the first shot 'hit the President in the throat.'" Kennedy aide David Powers, in the same limo as Kinney, was sure that the shot came from the right front—the grassy knoll—as was another Kennedy aide, Kenneth O'Donnell, who was in the limo with Powers. Soldier Gordon Arnold, on the grassy knoll, said "the shot came from behind me, only inches over my left shoulder. I had just gotten out of basic training . . . and I hit the dirt." According to Texas Senator Ralph Yarborough, who was two cars behind JFK, "immediately on the firing of the first shot I saw the man . . . throw himself on the ground . . . he was down within a second, and I thought to myself, 'There's a combat veteran who knows how to act when weapons start firing.'" (Yarborough himself was a World War II combat veteran.) Secret Service agent Lem Johns, in the limo behind Yarborough, later testified that "the first two [shots] sounded like they were on the side of me towards the grassy knoll. . . ."

JFK'S LIMO, WHICH accelerated to a speed of around 11 miles an hour after making the turn onto Elm, slowed down. Powers told my researcher that he felt they were riding into an ambush, which explains why JFK's limo initially slowed so much. John Connally turned to the right, because he thought the sound came from over his right shoulder. Not seeing JFK out of the corner of his eye, Connally started to turn back toward his left. Connally can be seen in the Zapruder film holding his Stetson hat well after JFK has already been hit in the throat; Connally's wrist would have been shattered at that point if both men had been hit by the same bullet.

1.65 seconds later: One or more shots were fired from above and behind JFK's limo. JFK's limo continued to slow as the driver looked toward the back seat. David Powers is adamant that "the same bullet that hit JFK did not hit John Connally," meaning one of these shots probably hit Connally.

Secret Service agent Glenn Bennett, in the limo with Powers and O'Donnell, "saw what appeared to be a nick in the back of President Kennedy's coat below the shoulder. He thought the President had been hit in the back."

At some point, a shot was fired that missed JFK's limo entirely and struck a curb on Main Street near the bridge that forms the triple underpass with Elm, Main, and Commerce. The shot knocked up a chip of concrete that struck an onlooker, James Teague.

5.91 seconds later: Lee Bowers, in the railroad tower behind the grassy-knoll parking lot, noticed a flash of "light or smoke" from the two men behind the fence overlooking the grassy knoll. Bowers said that he thought one of the men might have been standing on the bumper of a car backed up to the fence. This shot blew away a large portion of the President's skull, rendering him brain-dead, though his heart continued to beat.

Officer Hargis, riding on a motorcycle behind and slightly to the left of Kennedy, was splattered with blood and brain matter. Powers and O'Donnell are certain that shot came from the front, from the fence on the grassy knoll. It's possible that a shot was fired from above and behind at almost exactly the same time, hitting Kennedy in the back. Secret Service Agent Paul Landis, in the limo with Powers and O'Donnell, said he believed the final head shot came from the grassy knoll but that an earlier shot came from above and behind him (in the direction of the Book Depository). After a moment, JFK's limo finally sped toward Parkland Hospital, four miles away.

12:30:30 p.m.: On the fourth floor of the Book Depository, Victoria Adams later testified that "between 15 and 30 seconds" after the last shot, she and a friend left the window where they had been watching the motorcade. They went to the elevator, which "was not running," so she and her friend took the stairs "down to the first floor." She said in her police statement that "there was no one [else] on the stairs."

12:31 p.m.: A railroad yardman saw someone behind the fence on the grassy knoll "throw something in a bush." From the roof of the Terminal Annex Building near the Depository, J. C. Price saw a man (about twenty-five, with long dark hair) running full-speed away from the fence and toward the railroad yard. The man was carrying something in his right hand that "could have been a gun." He was wearing a white dress shirt, no tie, and khaki-colored trousers.

Dallas Police Chief Curry, driving the lead car, radioed to "get a man on top of that triple underpass and see what happened up there." Dallas Secret Service chief Forrest Sorrels later said that he "looked towards the top of the terrace to my right"—by the grassy knoll—"as the sound of the shots seemed to come from that direction." Sheriff Bill Decker, riding with Curry and Sorrells, radioed for all available men to head for the railroad yard behind the fence on the grassy knoll.

Photos clearly show that most of the crowd surged toward the grassy-knoll area, including many Dallas deputies. For example, Dallas Deputy Harry Weatherford "heard a loud report, which . . . sounded as if it came from the railroad yard." After hearing two more shots, he began "running towards the railroad yards where the sound seemed to come from." In fact, one researcher found that of the twenty deputies who gave statements, "sixteen thought the assassin had fired from the area of the grassy knoll" while three had "no opinion" and only one "decided the shots came from" the Book Depository.

12:31:30 p.m.: In contrast to the rush toward the grassy knoll, only one police officer, Marion Baker, headed into the Book Depository. He'd seen a flock of pigeons fly from the roof, and he wanted to check it out for a sniper. Baker first encountered Book Depository manager Roy Truly, who told the officer to follow him. (Truly said he initially thought the shooting had come from the area of the knoll.) Officer Baker later told the Warren Commission that while they were still "on the first floor there were two men . . . as we tried to get on the elevators, I remember two men, one was sitting . . . and another one between 20 or 30 feet away from us looking at us." Baker affirmed that both were "white men," but the two have never been identified and apparently were not employees of the Book Depository.

The elevators were not working when Baker and Truly got to them, so they took the stairs to the second floor. Author Michael Benson summarized testimony and documents showing that on the second floor, "between seventy-five and ninety seconds after the assassination," Officer Baker glimpsed Oswald "standing near a Coke machine in the building's lunchroom." Baker asked Truly if he knew the man; Truly said that Oswald worked for him. Baker and Truly then continued up the stairs. About thirty seconds later, "Oswald was seen drinking a Coke by Mrs. Elizabeth Reid," who worked on that floor. Officer Baker's initial report stated that Oswald had been "drinking a Coke," though for some reason, those words were later scratched out. Both "Reid and [Officer] Baker reported that Oswald was not breathing hard."

It's unlikely Oswald raced down all seventy-two steps of the eight flights of stairs from the far corner of the sixth floor's "sniper's nest," and bought a Coke, in the seventy-five to ninety seconds since the last shot. The "sniper's nest" was on the opposite corner of the building from the stairs, making Oswald's alleged feat even more difficult. Oswald was next seen looking calm as he passed clerical supervisor and "saunters out of the building."

Making any dash by Oswald down the stairs even more unlikely, if not impossible, was the fact that Victoria Adams had been walking down those same stairs at most just over thirty seconds after the last shot, and, as noted above, saw "no one on the stairs."*

---

*Adams's account was verified by her supervisor, Miss Garner, who later stated "that after Miss Adams went downstairs, she [Miss Garner], saw Mr. Truly and the policeman [Baker] come up" the same stairs.

12:32 p.m.: Dallas Deputy Seymour Weitzman ran to the knoll after hearing the shots. He was one of several law enforcement personnel who encountered someone behind the picket fence claiming to be a Secret Service agent, even though no real Secret Service agents were stationed there, or anywhere on the ground in Dealey Plaza. Dallas Police Officer Joe Smith ran to the knoll after hearing a woman scream, "They're shooting the President from the bushes!" Once Officer Smith was behind the fence, he noticed "the lingering smell of gunpowder," as did many of the witnesses on or near the knoll. Smith noticed a man near one of the cars, and, as he later testified to the Warren Commission, Smith pulled his pistol on him. The man then "showed me that he was a Secret Service agent." Smith later explained that the credentials "satisfied me and the deputy sheriff" who had joined him.

The Deputy, Seymour Weitzman, confirmed in his Warren Commission testimony that he had also met the fake Secret Service agent. Officer Smith later explained his regret at allowing the phony agent to leave, because—instead of looking like a typically clean-cut, suit-and-tie Secret Service agent—this man "had on a sports shirt and sports pants. But he had dirty fingernails and hands that looked like an auto mechanic's hands," indicating they were greasy. (His hands could have been dirty from having just quickly broken down a weapon.) Officer Smith searched the interior of a four-door, off-white 1960 or 1961 Chevrolet sedan parked by the fence, but not the trunk.

Deputy Seymour Weitzman also told the Warren Commission he saw "Secret Service, as well" behind the fence. Weitzman later said the man who he thought was Secret Service showed him ID and said that he had everything under control. Although Weitzman was one of the first people behind the fence, he found "numerous kinds of footprints that did not make sense because they were going in different directions."

Three other witnesses—Jean Hill, soldier Gordon Arnold, and Malcolm Summers—also saw what they thought were Secret Service agents on the knoll. Malcolm Summers, who gave a statement to authorities on the day of the assassination, confirmed to PBS in 1988 that "he encountered a man with a gun on the knoll." Summers said he was "stopped by a man in a suit and he had an overcoat—over his arm and . . . I saw a gun under that overcoat. And he [said], 'Don't you all come up here any further, you could get shot, or killed.'"

Behind the Book Depository, Police Sergeant D. V. Harkness met "several 'well-armed' men dressed in suits. They told Sergeant Harkness they were with the Secret Service."

There is a insurmountable problem with the Secret Service agents encountered by Officers Smith, Weitzman, and Harkness, and the other witnesses like Malcolm Summers: Secret Service Chief James Rowley later confirmed that all Secret Service agents in the area of Dealey Plaza were riding in the motorcade and went to the hospital with the President—none were stationed on the ground. That means NONE of the "agents" the witnesses encountered were actually Secret Service, including the one who showed Officer Smith and Deputy Weitzman a valid Secret Service ID.

Who were the men pretending to be Secret Service? Those behind the Book Depository could have included someone who fired from the Depository. As for those on the grassy knoll, twelve years later, journalist Michael Canfield talked to retired Deputy Seymour Weitzman, who'd "had a nervous breakdown" soon after the arrest of the Watergate burglars. Canfield asked that Weitzman's doctor be present during the interview, though Canfield said "Weitzman's memory seemed clear and sharp." Weitzman described the man who claimed to be a Secret Service agent and said the man "produced credentials and told him everything was under control." Deputy Weitzman said the man was of "medium height, [with] dark hair and wearing a light windbreaker." Canfield then "showed him a photo of Sturgis [Frank Fiorini] and [Bernard] Barker" because the government had investigated reports—later proved false—that Fiorini and E. Howard Hunt had been photographed in Dealey Plaza after JFK's murder.*

Instead of reacting to Fiorini's photo, Weitzman "immediately stated, 'Yes, that's him,' pointing to Bernard Barker." Just to be sure, "Canfield asked, 'Was this the man who produced the Secret Service credentials?' Weitzman responded, 'Yes, that's the same man.'" Weitzman even said he'd be willing "to make a tape recorded statement for official investigators," and he recorded a statement for Canfield, in which he reaffirmed the Barker identification.

In the late 1990s, when researchers showed Malcolm Summers a photo of Bernard Barker, he had identified Barker as the armed man he had encountered on the knoll moments after JFK was assassinated.

Could CIA agent and later Watergate burglar Bernard Barker have been one of the fake Secret Service agents in Dealey Plaza? Michael Canfield was party to a lawsuit involving E. Howard Hunt in which he and his coauthor obtained a sworn deposition from Barker. When their attorney asked Barker where he was on November 22, 1963, Barker initially remarked, "This is a question that came up during the Watergate Hearing," but review of Barker's Watergate testimony

---

*Claims that Hunt and Fiorini were two of the "three tramps" photographed in Dealey Plaza were investigated by the Rockefeller Commission and the House Select Committee on Assassinations and found to be groundless. The identities of the actual tramps were later released by the Dallas Police and confirmed by photos of the men.

reveals no such questioning. In Barker's deposition, he said that "I was working for the Agency, they know exactly everywhere I was, I reported to them daily." Barker claimed to be at home watching television at the time of the assassination, though he said no one but his family and friends could vouch for him that day. When Canfield's attorney asked if Barker "heard of the assassination via a news flash," Barker responded, "No." He stated, "I think I saw the parade, how the whole thing happened."

If Barker "saw . . . how the whole thing happened," he didn't see it on live TV, or even on the news later that night, because the motorcade wasn't broadcast live, even in Dallas. The Zapruder film, so well known today, wasn't shown on TV at all until almost twelve years after JFK's murder, and at the time of Barker's deposition, the film had appeared on TV only a handful of times. It was not the bright, colorful, and sharp restored version we're now used to, but a grainy, dark copy of the somewhat fuzzy eight-millimeter film that looked nothing like the high-quality videotape or sixteen-millimeter news footage shown on TV at the time.

12:32–12:33 p.m.: Behind the picket fence on the grassy knoll, Deputy Weitzman and Officer Smith were soon joined by three (of seven) railroad employees who had watched the motorcade from an overpass approximately fifty feet in front of the Presidential limousine. They had also heard shots coming from the grassy knoll. The railroad men also saw all the footprints on the ground and two muddy footprints on the bumper of a station wagon parked there. One of the railroad men said that near the "station wagon there were two sets of footprints . . . they could've gotten in the trunk compartment of this car and pulled the lid down, which would have been very easy." None of the trunks of the cars parked behind the knoll were searched.

According to Anthony Summers, "within minutes of the shooting" off-duty policeman John Tilson was driving near the knoll and "saw a man 'slipping and sliding' down the railway embankment behind the knoll." He later "described the man as '38–40 years, 5' 8" . . . dark hair, dark clothing.' Tilson comments that he looked like Jack Ruby, whom he knew, but does not claim it was Ruby." Officer Tilson said the man "had a car parked there, a black car. He threw something in the back seat and went around the front hurriedly and got in the car and took off." Tilson tried to follow the car but lost it. Around this time, a car was reported speeding through downtown Dallas, bearing a stolen Georgia license plate.

Journalist Robert MacNeil wrote that "a crowd, including reporters, converged on the grassy knoll believing it to be the direction from which the shots that struck the President were fired." He "saw several people running up the grassy hill beside the road. I thought they were chasing whoever had done the shooting and I ran after them."

At the Book Depository, James Worrell told police and the Warren Commission that he saw a man emerge from the back entrance of the Depository and run off down Houston Street, toward the south. He described the man as in his early thirties, 5' 8" to 5' 10", dark hair and average weight, in a dark sports jacket open in front with lighter-colored pants, no hat or anything in his hands.

Two witnesses, one of them a sheriff's deputy, saw "a light colored Nash (Rambler) station wagon" pull up in front of the Book Depository "and a white male came down the grass-covered incline between the building and the street and entered the station wagon after which it drove away in the direction of the Oak Cliff section of Dallas." Deputy Roger Craig also saw the incident and said "I heard a shrill whistle and I turned around and saw a white male running down the hill from the direction of the" Depository, while "a light colored Rambler station wagon" pulled over and the man "who had been running got into this car. The man driving this station wagon was a dark complected white male." Deputy Craig "reported this incident at once to a Secret Service officer, whose name I do not know"—though again, no real Secret Service agents were in the area. Craig saw Oswald at police headquarters later and thought that he had been the running man.

Some of the witnesses in Dealey Plaza soon started talking to authorities, and many of those on or near the grassy knoll said the shots came from there. Abraham Zapruder, filming the motorcade as he stood on a concrete step on the knoll, testified that the shots "came from back of me." On the knoll steps, not far from Zapruder, Emmett Hudson said, "The shots that I heard definitely came from behind and above me." Photos and films show a couple—the Newmans—and their two children on the knoll all on the ground because, as Mr. Newman said later, "I thought the [first] shot had come from the garden directly behind me," and "it seemed that we were in the direct path of fire."

Jean Hill was one of the closest witnesses to JFK when the shooting started. From where she stood, Hill was looking at the knoll from the other side of the street as her friend Mary Moorman took what would become a famous Polaroid photo of JFK. Hill said, "I frankly thought they were coming from the knoll . . . people shooting from the knoll." Summers found that "sixteen people, in or outside the Book Depository, indicated some shooting came from the knoll. They included the Depository manager, the superintendent, and two company vice presidents." Six witnesses, including three in the motorcade, said they smelled gunpowder around the knoll. Those in the motorcade were Senator Ralph Yarborough, Congressman Ray Roberts, and the Dallas mayor's wife, plus there were two police officers and a civilian who were on the ground near the knoll.

Those on or near the knoll tended to hear at least some shots from there, while others farther away reported one or more shots from the vicinity of the Book Depository. But even the number of shots witnesses reported—two, three, four, even five or more shots—varied widely. Several witnesses near the knoll said they heard only two shots, perhaps indicating the number fired from there. In an interesting parallel, investigator Josiah Thompson found that, "with no exceptions, all those witnesses who were deep inside the Depository (either at work or in hallways) report hearing fewer than three shots"—either just one shot or two.

Several witnesses and officers did direct attention to the Book Depository. However, the Depository had not attracted as much notice as the area behind the grassy knoll and was not sealed off until twenty-eight minutes after the shooting. A witness named Howard Brennan, whose statements to authorities would be very inconsistent, later became the star witness in making the case against Oswald. Though he initially appeared to have gone toward the knoll after the shots, he later claimed to have seen Oswald fire a shot from the Depository. As Anthony Summers notes, Brennan couldn't identify Oswald in a lineup on the night of November 22, even though a month later he said he could, and then, three weeks after that, said he wasn't sure. Finally, Brennan told the Warren Commission he was sure he had seen Oswald in the Depository window, even though Brennan's vision was questionable. The initial lookout for a suspect, apparently based on Brennan's description of the man in the window, was for a man older and heavier than Oswald. Dr. Gerald McKnight pointed out numerous other flaws in Brennan's testimony, rendering it worthless in placing Oswald in the "sniper's nest."

Two other witnesses later said they saw "a rifle being pulled back from a window" in the Book Depository. One was *Dallas Times Herald* photographer Bob Jackson, who would later win a Pulitzer Prize for his famous photo of Ruby shooting Oswald. The other was WFAA-TV cameraman Malcolm Couch, who was riding with Jackson in the press car, five cars behind JFK. Couch said he saw about a foot of rifle being pulled back into the window. (A shooter wouldn't need to extend the rifle out of the window at all in order to fire at JFK—unless he wanted to call attention to his position.) Neither Couch nor Jackson immediately contacted police about what he had seen, which even a Warren Commission counsel considered unusual, especially for a newsman.

Within minutes of the shooting, Oswald had walked out of the building without being noticed—and if Oswald could leave the building without being noticed, anyone else could, too. According to most accounts, Oswald walked north one block, then turned right and went east on Pacific. He swung back to Elm Street and paused in front of the Blue Front Inn, seven blocks east of the assassination site. He possibly boarded the Marsalis Street bus, on Griffin Street. When the bus became stalled in traffic, Oswald asked for a transfer and got off the bus at the same time as another passenger. Oswald headed south on Lamar Street. He paused in front of the Greyhound bus terminal, three blocks from where he had left the bus. He took a cab, which drove southeast down Zangs Boulevard and turned south onto Beckley.

12:35–1:00 p.m.: In separate incidents, police arrested or detained two men at the Dal-Tex building, across Houston Street from the Book

Depository. Some researchers believe that one or more shots may have been fired from a window of the Dal-Tex building near the corner of Elm and Houston, where the line of sight to JFK's limo would not have been obstructed by tree branches as it was from the Depository. Some witnesses stated that "when the shots were fired [at JFK], they sounded as if they came from the direction of the Dal-Tex building." One of the men arrested at the Dal-Tex was a young man wearing a black leather jacket and black gloves. He was later released, and no records were kept of his arrest.

The other man arrested at the Dal-Tex was Eugene Hale Brading (aka Jim Braden), from Los Angeles. Brading was on parole at the time, and some authors have alleged that he was a courier for the Mafia. Anthony Summers linked Brading to a gangster who "knew Jack Ruby well" and was "an acquaintance of both Carlos Marcello and Santo Trafficante." Brading sometimes did business from the seventeenth floor of the Pierre Marquette Building in New Orleans, and "in his work for Marcello, [David] Ferrie worked out of" a different office on the same floor. Some of Braden's activities the day before the assassination parallel those of Jack Ruby. After giving police only his "Jim Braden" alias, Brading would be released within hours.

In all, at least twelve men—possibly more—were detained by police, then released. In some cases, no records were kept about their detainment. In addition, some men from the Book Depository, besides Oswald, were questioned very closely by police.

12:35 p.m. (approx.): "Officer J. D. Tippit, who had been parked at" a Texaco service "station watching traffic . . . suddenly sped off towards Oak Cliff," according to "three attendants" at the station interviewed by former FBI agent William Turner. The station was located "on the Oak Cliff end of the Houston Street Viaduct that the fleeing Oswald traveled in a taxi . . . just a few blocks west of the triple underpass in Dealey Plaza."

12:37 p.m.: At Parkland Hospital, JFK was rushed into the trauma room, where faint signs of life were detected. The first doctor to see Kennedy, and the only one to see him before his clothes were removed, Dr. Charles J. Carrico, noticed a small, round bullet-entry wound (3–5 millimeters wide) in his throat, above his shirt and tie. Other doctors soon joined Carrico, and they noted the huge head wound, which they estimated to be about 35 square centimeters (by the time the autopsy on Kennedy is performed that night, this wound will be described as four times bigger). In their later statements they characterized this wound, at the right rear of the head, as an exit wound (indicating that the shot came from the front). At the small, round bullet-entry wound in his throat, a neat tracheotomy incision was made. Also, external cardiac massage was performed. Emergency room doctors had no immediate need to turn Kennedy's body over, so they didn't notice the wound in his back. Connally lay wounded in a second trauma room a few yards away.

JFK's limo was left unattended in the parking lot and was soon surrounded by people. Eventually someone, apparently a Secret Service agent, started scrubbing the blood off the President's limo, unintentionally removing what would have been crucial evidence.

12:40 p.m. (approx.): Jack Ruby was seen again at the *Dallas Morning News* building. "Hugh Aynesworth, reporter, *Dallas Morning News*," told the FBI that "shortly after" Jack Ruby had been "missed, people began to come to the office of the newspaper announcing the assassination of President John F. Kennedy and Ruby appeared shortly thereafter and feigned surprise at this announcement."

12:44 p.m.: The Dallas Police broadcast a description of the President's attacker, which sounded too old and heavy to be a good description of Oswald: white, 5' 10" , 160 pounds, thirty years old, armed with a .30-caliber rifle.

12:45 p.m.: Officer Tippit was ordered into the Oak Cliff area of Dallas, though some consider the veracity of this transmission problematic, since it was missing from some early accounts of the Tippit incident. Jack Ruby and Lee Harvey Oswald lived in different parts of the small Oak Cliff neighborhood.

12:45 p.m. (1:45 EST): J. Edgar Hoover called Robert Kennedy, who was having lunch at his home in Virginia, to tell him that "the President has been shot. I think it's serious. I am endeavoring to get details. I'll call you back when I find out more." RFK called CIA Director John McCone at Langley CIA Headquarters and asked him to come right over (it was only about a mile away).

12:50 p.m.: Secret Service agent Forrest Sorrels, who was in the motorcade, arrived at the Book Depository after leaving Parkland Hospital. He was able to enter the rear of the building without presenting any identification.

12:54 p.m.: Officer Tippit radioed that he was in the Oak Cliff area, and he was instructed to "be at large for any emergency."

12:58 p.m.: Police Captain Will Fritz arrived at the Book Depository after leaving Parkland Hospital. Twenty-eight minutes after the shooting, Fritz finally ordered the building sealed off.

12:59 p.m. (approx.): Two men working at a record shop in Oak Cliff said Tippit hurried into the shop, made a call, apparently got no answer, and hung up after about a minute and rushed from the store. Dallas reporter Earl Golz interviewed the two men, whose shop was one block from the Texas Theatre (where Oswald would be apprehended) and seven blocks from where Tippit would be killed. The men knew Tippit because he sometimes stopped in the store to use their phone.

1:00 p.m.: Despite the extreme severity of the President's head wound, which left him no chance of meaningful survival, the Dallas doctors had done everything humanly possible to save him, but to no avail.

John F. Kennedy received the last rites of the Catholic Church and was pronounced dead at Parkland Hospital.

CHAPTER 15

Officer Tippet Is Killed and Problems Arise for Marcello

I N NEW ORLEANS at 1 p.m. (CST, as are all times in this chapter unless noted), Carlos Marcello and David Ferrie were still in federal court, waiting for the judge to begin his charge to the jury. While they had a perfect alibi for JFK's murder, it's ironic that they also had no way to know for sure what had happened in Dallas. It would be up to Guy Banister, who was not in court, to monitor the news and field any reports from Dallas.

JFK's death would not be announced for another thirty minutes, but by 1:00 p.m. Lee Oswald must have realized that things had gone horribly wrong. Yet Oswald may have felt that he still had a mission to complete. We may never know how much of that mission was real, and how much had been simply made up or exaggerated by men like Ferrie and Banister. It most likely involved leaving work after lunch and going to a prearranged meeting at the Texas Theatre, as part of getting to Mexico and on to Cuba. As someone who had accepted the risks involved in defecting to Russia at the height of the Cold War, Oswald would have known the value of following orders and the danger of his current situation.

At 1:00 p.m. in the Oak Cliff neighborhood of Dallas, Earlene Roberts, the housekeeper at Oswald's rooming house, saw Oswald run inside. Also at 1:00, Dallas Police headquarters radioed the patrol car of Officer J. D. Tippit, but he did not answer. At 1:02, Roberts saw a Dallas Police car pull slowly up to the rooming house, park directly in front of it, sound its horn twice, and then slowly pull away. She said she saw two policemen in the car. However, ex-FBI agent William Turner points out that Tippit's uniform jacket "was on a hanger in the car's window," and she could have mistaken that for a second officer. The housekeeper, who had poor eyesight, said she thought the car's number was "107"—Tippit's number was "10."

At 1:05 p.m., Roberts saw Oswald run out of the rooming house. Oswald had probably changed shirts, to a long-sleeved rust-brown shirt with a white T-shirt beneath it. He was also probably carrying a concealed revolver by this time. The housekeeper last saw him waiting at a stop for a bus that would take him back downtown. At 1:08, Tippit radioed headquarters, but headquarters didn't reply.

Two witnesses at the Texas Theatre, Butch Burroughs and Jack Davis, said they observed Oswald inside the theater as early as 1:15, according to researcher Larry Harris. He wrote that "Burroughs, who was working the concession counter, remembered waiting on Oswald." However, sometime between 1:10 and 1:15—most likely around 1:12—Dallas Police Officer J. D. Tippit was shot at the 400 block of East Tenth Street, between Denver and Patton streets.

As described by researcher Michael T. Griffith, the official Warren Commission story says that after Tippit saw a man who matched the description of JFK's assailant that had been broadcast over police radio, Tippit "drove up slowly behind the man, pulled up alongside him, and then asked him to come over to the driver's window for what was described as having the appearance of a 'friendly chat.'" Oswald, the ex-serviceman turned killer, then pulled out his pistol, shot the officer, and fled.*

However, many other witnesses gave different accounts of Tippit's slaying. According to eyewitness Acquilla Clemons, Tippit was shot by a man who was "kind of short" and "kind of heavy," and wearing "khaki and a white shirt." This man then motioned another man with him to "go on." Another witness saw a man with a long coat, ending just about at his hands, looking at Tippit's body, then running to his car (described as gray, 1950–51, maybe a Plymouth) and driving off. Also, most witnesses say that the man who talked with Tippit had been walking west—toward Oswald's rooming house, not away from it.

Numerous problems with the evidence in the Tippit slaying have been noted for decades. For example, instead of immediately fleeing, the shooter took the time to empty four spent shells from his revolver at the crime scene. Two of the shells were made by Remington-Peters and two by Winchester-Western. However, of the four bullets taken from Tippit's body, just one was Remington-Peters and three were made by Winchester-Western. There were also problems with the chain of custody of the shells, as well as with the initial descriptions of the gun itself and a discarded jacket.

Noted journalist Henry Hurt pointed out that "one of the oddest assumptions of the Warren Commission was that Officer Tippit stopped Oswald because he was able to identify him as the man

---

*Remarkably, that scenario closely matches a scene in a then-forgotten 1948 film noir that court records show Johnny Rosselli helped to produce, *He Walked by Night*. The murderous ex-serviceman in Rosselli's film even kept one of his long-barreled weapons hidden away, wrapped in a blanket, just like Oswald is said to have done.

described in the police broadcasts that started about 12:45 p.m. . . . The description itself was of a 'white male, approximately thirty, slender build, height five feet, ten inches, weight 165 pounds,' believed to be armed with a .30-caliber rifle. This description missed Oswald by six years and about fifteen pounds." Michael Griffith points out that "the police description could have fit a good quarter to a third of the male population of Dallas." And yet "none of the witnesses who saw Tippit's assailant just before Tippit stopped him said the man was walking unusually fast or in any way acting strange or suspicious."

Witnesses sometimes changed their stories, possibly because they were intimidated or threatened. For example, two days after the Tippit slaying, a policeman told witness Acquilla Clemons that she might get hurt if she told anyone else what she saw, and she never spoke to the Warren Commission about it. As noted by Anthony Summers, witness "Warren Reynolds was shot in the head two days after telling the FBI he could not identify Oswald," and after his recovery Reynolds "agreed he thought the fleeing gunman had been Oswald after all." The chief suspect in the Reynolds shooting was a heroin addict named Darrell Wayne Garner. Though Garner drunkenly boasted of the shooting and confessed to being at the scene, he was released when provided with an alibi by Nancy Mooney, a former employee of Jack Ruby. Eight days later, Mooney was arrested; she "was later found hanged in her cell" by her pants, "presumably a suicide." Another Tippit slaying witness, Domingo Benavides, "was anonymously threatened after the Tippit killing," and "his brother Edward was murdered by an unknown assailant" soon afterward. Carlos Marcello's men in Dallas were very capable of having key witnesses intimidated or attacked.

Aside from Clemons, the Warren Commission did not hear from two other important witnesses. According to researcher Larry Harris,

"Frank Wright, who lived on the next block . . . heard gunshots, went out to see what was happening and saw a man standing near a police car. He insisted the man ran and jumped in a gray car parked beyond" Tippit's car "and sped away west on Tenth Street. Jack Tatum told House Assassination Committee investigators that he . . . had just passed a police car when the shooting broke out; Tatum paused and watched the gunman walk behind the squad car and take careful, deliberate aim before firing one more shot into Tippit." The House Select Committee on Assassinations said, "This action, which is commonly described as a coup de grace, is more indicative of an execution," something one might expect of an experienced hit man.

The key witness for the Warren Commission regarding Oswald and the Tippit slaying was Helen Markham. Larry Harris noted that while "publicly the Warren Report called 'Markham's . . . testimony reliable,'" in private memos, the Warren staff said, "This witness is very unsure of herself on most points." Staff attorney Joseph Ball "complained that her account was 'full of mistakes' and 'utterly unreliable,'" and "several years later Ball derided Markham publicly during a debate, called her an 'utter screwball.'" Warren attorney Wesley Liebeler "dismissed her story as 'contradictory' and 'worthless.'"

Even the Dallas Assistant District Attorney at the time, William Alexander, later told Anthony Summers that when it came to the Tippit slaying, "Oswald's movements did not add up then and they do not add up now. No way. Certainly he may have had accomplices." And when Oswald went to the Texas Theatre, "was he supposed to meet someone?" and "did he miss a connection?"

Jack Ruby lived just a few blocks from the Tippit murder scene. Jack Anderson, one of America's top investigative journalists in the 1970s, later obtained information from Johnny Rosselli on several occasions. Anderson wrote that Oswald had to be killed because, according to "Johnny Rosselli, . . . underworld conspirators feared he would crack and disclose information that might lead to them . . . so Jack Ruby was ordered to eliminate Oswald." Before Ruby had to do the job himself, he apparently tried to persuade one of his many police contacts to kill Oswald. In fact, the night of Tippit's death, Ruby met with one of Tippit's police-officer friends for more than an hour. According to Hurt, this officer had been "working privately as a guard at an Oak Cliff home when Tippit was murdered nearby."

Thousands of pages have been written just about the Tippit slaying, so we cannot cover here all of the evidence and the many problems with the theory of Oswald as a "lone assassin" of Tippit. The bottom line is that evidence and witnesses are so inconsistent that there are at least four possible explanations for his murder:

1. Oswald shot Tippit, just as the Warren Commission said he did.

2. Someone with Oswald might have shot Tippit.

3. While Tippit was talking to Oswald, the officer might have been shot by someone nearby who was unconnected with Oswald.

4. Oswald might have already been inside the Texas Theatre at the time of Tippit's death, meaning the officer had been shot by someone else.

At 1:22, officers on the scene of the Tippit shooting broadcast a description of the assailant, describing him as a white male about thirty years old, 5' 8", "black wavy hair," slender build, wearing a white jacket, white shirt, and dark slacks. William Turner cites Dallas

Police radio logs as saying that "shortly after 1:41 p.m., Sergeant Hill came on the air: 'A witness reports that he [the Tippit suspect] was last seen in the Abundant Life Temple about the 400 block. We are fixing to go in and shake it down.' On an alternate channel, Car 95 ordered 'Send me another squad [car] over here to Tenth and Crawford to check out this church basement.'" However, another call came in, erroneously reporting that the suspect was at a library, where police converged. Suddenly, police were called to the Texas Theatre, and the Abundant Life Temple was never searched. Reportedly, the Temple had recently been the site of activity by Cuban exiles.

According to the Warren Commission version, Johnny Calvin Brewer, the owner of a shoe store six blocks away from the slaying site, heard a report on the radio about the shooting. He looked up to see a man hide from a passing police car by stepping into his doorway. He followed the man, Oswald, who ducked into the nearby Texas Theatre. Brewer alerted the cashier, who called the police. However, some researchers think that Oswald had been inside the theater since shortly after 1:00 p.m., either having bought a ticket or using a ticket someone had bought earlier and given to him. As noted earlier, witness Jack Davis said that once in the theater, Oswald sat next to him for a few minutes; then Oswald moved to sit next to another person for a few minutes; then Oswald got up and went to the lobby, as though looking for someone. An alternate version proposed by some historians says that Oswald got worried when he couldn't find his contact, so he walked out to the lobby and looked around. He then went outside—onto the sidewalk—looking for his contact. Oswald saw a police car go by and ducked into the doorway of the shoe store, then went back into the theater to await his contact's arrival. In any event, police broadcast an alarm at 1:45 to converge on the Texas Theatre.

At approximately 1:48, police arrived at the theater, and once inside, the shoe store owner pointed out Oswald to the officers. However, Oswald was not the first patron approached. First, an officer frisked two men sitting in the center of the theater before proceeding to Oswald. Did one or more of the policemen hope Oswald would make a run for it, allowing them to shoot the possible cop-killer? Assistant DA William Alexander had gone to the theater and said the assumption at the time was that the person who killed Tippit had also killed JFK. Oswald was arrested between 1:51 and 1:55, after a scuffle. As noted by author Henry Hurt, "there is conflicting testimony among arresting officers about just what happened during the arrest," and "most of the dozen or so patrons scattered about the theater . . . were never canvassed and questioned in any inclusive fashion by the FBI or the Warren Commission." Other evidence calls into question what ID Oswald had on him at the time, and whether an additional wallet was found at the Tippit slaying scene. The Warren Report says that "officers found a forged Selective Service card with a picture of Oswald and the name 'Alex J. Hidell' in Oswald's billfold." Author Sylvia Meagher documented numerous problems with that claim, but that alias would soon be used to link Oswald to the rifle found on the sixth floor of the School Book Depository.

At the Texas Theatre, Oswald had something unusual with him: half of a box-top, as if he were supposed to meet someone with the other half. As noted, Oswald had sat next to at least two people in the theater, then moved, as if waiting for them to say a coded phrase or produce the other, matching half of the box-top. Later, dollar bills torn in half would be found in Oswald's room, indicating he had used the "matching half" technique before.

Antonio Veciana told my research associate how one of his CIA contacts (the CIA officer who originally recruited David Atlee Phillips for the CIA) used the technique of a torn-in-half dollar bill to identify his contact. CIA memos show they were using that technique in 1963, as part of the AMWORLD portion of the JFK–Almeida coup plan. The "matching half" technique was also used by the heroin ring Michel Victor Mertz shared with Marcello and Trafficante, most recently in a major bust that occurred in Laredo at the time of Oswald's return from Mexico.

Recall that John Martino said that Oswald was supposed to meet his "contact" at the Texas Theatre, and then later be eliminated. Martino himself was emblematic of how the mob manipulated Oswald, since he was both a CIA asset and a mob functionary for Santo Trafficante; Martino also knew Carlos Marcello. The use of movie theaters as clandestine meeting places for CIA missions was confirmed years later by David Atlee Phillips, the CIA officer Oswald had allegedly met with less than three months before the assassination. In his 1977 autobiography, Phillips described his own use of just such a technique, where he would meet a contact at a movie theater, whom he'd know because he carried with him a previously arranged item and recognized a prearranged coded phrase.

AT 2:00, OSWALD arrived at the Dallas Police station. He had $13.87 on him and may also have had David Ferrie's library card, as explained shortly. At 2:30, a police call went out to look for a 1957 Chevy sedan, last seen in the vicinity of the Tippit slaying. The alert said that the car's occupants should be checked for illegal weapons. Later, police searched Oswald's small apartment at the rooming house. In a sea bag they found a tiny Minox spy camera, three other cameras, a 15-power telescope, two pairs of field glasses, a compass, and a pedometer. There were also several rolls of exposed Minox film. (A November 27, 1963, memo shows that David Morales's Miami CIA station used Minox spy cameras.)

At approximately 3:00, police arrived at the home of Ruth Hyde Paine, where Oswald's wife, Marina, lived and Oswald had spent the previous night. Two weeks earlier, Marina had noticed what appeared to be Oswald's rifle wrapped in a blanket in the garage. The police found the blanket empty. The case against the ex-serviceman who kept his rifle wrapped in a blanket and shot a patrolman on the street seemed cinched, except for one more important piece of evidence.

The "magic bullet," the cornerstone of the "single bullet theory" required for one lone presidential assassin, was found at Parkland Hospital around 1:45, just before Oswald was arrested at the Texas Theatre. This was the almost pristine bullet that supposedly caused JFK's back and throat wounds and all of Connally's bone-shattering injuries. According to Henry Hurt, citing medical reports, it "'literally shattered' his fifth rib, leaving five inches of it 'pulverized,'" and then "struck Connally's right wrist" and "shattered the radius bone at the largest point"—all while, according to the Warren Commission's "single bullet theory," Connally continued to grip "his white Stetson hat" with that hand. The "magic bullet" then buried itself in Connally's thigh, from which it supposedly later fell out, emerging in almost perfect condition. Chapter Two noted numerous problems that showed why the single bullet theory was physically impossible, and the bullet mostly likely planted for a Parkland employee to find.

Around seventeen minutes before that "magic bullet" was found, Jack Ruby was at Parkland Hospital, where he spoke with noted journalist Seth Kantor. The time was approximately 1:28 p.m. Another witness saw also Ruby at Parkland around that time, though for some reason Ruby later denied being there.

The police and the Warren Commission seemed determine to pin Tippit's murder on the obvious suspect they had in custody, Oswald. According to author Larry Harris, the police lineups regarding Oswald and the Tippit slaying have been described as "a travesty. In the first two, the disheveled and bruised Oswald was paraded before witnesses (including Helen Markham) accompanied by two detectives and a jail clerk who were neatly attired in slacks and dress shirts." The next day's lineup, viewed by Tippit witness (William) Scoggins, "was even more outrageous: Oswald, two teenagers, and a Hispanic man." Despite that stacked line up, Harris pointed out that "an FBI report reveals that two days later, when FBI agents showed him a photograph of Oswald, Scoggins told them he couldn't be sure the person he observed on Nov. 22 was 'actually identical with Oswald.'"

AT 1:33 P.M., White House press aide Malcolm Kilduff in Dallas officially announced that JFK was dead. Five minutes later, at 1:38 p.m., CBS anchor Walter Cronkite told a national television audience the tragic news. It's often overlooked that just over a minute earlier, Cronkite had been telling his audience that "[r]egarding the probable assassin, the Sheriff's officers have taken a young man into custody at the scene, a man twenty-five years old we are rep—." Cronkite abruptly stopped describing the young suspect when he was handed a memo that confirmed JFK's death. Cronkite's emotional words reporting that the President was dead is an oft-repeated clip, but overlooked by most is that Cronkite's remark about the young man in custody didn't refer to the twenty-four-year-old Oswald's capture at the Texas Theatre. It couldn't have, since the newsman made his fateful pronouncement about JFK at 1:37 p.m.—but police weren't even called to the theater until 1:45, and the first officers didn't arrive until 1:48 p.m.

IN NEW ORLEANS, the trial of Carlos Marcello entered its final stages. At 1:30 p.m., Judge Herbert Christenberry "had just delivered his fifteen minute charge to the jury," according to John H. Davis, when "a bailiff suddenly strode into the courtroom and . . . handed the judge a note." After reading it, the shocked judge announced that JFK had been shot and might be dead. The judge "handed the case to the jury and called for an hour's recess."

For Marcello and David Ferrie, that hour would be their first chance to find out more about what had happened in Dallas. Guy Banister was not in his office that day during regular business hours, so he was probably available to tell them whatever he'd learned. While all three would have been happy at JFK's death, the fact that Oswald was still alive and in police custody presented a huge potential problem.

Court resumed session at 3:00. However, Robert Kennedy's lead Justice Department prosecutor on the case, John Diuguid, told me that while David Ferrie had been in the courtroom with Marcello's team before the break, Ferrie wasn't in court when everyone else returned. With remarkable speed, at 3:15 the jury delivered its verdict. The juror Marcello had bribed reportedly boasted later "that not only had he voted not guilty . . . but he had also convinced several of his fellow jurors to vote not guilty." Just to be sure he avoided conviction, Marcello had also made sure the key witness against him was threatened during the trial. Consequently, the jury found Marcello "not guilty" on both counts of perjury and conspiracy.

Marcello initially presided over a celebration of his victory. But Davis writes that Marcello left the party and "went to his office at the Town and Country" Motel, according to one source "looking as if he had something urgent on his mind." If Marcello didn't want to face far more serious charges than those he had just escaped, he had important loose ends left to deal with.

In Washington, DC, Harry Williams had returned from lunch to resume his meeting with the CIA officials. According to CIA Director John McCone's desk calendar, now at the National Archives, McCone had lunch that day, starting at 1:00 p.m. (EST), with Richard Helms, Lyman Kirkpatrick, and two other officials. By the time Williams's meeting resumed, everyone had heard that JFK had been shot. Williams told me that the highest official at the meeting at this time, apparently Lyman Kirkpatrick, began eyeing him with suspicion, as if some aspect of JFK's death made the CIA official think a Cuban exile was involved. Williams said he was trying to play it cool, but he felt that perhaps Kirkpatrick took his demeanor the wrong way. Within minutes, the meeting broke up with all plans on hold, and Williams returned to his room at Washington's Ebbitt Hotel.

SOMEONE IN THE Presidential party in Dallas called Robert Kennedy at his Hickory Hill estate in Virginia, to tell him his brother was dead. That was followed by a flood of calls—from Lyndon Johnson, Hoover, and others—over the four phones in RFK's large house. According to Richard Mahoney, while taking a break from the flurry of calls, Bobby confided to his press secretary Ed Guthman that "I thought they'd get one of us, but . . . I thought it would be me." Robert was apparently referring to the Mafia.

While CIA Director John McCone was en route to the estate, RFK made an intriguing call to CIA headquarters, according to journalists George Bailey and Seymour Freidin. (Freidin was the *New York Herald-Tribune*'s foreign-affairs editor, later revealed by Jack Anderson to have been a paid CIA informant in the 1960s.) Freidin said that RFK spoke to a high-level CIA official at headquarters about the shooting of JFK and demanded to know: "Did your outfit have anything to do with this horror?"

After John McCone arrived at RFK's estate, probably between 2:45 and 3:00 (EST), Mahoney writes that Robert "went out on the lawn with him. 'I asked McCone,' Kennedy was to tell his trusted aide Walter Sheridan, 'if they had killed my brother, and I asked him in a way that he couldn't lie to me and [McCone said] they hadn't. '" Mahoney points out that "McCone was one of Bobby's closest friends in the Administration, and this extraordinary question revealed a deep and terrible suspicion about the CIA, something born of some knowledge, or at least intuition, and not simply the incontinence of grief." Of course, neither McCone or RFK knew about the ongoing CIA–Mafia plots, or the assassination side of the Cubela (AMLASH) and QJWIN operations. RFK's question likely referred to some aspect of the JFK–Almeida coup plan that both men knew about, particularly the AMWORLD portion with exile leader Manuel Artime. Not long after the assassination, Arthur Schlesinger, Jr. notes, CIA Director McCone told RFK that "he thought there were two people involved in the shooting."

By 5:00 (EST), McCone was back at CIA Headquarters, meeting with officials who knew about the JFK–Almeida coup plan, including Richard Helms and Lyman Kirkpatrick. Helms told neither man that he had continued the CIA–Mafia plots to kill Fidel, or that a CIA officer had been meeting with Roland Cubela about Fidel's assassination at the very moment that JFK was shot.

IN PARIS, THAT CIA case officer had been meeting with Rolando Cubela (AMLASH). They had discussed Cubela's being provided with several items, including "two high-powered rifles with telescopic sights." According to the Church Committee, the case officer "tells AMLASH the explosives and rifles with telescopic sights will be provided. The case officer also offers AMLASH the poison pen device but AMLASH is dissatisfied with it. As the meeting breaks up, they are told President Kennedy has been assassinated."

IN HAVANA, FRENCH journalist Jean Daniel was having lunch with Fidel Castro, discussing JFK's proposal for talks between the two countries. When Castro was informed of Kennedy's death, he said three times, "This is very bad." (Other accounts have Castro saying "This is very bad news.")

IN MIAMI, JIMMY Hoffa called Frank Ragano, the attorney he shared with Trafficante, and gloated over the assassination of JFK. However, Hoffa's mood changed after he got a call from a Teamster official in Washington. Hoffa was furious that two Teamster leaders at the union's Washington headquarters had closed the office, lowered its flag to half-mast, and sent condolences to the President's widow. Hoffa yelled at his secretary for crying, hung up on the people in Washington, and left the building. In San Juan, Puerto Rico, FBI reports say a Teamster organizer told the Secretary-Treasurer of the local Teamsters Hotel and Restaurant Workers Union "We killed Kennedy." The Teamster organizer was an associate of Frank Chavez, a deadly henchman for Jimmy Hoffa. FBI reports also linked Chavez to Jack Ruby, and Chavez would later make a documented attempt to kill Robert Kennedy.

SHORTLY BEFORE 4:00 p.m. (EST) in Washington, DC, reporter Haynes Johnson had joined Harry Williams in his room at the Ebbitt Hotel. Williams had been helping Johnson with his forthcoming book on the Bay of Pigs. Haynes was also working closely with Manuel Artime on the book, even though at the time there was friction between Artime and Williams. Though Haynes was friends with both RFK and Williams, the journalist hadn't been told about the JFK–Almeida coup plan. In the hotel room, Williams was on the phone with Robert Kennedy, who told him that the JFK–Almeida coup plan was now on hold, so Williams wouldn't be leaving for Guantánamo the next day. Hearing that Haynes was also in the room, RFK then asked to speak to him, since he was also a friend of RFK's. As Haynes later wrote in a 1983 *Washington Post* article, Robert "was utterly in control of his emotions when he came on the line and sounded almost studiedly brisk as he said: 'One of your guys did it.'" Haynes didn't mention RFK's comment to Harry, and RFK never said anything about it—or said anything similar—to Williams.

It's important to stress that both Haynes Johnson and Williams agree that RFK said, "One of your guys did it"—killed JFK—to Haynes, not to Williams. Haynes confirmed that to me in 1992, and again in May 2007, and it's in his detailed 1983 *Washington Post* article. Williams said RFK never voiced any suspicion like that to him on that day or any other. A close Kennedy associate—who knew RFK, Haynes, and Williams—backed up Williams's statement.

Though historian Richard Mahoney didn't know about the JFK–Almeida coup plan when he wrote his 1999 book, he perceptively wrote that RFK's comment to Haynes Johnson "clearly was referring to embittered Cubans deployed by elements in the CIA" who might have been "acting at a deniable distance." The evidence indicates that

RFK's comment related to Manuel Artime's operations, which we now know had ties to associates of Carlos Marcello, Santo Trafficante, and Johnny Rosselli. That would also explain why RFK would make the "your guys" comment to Haynes and not Williams, due to the friction that had developed between Williams and Artime.

Haynes Johnson would later write that within a year or so after JFK's death, he heard that Artime was involved in the drug trade, something that was later confirmed by US officials. In addition, Haynes also wrote about one of Artime's protégés during Watergate, who became a major Miami drug lord when Trafficante was still powerful there.

AT 4:01 P.M. (EST) on November 22, 1963—only an hour after Oswald's arrival at Dallas Police headquarters, and just ten minutes after J. Edgar Hoover learned Oswald's name—Hoover called Robert Kennedy and was able to tell him he "thought we had the man who killed the President," and that Oswald was "not a communist." Hoover probably knew the latter because the FBI had assisted Naval Intelligence with its tight surveillance on Oswald. This information almost slipped out right after the assassination, when James Hosty, the Dallas FBI agent assigned to Oswald, allegedly told Dallas Police "officer Jack Revill on November 22 . . . that Oswald . . . had been under observation. When Revill protested that the information had not been shared with the Dallas Police, he was reminded of the FBI policy forbidding the sharing of information pertaining to espionage."

AT 7:00 P.M. (EST), NBC news anchor Chet Huntley introduced the audio portion of Oswald's August 21, 1963, interview with WDSU-TV in New Orleans. By 7:43, NBC was running the video portion of the interview as well, allowing millions of viewers to see and hear Oswald state, "I would definitely say that I am a Marxist" and then outlining the aims of the Fair Play for Cuba Committee. For many people, those comments cinched Oswald's guilt.

LIKE CARLOS MARCELLO, Santo Trafficante had a documented celebration the day that JFK was assassinated. Trafficante had earlier arranged to meet his lawyer, Frank Ragano, and Ragano's girlfriend—Nancy Young (later Ragano)—for dinner at Tampa's International Inn. JFK had delivered a speech there just four days earlier, and the irony was not lost on Trafficante or Ragano, who realized that in "the same hotel lobby I was crossing to meet Santo, Kennedy had shaken hands and waved at admirers" earlier that week.

Ragano found the normally crowded restaurant almost empty that Friday night. He says that "[a] smiling Santo greeted me at our table. 'Isn't that something, they killed the son-of-a-bitch,' he said, hugging and kissing me on the cheeks. 'The son-of-a-bitch is dead.'" Ragano noted that Trafficante's "generally bland face was wreathed in joy." As Trafficante drank Chivas Regal, he proclaimed, "This is like lifting a load of stones off my shoulders . . . now they'll get off my back, off Carlos's back, and off [Hoffa's] back. We'll make big money out of this and maybe go back into Cuba. I'm glad for [Hoffa's] sake because [Lyndon] Johnson is sure as hell going to remove Bobby. I don't see how he'll keep him in office." Ragano said that Trafficante "talked more excitedly than usual and it was unclear to me what he meant about returning to Cuba." Ragano didn't realize that Trafficante knew about the JFK–Almeida coup plan and that the US government had been making plans to invade Cuba for months.

After a Trafficante toast, Ragano's girlfriend arrived. Ragano says that "when her drink came, Santo and I raised our glasses again and Santo said merrily, 'For a hundred years of health and to John Kennedy's death.'" Then, Trafficante "started laughing" and began another toast. Horrified by the public spectacle, Ragano's girlfriend "banged her glass on the table and rushed out of the restaurant." Ragano stayed with the "jubilant" Trafficante, who "continued toasting in Sicilian to the bountiful times he was certain were coming."

Information uncovered after Ragano's death suggests why he might have toasted the President's death so heartily: Ragano may have had a small part in the payoff for the JFK hit. According to FBI reports, "in December 1963" an FBI source "witnessed a meeting between Santo Trafficante, Frank Ragano," and another Tampa mobster. The three argued over briefcases of money, with the mobster telling Trafficante the money was short by $200,000 because of the payoff the mobster had already made to the two men who killed JFK. The source was a prison inmate who sent a letter to an Assistant US Attorney in 1992, who then forwarded it to the FBI. The mobster he named was a business partner of one of Trafficante's closest relatives. Also, the club in Tampa where the source said the meeting occurred was well known for being linked to the Mafia. Confirmation for the meeting comes from the FBI file, which says that independent of the inmate, the FBI "had already received information regarding an incident similar to that reported by" the inmate.

AROUND 5:15 P.M. (EST), J. Edgar Hoover issued an internal memo stating that police "very probably" had Kennedy's killer in custody, calling Oswald a nut and a pro-Castro extremist, an "extreme radical of the left." Hoover soon began to exert pressure on senior FBI officials to complete their investigation and issue a factual report supporting the conclusion that Oswald was the lone assassin. Though it wasn't a federal offense for one person acting alone to kill a president, it WAS a federal offense for two or more people to conspire to "injure any officer of the US engaged in discharging the duties of his office." Thus, proclaiming Oswald the "lone assassin" kept it a local and not a federal prosecution—and kept it out of the hands of Robert Kennedy's Justice Department.

Hoover's early decision to pronounce Oswald a lone assassin— even before JFK's autopsy—no doubt signaled to many agents in the field how their investigation should proceed. There was a shift from agents pursuing every lead vigorously, to focusing on Oswald's guilt and claiming he had acted alone. In addition, because of the quick decision that there wasn't a conspiracy, there was no large manhunt in Dallas for other conspirators. Roads and airports weren't closed, making escaping the city far less difficult for those involved in the assassination. There are unconfirmed reports of various private planes taking off from small airports around Dallas, particularly Redbird, but nothing conclusive.

HOWEVER, IN NEW Orleans, the conspiracy would soon start to unravel. The mood at Guy Banister's office had been joyous earlier on November 22. Though his temporary secretary said Banister wasn't there "at all that day," she said that Banister's mistress, Delphine Roberts, was in the office. Roberts "received a call to inform her that the President was assassinated and to turn on the TV. When Roberts turned on the TV, she jumped with joy and said 'I am glad.'"

After the secretary left, that evening Banister finally made it in to the office after visiting a neighborhood bar. He was preceded by Jack Martin, a private-detective associate and drinking buddy of Banister's. According to Delphine Roberts, Martin arrived first and went to a filing cabinet. Banister soon entered and accused Martin of stealing files. They argued, and Martin yelled, "What are you going to do—kill me, like you all did Kennedy?" Banister then pulled out a pistol and struck Martin on the head several times, causing him to bleed. Martin later called an assistant District Attorney to say that Ferrie was a longtime colleague and tutor of Lee Oswald. Since Martin had fallen out with Ferrie over a fraudulent ecclesiastical order (the Holy Apostolic Catholic Church of North America) and was an alcoholic, there was some doubt at the time about his reliability. But Martin's actions would set off a chain of events that led to Ferrie's arrest by Monday, November 25.

However, on Friday evening, Ferrie had more to worry about than just Martin's accusations: David Ferrie's library card was apparently found on Oswald at the time of his arrest. According to an FBI report, Marcello's lawyer, G. Wray Gill, "stated that he had gotten word that Lee Oswald, when he was picked up, had been carrying a library card with David Ferrie's name on it." On Sunday, November 24, Gill would stop by Ferrie's residence and leave word that "Ferrie should contact him, Gill, and he would represent him as his attorney. In addition, Gill said that Jack Martin . . . had gone to the police and the FBI and said that Ferrie had stated in his presence that the President should be killed."

That was on Sunday, but according to the House Select Committee on Assassinations, "Oswald's former landlady in New Orleans, Mrs. Jesse Garner, told the committee she recalled that Ferrie visited her home on Friday—the night of the assassination—and asked about Oswald's library card." In addition, "a neighbor of Oswald's" in New Orleans also said "that Ferrie had come by her house after the assassination, inquiring if" her husband "had any information regarding

Oswald's library card." Within days, the Secret Service would ask Ferrie whether he had ever loaned Oswald his library card. But on Friday, November 22, Ferrie didn't want the authorities to connect him to Oswald in any way, so he took two young men with him on a sudden trip to Texas.

David Ferrie's travels and actions on the two-day trip were considered so bizarre and unusual by investigators that it's possible that his goal was to retrieve his library card. Ferrie needed the card, so that he could produce it if he were ever asked for it by investigators in New Orleans. Shortly before his death, Ferrie told the staff of New Orleans District Attorney Jim Garrison that "he had some business for [G. Wray] Gill to take care of" when he suddenly went to Texas.

Ferrie told the FBI that "he had been in New Orleans until at least 9:00 p.m. on November 22, celebrating Marcello's trial victory at the Royal Orleans" hotel. Ferrie suddenly decided to drive to Houston through a heavy rainstorm, accompanied by two young men. They visited a Houston ice-skating rink, where Ferrie "spent a great deal of time at a pay telephone, making and receiving calls," according to Anthony Summers. In the early morning hours of November 23, Ferrie checked in to the Alamotel in Houston, which was owned by Carlos Marcello. Congressional investigators confirmed that Ferrie made "a collect call . . . to the Town and Country Motel, Marcello's New Orleans headquarters." He also called Marcello attorney G. Wray Gill that weekend. While still registered at the Houston Alamotel, Ferrie drove to Galveston and checked into another motel there. Jack Ruby made several calls to Galveston around the time of Ferrie's arrival there. Congressional investigators couldn't understand why hotels in Houston and Galveston both listed Ferrie as staying there during the same twelve-hour period.

One explanation is that someone in Galveston or Houston may have been bringing David Ferrie his library card. For example, there were men in each city who had just come from Dallas, shortly before Ferrie's arrival. One was an associate of Jack Ruby, and the other was alleged mob associate Eugene Hale Brading, who had been arrested in Dealey Plaza just after JFK's assassination. I'm not asserting that either of those two men delivered Ferrie's card but simply explaining how it could have been done.

GUY BANISTER MIGHT have been able to use his law-enforcement or intelligence contacts to get someone on the Dallas Police force to pull the card. Banister could have evoked Ferrie's work for the CIA and with Varona's CIA-backed anti-Castro Cuban group, giving rise to the "for the good of the country" excuse offered to Dallas reporters to stop their reporting on Ferrie. Alternately, Marcello's associates might have been able to use their Dallas Police contacts to get the card. Mobster Joe Civello ran Dallas for Marcello, and Dallas Police Sergeant Patrick Dean boasted to Peter Dale Scott about his "longtime relationship" with Civello. Sergeant Dean was also good friends with Jack Ruby. In fact, according to Scott, "Dean would be in charge of security in the Dallas [Police Department] basement when Oswald was murdered" and later fail "a lie detector test about Ruby's access to" it. Homicide Captain Will Fritz—in charge of the Oswald investigation—was also "very close friends" with Jack Ruby, according to J. D. Tippit's attorney.

ACCORDING TO DALLAS FBI agent James Hosty, after JFK's murder in Dallas, "the Pentagon ordered us to Defense Condition 3, more commonly known as Def Con 3—the equivalent of loading and locking your weapon, and then placing your finger on the trigger. The power cells within Washington were in a panic." Peter Dale Scott points out that Hosty wrote "that at the time of Oswald's arrest, fully armed warplanes were sent screaming toward Cuba. Just before they entered Cuban airspace, they were hastily called back. With the launching of airplanes, the entire US military went on alert." Scott notes that "these planes would have been launched from the US Strike Command at MacDill Air Force Base in Florida." That was the very base that JFK had visited just four days earlier, for a secret session with the Strike Force Commander and other leaders. However, the Def Con 3 alert status soon diminished. *U.S. News & World Report* notes that "the Air Force and the CIA sent a 'Flash' worldwide alert for all" US surveillance flights "to return to their bases lest the Soviet Union be provoked."

On Friday afternoon and evening, national security concerns about JFK's assassination reverberated throughout the US government, as information, misinformation, and possible disinformation about Oswald started to be uncovered. Scott points out a declassified "cable from US Army Intelligence in Texas, dated November 22, 1963, telling the Strike Command (falsely) that Oswald had defected to Cuba in 1959 and was 'a card-carrying member of the Communist Party.'" Later, even Hoover would erroneously tell "Bobby Kennedy that Oswald 'went to Cuba on several occasions, but would not tell us what he went to Cuba for.'" It appeared that someone had fed disinformation about Oswald to the FBI and military intelligence, which served to incriminate him and focus attention on Cuba.

JACK RUBY CONSTANTLY stalked Oswald at the police station, while continuing to try to find a policeman willing to silence

Oswald for him. Ruby's association with hundreds of policemen made him well suited to the task. Ruby admitted later that he was packing a pistol when he went to police headquarters that night. At 6:00 p.m., Ruby was seen on the third floor of police headquarters by John Rutledge, a reporter for the *Dallas Morning News*. At 7:00 p.m., Ruby spoke to Detective August Eberhardt at Dallas Police headquarters, on the third-floor hallway. Finally, at some time after that and before 8:00 p.m., Ruby tried to open the door to Captain Fritz's office, where Oswald was being interrogated. However, two officers stopped him and one told him, "You can't go in there, Jack." If Ruby had managed to get into Fritz's office while Oswald was there, it's likely he would have done what he did finally do on Sunday—shoot Oswald.

Frustrated at his first attempt, Ruby regrouped. He called the home of his friend Gordon McLendon, owner of KLIF radio, who was close to David Atlee Phillips and had a connection to Marcello. Ruby then called a radio DJ, offering to help him set up a telephone interview with District Attorney Henry Wade. Around 9:50 p.m., Ruby even dropped by Temple Searith Israel, where Ruby seemed depressed when he talked with Rabbi Hillel Silverman. Ruby didn't mention JFK's assassination.

During Oswald's interrogation, around 10:30 p.m., one of the officers got a phone call from Ruby, who offered to bring them some sandwiches. The officer declined. By 11:30, Ruby was back at the police station, and a policeman spotted him among the throngs of reporters. Finally, after midnight, Ruby would get a chance to see Oswald—but he would be too far away to have a clear shot. Ruby was packing his pistol, and carrying some sandwiches, when he attended a third-floor briefing at Dallas Police headquarters. There, Chief

Curry and District Attorney Henry Wade announced that Oswald would be shown to newsmen at a press conference in the basement. Ruby attended the chaotic press conference in a basement assembly room, where Oswald was shown to reporters to counter stories that he had been beaten. When Wade said that Oswald belonged to the "Free Cuba Committee" (an anti-Castro group headed by Eladio del Valle, an associate of both Trafficante and Ferrie), Ruby—standing on a table in the back of the room—corrected him, saying that it was really the "Fair Play for Cuba Committee" (a Communist, pro-Castro group).

DURING THE ROWDY press conference, Oswald said in response to a question that he "didn't shoot anybody, no sir" and correctly stated that he had not been charged with shooting the President. Oswald also asked for someone to "come forward to give me legal assistance," possibly an appeal to one of his contacts, like Banister or Phillips, to clear him with the authorities. Two lawyers connected to Marcello received calls about representing Oswald, but Oswald never saw a lawyer while he was in custody.

Interestingly, Chief Curry later said that "one would think Oswald had been trained in interrogation techniques and resisting interrogation techniques," and that Curry believed Oswald could have been some type of agent. Curry's remark was based on the way Oswald handled himself during the twelve hours of interrogation that weekend, none of which were recorded or stenographically transcribed. Assistant DA Alexander said that he "was amazed that a person so young would have had the self-control he had. It was almost as if he had been rehearsed, or programmed, to meet the situation that he found himself in." For someone like Oswald, who had withstood

KGB pressure and scrutiny in Russia for years, dealing with the Dallas Police for a couple of days—until someone came forward to help him—would have presented few problems.

RICHARD D. MAHONEY wrote that "[s]ubsequent to the Kennedy assassination, Ruby, a man described by Rosselli himself as 'one of our boys,' stalked, murdered, and thereby silenced Oswald. This act shines out like a neon sign through the fog of controversy surrounding the President's death." Ruby continued trying to fulfill his obligation to Carlos Marcello throughout the weekend. After the press conference, Ruby went to the radio station, and left around 2:00 a.m., to meet a Dallas Police officer and his girlfriend, a dancer for Ruby, at Simpson's Garage. There are numerous discrepancies about the duration of the meeting and the participants, but the police officer said the meeting with Ruby lasted two to three hours. Some researchers have speculated that Ruby was trying to either persuade the officer to shoot Oswald, or to help Ruby find an officer who would.

THE TWO SHOOTERS supplied by Carlos Marcello returned to Joe Campisi's restaurant shortly after the shooting, where they remained until he helped them leave Dallas. Likewise, Michel Victor Mertz was also still in Dallas at this time. However, those three—and likely Bernard Barker—were probably not the only men in Dallas who had been working in Dealey Plaza for Marcello and Trafficante. Just as they'd carefully planned JFK's murder so it could take place in any of three cities, they probably had additional personnel assisting with JFK's murder in Dallas.

Johnny Rosselli's biographers confirm that "the FBI surveillance of Rosselli loses his trail on the West Coast between November 19 and

November 27." They added that "Jimmy Starr, the Hollywood gossip columnist and a friend of Rosselli's," told them, "What I heard about the Kennedy assassination was that Johnny was the guy who got the team together to do the hit."

There is an unconfirmed report of Rosselli being in Tampa on November 20, before flying to New Orleans the next day. Made years before the Tampa attempt became known to historians, that report comes from a pilot named W. Robert Plumlee, described by Congressional investigators as "an associate of John Martino." Plumlee told former FBI agent William Turner that Rosselli stayed in Tampa the night of November 20, before being flown in a private plane to New Orleans on November 21. He says the group then traveled to Houston, before going on to Dallas on the morning of November 22. Plumlee says the flight was authorized by "military intelligence" with "the CIA" in a supporting role, and it was apparently related to the CIA–Mafia plots to kill Castro.

Although Plumlee did talk to government investigators in the mid-1970s, some have criticized his credibility. However, three additional mob associates independently placed Johnny Rosselli in Dallas on November 22, 1963. Most of the accounts also include Chicago hit man Charles Nicoletti, whom the Associated Press said had joined the CIA–Mafia plots in the fall of 1963. Unfortunately, none of the accounts meet my usual standards for reliability and independent corroboration, so I consider those accounts only suggestive. It is worth noting that no solid alibi for either Rosselli or Nicoletti has emerged for November 22, despite the fact that these allegations have been public for many years.

Cuban officials have claimed that Trafficante bodyguard and henchman Herminio Diaz was in Dallas on November 22 and took part in JFK's murder. Diaz had recently become a CIA asset and as noted in Chapter Seventeen, would be linked to a CIA–Mafia plot to kill Fidel just over two weeks after JFK's murder. Diaz had a dark complexion, which could explain some of the witness statements from Dealey Plaza. Again, there is no independent corroboration or evidence for Diaz's involvement in JFK's murder, aside from the statement of a captured Cuban exile named Tony Cuesta. The Cuban exile also named Eladio del Valle—a drug trafficking associate of Trafficante and Roland Masferrer—as being part of the JFK plot. As noted earlier, in 1967 del Valle would be brutally murdered the same night that David Ferrie died.*

As for Lee Oswald as a possible shooter, any scenario for Oswald shooting the president simply doesn't make sense, either as a "lone nut" or as part of a conspiracy. Recall that the secret Naval Intelligence operation concluded that "Oswald was not the shooter [and was] incapable of masterminding the assassination or of doing the actual shooting." If Oswald had truly been a Communist, doing it for some ideological reason, he avoided claiming credit or making his ideological points when he had the chance at his Friday-night press conference. If Oswald hoped to get away, killing Kennedy and then trying to escape by bus and cab—to get to a rooming house where he had no car or driver's license—also makes no sense. Oswald would have known that once he left work, he would quickly be fingered for the crime, and he had no way to get out of Dallas without taking public transportation.

---

*One or more conspirators could have gotten into the Book Depository with a rifle by simply breaking into the lightly secured building the night before. They could have hidden on the roof or on one of the large, box-filled warehouse floors. It was also possible to enter the Depository shortly before the motorcade, through the back door in the loading dock area.

If Oswald were a lone Communist assassin, it makes no sense for the Mafia to have risked having Jack Ruby kill him in a police station, on live TV. It's also hard to believe the mob would have gone against decades of successful experience and hired someone like Oswald to kill JFK. The thought of the Mafia having an inexperienced hit man flee a major assassination using public transportation is ludicrous.

There were probably officials at the time—and even today—who thought that Oswald was a low-level US intelligence asset who "turned." Yet that scenario still doesn't make sense, in terms of him assassinating JFK. If Oswald had suddenly turned against the US, he blew his chance to expose the US to the world by keeping quiet about US anti-Castro efforts at his Friday-night press conference. Instead, after reviewing all the evidence for almost twenty-five years, my view is that Oswald was a low-level part of some US effort against Castro, and he had been told his cover must be maintained at all costs to avoid blowing an important operation, one that could cost lives if exposed.

Oswald was finally charged with killing JFK at 1:30 a.m. (CST); he had been charged with killing Tippit earlier, at 7:30 p.m. Anthony Summers writes that Assistant DA Alexander later said Oswald was charged with killing JFK because of his departure from the Book Depository, Frazier's story about Oswald bringing curtain rods to work that morning, and the "'Communist' literature found among Oswald's effects at the rooming house."

CHAPTER 16

Another Mafia Murder in Dallas

A S NIGHT FELL in Washington, DC, on November 22, 1963, Robert Kennedy went to Bethesda Naval Medical Center along with Jackie and a caravan that included the hearse with JFK's body. During the twenty-minute ride, RFK heard Jackie's account of the shooting. At Bethesda, the man really calling the shots was Robert Kennedy, from the family suite on the hospital's seventeenth floor. Robert was part of a group that included Jackie as well as JFK aides Dave Powers and Kenneth O'Donnell. RFK was no doubt shocked when he heard what Powers and O'Donnell had seen from their vantage point in the motorcade, in the limo directly behind JFK's.

As Powers told my research associate—and as Powers and O'Donnell both confirmed to former House Speaker Tip O'Neill—they clearly saw shots from the front, from the grassy knoll. Powers and O'Donnell had known and worked with RFK for years; the Attorney General would have trusted their observations. In addition, White House physician Admiral George Burkley—the only doctor at Bethesda who had also seen JFK at Parkland—later stated that he believed JFK had been killed by more than one gunman. All of this presented a dilemma for RFK: If Oswald had been shooting from the rear, as Hoover and the news were now reporting, who had been shooting from the front?

Entire books have been written about JFK's autopsy, which several government commissions studied over the course of thirty-five years, yet substantial controversies remain. The location and size of wounds on some autopsy X-rays and photos don't match what others show, or what some at Parkland or Bethesda observed. Even worse, crucial evidence is missing, ranging from photos and tissue samples to JFK's brain. At the root of these controversies is the fact that Robert Kennedy controlled the autopsy.

Only a few basic facts are not in dispute. All agree that the Bethesda doctors didn't realize JFK had been shot in the throat, since a tracheotomy incision obscured that wound. The Bethesda doctors did find JFK's small back wound, so they initially assumed he had been shot once in the back and once in the head, and that Connally had been hit by a separate shot. Not until the next day, Saturday, did lead autopsy physician Dr. James Humes learn about the throat wound, and he burned his first draft of the autopsy report on Sunday, November 24. Beyond those key points, much has been disputed over the years and remains controversial, ranging from what the autopsy doctors did or didn't do—and why—to what type of casket JFK arrived in.

Accounting for much of the controversy were the national security implications of the autopsy. The President's assassination was a nightmare scenario beyond anything contemplated for the Cuba Contingency Plans that Alexander Haig and others had been working on. Oswald was still alive, so the results of JFK's official autopsy would have to be part of a public trial—and there are many indications a hasty "national security" autopsy was performed before the "official" autopsy.

Robert Kennedy's concerns about the exposure of the Almeida coup plan would have been shared by other officials in the know, like Joint Chiefs Chairman General Maxwell Taylor, who had ultimate authority over a military facility like Bethesda. One of the main points of RFK's subcommittee's making the Cuba Contingency Plans—the one about the possible "assassination of American officials"—had been to avoid a situation in which the premature release of information could back the President into a corner and cause a crisis that could go nuclear. The thinking behind that planning appears to have been implemented to deal with JFK's death.

Some have tried to claim that shadowy generals, the CIA, or J. Edgar Hoover ran the autopsy without Robert Kennedy's knowledge, but much evidence shows that's simply not true. Several of the people at the autopsy made it clear that JFK's personal physician, Admiral Burkley, wielded a heavy hand at the autopsy on RFK's behalf. Francis O'Neill, one of two FBI agents present at the autopsy, told Congressional investigators that there was "'no question' that Burkley was conveying the wishes of the Kennedy family." Jerrol F. Custer, the radiology technician who took X-rays in the autopsy room with a portable X-ray machine, stated that Admiral Burkley said, "I am JFK's personal physician. You will listen to what I say. You will do what I say."

A laboratory technician at the autopsy, Paul O'Connor, said that "Admiral Burkley controlled what happened in that room that night, through Robert Kennedy and the rest of the Kennedy family." O'Connor said that when Burkley came into the autopsy room, he "was very agitated—giving orders to everybody, including higher-ranking officers."

Since the Commandant of the Bethesda facility, Admiral Calvin Galloway, was present in the autopsy room, Burkley sometimes conveyed RFK's wishes through him. James Jenkins, a navy man from Bethesda's clinical laboratory who assisted at the autopsy, said that the main autopsy physician "was probably being directed by Burkley through [Admiral] Galloway." One of the assisting autopsy physicians, Dr. J. Thorton Boswell, said that "Dr. Burkley was basically supervising everything that went on in the autopsy room, and that the commanding officer was also responding to Burkley's wishes." Dr. Burkley himself stated in his oral history at the JFK Library that "during the autopsy I supervised everything that was done . . . and kept in constant contact with Mrs. Kennedy and the members of her party, who were on the seventeenth floor."

Robert Kennedy was calling the shots to Dr. Burkley, and JFK military aide General McHugh later testified that "Bobby Kennedy frequently phoned the autopsy suite." According to Gus Russo, the Commander of Bethesda's Naval Medical School, Captain John Stover, said that "Bobby went so far as to periodically visit the autopsy room during the procedure." However, RFK also had someone— an individual I interviewed in 1992—assisting him in dealing with Burkley and the autopsy room. The presence of this very sensitive, confidential source at the autopsy has been confirmed by a Kennedy-authorized account, and his credibility is not only clear based on the public record but has been vouched for by numerous associates of John and Robert Kennedy. These include Secretary of State Dean Rusk, Harry Williams, and RFK's trusted FBI liaison Courtney Evans. It's significant that my source who assisted RFK at the autopsy was fully knowledgeable not only of the JFK–Almeida coup plan, but also about the Cuba Contingency Plans designed to protect it. The bottom line is that whatever went on at the autopsy most likely happened with the full knowledge, and probably at the ultimate direction, of

Robert Kennedy. Further proof of this concept is the fact that some of the most important missing evidence, such as JFK's brain, wound up under RFK's control.

Even such a basic fact as the time when the autopsy started has caused much debate and uncertainty over the past four decades. There was a delay of at least forty minutes, and possibly as much as an hour, between the arrival of JFK's body at the facility and the start of the autopsy. While that might not be very unusual in itself, something else was: There were two ambulances—one was a decoy supposedly meant to throw off reporters and sightseers who might have made it onto the base. After the ambulance that actually carried JFK's body arrived at the front of the building, the *Washington Post* reported that Admiral Galloway himself "pushed into the front seat and drove to the rear of the hospital, where the body was taken inside."

However, author David Lifton found that the men who were to guard the ambulance with JFK's body had lost sight of the ambulance as it sped away. The guards chased after the ambulance but couldn't find it. Much confusion on their part followed, before they finally arrived at the rear of the facility and found the ambulance at last. Oddly, Secret Service Agent Kellerman says the autopsy started at 7:30, while the casket team's report says JFK's casket was not carried in until 8:00 p.m. The two FBI agents say the first incision was made at 8:15 p.m.

In addition to the unusual timing discrepancies, there were also easy-to-document differences between how JFK's body looked at Parkland and how it looked (and was photographed) at the start of his autopsy in Bethesda. The most obvious example is JFK's throat wound, where the tracheotomy incision had been made. Dallas's Dr. Perry said that his small, neat incision was only 2–3 centimeters.

However, photos of JFK's body at the start of the autopsy show a very ragged incision, spread open in the middle, that was at least two or three times larger. JFK's official autopsy report said the incision was 6.5 centimeters when the autopsy began, while the lead autopsy physician, Dr. Humes, said under oath that it was 7–8 centimeters. The throat incision was not enlarged during the official autopsy, because, as assisting autopsy physician Dr. Pierre Finck later testified, the doctors had been ordered not to.

While the official autopsy was jammed with officers and other personnel, an earlier unofficial national security autopsy would have been conducted with only a few people present. This scenario could also explain other documented discrepancies. As the official account would evolve, JFK's back wound was supposedly caused by the complete "magic bullet" found at Parkland on a stretcher—no bullet (or substantial part of a bullet) was found at the autopsy. Yet Dr. Osborne—then a Captain and later an Admiral and the Deputy Surgeon General—told Congressional investigators he saw "an intact bullet roll . . . onto the autopsy table" when JFK was removed from his casket. Osborne reiterated to David Lifton that "I had that bullet in my hand and looked at it." He said it was "reasonably clean [and] unmarred," and "the Secret Service took it."

Dr. Osborne's account is confirmed to a degree by the account of X-ray technician Custer, who said that "a pretty good-sized bullet" fell out of JFK's "upper back," where his back wound was located. He said that when "we lifted him up . . . that's when it came out." Finally, the Commanding Officer of the Naval Medical School at the time, Captain John Stover, told author William Law, "Well, there was a bullet." To Lifton, "Stover confirmed there was a bullet in the Bethesda morgue" from JFK's body. However, Stover thought it was the bullet found on the stretcher at Parkland. But it wasn't, since that bullet was at the FBI laboratory, many miles away.

A brief national security autopsy before the official one, as well as national security concerns following the official autopsy, could also account for the many problems surrounding the autopsy photographs and X-rays. Douglas Horne was the Chief Analyst of military records for the congressionally created JFK Assassination Records Review Board for three years in the 1990s. In addition to the problem with JFK's throat wound, Horne recently wrote, "There is something seriously wrong with the autopsy photographs of the body of President Kennedy. . . . The images showing the damage to the President's head do not show the pattern of damage observed by either the medical professionals at Parkland Hospital in Dallas, or by numerous witnesses at the military autopsy at Bethesda Naval Hospital. These disparities are real and are significant."

Horne also cites FBI Agent Frank O'Neill, who "testified to the Review Board that the brain photos in the National Archives could not possibly be of President Kennedy's brain, because they showed too much remaining tissue; O'Neill testified that more than half of President Kennedy's brain was missing when he saw it at the autopsy following its removal from the cranium, and his objections to the brain photographs in the Archives were that they depict what he called 'almost a complete brain.'"

FBI Agent O'Neill made other interesting observations. Along with his colleague at the autopsy, Agent James Sibert, he doesn't believe in the "magic bullet" theory that was later proposed. Sibert says he looked at JFK's back wound from only two feet away. Measurements of the bullet holes in JFK's jacket and shirt show they were almost six inches below the tops of the collars, well below the neck. Agent Sibert says, "There's no way that bullet could go that low, then come up, raise up, and come out the front of the neck, zigzag and hit Connally, and then end up in a pristine condition over there in Dallas." Agent O'Neill concurs, saying, "Absolutely not, it did not happen."

O'Neill also recently revealed something that Secret Service Agent Roy Kellerman said to him at the autopsy: "He told me he [had] cautioned Kennedy that morning not to be so open with the crowds for security reasons. Kennedy told him that if someone wanted to kill him, all they would have to do was use a scope rifle from a high building." This statement was just one more indication of JFK's mindset following the Chicago and Tampa assassination attempts. When the events of the autopsy are considered in terms of the cloak of secrecy those attempts generated for national security reasons, it starts to provide a rationale for many, if not all, of the autopsy discrepancies.

WHAT HAPPENED AFTER the autopsy is well documented: JFK's body and funeral arrangements were put in the hands of Cyrus Vance's two trusted aides, Alexander Haig and Joseph Califano. Haig has written that he "was assigned the duty of helping with the preparations for the President's funeral [and] handling details concerning the burial site." Califano wrote that after JFK's murder, he went to the Pentagon and met Vance, who put him in charge of arranging JFK's burial at Arlington National Cemetery and told him to meet RFK there the next day.

Califano and Haig have always been careful to distance themselves from the most sensitive parts of Vance's work on RFK's plans to eliminate Castro, and neither ever admitted to knowing about the JFK–Almeida coup plan. Harry Williams confirmed that Al Haig did know about Commander Almeida. However, declassified files show that Califano and Haig both worked on the Cuba Contingency Plans for dealing with the possible "assassination of American officials." Vance's use of Califano and Haig is logical even if Califano had not yet been told about the JFK–Almeida coup plan, because Vance knew he could count on both men to follow orders, if any national security problems arose.

ON THE EVENING of November 22, my confidential Naval Intelligence source was called back to his office. Now that Lee Oswald's name had surfaced in JFK's murder, he and his co-workers were given new orders: to destroy and sanitize much of the "tight" surveillance file their group had maintained on Oswald since his return from Russia. At that point, it appeared that Oswald's file might become the subject of at least an internal military investigation, and, at worst, aspects of the surveillance might even be brought up or exposed at Oswald's trial or in a Congressional investigation. While national security was no doubt the overriding concern in the document destruction ordered by my source's superiors, it would also help to avoid embarrassment to those higher in the chain of command who had been aware of Oswald's special status.

CHICAGO BRIEFLY BECAME a focus of the assassination investigation very early on the morning of Saturday, November 23. A Mannlicher-Carcano found on the sixth floor of the Book Depository after JFK's murder might have a paper trail that could be traced, if authorities could determine where and how it had been purchased. According to historian Richard D. Mahoney, "CIA files . . . reveal that the first lead as to the location of the rifle came from the chief investigator of the Cook County Sheriff's Office, Richard Cain, a

Rosselli-Giancana confederate." The staff at Klein's, a major retailer of mail-order rifles, began searching their records and "on November 23 at 4:00 a.m., CST, executives at Klein's Sporting Goods in Chicago discovered the American Rifleman coupon with which Oswald had allegedly ordered the Mannlicher-Carcano," using the "Hidell" alias.

Since the rifle had been shipped to Lee Oswald's post office box, it appeared to many to cinch the case against Oswald. A CIA memo stated that Richard Cain, an Agency asset, was "deeply involved in the President Kennedy assassination case," but other details of his involvement—aside from his timely tip about the rifle—are lacking. Cain was also in a position to see if word of the recent four-man Chicago threat might surface in the news media, and to plant false information to deceive authorities and the media, such as claiming that Oswald had received support from the small Fair Play for Cuba Committee chapter in Chicago.

At 9:00 a.m. (EST) on November 23, 1963, CIA Director John McCone talked to Robert Kennedy. McCone was set to meet with new President Lyndon Johnson at 12:30 to start briefing him on the most pressing intelligence matters, so it's not hard to imagine that McCone and RFK must have discussed what McCone was going to tell LBJ about the coup plan with Almeida. At that point, LBJ had had no involvement in the plan and probably didn't even know it existed. Now, as President and Commander-in-Chief, he would have to be brought up to speed, and quickly.

McCone was about to find out a bit more about the AMLASH operation with Cuban official Rolando Cubela. According to Evan Thomas, on November 23 Desmond FitzGerald finally told "Walt Elder, the executive assistant to McCone, that he had met with Cubela in October and that one of his agents had been meeting with the Cuban turncoat the very moment Kennedy had been shot. However, he did not tell Elder that AMLASH had been offered a poison pen or promised a rifle." Even without knowing about the scoped rifles, "Elder was struck by FitzGerald's clear discomfort. 'Des was normally imperturbable, but he was very disturbed about his involvement.' The normally smooth operator was 'shaking his head and wringing his hands. It was very uncharacteristic. That's why I remember it so clearly.'" Just two days later, FitzGerald would tell Cubela's case officer to delete a reference to the poison pen in a memo, so McCone would continue to be in the dark about the assassination side of the Cubela operation.

After his talk with RFK on the morning of November 23, John McCone met with President Lyndon B. Johnson. It's very important to look at what McCone could have told LBJ in those early hours, since it would shape LBJ's opinions—and US policy—about JFK's murder and Cuba in the coming days, months, and years. Of course, even though McCone was CIA Director, he was limited in what he could reveal to LBJ because Richard Helms hadn't told McCone some crucial operations. McCone probably told LBJ the broad outlines of JFK's coup plan with Commander Almeida. McCone also could have informed LBJ about AMTRUNK, the so-far ineffective plan to try to find other Cuban military leaders willing to stage a revolt against Castro. McCone might have known what his aide had just learned about FitzGerald and Cubela (AMLASH); but, if not, McCone probably told LBJ the following day. However, anything McCone told LBJ about Cubela would have been incomplete, since McCone didn't know about the assassination side of the Cubela operation. As for the CIA–Mafia plots, McCone had learned about those only in August, and he had been falsely told they had ended in the spring of 1962—which is probably what he repeated to LBJ. Neither LBJ nor McCone would have known that the CIA–Mafia plots were continuing, or that CIA officer David Morales had been working with a mobster like Johnny Rosselli. They also didn't know that major Cuban exile leader Manuel Artime was part of the CIA–Mafia plots.

For LBJ, hearing all at once about the Almeida coup plan, AMTRUNK, Cubela/AMLASH, and what LBJ could have been told about the CIA–Mafia plots, all of those covert actions probably just seemed like different facets of one big CIA operation—one that might have backfired horribly against JFK. All that information would shape much of LBJ's outlook about the assassination, along with another bit of news that McCone reportedly conveyed to LBJ on either November 23 or at their meeting on November 24. According to historian Michael Beschloss, McCone told LBJ that "the CIA had information on foreign connections to the alleged assassin, Lee Harvey Oswald, which suggested to LBJ that Kennedy may have been murdered by an international conspiracy." Peter Dale Scott adds that "a CIA memo written that day reported that Oswald had visited Mexico City in September and talked to a Soviet vice consul whom the CIA knew as a KGB expert in assassination and sabotage. The memo warned that if Oswald had indeed been part of a foreign conspiracy, he might be killed before he could reveal it to US authorities." Scott says that "Johnson appears to have had this information in mind when, a few minutes after the McCone interview, he asked FBI Director J. Edgar Hoover if the FBI 'knew any more about the visit to the Soviet embassy.'"

According to Gus Russo, LBJ's former speechwriter Leo Janos said he heard the following from the spouse of an aide to Johnson: "'When Lyndon got back from Dallas, McCone briefed him' on the cause of the assassination, allegedly saying: 'It was the Castro connection.' The information was contained in a file McCone brought with him to LBJ's vice-presidential residence." "According to Janos, Johnson immediately called Senator Richard Russell, relayed to him McCone's conclusion, and asked, 'What do we do?' Russell replied, 'Don't let it out. If you do, it's World War III.' Johnson swore Russell to secrecy, and proceeded to destroy McCone's file."

However, it later emerged from CIA and FBI files that almost all of those reports had connections to associates of Santo Trafficante, Carlos Marcello, Johnny Rosselli, or David Morales. And those are just the reports we know about, the ones that were eventually declassified. There are indications that other versions of the same stories—from the same or similar mob-linked sources—are among the JFK assassination files still being withheld. Other versions of those reports were no doubt among the files destroyed, such as a report Alexander Haig describes in his autobiography: "Very soon after President Kennedy's death, an intelligence report crossed my desk. In circumstantial detail, it stated that Oswald had been seen in Havana in the company of Cuban intelligence officers several days before the events in Dallas . . . the detailed locale, precise notations of time, and more—was very persuasive. I was aware that it would not have reached so high a level if others had not judged it plausible . . . I walked it over to my superiors . . . 'Al,' said one of them, 'you will forget, as from this moment, that you ever read this piece of paper, or that it ever existed.' The report was destroyed."

As long as he lived, Haig—later Reagan's Secretary of State—expressed the belief that Castro was behind JFK's assassination, as does Califano today. However, neither man realized that stories like the one they saw were not only later discredited, but also linked to the Mafia. One CIA cable that weekend tried to urge caution in dealing with such reports, but it went unheeded, at least initially. The bottom

line was that high US officials like LBJ and McCone—and lower officials who gained power in later decades like Haig and Califano—were
left with the false impression that Castro had killed JFK. That mistaken impression has helped to essentially freeze US–Cuba relations
since the time of JFK's murder. However, at the time, it also served to
divert attention and suspicion away from the Mafia. As the following
chapter shows, Marcello and Trafficante would have their associates
like John Martino continue to spread false "Castro killed JFK" stories
that hinted at the JFK–Almeida coup plan, as a way to keep the pressure on US officials to stifle any truly full investigation of Oswald, his
associates, and of any other suspects in JFK's murder.

LATER REPORTS ABOUT the movements of Gilberto Lopez and
Miguel Casas Saez also fed the "Castro killed JFK" beliefs shared by
LBJ, McCone, and CIA Counter-Intelligence Chief James Angleton.
Lopez and Saez were reported to have crossed the border when it
reopened on November 23 (it had temporarily been closed right after
JFK's death). Both men were en route to Cuba, via Mexico City. Both
were later reported to have been in Dallas during JFK's assassination. Lopez had left Tampa sometime after November 20, and the
FBI concluded that on November 23 he crossed "the border at Nuevo
Laredo"—the same border crossing used by Oswald—"in a privately
owned automobile owned by another person." However, he wouldn't
check into his Mexico City hotel until Monday, November 25, and his
whereabouts on November 23 and 24 are unknown.

It's almost as if someone was keeping him on ice, just in case
some type of evidence emerged (perhaps photographic) proving that
more than one gunman was involved in Dallas, or in case Oswald
needed an accomplice to make the scenario of his guilt believable.

Lopez may well have been an unwitting asset for some US agency, while he was focused only on getting back to his native Cuba. But just as Oswald was manipulated by those with intelligence connections who were also working for the Mafia, the same could have been true for Lopez.

The actions of Miguel Casas Saez also appear to have been manipulated by someone wanting him to look suspicious. Some reports say that Saez flew out of Dallas on a private plane and made a mysterious airport rendezvous in Mexico City, where he transferred directly to a Cubana Airlines plane without going through Customs or Immigration. The plane had supposedly been waiting for him for five hours, and he then rode in the cockpit, thus avoiding identification by the passengers. The reports made Saez sound like a Cuban assassin, being given special treatment after fleeing Dallas. However, the House Select Committee looked into that account and found that it wasn't true. Other reports say that Saez left Dallas with two friends after JFK was shot and crossed the border Nuevo Laredo. Since many of the reports about Saez originated with David Morales's AMOT informants, the whole scenario is suspect, which is what the CIA and FBI eventually concluded. Still, either or both men would have made excellent patsies for JFK's death if anything had happened to Oswald or if someone else was needed to shoulder some of the blame. At the same time, each may also have been serving (or thought he was serving) some legitimate role for US intelligence.

TO RICHARD HELMS and his aides, it would have been clear that whatever CIA operation Oswald was involved with had been subject to a massive intelligence failure. John Whitten was Helms's Covert Operations Chief for all of Mexico and Central America. In a detailed report that he wrote soon after JFK's death, one kept classified for thirty years, Whitten said that after "word of the shooting of President Kennedy reached the [CIA] offices . . . when the name of Lee Oswald was heard, the effect was electric."

As the CIA's Deputy Director for Plans, essentially its highest operational official, Richard Helms was responsible. On November 23, 1963, Helms therefore had to take control of all the CIA's material on Oswald, both for national security reasons and probably to protect his own career. Historian Michael Kurtz has written that Hunter Leake, the Deputy Chief of the New Orleans CIA office at the time, told him "that on the day after the assassination, he was ordered to collect all of the CIA's files on Oswald from the New Orleans office and transport them to the Agency's headquarters in Langley, Virginia." Kurtz wrote that "[along with] other employees of the New Orleans office, Leake gathered all of the Oswald files. They proved so voluminous that Leake had to rent a trailer to transport them to Langley. Stopping only to eat, use the restroom, and fill up with gas, Leake drove the truck pulling the rental trailer filled with the New Orleans office's files on Oswald to CIA headquarters. Leake later learned that many of these files were . . . 'deep sixed.' Leake explained that . . . the CIA dreaded the release of any information that would connect Oswald with it. Leake thought that his friend Richard Helms, the Agency's Deputy Director for Plans, was probably the person who ordered the destruction of the files because Helms had a paranoid obsession with protecting the 'Company.'"

Leake's description of the Oswald files as "voluminous" makes sense, given the information from our independent source about the "tight surveillance" of Oswald, something not known to Kurtz at the time of his interview with Leake. (Professor Kurtz asked Helms about Leake's story, but Helms declined to confirm or deny Leake's account.) Buttressing Leake's credibility is the fact that no routine reports from the CIA's New Orleans office have ever surfaced about former defector Oswald's several well-publicized pro-Castro activities in New Orleans during August 1963, despite the CIA's interest in both former defectors and the Fair Play for Cuba Committee.

A SOMBER ROBERT Kennedy took time out from his family and official duties for a private meeting with Harry Williams, who told us the meeting occurred within two days of JFK's death. Almeida was still in Cuba, and his family was still outside of Cuba under US surveillance, but any plans for a coup were now on hold. Williams said that RFK "didn't say much," but told Williams that "things are going to change," now that RFK no longer essentially ran Cuban operations and policy for the United States. Williams said he already knew that RFK and "Johnson . . . hate[d] each other's guts," so RFK's role and the plans would no doubt be very different, if they continued at all.

IN A PHONE call recorded at 10:01 a.m. on November 23, J. Edgar Hoover admitted to Lyndon Johnson that "the case, as it stands now, isn't strong enough to be able to get a conviction." Yet the Saturday-morning newspapers were conveying just the opposite impression by establishing the basic "lone assassin" scenario that some people still believe today. In hindsight, it seems absurd to think that all the relevant information about the shooting, and an unusual former defector like Oswald, could be uncovered less than twelve hours after the shooting—and that clearly wasn't the case. However, investigations that touched on covert matters would have to be conducted in secret, so as not to alarm the public or back President

Johnson into a corner regarding possible retaliation against Cuba or the Soviet Union.

Journalists asked to withhold information from the public didn't have to be made aware of the JFK–Almeida coup plan, or the Cuba Contingency Plans to protect it. In those pre-Watergate times, they could simply be told that certain information was too sensitive, could compromise US operations, or might force a confrontation with the Soviets—and just a year after the Cuban Missile Crisis, this last explanation might be all that was required, since Oswald's Soviet and Cuba connections had been so widely reported.

As mentioned in Chapter One, when information linking Oswald to David Ferrie first started to surface during the weekend after JFK's murder, an NBC cameraman related that "an FBI agent said that I should never discuss what we discovered for the good of the country." That same phrase, "for the good of the country," would be used to stop Dave Powers and Kenneth O'Donnell from revealing they had seen shots from the grassy knoll, and it was probably used to silence others as well. Longtime television journalist Peter Noyes was told by several "members of NBC News who covered the events in Dallas [that] they were convinced their superiors wanted certain evidence suppressed at the request of someone in Washington."

It's unclear if Ferrie's name was surfacing because Oswald apparently had his library card, or because of the Jack Martin allegations, or for some other reason. But the "for the good of the country" comment helps to confirm CIA officer Leake's statements that Ferrie (and Guy Banister) was working for the CIA in 1963. Now, as a result of the Martin allegations, Ferrie was a wanted man. With Ferrie on the run, and Oswald still alive, Carlos Marcello would have known that his carefully orchestrated plan could still unravel.

Not all of the pressure on journalists in Dallas came from Washington; it also came from conditions on the scene. The intense competition among journalists and networks in Dallas for "scoops" also contributed to coverage that was often shallow or wrong, and stories that avoided the lengthy in-depth investigations that might have uncovered what had really happened in Dallas. However, just being involved in reporting on the assassination gave a huge boost to the careers of broadcasters. Texan Dan Rather's career-making scoop was his role as the first journalist to view and report on the Zapruder film, though so firmly entrenched by the weekend was the "official" story of the lone-assassin-shooting-from-behind that Rather claimed the home movie showed JFK's "head went forward with considerable violence" after he was shot. The public wouldn't get to see the film for themselves—and learn that JFK was pitched backward, not forward—for another twelve years.

Other later prominent newsmen covering—and at times involved in—the story include future PBS broadcasters Jim Lehrer and Robert MacNeil (as Oswald calmly left the Texas School Book Depository, MacNeil apparently asked him where he could find a phone), Bob Schieffer (who gave Oswald's mother a ride to Dallas), and Peter Jennings. While covering the assassination helped their careers, it sometimes impeded any questioning of the "official" version of the lone assassin, both at the time and for years to come.

In Dallas, Joe Campisi Sr. continued to hide the two European gunmen in his restaurant. Once it was deemed safe, Carlos Marcello told Jack Van Laningham that the two were whisked out of Dallas and taken back to Canada, using the same path that had originally brought them into the US. That presumably involved their going to Michigan to cross the border into Canada. In 1985, after hearing Marcello's remarks about the two on the FBI's undercover audio tapes, the FBI apparently took action. Van Laningham said that his FBI contact agent later told him that the FBI and "turned the matter over to the CIA, since it involved foreign countries." The CIA checked airline records and was able to confirm that "the two men had come into Canada, from Italy, on their regular passports."

Those two shooters were not the only Europeans involved in JFK's assassination. As noted earlier, a CIA memo said that French Connection heroin kingpin and assassin Michel Victor Mertz was in Dallas on November 22, the day of the shooting. The memo says he was "expelled from the US at Fort Worth or Dallas 48 hours after the assassination . . . to either Mexico or Canada." The CIA memo also indicated that Mertz had been using the alias of "Jean Souetre," a wanted French assassin. It also stated that "Souetre" had exchanged mail with a dentist in Houston, who had met the real Souetre on a trip to Europe.

The dentist later told investigators that he was interviewed by FBI agents who "told me that Souetre was in Dallas that day [of JFK's murder] and was flown out . . . as far as they were concerned, in a government plane. But there was no record whatsoever of the plane being there." The FBI couldn't find any record of Souetre's being "flown out" on a government plane, because the person in question was actually Mertz, who'd been posing as Souetre.

When Mertz was picked up by US authorities in Dallas, he had apparently switched to yet another cover identity, one guaranteed to get him deported back to familiar territory. Virgil Bailey, an INS investigator in Dallas in 1963, told researcher Gary Shaw years later about "picking up a Frenchman in Dallas shortly after the assassination of

President Kennedy." The man's description was very close to Mertz's, and he looked just a few years older than a cover identity Mertz often used. Based on age and description, the man Investigator Bailey remembered could not have been the real Souetre. Bailey also recalled that "the Frenchman . . . had been tried in absentia in France and was under a death sentence for collaboration with the Nazis during World War II." Mertz could have picked up that alias from either of two of his heroin associates, Joseph Orsini and Antoine D'Agostino, who had both earned "a death sentence in absentia" for Nazi collaboration. Bailey thought the man they arrested was "a chef or maitre d' in an unknown Dallas restaurant." It's possible the restaurant in question was Campisi's.

Bailey's supervisor at INS at the time, Hal Norwood, recalled other aspects of the story. Norwood described the arrest of an "individual who might have been French which occurred shortly after the killing of the President. The Dallas Police called INS and requested that they come to city jail to investigate a foreigner that they had in custody." Norwood thought Bailey "was one of the men he sent" to pick up the foreigner. "The man in question was a wanted criminal and shortly after INS took him into custody, the head of Washington INS investigations called requesting a pickup on the man. They were surprised that he was already a prisoner. . . . The Washington INS office was VERY interested in the man and called twice regarding him," according to INS supervisor Norwood.

Mertz could have used his intelligence connections to make sure the official paperwork was later suppressed. Something similar had been done in the recent Senate narcotics hearings, where Mertz's heroin associates had all been identified, but Mertz's name was completely missing from the hearings. The fact that the CIA discovered later that someone had been using the name of Souetre would also allow an official like Helms (or Angleton or Harvey) to ask INS officials to remove the information about the deportation from their files, on national security grounds.

Mertz likely used the name of one of his wanted associates to get picked up by the INS, but once in custody he could have used his intelligence connections to ensure he was deported to Canada, instead of to France, where his associate was wanted. It must have been deliciously ironic for Carlos Marcello to see the same INS that had once deported him, on the orders of Robert Kennedy, now fly his heroin partner and assassin Mertz out of Dallas shortly after JFK's assassination.

EVEN AS EVIDENCE tying Oswald to Cuba and Russia caused concern among officials in Washington, and would soon break in the press, Marcello continued the pressure to have Oswald killed. With the authorities still seeking David Ferrie, the whole plot could unravel and point to people working for Marcello. The godfather could make only limited efforts to contain Oswald's public statements and cooperation with police, which is why two attorneys linked to Marcello had been asked to represent the still lawyerless Oswald. (They were Clem Sehrt, an associate of Carlos Marcello who had known Oswald's mother since the 1950s, and Dean Andrews, who knew David Ferrie.) But only killing Oswald could guarantee his silence.

ON NOVEMBER 23, Jack Ruby continued to relentlessly stalk Oswald. We noted earlier Ruby's friendship with Dallas Police Sergeant Patrick Dean, Homicide Captain Will Fritz, and Police Chief Jesse Curry. At noon, Chief Curry called Captain Fritz to see if

Oswald could be transferred to the county jail—and the jurisdiction of the sheriff—at 4:00 p.m. Ruby was also at the police station at noon. At 1:30, Ruby placed a call from the Nichols Garage, next door to his Carousel Club, and told someone the whereabouts of Chief Curry, which must mean that Ruby was talking to or keeping tabs on Curry. At 3:00 p.m., Police Sergeant D. V. Harkness, expecting Oswald to be moved at 4:00 p.m., started clearing a crowd that was blocking a driveway entrance to the county jail. Harkness saw Ruby in the crowd. Sometime after 3:00, Ruby placed another call from the Nichols Garage, and when talking about the transfer of Oswald Ruby said, "You know I'll be there." An announcer for Dallas radio station KLIF said Ruby called him to offer to cover the transfer of Oswald for the station. Finally, at 4:00, Ruby was at the police station, expecting Oswald to be moved—but for some reason the transfer was called off and rescheduled.

However, at 7:30 p.m., Chief Curry inadvertently told two reporters wanting dinner—but not wanting to miss Oswald's transfer—that if they were back by 10:00 a.m. Sunday morning, "they won't miss anything." About an hour later, Ruby called his friend and business associate Ralph Paul, and someone overheard Paul saying, "Are you crazy? A gun?" Finally, at 10:20 p.m., Chief Curry announced at a press conference that Oswald would be moved the next morning, in an armored truck, which meant Ruby would have to wait until Sunday to complete his assignment.

However, Ruby began laying important groundwork on Saturday for the rationale he would use to be near police headquarters at the time of Oswald's transfer. Ruby's story would be that he had to wire $25 to one of his dancers, Karen Carlin. To begin preparing this cover story, Ruby had Carlin and several others go to the Nichols

Garage. All those involved in this meeting later gave authorities differ-ent accounts of what happened there. Carlin was willing to agree to whatever Ruby said, because the previous day, a Ruby associate had ordered her to meet him and threatened, "If you're not down here, you won't be around too long."

Karen Carlin arrived at the Nichols Garage before Ruby did; then Ruby called the parking attendant and told him to lend Carlin $5—and be sure to time-stamp the receipt—for which Ruby would reim-burse him. When Ruby arrived at the garage, his cover story was that he was supposed to loan Carlin another $25. Ruby claimed he didn't have the cash to lend and couldn't get it, ignoring the fact that his club and its safe were next door. The plan was for Ruby to wire Carlin the money the next day, from a Western Union office only one block from the police station where Oswald would be moved. The following day, Ruby's time-stamped Western Union receipt would be designed to "prove" that Ruby just happened to be near the police station when Oswald was being moved. It's clear this was only a cover story, since there were two Western Union offices much closer to Ruby's Oak Cliff apartment. There was no need for Ruby to go all the way downtown to use the Western Union office near the police station—except for the fact that Ruby had to silence Oswald.

ON NOVEMBER 24, 1963, at 10:00 a.m. (EST), CIA Director McCone met with President Johnson to tell him about "the Cuban situation," including "our operational plans against Cuba," accord-ing to McCone's notes. LBJ and McCone no doubt also discussed the latest information from Mexico City that seemed to implicate Fidel Castro in JFK's murder. Unaware that information would later be discredited, in another meeting that weekend, LBJ asked former JFK aide Ted Sorensen, "What do you think of the possibility of a foreign government being involved [in JFK's assassination]?"

IN SOUTH CAROLINA on November 24, white supremacist and Banister associate Joseph Milteer was having breakfast with his friend William Somersett, unaware that Somersett was an informant for the Miami police. Earlier, Milteer had told Somersett that "Oswald hasn't said anything and he will not say anything." Milteer also made it clear that, despite the initial reports of Oswald's stay in Russia and his seeming public support of Fidel Castro, "Oswald was not connected with Moscow, or any big Communist leaders." When the subject of JFK's murder came up again, "Milteer advised that they did not have to worry about Lee Harvey Oswald getting caught because he 'doesn't know anything.'"

However, as if he needed to make sure, Milteer excused himself so that he could telephone someone.

ON THE MORNING of November 24 in Dallas, Jack Ruby was spruced up, dressed in his finest, ready for the spotlight he was sure to occupy after he completed his assignment for Carlos Marcello. Ruby was undoubtedly nervous, but not about the length of time he might have to spend in jail after shooting Oswald. Under Texas law, for murders involving a "sudden passion," the sentence could be as brief as two years, with time off for good behavior, or sometimes even just probation, with no prison time. Instead, Ruby was probably worried only that after he pulled out his gun and started shooting at Oswald, he might hit a policeman or a policeman might start shooting at him. Getting into the police station basement where the transfer would take place would be no problem for Ruby, since the FBI later acknowledged that "as a result of his friendship with a number of police officers, Ruby had easy accessibility to the Dallas Police Department."

The executive director of the House Select Committee on Assassinations, former Mafia prosecutor G. Robert Blakey, said that "the murder of Oswald by Jack Ruby had all the earmarks of an organized crime hit." The Committee also found that Ruby's shooting Oswald wasn't "spontaneous," and that Ruby probably had help entering the basement of the police station for the transfer. The staffs of both the Committee and the Warren Commission focused particular attention on one of Ruby's police associates: Blakey "was convinced that Sergeant Patrick Dean had been the one who let Jack Ruby in the basement on the morning of the 24th."

Sergeant Dean refused to testify to Blakey's Committee and even told author Peter Dale Scott "of his longtime relationship with [Joe] Civello," the mobster who ran Dallas for Carlos Marcello. Scott also notes that Dean "was in charge of security in the Dallas basement when Oswald was murdered" and that Dean "later failed a lie detector test about Ruby's access to [the basement]." Dean also worked in narcotics, which Ruby was also involved in with Civello and Marcello.

As had apparently been planned the night before, at 10:19 a.m. (CST), dancer Karen Carlin in Fort Worth called Ruby's home, supposedly to ask him to send her money. It's doubtful that Ruby was there, since an earlier call to Ruby's home by his regular housekeeper was answered by someone who didn't seem to recognize her voice. At 10:45 a.m., Ruby was talking to a TV crew in front of the police station, before heading to the Western Union office. At 11:00 a.m., Sergeant Dean apparently removed police who had been guarding an interior door to the basement. Upstairs, in Detective Fritz's office, a small group of officials were questioning Oswald, but at 11:15 a.m.

they were told their time was up. However, the transfer car wasn't in position, so the group with Oswald had to slow its passage toward the basement. The basement was packed with at least seventy policemen and forty newsmen.

At Western Union, Ruby wired Carlin the money at 11:17 a.m. and then headed back to the police station, only a block away. The timing was tight for Ruby to have any hope of claiming a "sudden passion" defense, but he had plenty of associates who could signal when he should arrive. For example, only one minute after Ruby left the Western Union office, his attorney entered the police station and saw Oswald coming out of the jail elevator. Ruby's attorney turned to leave, telling a police detective, "That's all I wanted to see."

Even with the crowds of press and police, no one ever claimed to have seen Ruby actually enter the police basement, one more indication that he must have had help in doing so. Ruby most likely entered the basement from the alley that runs between the Western Union office and the police station. One officer claimed to have seen "an unidentified white male" walk down the ramp into the basement, past Officer Roy Vaughn, who was guarding the ramp. But that officer failed a polygraph test, while Officer Vaughn, who consistently said he had not let Ruby down the ramp, passed his polygraph test. Seven witnesses agreed with Vaughn.

AROUND 11:20 A.M., Oswald walked through the door, flanked by two Dallas Police detectives. As soon as he was visible, a car horn blew and is audible on the news broadcast of the transfer. At 11:21, Ruby surged out of the crowd and fired one shot into Oswald's abdomen. The basement erupted in pandemonium. As Oswald was rushed to Parkland Hospital, the apprehended Ruby appeared to police officer

Don Ray Archer as "being extremely agitated and nervous, continually inquiring whether Oswald was dead or alive." Oswald died at 1:07 p.m. It was only after Ruby was told that his victim was dead that "Ruby calmed down," according to Marcello's biographer, John H. Davis. Davis notes that even after an officer told Ruby, "'It looks like it's going to be the electric chair for you' . . . Ruby immediately relaxed and even managed a wan smile." Officer Archer said "it seemed at that time that Ruby felt his own life depended on the success of his mission, that if Oswald had not died, he, Jack Ruby, would have been killed."

Later that day, a Secret Service agent interviewed a "highly agitated" Karen Carlin. She blurted out to the agent that "Oswald, Jack Ruby, and other individuals unknown to her were involved in a plot to assassinate Kennedy, and that she would be killed if she gave any information to authorities." As Officer Archer had suspected, Ruby had apparently been threatened with death as well, and not just for himself. Ruby would soon be visited in jail by Marcello underboss Joe Campisi Sr. Ruby had last seen Campisi at his restaurant on the night before JFK's murder. Campisi was also close to Sheriff Bill Decker, in whose custody Ruby would spend most of the rest of his life, reportedly in a cell overlooking Dealey Plaza. When Ruby was later asked in a polygraph examination if "members of your own family are now in danger because of what you did," Ruby said "yes." Ruby's sister later testified that Ruby worried about their "brother Earl being dismembered [and] Earl's children [being] dismembered [and their] arms and legs . . . cut off." At the time, a Chicago mobster associate of Richard Cain was well known in the underworld for that type of Mafia retribution; years later, Johnny Rosselli's legs were cut off after Santo Trafficante had him murdered.

IN SOUTH CAROLINA, Joseph Milteer had completed his phone call and rejoined his friend William Somersett. After the radio broadcast the news about Oswald's death, Milteer told his friend, "That makes it work perfect . . . now we have no worry."

NOW THAT LEE Oswald was dead, Carlos Marcello would soon be free from worry. After Oswald's murder, David Ferrie returned to New Orleans and turned himself in to authorities. The FBI and Secret Service were investigating Jack Martin's allegations, and the news media had started to get wind not just of Ferrie, but even Marcello, as possibly being involved in JFK's death. However, Martin was an unstable individual and quickly backed away from his charges, and within forty-eight hours the entire incident had blown over. That was in spite of the fact that Ferrie admitted to the FBI he had "severely criticized" JFK and possibly said "he ought to be shot," and that he had "been critical of any President riding in an open car" and said that "anyone could hide in the bushes and shoot a President." Ferrie was also able to produce his library card when the agents asked, so he was released and the investigation dropped.

Former FBI supervisor Guy Banister was briefly interviewed by authorities, but not investigated. Statements by the local FBI to the press seemed to place responsibility for the whole incident on District Attorney Jim Garrison. The matter had been staunched before it could become national news, and the press and the authorities would soon forget the whole thing—at least for a few years.

Carlos Marcello had managed to emerge unscathed from the weekend crisis that could have exposed the roles of David Ferrie and Guy Banister in JFK's murder, and even led to the godfather himself. Marcello knew that Ruby was a long-time mob associate who could be trusted not to talk. But the godfather realized there were still avenues investigators could pursue that could lead to his associates. So, even as the government continued to scramble to deal with the aftermath of two assassinations—including the national security implications of JFK's murder and the coup plan that was on hold—Marcello, Trafficante, and Rosselli implemented plans to keep attention focused away from themselves, and toward Fidel Castro.

CHAPTER 17

Secret Investigations and Getting Away With Murder

I N THE COMING months and years, Carlos Marcello would have other close calls that could have exposed his role in the assassination; those would continue through the time of his 1985 confession to Jack Van Laningham and its almost deadly aftermath.

MARCELLO AND SANTO Trafficante used two basic strategies to conceal their roles in JFK's murder, at the time and for years to come. First, along with Johnny Rosselli, the two godfathers continued to exploit their work on the unauthorized CIA–Mafia plots to kill Fidel, to gain a measure of protection from close scrutiny. Those few CIA officials who knew about the plots would be loathe to look seriously at the possibility that their own operation was somehow involved in JFK's murder. To do so would cost their own careers, and perhaps even bring themselves and the Agency under suspicion. In addition, parts of the CIA–Mafia plots involving the mob bosses would continue in December 1963 and beyond.

Second, Marcello and Trafficante used the legitimate national security concerns surrounding the coup plan with Almeida to keep the pressure on US officials to withhold key information from investigators, the press, and the public, to protect the US government's ally high in the Cuban government. That pressure included continuing to have their men float "Castro killed JFK" stories that would find their way to occasionally receptive officials in Washington. Those stories would sometimes travel through government channels and other times through the press. Commander Almeida would remain high in the Cuban government and unexposed for decades, so protecting his life and his family would be a legitimate national security concern for a series of Presidents and CIA Directors, from 1963 until Almeida's death in 2009.

One unexpected benefit of the first two approaches for the mob bosses was that various US officials and agencies would use legitimate national concerns to hide a variety of intelligence failures and unauthorized operations—not just the CIA–Mafia plots—that could have been exposed in a truly wide-ranging investigation of JFK's assassination. National security concerns were also used to hide not just the "tight" surveillance of Oswald but the structure that allowed a massive program of domestic surveillance by a raft of agencies—including the CIA, FBI, and military intelligence—to be conducted on thousands of Americans in the 1960s, including some in the JFK investigation.

Finally, if their two main strategies failed, the two godfathers would not hesitate to resort to murder to keep their roles in JFK's murder hidden. That wasn't just a threat to help silence a long-time mobster like Jack Ruby—several murders would be carried out, including their gruesome slaying of Johnny Rosselli.

IN ADDITION TO Ferrie and Banister, in the weeks after JFK's murder more associates of Carlos Marcello were interviewed by authorities about JFK's murder. Even though at least a dozen of Marcello's associates and family members were interviewed or interrogated, the godfather would not be mentioned at all in the *Report* of the Warren Commission.

One of the consequences of Oswald's death was the creation of the Warren Commission. Sometimes misperceived as something solely created by LBJ so he could control the investigation, the Warren Commission was actually created due to the efforts of several Robert Kennedy associates. Neither President Johnson nor J. Edgar Hoover wanted the Warren Commission, whereas RFK's associates apparently saw a commission as preferable to having the whole investigation in the hands of LBJ and Hoover.

Within hours of Oswald's death, Hoover was talking to Nicholas Katzenbach, Robert's trusted Deputy Attorney General. While a devastated RFK was consumed with funeral preparations and family matters, Katzenbach was essentially running the Justice Department. However, Katzenbach focused on areas like civil rights and wasn't a specialist in the areas of organized crime or Hoffa, areas that were now especially relevant in light of Ruby's recent actions. Also, there is no evidence that Katzenbach was ever told about the JFK–Almeida coup plan, which had been withheld from all of RFK's associates who weren't actively involved in the Cuba operation.

Hoover's memo of his conversation with Katzenbach on the afternoon of November 24 says, "The thing I am concerned about, and so is Mr. Katzenbach, is having something issued so we can convince the public that Oswald is the real assassin." Katzenbach stated his feelings even more strongly in a memo the following day to LBJ aide Bill Moyers, declaring, "The public must be satisfied that Oswald was the assassin [and] that he did not have confederates who are still at large." He even wrote, "Speculation about Oswald's motivation ought to be cut off, and we should have some basis for rebutting thought that this was a Communist conspiracy or . . . a right-wing conspiracy to blame it on the Communists." In his private memo to Moyers, even Katzenbach notes that "the facts on Oswald seem [almost] too pat—too obvious (Marxist, Cuba, Russian wife, etc.)." Yet Katzenbach's main goal was "to head off public speculation or Congressional hearings." However, it's important to note that Katzenbach's concerns where shared by other high officials, all of whom were very concerned that rampant speculation about Oswald's ties to Russia or Cuba could trigger an dangerous confrontation with the Soviets, at a time when an untested President had just assumed office, and much of the nation was still in shock.

Even as RFK loyalists pushed for a Commission to investigate JFK's murder, Hoover and the FBI continued their investigation, which would later form the basis for much of the Commission's work. However, as mentioned in Chapter Two, author Henry Hurt found that an analysis of FBI documents eventually provided to the Warren Commission "showed that at least 60 witnesses claimed that the FBI in some way altered what the witnesses had reported," and more witnesses have reported discrepancies since that time.

In addition, in at least two instances, the FBI simply rewrote memos to completely change their meaning—something an FBI agent would do only on orders from the highest authority. We know this only because the National Archives eventually released the original, unaltered memos. In one case, a November 27, 1963, FBI memo about Ruby originally cited his link to Dallas mob boss Joe Civello. But in the version the Warren Commission published, the final three paragraphs of the memo, which cover Civello—and his ties to narcotics—are completely missing.

In another instance of FBI document tampering, the FBI was trying to make the case that Oswald used brown paper from the Book Depository to wrap the rifle he allegedly carried to work on the day JFK was shot. The published version of a November 30, 1963, FBI memo says that the Book Depository paper was "found to have the same observable characteristics as the brown paper bag" found on the sixth floor after the shooting. However, the National Archives eventually released the original version of the same FBI memo, which said the Book Depository paper was "found not to be identical with the paper gun case" found on the sixth floor. The bottom line is that Hoover was using national-security concerns to build a case against Oswald, avoid Ruby's Mafia ties, and hide anything that might embarrass him or the FBI.

Once President Johnson had been persuaded to appoint a Presidential Commission to investigate JFK's murder, LBJ pulled out all the stops in telling men like Senator Richard Russell why they should join the Warren Commission. LBJ told him, "We've got to take this out of the arena where they're testifying that Khrushchev and Castro did this and did that and kicking us into a war that can kill forty million Americans in an hour." President Johnson did the same with Supreme Court Chief Justice Earl Warren, whom he wanted to chair the Commission. The Warren Commission's real purpose was to end speculation about foreign involvement in JFK's murder, which it eventually did.

The creation of the Warren Commission was announced on November 29, 1963. According to historian Michael Kurtz, "Richard Helms personally persuaded Lyndon Johnson to appoint former CIA Director Allen Dulles to the Warren Commission." The other members were Georgia Senator Richard Russell, Kentucky Senator John

Cooper, Louisiana Congressman Hale Boggs, Michigan Congressman Gerald Ford, and disarmament official John J. McCloy.

However, before the Commission could begin gathering evidence, their final conclusion was preordained when J. Edgar Hoover leaked the FBI's own report and conclusions to the press on December 8, 1963. Hoover used his extensive media connections to make sure the FBI's conclusions—that Oswald acted alone, Ruby acted alone, the two had no connection, and there was no conspiracy in JFK's death—became front-page news.

At that point, the Commission couldn't really come to any other conclusion, since it would have to depend on Hoover's FBI for most of their investigative work. In addition, one of the seven men appointed to the Commission, Michigan Congressman Gerald Ford, went to one of Hoover's top aides, who wrote that Ford told him "he would keep me thoroughly advised as to the activities of the Commission. He stated this would have to be on a confidential basis." Five days later, Ford started delivering on his promise and was soon telling his FBI contact that "two members of the Commission [were] still not convinced that the President had been shot from the sixth floor window of the Texas Book Depository."

Allen Dulles knew a great deal about US efforts to assassinate Fidel using Trafficante, Rosselli, and Marcello, but he didn't tell the rest of the Commission. However, Earl Warren's son indicated that the Chief Justice learned something about the plots, and Gerald Ford indicated years later that he'd become aware of them as well, though there is no way to know how much they knew or if it was accurate.

Later, Chief Justice Warren and Congressman Ford were the only members of the Warren Commission who went to Dallas to interview Jack Ruby. They even denied the request of the Commission's expert on Ruby to accompany them. When Ruby begged Warren and Ford to take him to Washington for questioning away from Dallas, they refused.

CARLOS MARCELLO AND Santo Trafficante didn't want more situations like the Ferrie investigation, so even as the headlines were full of the FBI investigation and talk of the Commission, the godfathers' men quietly supplied a steady stream of stories implying that Castro had ordered JFK's death. This kept national security concerns alive in Washington, and the "Castro did it" stories of some—like John Martino—even contained hints of the JFK–Almeida coup plan. Other mob associates linked to such stories include Rolando Masferrer, Frank Fiorini, and Manuel Artime. The eager audience for these stories included officials such as CIA Director John McCone, J. Edgar Hoover, and Lyndon Johnson.

The stories spread by John Martino were especially provocative—and accurate, about matters the public wouldn't officially learn about for decades. Appearing in small-market newspapers and radio broadcasts, Martino's stories blamed Castro for JFK's murder while hinting at the JFK–Almeida coup plan. They were just detailed enough to draw the attention of US officials but not enough to become major news stories. The stories helped to force top officials into a continuing cover-up about JFK's assassination, in order to prevent a public outcry to invade Cuba and to avoid exposing Commander Almeida.

Martino's stories began just two days after Oswald's murder, when David Ferrie was essentially cleared of involvement in JFK's death. The more national security pressure the Mafia bosses could keep on officials to stifle the investigation the better, and the more Oswald looked like a Communist working for Fidel Castro, the more

Jack Ruby looked like a patriot (and not a mobster). Martino was touring the country as a prominent member of the far-right John Birch Society Speakers Bureau, ostensibly to promote his book *I Was Castro's Prisoner*. It's unlikely that David Atlee Phillips or others in the CIA were behind Martino's publicity efforts, because Martino's book actually mentioned the name of Phillips's associate, David Morales, a fact that the CIA wanted to keep secret.

Martino's phony stories started out mildly, claiming that Oswald had gone to Cuba in the fall of 1963 and had passed out pro-Castro literature in Miami and New Orleans. Those tales brought Martino a visit from the FBI on November 29, but he refused to identify his sources.

An article under Martino's name appeared in the December 21, 1963, issue of the right-wing journal *Human Events*, in which Martino took credit for revealing that "the Kennedy Administration planned to eliminate Fidel Castro . . . through a putsch, [and] the plan involved a more or less token invasion from Central America to be synchronized with the coup. A left-wing coalition government was to be set up, [and] the plan involved [the] US [military] occupation of Cuba." At the time, that was more than many high-ranking US officials in the Johnson administration knew about the coup plan.

Martino knew about the involvement of Manolo Ray's JURE exile group and wrote in the article that "Oswald made . . . approaches to JURE, another organization of Cuban freedom fighters, but was rejected." As previously noted, three months earlier Martino and Masferrer had been linked to the attempt to smear Ray's group by tying it to Oswald via Dallas JURE member Silvia Odio. When Martino's article was published, only the FBI and a handful of Odio's closest family and friends knew about Oswald's visit to her in Dallas, and nothing about it had appeared in the press.

In Martino's first major article, he only hinted that Oswald was working for Fidel Castro when he killed JFK. The following month, Martino revealed new details about the coup plan and implicated Fidel more directly, in a January 30, 1964, *Memphis Press-Scimitar* article headlined "Oswald Was Paid Gunman for Castro, Visitor Says." It quotes John Martino as saying, "Lee Harvey Oswald was paid by Castro to assassinate President Kennedy," and claiming that the murder was in retaliation for JFK's "plan to get rid of Castro." Martino described JFK's top-secret coup plan with remarkable precision, saying: "There was to be another invasion and uprising in Cuba . . . and the Organization of American States . . . was to go into Cuba [and help] control the country until an election could be set up." Martino even knew that "since the death of Kennedy, the work on an invasion has virtually stopped."

It's not hard to imagine the consternation Martino's increasingly provocative articles caused among high-ranking officials in Washington. They attracted the attention of J. Edgar Hoover, since FBI agents interviewed Martino yet again on February 15, 1964. In an era when Presidents and Congress treated Hoover and his FBI with deference, Martino basically thumbed his nose at the agents, declaring that "President Kennedy was engaged in a plot to overthrow the Castro regime by preparing another invasion attempt against Cuba." The frustrated FBI agents wrote that "Martino refused to divulge the sources of his information or how they might know what plans President Kennedy might have had."

Frank Fiorini, the future Watergate burglar under the name Frank Sturgis, was another Trafficante associate leaking information to the press implicating Fidel Castro in JFK's murder. However, none of these other leaks hinted at the JFK–Almeida coup plan, and Martino's stories were unique in that regard, probably because (by his own admission) Martino had actually been part of the assassination plot. In addition, Martino knew Marcello, Rosselli, and Trafficante, while Fiorini was simply a bagman for Trafficante. Fiorini's information implicating Fidel and the Cubans appeared in a Florida newspaper on November 26, 1963. In the article, Fiorini "claimed Oswald had been in touch with Cuban intelligence officials . . . and had been in touch with Castro agents in Miami." The FBI immediately interviewed Fiorini, who maintained he'd been misquoted. Later, Fiorini admitted he'd received his information from John Martino.

Other efforts to link Oswald and Ruby to Fidel were less sophisticated, though they sometimes echoed the information in the memo that so alarmed Alexander Haig. These additional efforts range from the fake "Pedro Charles" letter mailed to Oswald from Havana on November 28, 1963, to stories linking Ruby to Cuban plots. It's amazing how many dozens, sometimes hundreds, of pages of follow-up FBI and CIA memos were generated because of one or two obviously fake letters or stories. It's likely that even more phony information implicating Fidel, with hundreds of pages of official follow-up memos, remains unreleased.

NATIONAL SECURITY CONCERNS—that Castro might have been behind JFK's death in response to US actions against him—played a key role in the actions of LBJ, Hoover, and others. Hoover had almost certainly been told at least in general terms about the coup plan, by his good friend LBJ. As former FBI agent Harry Whidbee told *Vanity Fair*, "We were effectively told, 'They're only going to prove [Oswald] was the guy who did it. There were no co-conspirators, and there was no international conspiracy.'" An FBI supervisor at the time confirmed to

Vanity Fair that "[w]ithin days, we could say the [JFK] investigation was over. . . . The idea that Oswald had a confederate or was part of a group or a conspiracy was definitely enough to place a man's career in jeopardy."

Government officials conducted many secret investigations into JFK's murder, and not just because of all the phony mob-linked stories implicating Fidel Castro. Many leads and individuals couldn't be investigated publicly or revealed to the Warren Commission, both for national security reasons and to avoid exposing the unauthorized operations and intelligence failures of various agencies and officials. The CIA, Naval Intelligence, LBJ (he asked Richard Helms to conduct one for him), and the FBI all had their own internal, secret investigations of the JFK assassination. However, their results weren't shared between, or often even within, agencies.

As detailed in Chapter Two, my Naval Intelligence source said that after Oswald died, they quit shredding and sanitizing his surveillance files and began a lengthy investigation into the assassination. Naval Intelligence officially concluded that "Oswald was incapable of masterminding the assassination or of doing the actual shooting." But that investigation was not shared with most officials inside Naval Intelligence, and there is no indication it was ever shared with other branches of the military, the Joint Chiefs, or President Johnson.

Richard Helms had more suspicions about the possible involvement of CIA personnel in JFK's death than he ever acknowledged to the Warren Commission or to any of the later Congressional investigations. In a rarely noted television interview in 1992, Helms admitted that "we checked [to] be sure that nobody [with the CIA] had been in Dallas on that particular day [of JFK's assassination]." Helms said they not only checked "at the time" but later, "when the

Warren Commission was sitting." Those investigations have never been released, so there's no way to know if Helms suspected Barker or other agents.

Helms had the CIA conduct its own internal investigation into Oswald and JFK's assassination, a little-known fact first uncovered years later by Congressional investigators. Helms initially appointed an AMWORLD veteran, CIA officer John Whitten, to head the Agency's secret investigation, but as soon as Whitten asked Helms for "files on Oswald's Cuba-related activities," he was taken off the JFK investigation and reassigned. In Congressional testimony long after the fact, Whitten said that Helms hadn't told him anything about the CIA–Mafia plots to kill Fidel, and he was "appalled" when he heard about them twelve years later. Whitten also wasn't allowed to see the files on Oswald that CIA agent Hunter Leake had delivered from the CIA's New Orleans office to Helms, or told about the assassination aspect of the Rolando Cubela operation.

After Whitten was removed from the investigation, Helms replaced him with CIA Counterintelligence Chief James Angleton, under whom the internal CIA investigation seems to have been designed more to hide information than to uncover it. Angleton heard all of the claims from Mexico City that Oswald had killed JFK on Fidel Castro's orders and had access to other incendiary reports, like those concerning shadowy Cuban agent Miguel Cases Saez and young Cuban exile Gilberto Policarpo Lopez, both of whom went from Texas to Mexico City and then to Cuba. Not surprisingly, the paranoid Angleton concluded that Fidel had killed JFK and that both Saez and Lopez were involved, according to intelligence journalist Joseph Trento. Fifteen years later, when Congressional investigators got to see many of the files about Saez and Lopez, they exposed the numerous flaws in Angleton's conclusion.

In December 1963, one CIA memo says that President Johnson received a secret Agency report about Oswald and JFK's assassination. Angleton's conclusions probably fed Johnson's belief that Fidel had orchestrated JFK's assassination. In addition, Helms made Angleton his key contact with the Warren Commission, both for providing it information and for withholding material Helms didn't want the Commission to see. Hence, the Warren Commission saw nothing about the JFK–Almeida coup plan, AMWORLD, the surveillance of Oswald, any of his intelligence activities, or anything else that might have triggered a real investigation or cost Helms his job.

Richard Helms mysteriously dumped exile leader Tony Varona in January 1964 for unknown reasons. Congressional investigators found that "Varona . . . had to leave Miami in early 1964 and move to New York to seek employment," and a CIA memo from August 1964 noted a *New York Times* article about Varona headlined "Cuban Anti-Castro Chief by Day Selling Cars in Jersey by Night." Varona's quick fall from grace raises suspicions that someone in the CIA such as Helms, or perhaps even RFK, suspected that Varona was involved somehow in JFK's death. Helms had access to the Varona–Chicago Mafia payoff memos and would have known about Varona's long ties to Rosselli and Trafficante through the CIA–Mafia plots. Peter Dale Scott notes that an "agreement was in force from the mid-1950s to the mid-1970s, exempting the CIA from a statutory requirement to report (to the Justice Department) any criminal activity by any of its employees or assets." If Helms knew or suspected that Varona—or other CIA assets—had any involvement in JFK's death, he might simply have dealt with it himself.

It's important to point out that one of the first things Helms would do after becoming CIA Director a few years later would be to fire another Trafficante associate, Bernard Barker, because—as Helms later testified—Barker "was involved in certain gambling and criminal elements."

Robert Kennedy would also have close associates conduct secret investigations of his brother's murder for much of the rest of his life. For months after his brother's murder, associates described him as being "shattered," with some indicating he might have in some way blamed himself for his brother's death. RFK's secret investigations started the day JFK died, when the Attorney General called "Julius Draznin in Chicago, an expert on union corruption for the National Labor Relations Board," according to author David Talbot. He said that RFK "asked Draznin to look into whether there was any Mafia involvement in the killing of his brother." Draznin turned in his report three days after Ruby had shot Oswald. Draznin's report "detailed Ruby's labor racketeering activities [and] wide syndicate contacts." RFK later said that "when he saw Ruby's phone records, 'The list was almost a duplicate of the people I called before the [Senate] Rackets Committee.'"

Robert Kennedy conducted his own secret investigation of JFK's murder, using Walter Sheridan, the head of his "Get Hoffa Squad." Sheridan's widow later confirmed that her husband and RFK worked together on the secret inquiry. John Davis independently confirmed that Walter Sheridan had "conducted an informal investigation and concluded . . . Marcello might well have been involved." According to Sheridan's son, the search left Sheridan "convinced that President Kennedy had been killed by a conspiracy."

Those investigations are probably why, by 1966, RFK would tell his friend Richard Goodwin that he thought "that mob guy in New Orleans"—Marcello—was behind his brother's death, as Goodwin told me. The following year, after David Ferrie's name finally surfaced as a suspect in JFK's murder, RFK had his press aide, Frank Mankiewicz, conduct yet another secret investigation. Mankiewicz said he "came to the conclusion that there was some sort of conspiracy, probably involving the mob, anti-Castro Cuban exiles, and maybe rogue CIA agents." But when he tried to tell RFK, "it was like he just couldn't focus on it. He'd get this look of pain, or more like numbness, on his face. It just tore him apart."

In late 1963, that numbing pain was still constant for RFK, but he seemed determined to do something about Cuba and the coup plan. He seems to have become confident that the coup plan with Almeida was still secure enough to continue. My source, John H. Crimmins— Coordinator of Cuban Affairs for the US State Department—told me that "nothing ever surfaced" to make him think Castro was involved in JFK's murder, even after it "was looked at over the course of the days and weeks" after JFK's death. He felt the same way even decades later. Also, a formerly "top secret, eyes only" memo "from Gordon Chase of the National Security Council Staff" implies that McGeorge Bundy, the "President's Special Assistant for National Security Affairs," was able to provide some type of "assurances re Oswald" on December 3, 1963 which indicated that Oswald was not a Castro agent.

Commander Almeida was still safe and undetected, but the same wasn't true for one of his associates. A couple of rumors about the Almeida coup plan were reported to the CIA in the days after JFK's death, and it's possible that Fidel's agents in Miami might have heard the same or similar rumors. Perhaps out of caution, Commander Almeida left Cuba, in a way that would not arouse suspicion. On Thursday, November 28, 1963, a CIA memo was sent from the Miami station to McCone, reporting the "departure [of] 2 Britannias [airliners], probably for Algeria, with 170 Cubans aboard headed by Juan Almeida."

Commander Almeida's information, or his instinct, was correct because just two days later, on Saturday, November 30, a CIA memo revealed that "a Western diplomat . . . had learned [from someone in the Cuban government] that Che Guevara was alleged to be under house arrest for plotting to overthrow Castro." This wasn't just some rumor off the street because the CIA said the "source" of the information about Che's involvement "in an anti-Castro plot" was a "trained observer of proven reliability who is a member of the Western diplomatic community in Cuba." The timing of Che's arrest, just one day before the originally scheduled coup date, raises the possibility that Fidel had learned something about the coup and had arrested one of those he thought was responsible.

Che's house arrest probably lasted for only a short time, perhaps just a day or two. December 2 is one of Cuba's biggest holidays, the anniversary of the founding of the Cuban Army, whose first battle saw Almeida save his friend Che's life. As Commander of Cuba's Army, Almeida was also considered its founder, so the Cuban public would definitely notice if he didn't appear for the celebration. Apparently things had calmed down enough for Almeida to return from Algeria to be part of the celebration, something Almeida would not have done if he feared that he was returning home to the same fate as Che. The day after the big December 2, 1963, celebration, a CIA report says Almeida "expressed [his] despair" to a subordinate.

But at some point after that, Almeida communicated to Harry Williams that he was still willing to stage a coup against Fidel, if RFK and new President Lyndon Johnson would back him. RFK believed that a free and democratic Cuba would be the best memorial to his slain brother. Williams was ready as well, and he tried to use his contact in Cyrus Vance's office—Joseph Califano—to arrange a meeting with LBJ. Williams said that Califano told him that upon hearing Williams's name, LBJ had evoked the Kennedys' responsibility for the Bay of Pigs disaster and then declared, "I don't want to see any goddamn Cuban, especially that son of a bitch Williams." Apparently, LBJ had heard enough about the coup plan from McCone to worry that JFK's death was retaliation from Castro.

In the early weeks of January 1964, RFK decided to swallow his pride, put his own feelings aside, and plead his case personally to President Johnson. Their relationship had been terrible since 1960 and had worsened since JFK's death, because Robert Kennedy felt that Johnson had moved into the White House and asserted control too quickly. But Robert Kennedy's meeting with LBJ about the coup plan did not go well. Only the two of them were present, and RFK later told Williams that President Johnson listened sympathetically but made it clear that he would not continue with the plan. LBJ's decision also included ending the Cuban exile troop training program at Fort Benning, since those exiles' real purpose had been to be among the first US troops into Cuba after the coup. However, LBJ did agree to continue funding RFK's favored Cuban exile groups in case they proved useful in the future. This was LBJ's way of preserving his options and asserting control: Formerly, Cuban operations had essentially been run by Robert Kennedy through Army Secretary Cyrus Vance and Richard Helms. Now the CIA would take primary responsibility, with McCone reporting to LBJ, and RFK no longer had any role in Cuban operations.

RFK offered to back Williams with his personal fortune, but Williams felt they had both done—and sacrificed—enough, so he went back to being a mining engineer, far away from the intrigue of exile politics. Williams communicated the news to Almeida, who apparently ended any planning for a coup. According to Williams, RFK made sure Almeida's family—still outside of Cuba on a seemingly innocent pretext—was covertly sent "$3,000 that the family used. And then [in addition to that money] Bobby send them a pension. You know, they received a check every month. Out of the budget," apparently of the CIA. Almeida's first wife and two daughters reportedly never returned to Cuba to live, and those payments continued for decades. As for who in the Agency continued making those covert payments and monitoring the CIA's surveillance of Almeida's family, those files have not been released. However, at least initially, it was probably E. Howard Hunt and his aide Bernard Barker, since they had already been working on the top-secret operation.

A month after his meeting with President Johnson, RFK himself was expressing a different, more enlightened attitude about Castro. In an exchange with CIA official Desmond FitzGerald, RFK proposed seeking an accommodation with Fidel instead of trying to overthrow him. That was emblematic of RFK's development over the next four years, as he grew from being a tough bulldog of a prosecutor and protector of JFK to being one of the most progressive members of the Senate.

CIA OFFICIAL RICHARD Helms had not changed his feelings about Fidel, however. Files show that Helms combined the remnants of RFK's exile operation—Manuel Artime, Manolo Ray, and Eloy Menoyo—with his own CIA–Mafia and Cubela assassination plots. Hunt's friend Artime continued to get the lion's share of the money, which CIA accounts say totaled $7 million, while some former officials say it was several times that amount. With planes and ships going to his Central American bases full of CIA arms and supplies—and returning empty of cargo—Artime was also soon involved in drug trafficking with Santo Trafficante's organization.

A December 6, 1963, attempt to assassinate Fidel Castro involving Herminio Diaz—Trafficante's bodyguard and narcotics trafficker—was first documented in 2006 by author Larry Hancock. One CIA memo talks about "an assassination attempt on Fidel Castro after his TV appearance on 12/6," and FitzGerald or one of his men added a comment linking it to "continuing rumors of a plot to assassinate Castro which is connected with Herminio Diaz."

On the day after Diaz's attempt to kill Fidel, Helms approved a December 7, 1963, memo sending low-level Cuban official Rolando Cubela a weapons cache of shotguns, pistols, grenades, "C-4 [explosives]," and "rifles with scopes." The material, especially appropriate for an assassination attempt, was slated to be delivered in January 1964 under David Morales's supervision. Morales remained good friends with Johnny Rosselli, and in 1964 Morales made at least one trip to visit the Mafia don in Las Vegas. Rosselli continued to split his time between Las Vegas and Los Angeles, where he moved into a large, lavish apartment on Beverly Glen, near Beverly Hills. Prospering in the immediate years after the JFK assassination, Rosselli even joined the prestigious L.A. Friars Club and was soon bilking stars of the era, including Milton Berle and Phil Silvers, in an elaborate poker scam.

Helms kept other aspects of the CIA–Mafia plots going as well, retaining European assassin recruiter QJWIN on the CIA payroll in December and for several months thereafter—until reports about Trafficante's associate Michel Victor Mertz surfaced in Europe and to the CIA, at which point QJWIN was fired. As for Mertz, the Warren

Commission never learned about him, though the FBI gave them—with no explanation—a few memos showing the Bureau had checked for airline passengers in Dallas named Mertz on November 22, 1963. Aside from having $1 million in heroin stolen from in France near the one-year anniversary of JFK's death, Mertz prospered and lived extremely well after the assassination. According to one report, one of his homes was "a gigantic estate in the Loiret region near Orléans, measuring about five miles on one side by about six or seven miles on the other." In Paris, Mertz had a swank townhouse on Boulevard Suchet, an area also home to the Duke and Duchess of Windsor. Even after his heroin network was busted at Fort Benning, Georgia, in 1965, and Mertz was profiled in a Pulitzer–Prize-winning heroin exposé by *Newsday*, Mertz served only a brief, comfortable detention in France a few years later. While the man whose alias Mertz used in 1963—Jean Souetre—eventually talked to journalists and allowed himself to be photographed, Mertz remained reclusive and threatening to investigators until his death on January 15, 1995. Even his death was kept relatively secret for such a notorious figure, hindering efforts to get US government files about him released.

A far more lowly member of the heroin network Mertz shared with Trafficante and Marcello did not live nearly as long. Rose Cheramie's statements about a plot to kill JFK were finally taken seriously by authorities after JFK's assassination. On Monday, November 25, she revealed new information about her sometime boss, Jack Ruby, to Louisiana State Police Lieutenant Francis Fruge. Fruge investigated and confirmed her claims about a heroin ring operating in Texas and that she had worked for Ruby as a B-girl. But authorities in Houston lost track of the heroin courier Cheramie had identified and closed the case. Congressional investigators found that in 1965, Cheramie had tried to tell the FBI "about a heroin deal operating from a New Orleans ship," and even though "the Coast Guard verified an ongoing narcotics investigation of the ship," the FBI had decided not to pursue the case. One month after she contacted the FBI, Cheramie was found mortally wounded under unusual circumstances on a desolate road in Texas, and she died on September 4, 1965.

CARLOS MARCELLO, SANTO Trafficante, and most of their associates prospered after JFK's murder. According to historian Richard Mahoney, "[a]s Bill Hundley, head of the [Justice Department's] Organized Crime Section, put it, 'The minute that bullet hit Jack Kennedy's head, it was all over. Right then. The organized crime program just stopped, and Hoover took control back.' Marcello had been right: Cut the dog's head off and the rest of it would die." More confirmation for the success of Marcello's approach comes from the FBI's "own electronic surveillance transcripts" of a "conversation between Sam Giancana and a lieutenant" two weeks after JFK's death, in which the lieutenant told Giancana: "I will tell you something, in another 2 months from now, the FBI will be like it was 5 years ago."

That wasn't completely true, and the FBI did step up its efforts against organized crime after JFK's murder. Also, while Robert Kennedy remained Attorney General, there were still prosecutions to continue against Marcello, for jury tampering, and multiple counts against Jimmy Hoffa. In 1964, the juror Marcello had bribed for his November 22, 1963, acquittal went to the authorities, since Marcello had paid him only $1,000 instead of the promised $25,000 (which would have attracted too much attention to the juror). Shortly after that, the US Attorney in New Orleans learned that Marcello "had threatened to kill" the government's main witness during the same trial.

In late 1964, RFK resigned as Attorney General to run for the US Senate in New York, but he left the Justice Department in the hands of his trusted deputy, Nicholas Katzenbach, who announced on October 6, 1964, that Carlos Marcello had been indicted for conspiracy and obstruction of justice, including "seeking the murder of a government witness." Four weeks later, RFK won his race to become a New York senator. Marcello would not be tried until the following year, and he would be found "not guilty" on August 17, 1965. John H. Davis wrote that "Carlos Marcello was well on his way to becoming the wealthiest and most influential Mafia leader in the US," and his organization's "estimated annual income of two billion dollars [made] it by far the largest industry in Louisiana."

Jimmy Hoffa was not so lucky, and by the spring of 1964, Robert Kennedy's Justice Department and the head of his "Get Hoffa Squad," Walter Sheridan, had finally succeeded in convicting Jimmy Hoffa for the first time. Hoffa would also be convicted on separate charges, in Chicago, and only a flurry of appeals delayed the start of his long prison sentences.

In 1964, Jack Ruby faced murder charges for killing Lee Oswald. In the press at that time, Ruby was not connected to the Mafia or considered any type of mobster, which would remain true for more than ten years. Melvin Belli eventually took over Ruby's defense; his law partner had first been called on November 24, 1963, by someone from Las Vegas connected with mobsters who'd had casinos in Havana. The call didn't come from Johnny Rosselli, but it did come from his Las Vegas headquarters hotel, the Desert Inn. The Las Vegas caller wanted Belli to defend Ruby, who was described as "one of our guys." Belli was close to Los Angeles gangster Mickey Cohen, who was a good friend of Carlos Marcello. A CIA memo says that Belli "was reportedly involved in illicit drug traffic." Belli took Ruby's case and kept any mention of Ruby's Mafia contacts out of the trial. Instead of using the "sudden passion" defense available in Texas—which can result in a sentence as short as two years served, or even just probation—Belli use a bizarre "psycho-motor" defense that had never been attempted before, and they lost. Jack Ruby received his death sentence in Dallas on March 14, 1964.

EVEN WHILE RUBY'S trial was going on, and after it ended, several Warren Commission staff members tried to do a thorough investigation of Jack Ruby's Mafia ties and Cuban gunrunning, but they were stymied. The FBI intimidated several witnesses who tried to talk about Ruby's gunrunning, while FBI agents relied on Ruby's mob associates to say that Ruby had no mob associates. After the two staffers investigating Ruby wrote a long memo to the the Commission's General Counsel outlining numerous problems and stonewalling by the FBI and by Richard Helms, they were barred from interviewing Ruby in Dallas. The resulting interview by Earl Warren and Gerald Ford was marked by Ruby's saying, "Unless you get me to Washington, you can't get a fair shake out of me." Anthony Summers writes that "repeatedly, eight times in all, [Ruby] begged the Chief Justice of the US to arrange his transfer to Washington for further questioning and lie-detector tests." Warren and Ford refused, even when Ruby pleaded with them, saying, "Gentlemen, my life is in danger." Given Sheriff Decker's mob ties and Marcello's control of Dallas, Ruby's concerns were all too real.

THE WARREN COMMISSION staff lost another important source of information when mob associates of Trafficante's and Rosselli's framed Chicago Secret Service agent Abraham Bolden. Using information provided by two criminals he'd put in jail, Bolden was arrested on the day he went to Washington to tell Commission staff about the Secret Service's laxity, as well as the Chicago and Tampa attempts. One of Bolden's accusers worked for Sam DeStefano, a notorious associate of Richard Cain, the Chief Investigator for in the Cook County/Chicago sheriff's office. Richard Cain's brother, Michael, told me that Richard Cain had the "motive, means, and opportunity" to frame Bolden. Cain was part of the Chicago Mafia and had worked with Rosselli and Trafficante on the CIA–Mafia plots. Bolden was sentenced to six years in prison, even though his main accuser later admitted to committing perjury against him. Bolden's judge told the jury before their deliberations that Bolden was guilty, but even after that misconduct resulted in a mistrial, the same judge was allowed to conduct Bolden's second trial. The result was another conviction, and Bolden has been fighting to clear his name ever since his release from prison.

SOME OF THE many shortcomings of the Warren Commission were covered in Chapters 1 and 2. They are too numerous to cover here, though Professor Gerald McKnight's *Breach of Trust* (2005) details the most definitive account of their many problems. Basically, the Commission was not given much crucial information and had to rely on the FBI for most of their investigative work. Like the CIA, the Bureau withheld much crucial information from the Commission— including the Tampa attempt, and much about Cuban exiles tied to Trafficante and Rosselli. Instead, the FBI flooded the Commission staff with reports of wild allegations and irrelevant paperwork. That's why you'll find Jack Ruby's mother's dental records in the twenty-six volumes of supporting evidence for the one-volume *Warren Report* but nothing about the JFK–Almeida coup plan, the CIA–Mafia plots, or the threat against JFK by Marcello and Trafficante that informants reported to the FBI in 1962. Like Marcello, neither David Ferrie nor Guy Banister—who died of natural causes on June 6, 1964—is mentioned even once in the *Warren Report*.

I noted in early chapters the Commission's internal struggles over their conclusion, but another problem surfaced just as the Commission had hoped to be wrapping up. Commission staffers and the FBI were under pressure to resolve the matter of Silvia Odio's visit from Oswald and two exiles a couple of months prior to JFK's murder. On September 16, 1964, the FBI apparently got a break. An anti-Castro soldier of fortune named Loran Hall allegedly told "the FBI that he" and two friends "were the people who visited Silvia Odio." The soldier of fortune knew Santo Trafficante and had been under house arrest with the mob boss in Cuba in 1959, before being asked to join the CIA–Mafia plots to kill Castro in the spring of 1963. Hall's convenient claim came just in time for the Warren Commission's last meeting, two days later.

At that final meeting, three of the Commission members, led by Georgia Senator Richard Russell, tried to include a dissenting opinion about the "magic bullet" theory. However, effort failed, and the report was issued with no dissent. Over the next two days, Hall changed his story and denied having visited Odio, as did his two friends, but it was too late to change the Commission's Final Report.

THE *REPORT* WAS submitted to President Johnson on September 24, given to Hoover the following day, and released to the public on September 28, 1964. The press widely proclaimed the *Warren Report*, as it came to be known, to be the definitive account of Oswald's guilt as a lone assassin.

IN ADDITION TO his anti-Castro duties, E. Howard Hunt later admitted that during the 1960s, one of his duties for the CIA had been press and publisher relations. Both Richard Helms and his protégé Hunt played behind-the-scenes roles with the press and publishers during 1964 and afterward, and that likely applied to the reporting of matters relating to the CIA, Cuban exiles, and JFK's assassination. Hunt later wrote that the Church Committee "identified me as an important figure in the [CIA's press] operation, pointing out [that] one of my ongoing responsibilities [was] to get certain books reviewed by particular writers who would be either sympathetic or hostile to works we hoped to popularize or suppress." Hunt admitted that "[m]ost of my work involved publishing and publications, in which we supported an entire division of [one publisher] and subsidized books that we felt the American public should read." Hunt acknowledges that the CIA "also ran a couple of national newswire services."

The authors of two early books about JFK's assassination, Thomas Buchanan and Joachim Joesten, a left-wing European journalist and concentration-camp survivor, were the targets of CIA attempts to discredit them. The CIA even dug up Nazi files to use against Joesten, foreshadowing the more extensive efforts Helms and the CIA would launch against *Warren Report* critics just two years later. After the first wave of well-researched, bestselling books critical of the Warren Commission emerged in 1966, early the following year, the CIA issued a fifty-three-page memo detailing how CIA officials could attack critics and bolster the "lone nut" theory in the press.

In the 1970s, the Senate Church Committee was able to document that "the CIA maintained covert relationships with about 50 American journalists or employees of US media organizations" from the 1960s to the mid-1970s. However, Carl Bernstein, in a major piece for *Rolling Stone*, was able to document there were actually "400 journalists who maintained covert relationships with the Agency." Bernstein wrote that even that figure "refers only to those who were 'tasked' in their undercover assignments or had a mutual understanding that they would help the Agency or were subject to some form of CIA contractual control. It does not include even larger numbers of journalists who occasionally traded favors with CIA officers in the normal give-and-take that exists between reporters and their sources." In E. Howard Hunt's final autobiography, he confirmed Bernstein's much higher figures and the other information in his article.

In the mid-1960s, Hunt, and his assistant Bernard Barker, was still involved with the Manuel Artime side of the CIA–Mafia plots, which had now been officially merged with the Rolando Cubela assassination operation. RFK's liberal exile leader Manolo Ray was no longer working with the CIA, and Eloy Menoyo had been captured while on a mission into Cuba and had been given a life sentence.

However, the CIA started getting reports from Trafficante associates showing that the Cubela operation was insecure. In addition to the mob-linked security breaches surrounding the Cubela operation, Fidel Castro's intelligence agents had actually penetrated Artime's group a year earlier. Richard Helms was no doubt livid when he saw a January 25, 1965, article in *The Nation* that gave an all-too-accurate description of the expensive scope of Artime's operation.

That publicity, various problems with Artime, and the insecurity of Cubela's operation due to Trafficante's associates proved too much for Helms, and he began the gradual process of shutting down Artime's operation. Harry Williams had one last encounter with his former colleague Manuel Artime, after Artime's CIA-backed operations had been ended, in part because of financial irregularities. In Miami, Williams happened to drop by a friend's house—and was surprised to find Artime, Hunt, and Barker there, along with a Trafficante associate. Williams told me "they were planning the selling of the equipment" for Artime. He advised them not to, and after declining their offer to join their venture, he quickly left. Instead, Artime, Hunt, and Barker sold the supplies and apparently kept the money.

On February 28, 1966, Rolando Cubela (AMLASH) was arrested in Cuba, due in part to information from Fidel's agent in Artime's camp. Two CIA cables in the following weeks mentioned or alluded to Almeida, with one expressing relief that none of the "real military leaders" in Cuba had "been arrested or detained." When the *New York Times* reported on March 6, 1966, that Cubela planned "to shoot Premier Castro with a high-powered telescopic rifle and later share [power] with Mr. Artime," LBJ's Secretary of State, Dean Rusk, asked Richard Helms if that was true. Helms lied to him, saying, "The Agency was not involved with Cubela in a plot to assassinate Fidel Castro, nor did it ever encourage him to attempt such an act."

Richard Helms officially became CIA Director on June 30, 1966, putting him in an even stronger position to ensure that his unauthorized activities under JFK and LBJ were not exposed. In addition to firing Bernard Barker, Helms made sure that six CIA veterans of AMWORLD and his sensitive anti-Castro operations were reassigned to Laos in 1966, where the United States had been waging a secret war for years. These included Artime's deputy Rafael "Chi Chi" Quintero, former Miami CIA Chief Ted Shackley, and David Morales (after an assignment in South America involving the capture of Che Guevara).

1966 BROUGHT A wave of new challenges for Carlos Marcello and his associates, in addition to the spate of bestselling books critical of the *Warren Report* (though all of them avoided any mention of the Mafia). In May 1966, Sam Giancana left the country, after using his work on the CIA–Mafia plots to avoid spending another year in jail for refusing to testify about the Mafia to a grand jury after being granted immunity. His old pal Johnny Rosselli was not so lucky, when the FBI got a tip that his real name was Filippo Sacco and he wasn't a US citizen. William Harvey tried to get the CIA to aid Rosselli, but to no avail, and Harvey was forced to resign from the CIA the following year.

Apparently, the younger FBI agents in New Orleans had grown tired of seeing Marcello literally get away with murder. After Marcello went to a Mafia summit in New York that included Trafficante and attorney Frank Ragano, Marcello returned to New Orleans on October 1, 1966. Apparently hoping to force Hoover to take action against Marcello, an FBI agent staged a public confrontation with the godfather at the airport. Accounts vary as to the reasons for what happened next, but the physical act was well documented by witnesses and a photographer: Marcello took a swing at the FBI agent and hit him. The resulting arrest and charges would dog Marcello for years, eventually sending him to a short stay in federal prison.

Marcello—and Trafficante—was dealt another blow on October 5, 1966, when the Texas Court of Appeals ordered a new trial for Jack Ruby. Two months later, the same court would order a change of venue to Wichita Falls, Texas, away from Dallas and its mob-affiliated sheriff. Three days after winning that appeal, Ruby was diagnosed with cancer and died on January 3, 1967, before his trial could begin.

In November 1966, the *New York Times* was one of several major American newspapers and magazines investigating the JFK assassination anew. The *Times* wrote to a New Orleans Police Lieutenant, listing thirty-two questions about the assassination, primarily focused on David Ferrie but also including Carlos Marcello. The police chief gave a copy of the letter to New Orleans District Attorney Jim Garrison, who then had Ferrie brought in for questioning in December 1966.

Garrison tried to conduct his investigation in secret at first, but it was leaked to the media, resulting in a firestorm of publicity that centered on Ferrie. At the height of the controversy on February 22, 1967, David Ferrie died, an apparent suicide. That same night, Ferrie's friend Eladio del Valle—an associate of Trafficante and Masferrer— was murdered in Florida. In the weeks and months that followed, Garrison's investigation was targeted by a variety of people offering to help, some of whom should have been investigated themselves, such as a bitter Cuban exile named Alberto Fowler and Trafficante associates Rolando Masferrer and Loran Hall.

After Ferrie's death, Garrison focused on Clay Shaw, a coworker of Fowler. RFK asked his close associate Walter Sheridan to go to New Orleans and look into Garrison's charges. However, Sheridan felt that Garrison was a fraud, and he soon began to undermine Garrison's investigation in various ways, which included producing an NBC News special critical of Garrison. Recently released FBI files show that in the late spring of 1967, Garrison twice privately considered indicting Marcello for the assassination of JFK but decided not to. Instead,

Garrison's investigation wound up becoming a media circus, and Clay Shaw was eventually acquitted.

In 1967, amid the Garrison firestorm, to pressure the CIA to help him, Johnny Rosselli began leaking information to columnist Jack Anderson, who was not yet the journalist superstar he would become before the Watergate scandal, five years later. Rosselli's leaks to Anderson hinted at the CIA–Mafia plots, though the Mafia don attempted to tie them to Robert Kennedy. No other reporters followed up on Anderson's stories, but President Johnson asked CIA Director Richard Helms for a report on the plots and any links they might have had to JFK's assassination. Helms met with RFK around this time, and the resulting Inspector General's report delivered by Helms contained no information about the JFK–Almeida coup plan or AMWORLD, Rosselli's work for the CIA in the summer and fall of 1963, or the 1959 CIA–Mafia plots involving Jimmy Hoffa. In July 1967, CIA official Desmond FitzGerald, who had overseen the CIA–Mafia plots in 1963, died of natural causes.

Carlos Marcello would increasingly become the focus of unwanted attention in 1967 and the first half of 1968. On May 6, 1967, author Ed Reid showed a copy of the manuscript for his new book to the Los Angeles FBI Bureau. It mentioned for the first time Marcello's fall 1962 assassination threat against JFK, heard by Ed Becker. Someone high in the Los Angeles mob learned about Reid's manuscript, because the very next day the Mafia's most powerful attorney—Sidney Korshak—provided the FBI with derogatory information about Becker.

Early in 1968, Senator Robert Kennedy began offering behind-the-scenes help to journalist Michael Dorman for an article about Carlos Marcello. According to one account, "Dorman received RFK's personal attention, meeting with the Senator in his office." Dorman told author Gus Russo that "Robert Kennedy was enthusiastic about the article" and even offered to have one of his aides assist Dorman.

In March 1968, Robert Kennedy officially entered the race for the presidency. Just as his late-starting campaign was building impressive momentum, by winning the all-important California primary, he was tragically assassinated on June 4, 1968. His convicted assailant, Sirhan Bishara Sirhan, was first represented by Johnny Rosselli's Los Angeles attorney, whose defense strategy included admitting in court that Sirhan had fired the fatal headshot (a claim some experts still contest today). Sirhan's co-counsel was a lawyer whom David Scheim writes "had represented many Mob clients and had once been investigated himself by . . . Robert Kennedy." Years later, Robert Kennedy's friend and biographer Jack Newfield wrote that Joe Marcello, Carlos's younger brother, made this remark about the Kennedys to FBI informant Joe Hauser: "We took care of 'em, didn't we?"*

IN THE EARLY 1970s, the fifty-nine-year-old Carlos Marcello was continuing to expand his criminal empire, even as he diversified into more legitimate businesses. Marcello still ordered contract killings, even while appealing his assault conviction and two-year sentence for slugging an FBI agent. Mississippi's *Sun Herald* reported that in just the first two months of 1970, Marcello's hits included the murders of Jack Howard Joy and Donald Lester "Jimmy" James—and as usual for Marcello, "no one [was ever -] convicted of [either] murder."

Marcello was under pressure because he'd been convicted of assaulting the FBI agent, and his appeals were running out. However,

---

*For extensive documentation about the criminal ties of Sirhan and some of his brothers, as well as FBI reports that Jimmy Hoffa had put a bounty on RFK, see *Legacy of Secrecy*.

Marcello had backed Nixon for years, and one of Marcello's "fixers" was close to President Nixon's own fixer, former mob attorney Murray Chotiner. According to John H. Davis, Marcello "and his lawyers pulled every string at their command to get Carlos's two year sentence reduced...to six months and made arrangements for him to spend that time at the Medical Center for Federal Prisoners in Springfield, Missouri." That was in stark contrast to his old friend Jimmy Hoffa, who was doing hard time at the Lewisburg Federal Penitentiary.

Marcello entered the Springfield facility on October 14, 1970. Since it was one of the least secure and most comfortable federal prisons, allowing more phone calls and visitors than others, Marcello had no trouble running his empire from prison. When he was released on March 12, 1971—after serving just five months—Marcello emerged much healthier and more fit, ready for what would be his most prosperous decade.

Even before Marcello entered prison in 1970, reporters whispered among themselves that the New Orleans godfather was tied to JFK's murder. Television journalist Peter Noyes recalls covering a Marcello court appearance in 1970, when "a newspaper reporter [told him] 'There's been a lot of talk about that guy being involved in the Kennedy assassination.'" In fall 1971, Noyes learned from the Los Angeles Chief Deputy District Attorney that the Senate Judiciary Committee was holding secret hearings into the assassinations of John and Robert Kennedy. These were prompted by California Senator George Murphy's speech in which he said "the killers of John and Robert Kennedy may have acted under orders from someone else." An aide to Murphy confirmed the secret hearings to Noyes, who began writing a book about the assassinations, *Legacy of Doubt*.

At sixty-five, Johnny Rosselli was facing five years in prison after being caught and convicted for his Friars Club cheating scheme and immigration violations. The INS was also again trying to deport him. A CIA memo says that "on November 18, 1970 . . . Mr. Helms flatly refused to intercede with INS on Rosselli's behalf." However, the CIA admits "meeting with INS regarding the status of the deportation proceedings [in] March 1971," and the INS deportation efforts were halted at that time, after Rosselli entered prison on February 25, 1971.

Rosselli had forced Helms to intervene by resuming his leaks to muckraking columnist Jack Anderson. On January 18, 1971, Anderson ran the first of two new articles about the CIA–Mafia plots, asking again, "Could the plot against Castro have backfired against President Kennedy?" The new articles discussed "six [CIA] attempts against Cuba's Fidel Castro," including those involving rifles. Anderson said the Castro assassination plot he was writing about "began as part of the Bay of Pigs operation . . . to eliminate the Cuban dictator before the motley invaders landed." Anderson's linking the Bay of Pigs and the CIA–Mafia plots to JFK's assassination would hit President Nixon especially hard, since it referred to events during his tenure as Vice President. Nixon's alarm at the time was confirmed by long-secret Senate Watergate Committee files that I published for the first time in 2012.* Nixon's Attorney General John Mitchell, also Nixon's de facto campaign manager, was reportedly in tears after talking with former Howard Hughes aide Robert Maheu about the plots.

In addition, Jack Anderson wrote that the plots continued until March 1963 and for the first time named some of the participants: Rosselli, Harvey, and Maheu. However, Anderson's column didn't

---

*For more about this, see the updated, trade paperback edition of *Watergate: The Hidden History* (2013).

mention Trafficante, Giancana, Marcello, or David Morales—meaning that someone as knowledgeable as Helms would realize Rosselli had more bombshells to drop, if he chose.

Soon after the Rosselli-Anderson articles, E. Howard Hunt began working as a White House consultant. The conventional wisdom is that Nixon formed "the Plumbers" with Hunt, to plug leaks like these of Daniel Ellsberg and the Pentagon Papers. However, Hunt began working for Nixon—and recruiting former colleagues like Bernard Barker—in mid-April 1971, before the Pentagon Papers were first published. Clearly, as a veteran of the CIA–Mafia plots that Nixon had begun back in 1960, Hunt's first priority was to make sure that Nixon's role in those plots didn't surface. Testimony shows that Hunt was even ordered by the White House to look into assassinating Jack Anderson.

Later in 1971, CIA official David Atlee Phillips was apparently overseeing a new assassination attempt against Fidel Castro, once more involving Cuban exile Antonio Veciana. The site was Chile, which had a new socialist government. The attempt failed, but Fidel was apparently so angry that he ordered the compilation of a huge Dossier of the CIA's attempts to kill him. The Dossier—with extensive details, including photos of captured weapons and assassins—began when Nixon was Vice President in 1960 and continued under Nixon's Presidency.

As the new Senate Watergate files indicate, and Watergate burglar Frank Fiorini confirmed in a long-overlooked published interview, the Watergate break-ins were all about trying to see if that Dossier had fallen into the hands of Nixon's enemies. The first break-in involving Hunt, Barker, Fiorini (using the name Frank Sturgis), and the other "Plumbers" occurred at the Chilean Embassy in Washington. That burglary, which

Nixon talked about on a White House tape, occurred two weeks before the first Watergate break-in. As Trafficante later revealed to the Chief Investigator for his attorney, that's also why almost all of the Watergate burglars were veterans of the CIA–Mafia plots.

Remarkably, six months before the first Watergate break-in, President Nixon had received a new Mafia bribe of $1 million involving Jimmy Hoffa. Just as in 1960, this new Mafia–Hoffa bribe again involved Carlos Marcello, Santo Trafficante, and New Jersey mobster Tony Provenzano. As documented by the FBI and *Time* magazine, the bribe was for Hoffa's release from prison, only with the condition that he couldn't return to the Teamsters for eight years. The mob bosses preferred to deal with Hoffa's easygoing replacement, Frank Fitzsimons, instead of the volatile Hoffa, hence the special stipulation barring Hoffa from the Teamsters.

In late 1973, Hoffa—angry that Nixon had kept him from the Teamsters—tipped Senate Watergate Committee investigators about Nixon, Johnny Rosselli, and the CIA–Mafia plots. Committee investigators interviewed Johnny Rosselli in a secret session about those plots. However, for reasons that are still unclear, that part of the investigation was shut down in early 1974 and was withheld from the press. However, following Nixon's resignation in August 1974, leaks about assassinations coming from new President Gerald Ford resulted in news articles that caused Ford to create the Rockefeller Commission on January 4, 1975, to investigate CIA activities, including assassination plots and JFK's assassination. However, the Rockefeller Commission was stacked with conservative establishment figures like Ronald Reagan, so Congress created their own investigating committees: the Pike Committee (originally the Nedzi Committee) and the far better-known Church Committee, named for liberal Senator

Frank Church, of Idaho. Their goal was to investigate CIA operations, domestic surveillance, and assassination plots.

In the case of each of those Committees, all the files about JFK–Almeida coup plan—and its infiltration by the Mafia—were withheld from Congress. That was ostensibly to protect Almeida, still a very high official in Cuba, from being exposed as a US asset. It also prevented the exposure of intelligence failures by agencies like the CIA and potentially embarrassing revelations about officials of both parties. For example, while crucial information was being withheld from the Church Committee, former Warren Commission member Gerald Ford was President, his Chief of Staff was Donald Rumsfeld, his senior White House adviser, Dick Cheney, and later, his CIA Director was George H. W. Bush. All four men had been part of the Nixon Administration during the Watergate scandal, which had involved numerous veterans of the anti-Castro plots, including those linked to the Mafia.

Of course, Marcello, Trafficante, and Rosselli had the most to fear if their roles in JFK's assassination were exposed by the Congressional investigations. The godfathers would try to prevent that at any cost, even if it meant murdering some of their own.

CHAPTER 18

Mafia Murders, Confessions, and a Million Files Still Secret

T HE CIA–MAFIA PLOTS to kill Fidel Castro became front-page news in June 1975. Even as the Rockefeller Commission issued its final report on June 11, 1975, the Senate Church Committee intensified its efforts. On June 13, the Church Committee again grilled Helms, this time exclusively about CIA assassination plots, including those with the Mafia. He testified in closed session, so the public had no way to know what he said—or didn't say. Carlos Marcello and Santo Trafficante would have been extremely concerned, since Helms's revelations about the CIA–Mafia plots could lead to the exposure of their roles in JFK's murder. In the short term, Trafficante had the most to lose, since he'd played a much bigger role in the CIA–Mafia plots. Trafficante would have been especially worried when Sam Giancana was subpoenaed and slated to testify on June 26.

On June 19, 1975, Sam Giancana became the first of several Congressional witnesses to be murdered. The former mob boss was cooking a late-night meal for a trusted friend visiting his home in Chicago's Oak Park neighborhood. His friend shot Giancana seven times with a silenced .22-caliber pistol, an unusually small gun for a mob hit. Five of the shots were around Giancana's chin and mouth, a sign that Mafiosi shouldn't talk.

The gun was eventually traced to Florida, and some pointed the finger at Trafficante. One government informant, Charles Crimaldi, said that Giancana was killed by someone who worked for the CIA, though the hit man was acting on his own and not at the request of officials. Since several CIA assets and officials also worked with the Mafia, the hit man could have been someone with ties to both the mob and the Agency.

Giancana's murder made headlines across the country, adding urgency to the Committees' investigations. The day after Giancana's death, CIA Director William Colby testified about CIA assassination plots, followed four days later by Johnny Rosselli. The transcripts—kept secret until the 1990s—show that Rosselli had mastered the art of saying a lot while revealing little, sticking to an incomplete version of the CIA–Mafia plots that mirrored the whitewashed version Helms had promulgated in his own testimony and in the 1967 Inspector General's Report. On June 25, William Harvey testified to the Church Committee about the CIA–Mafia plots, followed by more testimony from Helms on July 17 and 18, both in closed sessions.

Jack Anderson wrote once more about Rosselli on July 7, and *Time* magazine ran an article touching on the original 1959 CIA–Mafia plots that Jimmy Hoffa had brokered—a story Hoffa himself had just leaked to someone with the Church Committee. Hoffa was now in the crosshairs of the Committee, because of *Time*'s article about the 1959 CIA–Mafia plots.

Carlos Marcello and Santo Trafficane couldn't afford to let Hoffa testify, continue his leaks to Committee staff, or continue his efforts to rejoin the Teamsters. According to the CAMTEX FBI file, Marcello summoned Hoffa to Churchill Farms for a conference shortly before his disappearance, but Hoffa refused to back down.

On July 30, 1975, Jimmy Hoffa was spotted leaving a restaurant near Detroit, headed for what he thought was a meeting with New Jersey mobster Tony Provenzano, an associate of Carlos Marcello's. Hoffa was never seen again, and his body has never been found.

Government informant Crimaldi said that "he had heard information that the same man that killed [Giancana] took care of Hoffa for the same reason: he knew about the Castro plots [and] it had been Hoffa who was the original liaison between the CIA and the [Mafia]." Hoffa was killed the same day Senator George McGovern released to the US news media an updated copy of the Cuban Dossier of CIA assassination attempts against Castro, which McGovern had recently received in Cuba.

Johnny Rosselli used Jack Anderson to ensure he didn't meet the same fate as Giancana and Hoffa. Anderson's September 1, 1975, column claimed that Rosselli had avoided deportation because of his war record, helping Rosselli show Trafficante and Marcello that he wasn't getting preferential INS treatment because he was testifying. Rosselli was back in front of the Church Committee on September 22, ten days after Helms had faced the Committee yet again.

Trafficante's old associate Rolando Masferrer—who was on the fringe of the JFK plot—was killed in a spectacular car bombing on October 31, 1975. His death could have been related to the Church Committee hearings or to the general upsurge of violence in Miami's exile community, fueled by politics and the expanding drug trade. A current article about JFK's assassination was on Masferrer's desk when he died. John Martino, Masferrer's mutual associate with Trafficante, had died of natural causes on August 3, 1975, three days after Hoffa disappeared. In declining health, Martino had finally confessed his role in JFK's murder to two friends, his business partner and reporter John Cummings. The Church Committee apparently never learned about Martino or his published statements about the Kennedys' 1963 coup and invasion plan.

William Harvey, who had already testified to the Church Committee but had not revealed all he knew about the CIA–Mafia plots, died on June 9, 1976. Long out of the CIA, he had worked most recently at a book publisher, where he reportedly scrubbed information about Johnny Rosselli and the Miami CIA station from the memoir of an Army Ranger stationed there in 1963 (it was restored for a later edition).

In addition to the main Senate Church Committee, there was a subcommittee with Senators Gary Hart and Richard Schweiker that was devoted exclusively to exploring JFK's assassination. Their report was issued on June 23, 1976, but Schweiker was determined to forge ahead with the investigation, which included the possibility of more interrogation of Johnny Rosselli by increasingly knowledgeable Senate staffers.

Rosselli had a problem he could have discussed only with his attorney, Tom Wadden: During intense questioning, he had reportedly given Congressional investigators Santo Trafficante's name in relation to JFK's assassination. Rosselli had to explain to Wadden why that, or further testimony, was so dangerous. According to historian Richard Mahoney, Rosselli confessed to Wadden his "role in plotting to kill the President"—something Wadden revealed only much later, to RFK's former Mafia prosecutor William Hundley.

On July 16, 1976, Rosselli had dinner with Trafficante and told the godfather he'd had to mention his name during his most recent testimony. Twelve days later, on July 28, 1976, Rosselli was seen alive in public for the last time. Once it was clear Rosselli was missing, Senator Schweiker asked the FBI to look into the matter.

Rosselli's body finally turned up on August 7, 1976, in a fifty-five-gallon oil drum, found in a canal near Miami. Rosselli had been shot and stabbed, his legs cut off, and his body stuffed in the oil drum. It was shot with holes, so it wouldn't float, then weighted with chains, but somehow it was still discovered. The police were officially baffled, and E. Howard Hunt suggested that Fidel had killed Rosselli. However, three of Rosselli's associates said that Trafficante had ordered the gruesome slaying. Rosselli's murder was the kind of headline news that even the most jaded or intimidated reporter couldn't ignore, especially after Jack Anderson revealed information he had to keep secret while Rosselli was alive. In his September 7, 1976, column, Anderson wrote that Rosselli had said those involved in the CIA–Mafia plots had killed JFK and even hinted that shots from the grassy knoll were part of that plan.

The Senate Church Committee hearings had overshadowed those in the House by the Pike Committee, but on September 17, 1976—amid the furor created by Rosselli's murder—the House created the Select Committee on Assassinations. Unfortunately, the investigation's first nine months were hampered by problems in settling on a chief counsel to direct the probe and determining which member of Congress would chair the Committee. Not until the summer of 1977 did the House Select Committee finally have its permanent general counsel, G. Robert Blakey, creator of the RICO racketeering law and a former Mafia prosecutor for Robert Kennedy.

Santo Trafficante had been interviewed once by the Church Committee, with no record kept at Trafficante's request, but he couldn't count on such consideration from the new House Select Committee. Hit man Charles Nicoletti, an associate of Johnny Rosselli's and a veteran of the CIA–Mafia plots with Trafficante, was slated to talk to Congressional investigators. But on March 29, 1977, Nicoletti was "the victim of a mob assassination" in Chicago, according to the *Miami Herald*. They said Nicoletti "was pulled from his burning car . . . after being shot three times in the back of the head at point-blank range." The article mentioned that Nicoletti had once "been responsible for drawing up CIA-ordered plans for the assassination of Castro . . . in October, 1963," though at that time, Nicoletti's mob superiors were far more focused on assassinating JFK than Castro.

Gaeton Fonzi, an investigator for the Church Committee, had gone to work for the new House Select Committee on Assassinations. On the same day that Nicoletti died, Fonzi was in south Florida to interview George DeMohrenschildt, the sophisticated White Russian who had been Oswald's best friend for a time. DeMohrenschildt had known not only Jackie Kennedy but also George H. W. Bush. Even as Fonzi spoke to DeMohrenschildt's daughter about arranging the interview, DeMohrenschildt was meeting with a writer for the *Wall Street Journal*, Edward Epstein, telling Epstein he'd informed Dallas CIA official J. Walton Moore about Oswald's activities. That evening, before Fonzi could meet him, DeMohrenschildt committed suicide by putting the barrel of a .20-gauge shotgun in his mouth and pulling the trigger.

About a week later, Fonzi had also planned to set up an interview in Miami with former Cuban president Carlos Prio, also an associate of Trafficante's. On April 5, 1977, before Fonzi could interview him, Prio committed suicide by shooting himself in the heart with a .38 pistol.

That fall, Fonzi tried to arrange an interview with Cuban exile Manuel Artime after being tipped that Artime had "guilty knowledge" of JFK's assassination. Artime, one of E. Howard Hunt's best friends and a supplier of "hush money" to Hunt and the other Watergate burglars, had become a player in Miami's exploding drug market. Fonzi's partner talked to Artime in early November about scheduling an interview, but Artime entered the hospital the following week, was diagnosed with cancer, and died two weeks later, on November 18, 1977, at only forty-five.

The following spring, Fonzi tried to track down David Morales, though the CIA made it difficult for the House Select Committee to determine even Morales's CIA position in 1963. Two weeks after David Atlee Phillips and Antonio Veciana testified to the Select Committee in executive session—and after Morales was added to the list of CIA personnel the Committee wanted to interview—Morales died, apparently of natural causes, on May 8, 1978.

In less than three years, Congressional investigations had been thwarted by the deaths of at least nine actual or potential witnesses, from the sensational murders of Rosselli, Giancana, and Hoffa to the unexpected deaths of Morales, Artime, and DeMohrenschildt. Those important witnesses died before they could testify fully or, in most cases, testify at all. Surprisingly, even after Harry Williams had seen those headlines, he still volunteered to talk to the House Select Committee, but he never heard back from them.

THE REMAINING PROBLEMS for Fonzi, Blakey, and the rest of the Committee centered on the CIA and the Mafia, as well as on critical files being withheld from them by the CIA, FBI, Secret Service, and Naval Intelligence (and Marine Intelligence). Richard Helms faced charges about lying to Congress that needed to be resolved before he could testify. After a major White House meeting about the issue in July 1977, Helms agreed to plead guilty to making a false statement to Congress and was fined $2,000 on November 4, 1977. Later that day, he went to a CIA reception where his current and former CIA colleagues donated an even larger amount.

Santo Trafficante had primarily pleaded the Fifth in his first House Select Committee appearance on March 16, 1977, but Blakey arranged to grant him and Marcello limited immunity, in an effort to get them to talk. The situation was complicated because Trafficante was under indictment for charges relating to the FBI's BRILAB investigation, which had grown out of the Watergate-era prosecution of Nixon's former attorney general, Richard Kleindienst. Carlos Marcello didn't realize his new business partner, Joe Hauser, would soon be a wired FBI informant for that operation. Nonetheless, Trafficante testified on November 14, 1977, and September 28, 1978, and Marcello testified in January 1978. Both gave cautious statements and denied having anything to do with JFK's murder.

The same month that Trafficante testified for the last time, author Dan Moldea had a revealing exchange with Frank Ragano, Trafficante's former attorney who had gone through a very acrimonious split with the Tampa godfather. Possibly as part of a Teamster effort to suppress Moldea's book, Ragano had offered Moldea a large sum for the rights to it. As part of their back and forth, in September 1978 Moldea had his attorney ask Ragano about his book's theory that Hoffa, Marcello, and Trafficante were behind JFK's murder. Moldea said "that Ragano . . . corroborated my conclusions."

Bernard Barker had been released from prison for his Watergate crimes in June 1974, but by 1978 he was being investigated by the

House Select Committee on Assassinations. According to a formerly secret Committee memorandum about Barker, "he was closely examined under oath by the [Committee about] allegations under investigation by the Committee that Barker associates . . . Hunt and [Frank] Sturgis [aka Fiorini] were in Dallas on November 22, 1963." We can't tell if the Committee investigated Barker's possible presence in Dallas that day, because according to the National Archives website, Barker's entire Committee testimony on August 29, 1978, remains withheld. That is highly unusual, since even the testimony of far more senior CIA figures like Richard Helms, E. Howard Hunt, and David Atlee Phillips has been released in full. For CIA figures, testimony can be released with any sensitive terms or identities censored, so it's remarkable that all of Barker's Committee testimony remains secret.

Even though the Committee conducted an investigation of Barker, it's not mentioned in the Committee's *Final Report* or in any of their supporting volumes. A six-page Committee memorandum about Barker, recently discovered among the million-plus pages of JFK files on the Mary Ferrell Foundation website, is the only indication Barker was investigated by the Committee. However, the memorandum's biography of Barker does not mention the FBI report of Barker's gangster activity in Cuba, which may not have been provided to the Committee. There is no indication in the memo that the Committee investigated Barker's Mafia ties. The CIA withheld much material from the Committee about the roles of Barker (and Hunt and Helms) in the JFK–Almeida coup plan and the CIA–Mafia plots. A CIA Office of Security memo says that "3 sealed envelopes" were deleted from the Barker file given to the Committee.

On April 22, 1978, Secretary of State Cyrus Vance—a veteran of the JFK–Almeida coup plan—had his representative meet with

Commander Juan Almeida at the UN in New York. A short time later, CIA officer George Joannides was assigned to be the Agency's new liasion with the House Select Committee. Joannides had worked with David Atlee Phillips in 1963, running the DRE exile group involved in the altercation with Oswald. The Committee wanted to interview the CIA agent running the DRE in 1963, but Joannides claimed he couldn't be found. It appears that some high CIA official, probably Ted Shackley, was using Joannides—and the excuse of protecting Almeida—to withhold important information from the Committee.

As the House Select Committee on Assassinations rushed to finish its work on the JFK assassination, acoustic tests indicated there had been at least one shot from the grassy knoll. Those highly technical findings have been the source of much debate ever since, so I have not factored them into my conclusions. When the House Committee submitted its *Final Report* on March 29, 1979, its ultimate conclusion about JFK's murder was that it was likely a conspiracy, involving at least one shot from the grassy knoll. In addition:

> The Committee found that Trafficante, like Marcello, had the motive, means, and opportunity to assassinate President Kennedy.

For both Marcello and Trafficante, the Committee "was unable to establish direct evidence of Marcello's complicity." It could just as well have added "because of all the material the CIA, FBI, and other agencies withheld." Investigator Gaeton Fonzi later wrote a book-length account of all the Agency stonewalling the Committee had faced, called *The Last Investigation*. The Committee also recommended the Justice Department investigate the possible involvement of Marcello and Trafficante in JFK's murder.

BY 1981, CARLOS Marcello was feeling the full force of the FBI's BRILAB undercover operation. Facing the biggest legal battle of his life, Marcello was under indictment in Louisiana for trying to bribe state officials in a multimillion-dollar insurance scam. In Los Angeles, he'd been indicted for trying to bribe a federal judge. Even worse, much of the evidence was in the godfather's own words, recorded by a bug and phone taps the FBI had finally placed in Marcello's office at the Town and Country Motel. They were augmented by secret recordings made by convicted insurance swindler Joe Hauser, who wore a wire for the FBI in hopes of securing an early release. He was aided by two undercover FBI agents, who pretended to be crooked businessmen.

In Miami, Santo Trafficante was under indictment for a $1 million labor union fraud scheme. Both Trafficante and Marcello were also hit with RICO racketeering charges, using the statute that G. Robert Blakey had helped create. Trafficante would avoid conviction, but Marcello's luck had finally run out.

Marcello's BRILAB battles were covered by the press in New Orleans, and by some national media like the *New York Times*, but the coverage rarely mentioned his name in conjunction with JFK's assassination. The 1,200 hours of BRILAB recordings, along with unrecorded information from Hauser, contained tantalizing hints about Marcello and the assassination. They weren't mentioned in the press and were barred from the trial, at Marcello's lawyers' request, so they wouldn't prejudice the jury. Still, the jury was able to hear hours of Marcello discussing the blatant corruption and crimes he had been committing for years.

Marcello was convicted in Louisiana on August 4, 1981, and in Los Angeles on December 11, 1981. The following year, he was sentenced to seven years for the Louisiana counts and ten years for the

Los Angeles counts. His powerful attorneys did everything they could, but on April 15, 1983, Marcello's BRILAB appeal was denied and he was ordered to begin serving his sentence immediately.

At age seventy-three, Marcello faced seventeen years in prison. He was initially sent to familiar territory: the US Medical Center for Federal Prisoners, in Springfield, Missouri, where Marcello had spent six months a decade earlier. The prison and its park-like grounds were designated as level one, meaning it was one of the least secure and most comfortable federal prisons. But after a year, Marcello was transferred to the far more secure federal prison in Texarkana, Texas, an imposing level-three facility where most prisoners had few comforts. However, Marcello was not like most other prisoners, and he soon found ways to receive extraordinary privileges.

As DETAILED IN Chapter Three, by December 1985, Jack Van Laningham was Carlos Marcello's cellmate at Texarkana, as part of the FBI's highly secret CAMTEX undercover operation. Van Laningham had placed a court-authorized, bugged transistor radio in their cell, and the Bureau was recording everything the two said there. Supervising the operation was FBI agent Thomas Kimmel. Agent Tom Kirk worked undercover, pretending to be a sleazy businessman with a friend in the Bureau of Prisons who—for the right price—could get Marcello transferred to a nicer prison and, eventually, even released. While Carlos was in prison, his younger brother, Joe*, ran the parts of Carlos's empire that the godfather couldn't run from prison.

Carlos Marcello had grown close to his trusted cellmate Jack Van Laningham, and it was on December 15, 1987, that FBI files confirm

---

*All references to Joe Marcello refer to Carlos's younger brother, NOT to Carlo's son, who was also named Joe.

that the godfather made his dramatic confession to having ordered JFK's assassination, to Van Laningham and other witness: "Yeah, I had the son of a bitch killed. I'm glad I did. I'm sorry I couldn't have done it myself."

That night, in their cell, Marcello said, "Jack, you can never mention to anybody that I had Kennedy killed." Van Laningham tried to mollify the godfather and reassured him his secret was safe, all while knowing the FBI was recording their coversation through the bugged transitor radio.

Van Laningham was even more nervous about his undercover role after Marcello's admission. Agent Kirk told him that they had heard Marcello's remarks in the cell and that "it had even gone as far as the Attorney General." Van Laningham offered to take a lie detector test about Marcello's admission, and he wanted to drop out of CAMTEX. But Agent Kirk convinced him to stay. Marcello's family had paid the first bribe, and the godfather wanted Jack to be the first to go to the nicer level-two Seagoville Prison near Dallas, where Marcello would join him a few days later.

Though Van Laningham was still afraid, he also wanted to know more about what Marcello had done to JFK. The next time Marcello brought up the Kennedys and his deportation while they were in their cell, Jack encouraged him to talk about his hatred of the Kennedys. That resulted in Marcello's making a few more revelations about the assassination, including the two hitmen he imported from Europe, which were all recorded by the FBI's bugged radio.

Van Laningham said in his FBI file that "on the 17th of December [1985] I was packing, to leave the next day" for Seagoville Prison, when "Marcello told me to sit down, that he had something to talk to me about. He said we have become good friends and I want to tell you a story; he was dead serious and I was scared. He said a Priest came to visit him from Italy, years before. The Priest was old Mafia. 'My son,' he said, 'if your enemies get in your way, you bury them in the ground, the grass grows over them, and you go on about your business.' He was telling me that if I crossed him, the grass would grow over me, as I would be dead. My god, if he had murdered the President, he would have no trouble with me."

After Marcello joined Van Laningham at the Seagoville prison, Joe Marcello was supposed to pay another bribe to have Marcello moved from Seagoville to the federal facility at Fort Worth, which John H. Davis described as "the paradise of the federal prison system, [a] minimum-security level-one facility." After the godfather was moved to Fort Worth, a final bribe—$1 million—was to be paid to Kirk, for Marcello's early release from prison.

Van Laningham said that Marcello was grateful for what Van Laningham was doing and told him "that after we were out, he was going to take me into his organization." Marcello complained to Van Laningham about the "running of his organization," by his brother, Joe Marcello, who lacked the ability to run such a huge criminal empire.

Soon Van Laningham was transferred to a federal prison in California, where he began helping the San Francisco FBI. Marcello's family member paid the bribe, and Marcello was moved to the Fort Worth facility. However, when it came for Joe Marcello to pay the final bribe, to get his older brother released from prison, it wasn't paid. Van Laningham heard that Joe "did not want [Carlos] out of prison, as he would have gotten kicked out of his soft job . . . he would have become a nothing."

Still, two bribes for the prison moves had been paid, so Van Laningham thought the FBI would soon file charges. Van Laningham said in his FBI file that Carlos Marcello and his brother Joe "could have been convicted a dozen times with all the evidence that we put together."

WHILE MARCELLO SAT in prison, his old partner Santo Trafficante made a startling confession to his old attorney. On March 13, 1987, the seventy-two-year-old Trafficante called Frank Ragano to arrange a meeting for the following day. Trafficante had brought Ragano back into the fold, after smoothing over their acrimonious split in the 1970s, and in 1986 Ragano had helped Trafficante beat a federal RICO prosecution. But the Tampa godfather had fallen seriously ill, was facing risky surgery, and wanted to talk to his old confidant one last time.

During an hour-long drive in Ragano's car, away from family and any possibility of government bugs, Trafficante mused about his criminal career and their long association. According to Ragano, when the subject of John and Robert Kennedy came up, Trafficante said (in Italian), "Goddam Bobby. I think Carlos fucked up in getting rid of John—maybe it should have been Bobby." Ragano later claimed he was stunned that Trafficante was admitting a role in JFK's murder. While I think Ragano was accurately reporting what Trafficante said, information I've cited earlier indicates that Ragano already knew about Trafficane's role in JFK's assassination.

Four days later, on March 17, 1987, Santo Trafficante passed away. Ragano held a news conference in front of the Trafficante family home in Tampa's posh Parkland Estates. In discussing Trafficante's illness, Ragano mentioned his meeting with Trafficante four days earlier, as documented in a *Tampa Tribune* article published the following day. Ragano wouldn't reveal Trafficante's confession to the public until 1992, and it wouldn't be detailed fully until his 1994 autobiography was published.

Trafficante's family remained silent when Ragano's allegation first surfaced, but in 1994 they denied Ragano's account to Anthony Summers and other journalists. They claimed Trafficante had been receiving medical treatment in Miami on March 13 and therefore couldn't have been in Tampa, where Ragano says his meeting took place. However, while medical records prove that Trafficante was in Miami receiving dialysis on March 12 and March 14, no medical records place him there on March 13.*

Just over two months after Trafficante's death, CAMTEX came to an end. By May 21, 1987, it was clear that Marcello's family was never going to pay the final bribe for Marcello's release. That night, federal marshals removed Marcello from his comfortable room at the Fort Worth prison. John H. Davis writes that Marcello was then "driven under heavily armed escort (back) to the federal prison at Texarkana."

To Marcello, his family, and his attorneys, the sudden move from level-one Fort Worth to the remote level-three Texarkana must have seemed like a nightmare. They no doubt tried to contact Kirk for an explanation, but his undercover role for CAMTEX had ended.

For Carlos Marcello, the move would have been a crushing, devastating blow. And who was to blame? His brother Joe? Agent Kirk's undercover businessman? Jack Van Laningham?

A FORMER FRIEND of Joe Marcello told me that he was with Joe when Carlos first learned his cellmate—Jack Van Laningham—was an

---

*Ragano later admitted to G. Robert Blakey that he hadn't been able to remember the exact day during that time period when Trafficante made his statement, so he simply picked the most likely possibility to use in his book.

informant for the FBI. Joe Marcello's friend was not a criminal, just a salesman who dealt with one of the legitimate businesses Joe Marcello managed for his brother's empire in the mid-1980s. For obvious reasons, the salesman does not want his name used.

The salesman and his family were with Joe Marcello at his restaurant one afternoon, for a holiday meal. The salesman thought it odd that Joe would have such a meal with him, instead of with his family. Early in the meal, someone came out from the back of the restaurant and whispered to Joe Marcello. Joe excused himself, and an unusually long amount of time passed, more than an hour, with no sign of Joe.

Finally, an apologetic Joe Marcello re-emerged. He explained that he'd had to deal with something extremely serious—they had just learned that the inmate "next to" Carlos Marcello in prison was "an informant for the FBI." Joe said nothing more, but the salesman thought it so unusual that he told another family member about it.

JACK VAN LANINGHAM knew nothing about that, when he called Carlos Marcello's office in April 1988, shortly after Easter. Van Laningham, still in prison in California, was simply curious about what had happened to Marcello and assumed his secret was still safe. But the FBI's CAMTEX file shows that the person Van Laningham spoke with at Marcello's office "indicated to him in a very angry tone of voice that Mr. Marcello knew what he had done and of his cooperation with the FBI [and] hung up the phone."

Van Laningham was frantic and remembered Marcello's threat to him, after the godfather's outburst about ordering JFK's assassination. He knew enough about Marcello's associates and connections to realize he was in danger, especially while he remained in prison.

Fearing for his life, Van Laningham wrote the first of a series of increasingly frantic letters to the Justice Department in Washington. He listed the important information he had obtained for the FBI, including Marcello's JFK confession. Van Laningham said that "[Agent] Kirk told me during the investigation that the Attorney General knew what was going on. And that I would be released when the case was over. . . . I did a good job and I put my life on the line for you."

Van Laningham also told the Justice Department, "Marcello knows all about what we did to him. He will never rest until he pays me back." He pointed out that for almost two years, "I have worked with the San Francisco FBI." He pleaded with the Justice Department, saying, "You are responsible for me." He pointed out "It has been two years [since his work against Marcello and] why they have not been arrested?"

After recieving no reply, Van Laningham wrote to FBI headquarters in Washington, saying "the Justice Department has all of the evidence that we gathered . . . the bribe money that was paid to an undercover FBI Agent . . . all the tapes with hundreds of hours of conversations." He reminded them about Marcello's JFK confession "that he had John Kennedy murdered," adding, "I believe that your office should make Senator Kennedy aware of this evidence." Van Laningham reiterated his willingness to "go on the stand against [Carlos and his brother Joe] any time that I was asked to do so."

San Francisco FBI Agent Carl Podsiadly weighed in on his behalf. Van Laningham also volunteered to take a lie-detector test about Marcello's JFK confession. Finally, Van Laningham also threatened to tell the news media about his FBI work and about the Justice Department's reluctance to prosecute Carlos Marcello or his brother.

Unknown to Van Laningham, in mid-1988 John H. Davis had been in contact with the FBI regarding his upcoming biography of

Carlos Marcello, scheduled for release in January 1989, since he was seeking the release of FBI files and the BRILAB surveillance tapes of Marcello. PBS and journalist Jack Anderson were also working on major television specials for the twenty-fifth anniversary of JFK's assassination in November 1988, which would include information linking Marcello to JFK's murder.

A high official in the Reagan–Bush Justice Department apparently decided it was better not to add Van Laningham's explosive Marcello confession to the mix. By September 1988, Van Laningham had been given a firm release date in January 1989, ending any talk of his going to the press—and any chance his explosive information could be added to Davis's book.

HALF A DOZEN television specials aired around November 22, 1988, several featuring information about the Mafia, with two specifically highlighting Marcello. However, none of the journalists knew the FBI was sitting on a trove of secret reports and tapes that included Marcello's confession. The most influential program was Jack Anderson's November 2, 1988, TV special, *American Exposé: Who Murdered JFK?* It focused extensively on Marcello, Trafficante, and especially Rosselli, though it sometimes appeared to endorse Rosselli's false claim that Castro was involved in JFK's murder.

Anderson's documentary revealed that much information—especially from the CIA—remained unreleased. His special, and the other programs and articles that appeared by November 22, 1988, started to generate a movement calling for the release of all the JFK assassination files. The movement was further fueled by the January 1989 release of John H. Davis's Marcello biography, *Mafia Kingfish: Carlos Marcello and the Assassination of John F. Kennedy*. Unlike most other books and articles published at the time, it presented Marcello not as one of many suspects in JFK's murder but as THE suspect. Even with so much material still withheld, Davis came remarkably close to outlining how Marcello had murdered JFK, something that would have seriously alarmed Marcello and his men.

The push to release the files accelerated rapidly when director Oliver Stone announced plans to dramatize the case in his film *JFK*. Essentially, the attention generated by the twenty-fifth anniversary coverage reignited public interest in JFK's murder, eventually leading to action by Congress.

In January 1989, Jack Van Laningham was paroled from federal prison and sent to a halfway house in Tampa, Florida, where Trafficante's mob family was still active. Van Laningham started trying to put his life back together. Regarding the situation with Carlos Marcello, he made a call to Marcello's office, in hopes of reaching some type of accommodation. Since Marcello remained in prison, his organization was still being run by Joe Marcello and underbosses like Frank Caracci, who'd met with Jack Ruby six weeks before JFK's murder.

A few days after his call to Marcello's office, Van Laningham had left work and was walking back to the half-way house. On a relatively deserted road, a car pulled up and two men got out. The two looked like mob "torpedoes" but initially seemed as if they were going to give him something—until they began savagely beating him.

While one of the men held the stunned Van Laningham on the ground, the other looked around and—seeing no one in the area—went back to the car to get his gun. Van Laningham was sure he was going to die.

Suddenly, a car pulled onto the street, and the driver—spying Van Laningham on the ground—stopped and called out. The two hitmen jumped in their car and sped off while the driver helped him to his feet.

Van Laningham was helping the Tampa FBI at the time, and he reported the attack to them. Finally, the FBI gave Van Laningham a lie-detector test, not only about the attack but also about Carlos Marcello's JFK confession, and he passed. He was eventually released from parole and kept a very low profile for twenty years, until he was finally located by NBC News, to appear in my 2009 special (*Did the Mob Kill JFK?*) that NBC produced for the Discovery Channel.

IN JANUARY 1989, Carlos Marcello also had the first of several small strokes. The godfather was transferred to Rochester, Minnesota's, Medical Center for federal prisoners. There, on February 27, 1989, while Marcello was "in a semi-coherent state," an attendant over-heard him say, "That Kennedy, that smiling motherfucker, we'll fix him in Dallas." The FBI didn't ask Marcello about his statement until September 6, 1989, when he denied "any involvement in the assassination of President Kennedy." Apparently, the Bureau didn't question Marcello at that time about his earlier remarks to Van Laningham.

By that time, the debilitating effects of Marcello's strokes, compounded by Alzheimer's, were clear. One of the CAMTEX FBI officials told us he had not noticed any signs of the latter four years earlier, while listening to all of the Bureau's undercover Marcello tapes in 1985 and 1986. Agent Kimmel said he thought a few of Marcello's remarks showed such indications; however, they weren't enough to stop the dangerous CAMTEX undercover operation, which continued until May 1987. It's important to note that both Van Laningham and Agent Kirk were risk-ing their lives for the FBI at that time, something the Bureau would not have allowed if Marcello had shown serious signs of being senile.

Marcello's statements, noted by Van Laningham in the FBI files, are usually accurate and consistent with facts not well known at the time. Van Laningham said Marcello was mentally "sharp" with no signs of Alzheimer's while he knew him, and the aging godfather demonstrated a firm grasp of complex criminal matters in the 1985 and 1986 accounts. The earliest documented sign of Alzheimer's was noted by John H. Davis, who indicated that by January 1, 1988, those visiting Marcello had begun to notice signs of the disease.

Carlos Marcello was released from prison on October 6, 1989, after his BRILAB conviction was reversed unexpectedly. The government decided not to retry him, so Marcello, increasingly incapacitated from the strokes and his Alzheimer's, returned to Louisiana. By the time of his strokes, Marcello's empire had begun to break apart.

After spending his final years at home, his mind ravaged increasingly by disease and strokes, Carlos Marcello died on March 2, 1993, at age eighty-three. He reportedly died peacefully at his home, a far cry from the bloody executions he had ordered for so many victims. A number of his obituaries, such as the one by Associated Press, noted that "Marcello's name was often mentioned in connection with the assassination of [JFK], but he was never charged."

IN 1989, COMMANDER Juan Almeida was still a revered figure in the Cuban government, and his secret work for JFK had not been exposed. However, some of his protégés were caught up in a major drug scandal in 1989. One may have bartered for his life by revealing Almeida's work for JFK, because soon after the trials, Almeida largely disappeared from view in Cuba. There was no official explanation, though Almeida's absence was noted by exiles and journalists.

It was after Almeida's disappearance that JFK's Secretary of State Dean Rusk first revealed JFK's fall 1963 coup plan to me. With Almeida assumed dead, and with the 1992 passing of former exile (and Trafficante associate) Tony Varona, Harry Williams began telling Thom Hartman and me details about the coup plan. Williams revealed Bernard Barker's work for Trafficante, and that he eventually learned both were involved in JFK's assassination. Williams for the first time also named Almeida, whose identity as the coup leader was soon confirmed by a former JFK and RFK associate who later became a prominent Washington official.

Later in 1992, Congress unanimously passed the JFK Act, which created the JFK Assassination Records Review Board to identify and release the remaining files. In November 1994, I informed the Review Board very generally about JFK's 1963 "plans for a coup in Cuba," without revealing Almeida's identity.

By 1995, Commander Almeida had resurfaced in Cuba, perhaps because his presence was needed to help stabilize the country, which was in dire financial straits after the fall of the Soviet empire. No official explanation for Almeida's return, or his several-year fall from grace, was ever given. Harry Williams passed away on March 10, 1996, after Thom and I had extensively interviewed him as a confidential source more than half a dozen times. Though his own extensive CIA and FBI files remain unreleased, he lived to see a few declassified AMWORLD memos about himself, which detailed and confirmed information he had first revealed to us four years earlier.

In 1997, the Review Board declassified hundreds of pages of military files about JFK's 1963 "Plans for a Coup in Cuba" from the files of the Joint Chiefs of Staff and Joseph Califano, but none named Almeida—they referred only generally to the high-ranking Cuban military officials who would lead the coup. However, after being contacted by a JFK Review Board official in late 1997 and 1998, I confidentially provided the official with the first information naming Almeida and AMWORLD, which the official tried to get released. The Board's mandate expired in September 1998, and though it had declassified more than 4.5 million files, NBC News reported on September 29, 1998, that "millions" of pages remain unreleased.

DAVID ATLEE PHILLIPS died in 1988. Shortly before Phillips's death, he told an associate that in JFK's murder, "there was a conspiracy, likely including American intelligence officers." According to Phillips's nephew, musician Shawn Phillips, when his father asked a dying David Atlee Phillips by phone "Were you in Dallas on that day?" David Atlee Phillips answered, "'Yes,' and then hung up." Was Phillips confessing to JFK's murder? AMWORLD operations were sometimes conducted out of Dallas in 1963. Also, Phillips grew up in Fort Worth and had friends and former classmates in the area, so it's hard to believe Phillips would have met Lee Oswald in public, in Dallas, less than three months before JFK's murder, if he knew Oswald was going to be blamed for the assassination. As with William Harvey, and E. Howard Hunt, only the release of the remaining JFK assassination files might clarify the matter.

Richard Helms died on October 23, 2002, having successfully maintained his decades-long cover-up in the public eye and largely rebuilt his reputation in the process. E. Howard Hunt, his former pro-tégé, died on January 23, 2007. In his posthumously published auto-biography, Hunt admitted that David Atlee Phillips had run Alpha 66, Antonio Veciana's group, for the CIA, and that if Richard Helms was involved in something negative, "he would lie about it later."

Hunt limited his JFK assassination comments in his book to speculation, some of which was inconsistent with remarks he made to his son in a so-called "confession" tape. Other of Hunt's claims are demonstrably false. Hunt tried to make millions selling his story to actor Kevin Costner before his death, and some of Hunt's account appears to have been cribbed from existing JFK conspiracy books, as he speculated about a large conspiracy that could have included LBJ, Cord Meyer, William Harvey, David Phillips, David Morales, Frank Fiorini, and French hit man Lucien Sarti. Most tellingly, Hunt never mentioned—in his autobiography or in his son's tape—the documented Mafia ties of his best friend Manuel Artime and former assistant Barker, or their work on the CIA–Mafia plots. Whether Hunt was involved in the assassination, or was used by Barker on behalf of Trafficante, might only be known when the remaining JFK assassination files are released.

Bernard Barker died on June 5, 2009. On September 11, 2009, Commander Almeida passed away in Cuba, with his work for John and Robert Kennedy never having been publicly exposed to the Cuban people. In the last years of Almeida's life, after Fidel Castro's illness forced him to step down, Almeida had very high profile in Cuba.

After serving twenty-one years in a Cuban prison, former exile leader Eloy Menoyo was released in 1986, the same year Senator

Edward Kennedy engineered the release of the last Bay of Pigs prisoner. Menoyo later returned to Cuba to work for peace and died in 2012. Former exile leaders Manolo Ray and Antonio Veciana are still alive, in Miami and Puerto Rico, respectively. Several Cuban-exile military veterans of AMWORLD and JFK's Cuban-American training at Fort Benning have formed CAMCO, an outreach to military leaders inside Cuba.

Standing in the way of any true normalization between the US and Cuba is the continued withholding of so many JFK assassination files. The respected Washington think tank OMB Watch found that "well over one million CIA records" pertaining to JFK's assassination remain unreleased. But despite the 1992 law requiring their release, the CIA intends to keep those records secret until at least 2017 and has reserved the right in court filings to keep them secret even longer. With Almeida's death, there is no longer any legitimate national security reason for so many files to be withheld.

As of September 16, 2013, the National Archives has refused to tell the public or journalists exactly how many JFK assassination files (and tapes) are still secret. Until all the files are released, former officials and CIA personnel will continue to say or imply that Fidel killed JFK, thus perpetuating the fifty-plus-year Cold War with Cuba.

Only public pressure on Congress and the White House can get the remaining JFK files released. They are important not just for history but also for our democracy. And for framed ex–Secret Service Agent Abraham Bolden, still fighting for a pardon after almost fifty years, they represent his last chance for justice.

SELECTED GOVERNMENT DOCUMENTS

This memo refers to the FBI's CAMTEX undercover operation that targeted godfather Carlos Marcello in prison, and obtained his confession to JFK's murder. It calls FBI informant Jack Van Laningham "DL 2918-OC" and talks about the Title III electronic surveillance of Marcello.

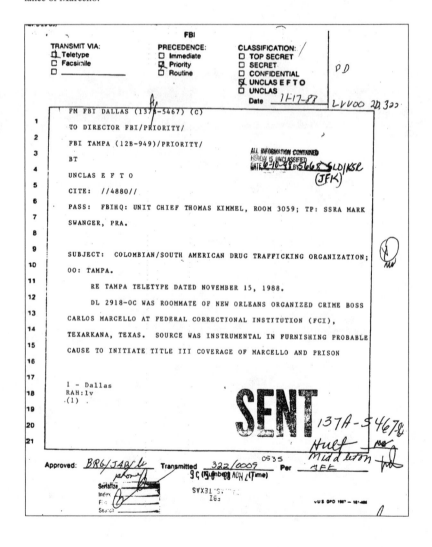

This May 29, 1963 memo was issued just over two weeks after Cuban Army Commander Juan Almeida, the third most powerful official in Cuba, offered to stage a "palace coup" against Fidel Castro, if President Kennedy would back him.

TOP SECRET ~~SEN.~~ ~~THE~~

THE JOINT CHIEFS OF STAFF
WASHINGTON 25, D. C.

CM-605-63

29 MAY 1963

MEMORANDUM FOR THE DIRECTOR, JOINT STAFF

SUBJECT: Actions Related to Cuba (U)

    1. In connection with study of the courses of action related to Cuba, I would like the Joint Staff as a matter of priority to make an examination of the pros and cons of an invasion of Cuba at a time controlled by the United States in order to overthrow the Castro government. The report should develop conclusions for submission to the Secretary of Defense.

    2. Concurrently, I would like the Joint Staff to develop and submit an outline plan for the preliminaries leading up to such an invasion. Included therein should be (a) a proposed date for D-Day, (b) a possible sequence of incidents out of which the invasion could develop, and (c) the requirements that would have to be satisfied to make any cover plan plausible.

(Sgd) MAXWELL D. TAYLOR

MAXWELL D. TAYLOR
Chairman
Joint Chiefs of Staff

After months of careful planning, the date for the JFK–Almeida coup was set for December 1, 1963, as shown by the memo sent by CIA Director John McCone to the Miami CIA Station, on the morning of November 22, 1963. The secret coup plan, and the code-name for part of it—AMWORLD—was withheld from the Warren Commission and the five later US government committees that investigated JFK's murder.

In case it appeared that Fidel Castro had found out about the JFK–Almeida coup plan, and retaliated by the "assassination of American officials," Robert Kennedy had a subcommittee of the National Security Council make plans about how to handle such a situation. The thinking behind those plans would cause some of the secrecy and controversy surrounding JFK's assassination.

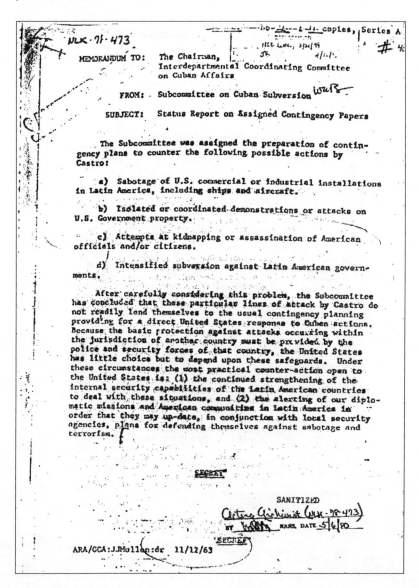

NLK·71·473

.... copies, Series A

MEMORANDUM TO: The Chairman,
                  Interdepartmental Coordinating Committee
                  on Cuban Affairs

        FROM: Subcommittee on Cuban Subversion

        SUBJECT: Status Report on Assigned Contingency Papers

        The Subcommittee was assigned the preparation of contin-
gency plans to counter the following possible actions by
Castro:

        a) Sabotage of U.S. commercial or industrial installations
in Latin America, including ships and aircraft.

        b) Isolated or coordinated demonstrations or attacks on
U.S. Government property.

        c) Attempts at kidnapping or assassination of American
officials and/or citizens.

        d) Intensified subversion against Latin American govern-
ments.

        After carefully considering this problem, the Subcommittee
has concluded that these particular lines of attack by Castro do
not readily lend themselves to the usual contingency planning
providing for a direct United States response to Cuban actions.
Because the basic protection against attacks occurring within
the jurisdiction of another country must be provided by the
police and security forces of that country, the United States
has little choice but to depend upon these safeguards. Under
these circumstances the most practical counter-action open to
the United States is: (1) the continued strengthening of the
internal security capabilities of the Latin American countries
to deal with these situations, and (2) the alerting of our diplomatic missions and American communities in Latin America in
order that they may up-date, in conjunction with local security
agencies, plans for defending themselves against sabotage and
terrorism.

                                   SECRET

                                             SANITIZED

                                   BY ____ NARS. DATE 5/6/80

                                           SECRET
ARA/CCA:JJMullen:dr   11/12/63

JFK had barred the Mafia from the coup plan, or from reopening their casinos in Cuba if the coup were successful. But this file shows that John Martino—an associate of godfathers Carlos Marcello and Santo Trafficante—was one of a dozen mobsters who managed to learn about the top secret coup plan (See last three lines of first paragraph). They linked JFK's assassination to the coup, triggering even more official secrecy about JFK's murder.

/6

Commission No. *657*

UNITED STATES DEPARTMENT OF JUSTICE

FEDERAL BUREAU OF INVESTIGATION

In Reply, Please Refer to
File No.

Miami, Florida

RE: LEE HARVEY OSWALD;
     INTERNAL SECURITY - RUSSIA - CUBA.

On February 15, 1964, John V. Martino, born August 3, 1911, at Atlantic City, New Jersey, and resident, with his family, at 2326 Alton Road, Miami Beach, Florida, stated he was aware of the article which had appeared in the Memphis, Tennessee, "Press-Scimitar," on January 30, 1964. Mr. Martino said he had been interviewed by Kay Pittman of the "Press-Scimitar" on the day before he gave a lecture in Memphis on the situation in Cuba. With regard to the content of the newspaper article, Mr. Martino said it had been completely twisted by the reporter, and he had reprimanded her for it while in Memphis. He said, specifically, that he had never stated that Oswald had been paid to assassinate President Kennedy. He said he does not work with the Cuban underground, as quoted in the article, although he has sources of information concerning activities in Cuba. He said he was quoted correctly in the statement that his sources informed him that President Kennedy was engaged in a plot to overthrow the Castro regime by preparing another invasion attempt against Cuba.

Martino refused to divulge the sources of his information or how they might know what plans President Kennedy might have had. He said it was the opinion of his sources,

ANNOTATED BIBLIOGRAPHY

T his is a selected Annotated Bibliography of the source material used in *The Hidden History of the JFK Assasssination*. Far more books, documents, and articles were consulted than can be listed here, but the exact source for most quotes can be found using Google. My previous books dealing with JFK's assassination, each had approximately 2,000 endnotes, with almost every paragraph, sometimes every line end noted. This book highlights just the most important references, in an easier-to-read format. More references will be available after November 10, 2013 at thehiddenhistoryofthejfkassassination.com.

More detailed information about any of the topics covered in this book can be found in my earlier books. *Ultimate Sacrifice* (2008 updated Counterpoint trade paperback, 952 pages) covers JFK's plan for a fall, 1963 coup in Cuba in great detail, as well as all of the events leading up to JFK's assassination. *Legacy of Secrecy* (2009 updated trade paperback, 923 pages) has new material about JFK's murder especially its aftermath and the cover-ups that followed. *Watergate: The Hidden History* (2013 updated trade paperback, 808 pages) dedicates several chapters to JFK's murder in the historical context of the CIA careers of Richard Helms, E. Howard Hunt, Bernard Barker, and Mafia don Johnny Rosselli. The trade paperback of each contains important material not in the hardback editions.

I've listed the most important, well-documented books related to JFK's assassination that have stood the test of time. Some are not yet available as eBooks, and others are out of print, but copies can be found online.

All government files cited in this book have been declassified and are available at the National Archives. Of their 4.5 million pages of JFK assassination files, they have only a few hundred pages online, most related to the plans for a coup in Cuba, at http://www.archives.gov/research/jfk/

However, almost a million pages of JFK assassination files can be viewed online at maryferrell.org by using document numbers or other information that I've provided. A Google search for documents using some or all of that information will often locate the document.

Other sources of documents online include the Harold Weisberg Collection at Hood College (http://jfk.hood.edu/index.shtml?home.shtml); JFK Lancer at www.jfklancer.com/; JFK Facts at http://jfkfacts.org; and The National Security Archive at http://www2.gwu.edu/~nsarchiv/

GOVERNMENT REPORTS:

Reports from government committees and commissions used in the preparation of this book include:

- JFK Assassination Records Review Board *Final Report* (1998) online at http://www.history-matters.com/archive/contents/contents_arrb.htm

- House Select Committee on Assassinations *Final Report* (1979) at http://www.history-matters.com/archive/contents/hsca/contents_hsca_report.htm

- House Select Committee on Assassinations twelve volumes of supporting evidence and testimony: http://www.history-matters.com/archive/contents/hsca/contents_hsca_vols.htm

- Twenty-six volumes of Warren Commission hearings and exhibits, much more useful than the woefully incomplete one-volume *Warren Report*. All twenty-six volumes can be found online at: http://www.history-matters.com/archive/contents/wc/contents_wh.htm

- Two volumes of the Senate Church Committee: Church, Senator Frank. *Alleged Assassination Plots Involving Foreign Leaders.* (New York: W.W. Norton & Company, 1976) and Church Committee Report, Vol. V, officially *The Investigation of the Assassination of President John F. Kennedy: Performance of the Intelligence Agencies.* Both can be found online at: http://www.history-matters.com/archive/contents/contents_church.htm

- Senate Committee on Government Operations, Permanent Subcommittee on Investigations: *Organized Crime and Illicit Traffic in Narcotics*, 1963.

- Investigation of Improper Activities in the Labor or Management Field, Senate Select Committee Hearings, 1959.

INTERVIEWS:

This book draws on interviews with more than fifty individuals, conducted over the past 23 years, starting with JFK's Secretary of State, Dean Rusk, in 1990 and continuing through 2013. Several of the most important interviews with non-confidential sources are listed below (only a half-dozen sources still remain confidential). All other interview subjects are named in the text.

A dozen interviews were conducted with CAMTEX FBI informant Jack Van Laningham, from August 2009 through 2012. In addition, Van Laningham was the subject of a professionally-filmed Oral History, in which he discussed every aspect of CAMTEX and his time with Carlos Marcello over two days. Additional CAMTEX interviews include those with FBI supervisor Thomas Kimmel; with another FBI official who heard all of the CAMTEX tapes of Marcello; and the source with Joe Marcello when Carlos found out Van Laningham was an FBI informant.

Here is a small selection of additional interviews cited in the book, most conducted by me but some by my research associate, Thom Hartmann:

- JFK's Secretary of State, Dean Rusk 1-8-90.

- JFK aide Dave Powers, 6-5-91, at the John F. Kennedy Presidential Library.

- John Crimmins, JFK's Coordinator of Cuban Affairs for the US State Department, 3-6-95, 3-8-96, 4-18-96.

- JFK aide Richard Goodwin, who confirmed that Robert Kennedy told him "that mob guy from New Orleans"—Carlos Marcello—was behind JFK's assassination. 4-15-98.

- RFK's top Cuban exile aide, Enrique "Harry" Ruiz-Williams (Harry Williams): 2-24-92; 4-92; 11-13-92; 7-24-93; plus four telephone interviews. Former FBI agent William Turner provided me with a transcript of his interview with Harry Williams on 11-28-73.

- Interviews with other Cuban exile leaders include Antonio Veciana, who met with Oswald in 1963, when killing Castro was discussed (6-2-93), and an online interview with Cuban exile leader Manolo Ray, 2-9-06.

- Justice Department Mafia and Hoffa prosecutors for Robert Kennedy have been especially helpful over the years. In addition to several talks with Ronald Goldfarb and G. Robert Blakey, others interviewed include Marvin Loewy, Thomas Kennelly, and John Diuguid, Marcello's Justice Department Prosecutor in November, 1963.

- Interviews about the attempt to kill JFK in Tampa, Florida, on November 18, 1963, four days before Dallas: Phone interview with J. P. Mullins, Tampa Police Chief in November 1963, on 12-10-96. Phone interview with the former Chief of the Florida Police Intelligence Unit, who helped to provide security for JFK in Tampa, 12-10-96. Interview with the former Mrs. Gilberto Lopez, 3-2-96.

- Interviews about the plot to kill JFK in Chicago on November 2, 1963, three weeks before Dallas: Interview with ex-Secret Service Agent Abraham Bolden 4-15-98; Interviews with JFK's Press Secretary, Pierre Salinger 4-3-98 and 4-10-98; Phone interviews with Jim Allison, who witnessed Jack Ruby receiving a payoff of approximately $7,000 in Chicago, several weeks before JFK was almost killed in that city: 4-14-98, 4-15-98 and 4-16-98.

DOCUMENTS:

Many thousands of pages of files were used in the preparation of this book, but here are some of the most important:

- FBI files about CAMTEX, Jack Van Laningham, and Carlos Marcello at the National Archives include: Letter from Van Laningham to Carl Podsiadly, FBI, San Francisco office, 6-88; Letter from Van Laningham to Justice Department, 4-6-88; FBI Marcello confession memo, DL 283A-1035-Sub L, 3-7-86; Priority FBI memo from Dallas office to FBI Director, 11-88; FBI contact investigation 3-7-86, report dictated 3-6-86, FD-302 declassified 6-98; Letter from Senior Case Manager, Federal Correctional Institution, Dublin, CA, to FBI agents, 6-21-88; Letter from Van Laningham to FBI headquarters in Washington, 4-18-88; Priority FBI memo from FBI San Francisco Office to FBI Director, Washington, 9-88, available at the National Archives. FBI record numbers include 124-10182-10430 and 124-1019310471.

- All of the Warren Commission Documents, approximately 50,000, were reviewed on microfilm.

- HSCA: 180-10090-10232 is the Cuban Dossier of CIA attempts to kill Fidel Castro.

- CIA 1961 Inspector General's Report on the Bay of Pigs.

- CIA 1967 Inspector General's Report on the CIA-Mafia plots.

- FBI memo about Trafficante-Ragano meeting 12-63 about money for JFK's assassination: FBI 124-10273-10448.

Memos about the JFK-Almeida coup plan:

- Army document, Summary of plan dated 9-26-63, Califano Papers, Record Number 198-10004-10001, declassified 10-7-97.

- Army copy of Department of State document, 1963, Record Number 198-10004-10072, Califano Papers, Declassified 7-24-97.

- The following is just one of many: Joint Chiefs of Staff document, dated 12-4-63 with 11-30-63 report from Cyrus Vance, Record Number 202-10002-101116, declassified 10-7-97.

- Joint Chiefs of Staff document, dated 12-4-63 with 11-30-63 report from Cyrus Vance, 80 total pages, Record Number 202-10002-101116.

- Joint Chiefs of Staff document 5-1-63 (revised 5-13-63) "Courses of Action Related to Cuba," Record Number 202-10002-10018, declassified 7-23-97.

- CIA 104-10315-10004, 6-28-63 AMWORLD memo, declassified 1-27-99.

- CIA memo, AMWORLD 11-22-63, #84804, declassified 1993.

- CIA memo 2-20-61, page 28 of CIA Sensitive Study, 1978, CIA 104-10400-10200, declassified 10-31-98.

- CIA memo 3-17-61, page 29 of CIA Sensitive Study, 1978, CIA 104-10400-10200, declassified 10-31-98.

- CIA 104-10400-10200, declassified 10-31-98, page 39 citing information from 12-3-63.

- CIA Dispatch from Chief of Station Caracas to Chief, SAS, 2-28-64.

- CIA cable to Director, 12-10-63, CIA 104-10076-10252.

- CIA #104-10098-10093, 10-31-63 AMWORLD Dispatch, declassified 6-20-96.

- NARA 1994.03.08.09:46:690007 CIA/DCD File on Bernard Barker, declassified 3-8-94.

- 12-6-63 CIA Document, from JMWAVE to Director, released during the 1993 CIA Historical Review Program.

- 1964 AMWORLD files, including CIA 104-10308-10080, 104-10308-10084, 104-10308-10098, and many others.

- *Foreign Relations of the United States*, Volume XI, Department of State.

About the Cuba Contingency Plans to deal with the possible assassination of American officials in the fall of 1963:

- John F. Kennedy Presidential Library, NLK 78-473, declassified 5-6-80.

- Department of the Army documents dated 9-14-63 and 9-27-63, provided by the State Department, in SSCIA record number 157-10005-10372 dated 3-27-76, declassified 2-18-94.

Memos discovered in 2012 about the CIA-Mafia plots, Johnny Rosselli, and Watergate:

- Senate Watergate Committee memo, to Senator Ervin, Subject: Relevance to S. Res. 60 of John Rosselli's testimony about his CIA activities, 12-73.

- Senate Watergate Committee staff "Interview of John Rosselli" (Johnny Rosselli), 2-20-74.

- Robert Kennedy phone logs at the National Archives. In addition to 25 calls from Harry Williams to Robert Kennedy during 1963, they also document 13 phone calls from 7-31-62 to 10-22-62.

- CIA document about Gilberto Lopez, 12-3-63, document ID 1994.04.06.10:28:12:530005, declassified 4-6-94; many memos about Lopez in the CIA's Russ Holmes Work files. Miguel Casas Saez document 1-27-64, F82-0272/1, declassified 8-16-83; CIA memo about Saez released 8-16-93, still partially censored.

- Warren Commission draft memo about Oswald's ability to go to Mexico City on 11-22-63 by David Belin, 7-11-64.

- CIA memo, 1-4-67: "Countering Criticism of the Warren Report," CIA 104-10404-10376; CIA 104-10009-10024.

- About the bullet in Oswald's rifle and the plan for a coup in Cuba.

- FBI airtel to "Director, FBI" from "SAC, San Antonio" 11-8-63; HSCA #1801007810062, declassified 11-29-93; HSCA #1801007810066, FBI document to "Director, FBI" from "SAC, San Antonio"; to Director, SAC, Dallas, and Miami; from SAC San Antonio; 10-25-63 HSCA #180-10078-10069-1, declassified 11-29-93; also see Ray and Mary La Fontaine, "The Fourth Tramp," *Washington Post* 8-7-94.

ARTICLES:

Of the hundred-plus articles cited in the text, the following are some of the most important:

"A Presumption of Disclosure: Lessons from the John F. Kennedy Assassination Records Review Board," by OMB Watch, available at ombwatch.com

Bernstein, Carl, "The CIA and the Media," *Rolling Stone*, 10-20-77.

Black, Edwin, article about the attempt to kill JFK in Chicago on 11-2-63, *Chicago Independent*, 11-75.

"Cuban Exiles in New Drive for Unity to Topple Castro," *The New York Times*, 5-11-63, citing 5-10-63 AP report.

Johnson, Haines, "One day's events shattered America's hopes and certainties." *Washington Post* 11-20-83; "Rendezvous with Ruin at The Bay of Pigs," *Washington Post* 4-17-81; "The CIA's Secret War on Cuba," *Washington Post* 6-10-77, B1; "The New Orleans Plot," *Washington Sunday Star*, 2-26-67.

Kohn, Howard, "Execution for the Witnesses." *Rolling Stone* 6-2-77.

MacPherson, Myra, "The Last Casualty of the Bay of Pigs," *Washington Post* 10-17-89.

Malone, William Scott, "The Secret Life of Jack Ruby," *New Times* 1-23-78.

Morley, Jefferson, "The Good Spy," *Washington Monthly* 12-03; "What Jane Roman said;" originally *Washington Post*.

Newfield, Jack, "I want Kennedy killed," *Penthouse* 5-92.

Summers, Anthony and Robbyn, "The Ghosts of November," *Vanity Fair*, December 1994.

Szulc, Tad, Cuba Contingency Plan article by Tad Szulc in the *Boston Globe* 5-28-76 and a slightly different version of the same article in *The New Republic* 6-5-76; Tad Szulc, "Cuba on our Mind," *Esquire*, February 1973; "Castro Reported Quarreling Again with Red Backers," special to the *New York Times*, 9-2-63.

Tampa attempt to kill JFK on November 18, 1963: "Threats on Kennedy Made Here," *Tampa Tribune* 11-23-63; "Man Held in Threats to JFK," *Miami Herald* 11-24-63; Mary Everett, "Charm takes over in Tampa," *St. Petersburg Times* 11-11-99; Skip Johnson and Tony Durr, "Ex-Tampan in JFK Plot?" *Tampa Tribune* 9-5-76; Rory O'Connor, "Oswald Visited Tampa," *Tampa Tribune* 6-24-76; Tim Gratz and Mark Howell, "The Strange Flight of Gilbert Lopez," *Key West Citizen* 11-20-03.

BOOKS:

These books are among the most important of the hundreds cited in the text:

Benson, Michael. *Who's Who in the JFK Assassination*. (New York: Citadel Press, 1993)

Blakey, G. Robert, and Richard N. Billings. *The Plot to Kill the President*. (New York: Times Books, 1981)

Cain, Michael. *The Tangled Web: The Life and Death of Richard Cain, Chicago Cop and Mafia Hitman*. (New York: Skyhorse Publishing, 2007)

Davis, John H. *Mafia Kingfish: Carlos Marcello and the Assassination of John F. Kennedy*. (New York: Signet Books (pb), 1989)

Davis, John H. *The Kennedy Contract*. (New York: Harper Paperbacks, 1993)

Fensterwald, Bernard, and Michael Ewing. *Coincidence or Conspiracy?* (New York: Zebra Books, 1977)

Fonzi, Gaeton. *The Last Investigation*. (New York: Thunder's Mouth Press, 1993)

Goldfarb, Ronald. *Perfect Villains, Imperfect Heroes: Robert F. Kennedy's War Against Organized Crime* (New York: Random House, 1995)

Hancock, Larry. *Someone Would Have Talked*. (Southlake, Texas: JFK Lancer Productions and Publications, 2010)

Hinckle, Warren, and William W. Turner. *Deadly Secrets: The CIA-Mafia War against Castro and the Assassination of JFK*. (New York: Thunder's Mouth Press, 1992)

Hurt, Henry. *Reasonable Doubt* (New York: Henry Holt, 1987)

Kaiser, David. *The Road to Dallas: The Assassination of John F. Kennedy*. (Cambridge, Massachusetts: Belknap Press of Harvard University Press, 2008)

Kantor, Seth. *The Ruby Cover-Up*. (New York, Zebra Books, 1978). Later edition of the book originally titled *Who Was Jack Ruby?*

Krüger, Henrik. *The Great Heroin Coup: Drugs, Intelligence, and International Fascism*. (Boston: South End Press, 1980)

Kurtz, Michael L. *The JFK Assassination Debate*. (Lawrence, Kansas: University of Kansas Press, 2006)

Law, William Matson. *In the Eye of History* (Southlake, TX: JFK Lancer Productions, 2005)

Lifton, David S. *Best Evidence: Disguise and Deception in the Assassination of John F. Kennedy*. (New York: Carroll & Graf, 1988)

Mahoney, Richard D. *Sons & Brothers*. (New York: Arcade Books, 1999)

Meagher, Sylvia. *Accessories after the Fact*. (New York: Vintage Books, 1992)

Moldea, Dan. *The Hoffa Wars*. (New York: S.P.I. Books, 1993)

Newman, John. *Oswald and the CIA* (New York: Carroll & Graf, 1995)

Staff of *Newsday. The Heroin Trail*. (New York: New American Library, 1992)

Noyes, Peter. *Legacy of Doubt*. (New York: Pinnacle Books, 1973; see also newer edition)

Powers, Thomas. *The Man Who Kept the Secrets: Richard Helms and the CIA*. (New York: Knopf, 1979)

Ragano, Frank, and Selwyn Raab. *Mob Lawyer*. (New York: Scribners, 1994)

Rappleye, Charles, and Ed Becker. *All American Mafioso: The Johnny Rosselli Story*. (New York: Doubleday, 1991)

Russell, Dick. *The Man Who Knew Too Much*. (New York: Carroll & Graf, 2003) has some new material; the original hardback (New York: Carroll & Graf, 1992) has some material not in the later edition.

Scheim, David. *The Mafia Killed President Kennedy*. (New York: S.P.I. Books, 1992)

Scott, Peter Dale. *Crime and Cover-Up: The CIA, the Mafia, and the Dallas-Watergate Connection*. (Santa Barbara, California: Open Archive Press, 1993)

Scott, Peter Dale. *Deep Politics and the Death of JFK*. (Berkeley, California: University of California Press, 1993)

Summers, Anthony. *Conspiracy*. (New York: Paragon House, 1989)

Summers, Anthony, with Robbyn Swan. *The Arrogance of Power: The Secret World of Richard M. Nixon*. (New York: Viking Press, 2000)

Talbot, David. *Brothers*. (New York: Free Press, 2007)

Thompson, Josiah. *Six Seconds in Dallas*. (New York: Bernard Geis, 1967)

Valentine, Douglas, *The Strength of the Wolf: The Secret History of America's War on Drugs* (London, New York: Verso, 2004)

ACKNOWLEDGEMENTS

T his book builds on 25 years of research, and the work that led to my three earlier books about President Kennedy's life and death. When I'd said something as concisely and accurately as possible in a previous book, I sometimes adapted that wording for this book. So, before I thank the many people who made this book a reality, I want to thank those who helped my previous books come to fruition. There isn't room to name them all, but their efforts are both appreciated and remembered.

Someone who has been there to shape and mold all of my books is Charlie Winton, Counterpoint's founder and CEO, and this one is no exception. A literary editor in the truest sense of the word, he helps to bring my often diffused work into sharp focus, and it's always the better for it.

Kelly Winton is following in her father's footsteps at Counterpoint and guided an ever-expanding book—that grew by more than 50%—seamlessly through a tight production schedule. She coordinated an effective team that included Peg Goldstein's excellent copyediting, Megan Jones' attractive interior layout, Charles Brock's sharp cover design, and Sara Walker's accurate proofreading. Publicity expert Lorna Garano is already laying plans to spread the word out about the book, and Judy Klein is always working to bring the book to other countries.

Brad Strickland, an excellent writer himself, always helps my prose to read more smoothly. Ashley Zeltzer's amazing photography is stunning.

This book might not exist if not for Jack Van Laningham, a true America hero who risked his life while helping the FBI. Thanks also go to Jack's son, Craig, for allowing me to provide the proof that backs up his father's amazing story.

The best research partner anyone could ever have is Thom Hartmann, who helped with the first six years of research and has remained a staunch supporter and friend ever since. Wife Louise Hartmann and producer Shawn Taylor make Thom's radio and TV shows a pleasure to be part of, and check out their many great projects at thomhartmann.com.

My father, Clyde Waldron, is my partner in the book writing business, and I couldn't do it without him. George and Leonardo DiCaprio, and Earl Katz, have also been great supporters, and—along with Robert De Niro—will soon bring Jack Van Laningham's story to the screen.

Ron Goldfarb, a long-time friend and supporter, was a great help in getting this book off the ground. It is truly an international effort, and research help came from Stephane Risset in France, Paul Byrne and John Simkin in England, and Kate Willard in Australia. Henry Rosenbloom and his crew at Scribe always do a great job in presenting my work in Australia.

Special thanks is due to several key sources for this book, including Daniel Sheehan (whose own autobiography has just been released), Travis Kiger, Casey Quinlan, Thomas Kimmel, and others who wish to remain anonymous.

I continue to rely on the work and expertise of several great writers and researchers: Dan Moldea, Peter Dale Scott, Anthony Summers and Robbyn Swan, the late John H. Davis, John Newman, Dick Russell, and William Turner—I encourage our readers to Seek out their work. Mike Cain was a source of valuable information about the Chicago Mafia, while Gordon Winslow is a fountain of information about Cuban exiles. Vince Palamara contributed valuable work about the Secret Service, and Larry Hancock and Stuart Wexler are always sharing new discoveries. Because historian Gerald McKnight demolished the Warren Commission with his book *Breach of Trust*, I didn't have to.

Liz Smith (at wowowow.com) remains an icon of American journalism, who isn't afraid to report the truth. Mark Crispin Miller advances a variety of progressive stories at this excellent site (markcrispinmiller.com), as does Mark Karlin (buzzflash.com).

Rex Bradford and the Mary Ferrell Foundation do a remarkable job a making one million assassination files available online. Also great online resources are the National Security Archive; JFK Lancer, run by Debra Conway and Sherry Fiester; and Bill Kelly's jfkcountercoup.blogspot.com.

Susan Barrows and Chris Barrows are always unfailingly helpful, while Jim Steranko's interest and encouragement have been part of this project since the start.

To all of these great people—and anyone I might have forgotten—I give my warmest thanks for your help in making this book possible.

LAMAR WALDRON
SEPTEMBER 17, 2013

INDEX